PassKey EA Review
Part 1: Individuals

IRS Enrolled Agent Exam Study Guide 2012-2013 Edition

Authors:
Collette Szymborski, CPA
Richard Gramkow, EA
Christy Pinheiro, EA ABA®

PassKey Publications
Elk Grove, CA 95758

Recent Praise for the PassKey EA Review Series

Ralph P. Mendoza (Queens, New York) This book did a great job of preparing me for the exam. I passed Part One on my first try.

Michael Mirth (North Las Vegas, Nevada)
The workbook is wonderful. I have timed myself to 3½ hours and have been able to complete each part in the time allowed. I believe I will pass the exam with no problems, and you can tell that the authors have a lot of experience in this field.

Sung Hyon (Aurora, Colorado)
Easy to understand and comprehensive. This book is one of the best EA review books I've found. I downloaded a sample PDF file from the publisher's website and liked how it read. I'd recommend this book.

Chris Davidson (Orange County, California)
I wanted to purchase a book with an easy writing style, so I could enjoy the process of preparing myself for the test. Text is bolded and bulleted to break the monotony. The examples (a big learning boost for me!) are completely enclosed in a box, so they clearly stand out. Each [unit] is followed by questions, complete with an explanation as to why the answer is correct. I showed the book to a CPA friend last night, and he went online immediately and ordered it! I HIGHLY recommend this book!

Cynthia Adcock (Manchester, Tennessee)
After using both the book and the audio book, I had no problems passing all three parts of the exam. It's a wonderful tool for anyone studying to become an Enrolled Agent.

J. Lancaon (San Francisco, California)
I passed all three parts of the EA exam! I have passed all parts of the EA exam using your book (thank you), and have recommended other coworkers use your book for their studying. The content of the tax material is right on point so that there were no surprises on the exams.

M. Avila (Las Vegas, Nevada)

This is a great low-cost study guide; I used it along with the IRS Pubs to pass. There are not many books available for this program at an affordable price.

A. Engbretsen (Jacksonville, Florida)

I purchased this item to use alongside classroom training that I am receiving. It has been so helpful, especially since I found out that the teacher uses the book to find his teaching material! Definitely recommend!

Do you want to test yourself?
Then get the PassKey EA Exam Workbook!

PassKey EA Review Workbook:
Three Complete Enrolled Agent Practice Exams

This workbook features three complete Enrolled Agent practice exams, with detailed answers, to accompany the PassKey EA Review course books. Take three full, 100-question exams on Individuals, Businesses, and Representation.

All of the answers are clearly explained in the back of the book.
Test yourself, time yourself, and learn!

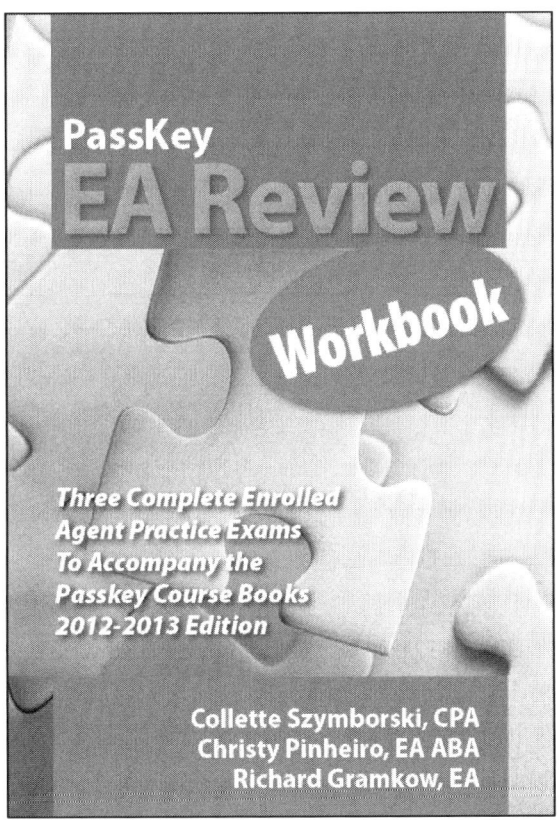

Editor: Cynthia Willett Sherwood, MSJ

PassKey EA Review, Part 1: Individuals, IRS Enrolled Agent Exam Study Guide 2012-2013 Edition

ISBN: 978-1-935664-15-4

First Printing. PassKey EA Review
PassKey EA Review® is a U.S. Registered Trademark

All Rights Reserved ©2012 PassKey EA Review DBA PassKey Publications. Revised and updated every year to updated IRS EA Exam specifications. United States laws and regulations are public domain and not subject to copyright. The editorial arrangement, analysis, and professional commentary are subject to this copyright notice. No portion of this book may be copied, retransmitted, reposted, duplicated, or otherwise used without the express written approval of the publisher. Questions for this study guide have been taken from previous IRS Special Enrolled Agent examinations and from current IRS publications. The authors have also drafted new questions.

Tammy the Tax Lady® is a trademark of PassKey Publications.

PassKey Publications, PO Box 580465, Elk Grove, CA 95758

www.PassKeyPublications.com

Part 1: Individuals

Tammy the Tax Lady®

Table of Contents

Introduction 11

Essential Tax Figures for Tax Year 2011 17

Unit 2: Filing Status 35

Unit 3: Determining Residency and Tax Home 57

Unit 4: Exemptions and Dependents 73

Unit 5: Due Dates, Estimates, and Extensions 101

Unit 6: Types of Taxable and Non-taxable Income 117

Unit 7: Rental and Royalty Income 189

Unit 8: Adjustments to Gross Income 213

Unit 9: Individual Retirement Arrangements 251

Unit 10: The Standard Deduction and Itemized Deductions 273

Unit 11: Tax Credits 341

Unit 12: Basis of Property 387

Unit 13: Capital Gains and Losses 411

Unit 14: Non-Recognition Property Transactions 435

Unit 15: The Estate Tax 465

Unit 16: The Gift Tax 477

Introduction

Congratulations on taking the first step toward becoming an Enrolled Agent, the most widely respected professional tax designation. Enrolled Agents are licensed to practice by the Internal Revenue Service. You are taking the first step to an exciting and rewarding career as a tax professional!

This study guide is designed to help you prepare for the IRS Enrolled Agent's exam. Although designed to be a comprehensive guide, we still recommend that you study IRS publications, and also try to learn as much as you can about tax law in general so that you are well-equipped to take the exam.

Enrolled Agents have passed all three parts of the exam, which is formally called the *IRS Special Enrollment Examination* or "*SEE*." The exam covers all aspects of federal tax law, including the taxation of individuals, corporations, partnerships, exempt entities, ethics, and IRS collections and audit procedures.

This book is designed for the 2012 to 2013 testing season. Prometric will begin testing candidates on May 1, 2012. The testing window closes on **February 28, 2013**. Any candidate taking the Enrolled Agent exam during this time period will be tested on **2011 tax law**.

These are the average pass rates for the IRS Enrolled Agent's exam, according to Prometric:

Pass Rate: Part 1: 42%
Pass Rate: Part 2: 45%
Pass Rate: Part 3: 70%

The IRS Enrolled Agent's exam is exclusively administered by Prometric, and exam candidates can find valuable information on Prometric's IRS/EA Exam website at:

http://www.prometric.com/IRS

Candidates can easily sign up for the exam online and schedule convenient exam dates to accommodate their schedules.

Prometric has designed the exam with content derived from input by experts from the Enrolled Agent community. Each exam section is formatted with multiple choice questions. There are no essay questions or questions requiring written answers. At the time of this book's publication, the EA exam has 100 questions per part.

Computerized EA Exam Format
Part 1: Individual Taxation-100 Questions
Part 2: Business Taxation-100 Questions
Part 3: Representation, Practice, and Procedures-100 Questions

An exam-taker is given 3.5 hours to complete each part. The actual seat time is four hours to allow for a tutorial and survey at the end. There are multiple versions of each exam. Each year, the exam is updated and new questions are added. If you fail an exam section, do not expect the questions to be identical the next time you take the exam.

Each exam question is equally weighted. A panel of subject matter experts comprised of Enrolled Agents and IRS representatives developed the definition of the minimally qualified candidate. The IRS has set a scaled passing score at 105, which corresponds to the minimum level of knowledge deemed acceptable by those persons who will be practicing before the IRS.

Failing candidates are provided a scaled score value so that they may see how close they are to being successful. Candidates with a score of 104 are very close to passing. Candidates with a score of 45 are far from being successful. Candidates receive their exam results before leaving the test site.

The test has been designed to identify those who passed, NOT to rank the scores of exam-takers. Scaled scores are determined by calculating the number of questions answered correctly from the total number of questions in the examination and converting that sum to a scale ranging from 40 to 130. Scores are scaled because there are "sample" questions that the IRS adds to each candidate's exam. These "sample" questions do not count toward the score.

The IRS has previously thrown out questions or allowed multiple answers for about five questions per exam, per part. This is no longer the case. When a candidate takes the exam, scores are given immediately after completion of the section. Prometric will not tell the candidates the questions that they got correct or missed—exam-takers will only receive a score report reflecting whether or not they passed.

Old EA exam questions will no longer be released or published by the IRS. Therefore, you will not be able to anticipate exactly what will be on the exam. Be prepared to be tested on anything that is in the IRS publications.

In addition to this study guide, we highly recommend that all exam candidates read:

- **Publication 17,** *Your Federal Income Tax* (for Part 1 of the exam), and
- **Circular 230,** *Regulations Governing the Practice of Attorneys, Certified Public Accountants, Enrolled Agents, Enrolled Actuaries, and Appraisers before the Internal Revenue Service* (for Part 3 of the exam).

Anyone may download these publications for free from the IRS website or may call the IRS directly and receive a copy in the mail.

If an exam-taker requires special accommodations for a disability, he or she must contact a Prometric test center in advance. For example, a blind or deaf candidate could have a special proctor administer the exam upon request. However, no accommodations will be made for EA candidates with limited English skills. According to the official IRS Bulletin, "difficulty understanding English" is **not** considered a disability for the purposes of the EA examination.

Prometric's policy is to prohibit candidates from bringing in anything, including bottles of water, to the test center to minimize the opportunities for cheating. A second reason for prohibiting water is to avoid the possibility of computers being damaged inadvertently.

The examination is offered throughout the year, providing candidates the opportunity to find a time that fits their schedules. The test will be offered at approximately 290 Prometric Testing Center sites throughout North America, in a highly secure, professional testing environment.

If necessary, candidates are able to re-take each part of the examination several times each year, and there is no longer a deadline for registering. Candidates now apply online throughout the year and pay with a credit card.

It is beneficial for candidates to register and schedule as far in advance as possible. Allowing a longer lead time between scheduling and testing will enable candidates to choose a test date and time that is convenient. If space permits, a candidate may register and schedule up to two days prior to a test date. Candidates are no longer required to take the entire exam in one sitting.

Once the EA Exam candidate passes the test, he or she must undergo a background check and complete an application prior to enrollment. This includes a review of the candidate's tax transcript. Failure to timely file or pay personal income taxes can be grounds for denial of enrollment. A person may not practice as an Enrolled Agent until the application process is complete and the IRS approves the EA's application and issues the candidate a Treasury Card.

Just like CPAs and tax attorneys, EAs can handle any type of tax matter and represent their clients' interests before the IRS. Unlike CPAs and tax attorneys, Enrolled Agents are tested directly by the IRS and Enrolled Agents focus exclusively on tax accounting.

Successfully passing the EA Exam can launch you into a fulfilling and lucrative new career. The exam requires intense preparation and diligence, but with the help of PassKey's comprehensive EA Review, you will have the tools you need to learn how to become an Enrolled Agent.

We wish you much success.

Nine Steps for the IRS EA Exam

STEP 1-Learn

Learn about the Enrolled Agent designation. An Enrolled Agent (EA) has passed a three-part test covering all aspects of federal taxation and has passed an IRS background check. As a result, an EA can represent people before the Internal Revenue Service, just like attorneys and CPAs.

STEP 2-Gather information

Gather information about the Special Enrollment Examination. The IRS publishes basic information about becoming an Enrolled Agent on the Enrollment Overview page of its website. Additionally, candidates will find important information about registering, scheduling, fees, and the format of the EA Exam from the Prometric/IRS website. Prometric administers the Special Enrollment Exam on behalf of the IRS. Candidates will want to download the *"Enrolled Agent Candidate Information Bulletin"* from the Prometric site.

STEP 3-Sign up with Prometric

Sign up to take the Special Enrollment Examination. The easiest way is to sign up online. Candidates sign up for the test using IRS Form 2587 or by using the online Form 2587 found on the Prometric/IRS website. The online form is easier and more secure. The fee is $101 for each part of the exam.

STEP 4-Choose a test site

Choose a test site and test date with Prometric. There are test sites throughout the United States and all over the world. Choose a site that's convenient for you.

STEP 5-Adopt a study plan

Adopt a study plan that covers all the tax topics on the Special Enrollment Examination. Approach each study unit at a pace of three to four hours each. A good rule of thumb is to study at least 60 hours for each of the three exam sections, committing at least 15 hours per week. Start well in advance of the exam date. There's absolutely no point in cramming at the last minute, especially for a test covering something as hard as taxation. Take your time. Try focusing on the "big picture," especially in areas of taxation that might be new to you.

STEP 6-Get plenty of rest, exercise, and good nutrition

Get plenty of rest, exercise, and good nutrition in the two weeks before the EA exam. Don't focus on studying. Instead, review your notes to get an overall feel for the main points of the test. Don't cram in the last two weeks. It will prove counterproductive.

STEP 7-Test day has arrived!

On test day, don't forget your driver's license, ID, or passport! Arrive early to the test site, sign in, and get situated. Have breakfast or lunch, and go to the bathroom before entering to take the exam, because any breaks you take will cut into your exam time. Although you will be able to leave the test center to go to the restroom or take a quick break, the clock does not stop on the exam. You won't be able to bring anything into the test room except glasses and an ID, so make sure you eat and go to the bathroom BEFORE the test. If you need accommodations for a medical condition or a disability, call the test site in advance. The testing site will give each candidate scratch paper, pencils, and a calculator. A candidate cannot bring his or her own paper or calculator.

STEP 8-During the exam

During the exam, do not speak with other students or you may be asked to leave the testing center. Also, with the computer-based test format, the exam questions may differ slightly from what other test-takers have seen. Don't fuss over one question. If you are unsure, just guess and move on! You can always go back at the end if you have time. The exam will allow you to review all your answers if you have time left over. Your scores will be available immediately after the exam. Candidates are not penalized additional points for wrong answers, so it is better to answer every question rather than leave one blank.

Step 9-Congratulations! You passed!

Now you must begin the process of applying for your EA designation through the IRS. You must submit your application fee and IRS Form 23 to the IRS in order to become an Enrolled Agent. Each application is examined by the IRS and each applicant is investigated for suitability. This process takes about three months.

Exam candidates can download IRS **Form 23** at *www.IRS.gov*. Incomplete applications will not be processed. The most common delays are due to:

- Lack of an original signature on IRS Form 23 (NO PHOTOCOPIES)
- Unsigned check for the application fee
- Missing application fee

- Incomplete or unfinished applications

*Note: Although it is not required, it is easier for the IRS to process your Enrolled Agent application (**Form 23**) if you include copies of your Prometric score reports. Candidates who do so tend to get their applications processed much faster.

After the application is processed, the IRS will issue you a Treasury Card. Once you have your Treasury Card and your enrollment number, you are officially an Enrolled Agent!

Essential Tax Figures for Tax Year 2011

These are the most common figures you will see on the IRS Enrolled Agent exam. Although you do not have to memorize exact figures most of the time, the following basic figures are necessary and you should know them. Here's a quick summary of all the essential tax figures for the current exam cycle:

Income Tax Return Filing Deadline: April 17, 2012 (due date for tax returns and extensions)[1]

The Personal Exemption: $3,700, (up $50 from 2010)
Note: In 2011, the personal exemption and itemized deductions do NOT phase out at higher income levels, as in previous years.

2011 Social Security Taxable Wage Base: $106,800

2011 Medicare Taxable Wage Base: No limit

The Annual Gift Tax Exclusion: $13,000 (unchanged from 2010)

2011 Standard Deduction Amounts
- Married Filing Jointly (or Qualifying Widow/Widower) $11,600
- Head of Household $8,500
- Single $5,800
- Married Filing Separately $5,800
- Dependents $950
- Blind taxpayers and senior citizens (over 65) qualify for an increased standard deduction. Additional amounts for 2011 (per taxpayer) are:
    - $1,450 for Single or Head of Household
    - $1,150 for Married Filing Jointly, Married Filing Separately, or Qualifying Widow

Section 179 Expense: $500,000 of qualified expenditures/phase-out at $2 million

Mileage Rates 2011
- **Business Miles**
    - Before 7/1/2011: 51 cents per mile
    - After 6/30/2011: 55.5 cents per mile
- **Medical or Moving Miles**
    - Before 7/1/2011: 19 cents per mile
    - After 6/30/2011: 23.5 cents per mile
- **Charitable Purposes:** 14 cents per mile (unchanged from 2010)

---

[1] Note that the *normal* filing deadline for individual returns is April 15. However, April 15, 2012 is a Sunday and April 16, 2012 falls on Emancipation Day, which is a federal holiday in the District of Columbia (Washington, D.C.)

Retirement Plan Contribution Limits For 2011: Traditional or Roth IRA: $5,000 ($6,000 for taxpayers age 50 and over)

2011 Roth IRA Phase-Out AGI limits
- Married Filing Jointly: $169,000 to $179,000
- Single or Head of Household: $107,000 to $122,000
- Married Filing Separately: $0 to $10,000

Tax Year 2011 Earned Income Tax Credit (EITC) Income Thresholds
Earned income and adjusted gross income (AGI) must each be less than:
- $43,998 ($49,078 MFJ) with three or more qualifying children
- $40,964 ($46,044 MFJ) with two qualifying children
- $36,052 ($41,132 MFJ) with one qualifying child
- $13,660 ($18,740 MFJ) with no qualifying children

Tax Year 2011 Maximum EITC credit:
- $5,751 with three or more qualifying children
- $5,112 with two qualifying children
- $3,094 with one qualifying child
- $464 with no qualifying children

Investment income must be $3,150 **or less** for the year in order to qualify for the EITC.

The **Adoption Credit** is refundable in 2011: $13,360 (maximum credit)

2011 Education Credits and Deductions
- The American Opportunity Credit is a maximum annual credit of $2,500 per student.
- The Lifetime Learning Credit is a maximum of $2,000 per return.
- The Tuition and Fees Deduction is a maximum of $4,000 in 2011.
- The Student Loan Interest Deduction is a maximum $2,500 of qualified loan interest paid in 2011.

New Tax Law Affecting Individuals for 2011

Adoption Credit: In 2011, as in 2010, the Adoption Credit is refundable. This provision expires in 2012. The maximum Adoption Credit is $13,360 in 2011. Taxpayers who adopt a "special needs" child may claim the credit, even if they have no adoption expenses.

Advance EITC: Starting in 2011, Advance EITC is no longer available.[2]

Alternative Minimum Tax (AMT): The AMT exemption amount in 2011 has increased to $48,450 ($74,450 if Married Filing Jointly or a Qualifying Widow(er); $37,225 if Married Filing Separately).

Capital Gains and Losses: Effective in 2011, capital gains and losses are no longer reported directly on Schedule D. The IRS has introduced the new Form 8949, *Sales and Other Dispositions of Capital Assets*. This form is used to list all capital gain and loss transactions; the subtotals are then carried over to Schedule D.

Due Date: The due date for 2011 tax returns is April 17, 2012. The customary tax filing deadline is April 15, 2012, but this is a Sunday and April 16, 2012 falls on Emancipation Day in the District of Columbia, (Washington D.C.)

EITC Penalty Increased: There is a $500 penalty for each failure to comply with EITC due diligence requirements. The penalty was increased from $100 to $500 per return. Preparers are also now required to fill out and attach Form 8867, *Paid Preparers Earned Income Credit Checklist*.

E-File Mandate: A new law requires most tax preparers to e-file income tax returns prepared and filed for individuals, trusts, and estates. The mandate applies to any paid preparer who anticipates filing 11 or more Forms 1040 and/or 1041 during the year. Business and payroll tax returns are not included in this mandate.

Form 1099-K: Starting in 2011, Payment settlement entities (PSE) may have to report merchant card payments and third network payments on new **Form 1099-K**, *Merchant Card and Third-Party Payments*. This means that a business that receives credit card payments or third party payments will now be required to report the gross amount from **Forms-1099-K**.

Health Savings Accounts (HSAs) and Archer MSAs: The additional tax on distributions from HSAs and Archer MSAs not used for qualified medical expenses increased to 20%.

---

[2] The Education Jobs and Medicaid Assistance Act of 2010 permanently repealed the Advance EITC.

Beginning in 2011, only drugs that are prescribed by a doctor (including insulin) are qualified medical expenses. Over-the-counter medications no longer qualify.

Household Employees; Wage Threshold: For 2011, the social security and Medicare wage threshold for household employees remains unchanged at $1,700. This means that taxpayers who paid a household employee cash wages of less than $1,700 in 2011 do not have to report and pay social security and Medicare taxes on that employee's 2011 wages.

Mandatory EFTPS: Businesses must make deposits using the Electronic Federal Tax Payment System (EFTPS); Federal Deposit Coupons are no longer an option. Small businesses that have less than $2,500 in quarterly tax liabilities can choose to pay using a paper check when they file their quarterly returns.

Mandatory PTIN: Starting in 2011, all paid preparers are required to have a Preparer Tax Identification Number (PTIN) before preparing returns.

SE Health Insurance: The SE Health Insurance deduction no longer offsets SE Tax, as it did in 2010. In 2011, it is allowed only as an above-the-line deduction on Page 1 of Form 1040.

Self-employment and Payroll Tax Changes: 2011 saw a temporary decrease in the employee's share of payroll tax. Social Security was withheld from wages at the rate of 4.2% (down from 6.2%). There was no change to Medicare withholding. The same reduction applies to net earnings from self-employment—the temporary rate was 10.4% (down from 12.4%), up to the Social Security wage limit of $106,800. As a result of this change, the overall self-employment tax was reduced from 15.3% to 13.3%.

Standard Mileage Rate: In 2011, the standard mileage rate may be used by a vehicle used for hire, such as a shuttle or a taxicab.

Energy Credits: There are changes to the non-business energy property credit for tax year 2011; the amounts are less than what was allowed in previous years.

Health Coverage Tax Credit (HCTC): A refundable credit that pays 72.5% of qualified health insurance premiums for eligible individuals and their families. In 2011, there is an additional 7.5% retroactive credit.

Estate Tax: For 2011, the estate tax has been reinstated, and the combined exclusion for estate and gift tax is $5 million. A new provision in 2011 allows for "portability" where a predeceased spouse's unused estate tax exclusion may be transferred to the surviving spouse.

Unit 1: Preliminary Work and Individual Taxpayer Data

> **More Reading:**
> Publication 17, *Your Federal Income Tax*
> Publication 519, *U.S. Tax Guide for Aliens*
> Publication 501, *Exemptions, Standard Deduction, and Filing Information*

Use of Prior Years' Returns for Comparison

Enrolled Agents are required to perform due diligence. When a professional preparer sits down to prepare a tax return for a client, he is expected to perform due diligence in collecting, verifying, and gathering taxpayer data. EAs are also expected to review prior year tax returns for compliance, accuracy, and completeness.

A tax professional is required by law to notify a taxpayer of an error on his tax return. A tax professional is also required by law to notify the taxpayer of the consequences of *not* correcting the error. However, a tax professional is not required to actually correct the error.

Example: Terrence Jones is a taxpayer who goes to Janice Smith, EA in order to prepare his tax returns. Terrence is a new client who has always prepared his own tax returns. When Terrence makes his tax interview appointment, Janice tells him to bring his prior year return. When Terrence arrives for his appointment, Janice notices that Terrence made a large error on his prior-year, self-prepared tax return when calculating his Mortgage Interest Deduction. Janice is required to notify Terrence of the error, as well as the consequences of not correcting the error. She encourages Terrence to file an amended tax return in order to correct the mistake. Terrence declines because he does not want to pay for an amended tax return for the prior year. Janice notes in her work papers that Terrence has declined to amend his return, even though she has warned him of the consequences. Janice has therefore fulfilled her professional obligation to notify the taxpayer of the prior year error.

Most tax practitioners use professional tax software to prepare their clients' tax returns. Tax professionals must be knowledgeable about tax law as well as the application of the law as it relates to their particular software program.

Tax software is NOT a substitute for competency and understanding of tax law. In other words, you, as a tax professional, must understand how tax law applies to each individual client.

Tax returns are now primarily filed electronically; tax practitioners have led the way toward a future of completely electronic returns. E-filed returns are also called "paperless" tax returns.

E-filed returns also reduce human error. E-file regulations are tested heavily on **Part 3** of the Enrolled Agent exam. For **Part 1** of the exam, you may not see any questions about the IRS e-file program, but you must know that it exists and that the majority of taxpayers and tax professionals now file this way.[3]

Taxpayer Biographical Information

Tax preparers are expected to collect biographical information. Examples of necessary biographical information include date of birth, marital status, dependents, a client's legal name, and address. All of this information is required in order to prepare an accurate tax return.

Taxpayer biographical information is considered highly sensitive and confidential. Severe preparer penalties exist for preparers who do not protect taxpayer biographical information. Wrongful disclosure of taxpayer information is a criminal offense.

> ***Important Tip:** The U.S. Internal Revenue Code makes it a federal crime for tax professionals who "knowingly or recklessly" disclose confidential taxpayer information to third parties or who use such information for any non-preparation purpose. Exceptions apply for disclosures mandated by law or a court or for disclosure for use in preparing state or local tax returns. Generally, in order for the criminal penalties to apply, criminal intent must be proven. Ordinary preparer negligence does not qualify as "criminal intent." This law became effective in 1997. You will be tested more on client privacy and disclosure rules on Part 3 (Ethics) of the exam.

A tax preparer is also required to determine a taxpayer's residency. In other words, the preparer must determine whether or not the taxpayer is considered a *resident* or *non-resident*.

The rules for determining residency for tax purposes are completely different than what is established under current immigration law. A person who has a "green card" or a "student visa" may still be considered a resident of the United States for tax purposes, even if he does not have a Social Security Number.

There are numerous examples of when this may occur. A common example is when a soldier marries a foreign spouse and brings him or her to the United States. Usually, the spouse must wait to be assigned a Social Security Number. However, the couple may still file a joint tax return by requesting an Individual Tax Identification Number (ITIN) from the IRS for the foreign spouse. ITINs are also requested for parents adopting a foreign child while they wait for the adoption to become final.

Taxpayer Identification Numbers (TINs)

IRS regulations require that each individual listed on a U.S. federal income tax return have a valid Taxpayer Identification Number (TIN). The types of TINs are:

- Social Security Number (SSN)

---

[3] A new e-file mandate requires most paid preparers to electronically file federal income tax returns prepared and filed for individuals, trusts, and estates. This law went into effect starting Jan. 1, 2011.

- Individual Taxpayer Identification Number (ITIN)
- Adoption Taxpayer Identification Number (ATIN)

An Employer Identification Number (EIN) is also a type of identifying number, but it is used for entities and businesses. The Employer Identification Number will be covered and discussed at length in Part 2, Businesses.

One of the first things a tax professional should do when preparing an individual's tax return is to ask for a Social Security card for each person who will be listed on the return. Then the tax preparer should verify the accuracy of the Social Security Number and the spelling of the individual's name by ensuring that the information on the tax return matches the Social Security card.

An SSN, ITIN, or ATIN is required for the taxpayer, the taxpayer's spouse (if married), and any dependent listed on the tax return.

Any taxpayer who is not eligible for a Social Security Number must request an Individual Taxpayer Identification Number. The issuance of an ITIN does not:

- Entitle the recipient to Social Security benefits or the Earned Income Tax Credit[4] (EITC)
- Create a presumption regarding the individual's immigration status
- Give the individual the right to work in the United States

Taxpayers who cannot obtain an SSN must apply for an ITIN if they file a U.S. tax return or are listed on a tax return as a spouse or dependent. These taxpayers must file **Form W-7**, *Application for Individual Taxpayer Identification Number*, and supply documentation that will establish foreign status and true identity. A federal tax return must generally be filed along with **Form W-7**.

> **Example:** Kamala is a U.S. citizen and has a Social Security Number. In January 2011, Kamala marries José Martinez, a citizen of Mexico. José has one child from a prior marriage named Graciela. Kamala decides to file jointly with Jose in 2011 and also claim her stepdaughter Graciela as a dependent. In order to file jointly and claim the child, they must request ITINs for José and Graciela. They must file **Form W-7**, *Application for Individual Taxpayer Identification Number*, and supply the required documentation.

Adopted children may be claimed as dependents even if they do not have a Social Security Number yet. If the taxpayer is unable to secure a Social Security Number for a child until the adoption is final, he may request an Adoption Taxpayer Identification Number (ATIN). The ATIN may NOT be used to claim the Earned Income Tax Credit.

A taxpayer should apply for an ATIN only if he is adopting a child *and* meets all of the following qualifications:

---

[4] The IRS uses both the terms "EIC" and "EITC." "EIC" stands for "Earned Income Credit" and "EITC" stands for "Earned Income Tax Credit." They mean essentially the same thing.

- The child is placed in the taxpayer's home for legal adoption.
- The adoption is a domestic adoption OR the adoption is a legal foreign adoption and the child has a Permanent Resident Alien Card or Certificate of Citizenship.
- The taxpayer cannot obtain the child's existing SSN even though he has made a reasonable attempt to obtain it from the birth parents, the placement agency, and other persons.
- The taxpayer cannot obtain an SSN for the child from the Social Security Administration for any reason (for example, the adoption is not final).

An ATIN can be requested for an adopted child using IRS **Form W-7A,** *Application for Taxpayer Identification Number for Pending U.S. Adoptions.* The dependent must meet the dependency qualifications (covered next) in order to be claimed as a dependent on the taxpayer's tax return.

The Preparer Tax Identification Number (PTIN) is also an identifying number, but it is used exclusively by tax preparers to identify themselves on a taxpayer's return. It is not an identifying number for taxpayer use.

Generally, anyone who files a tax return or claims a dependent must have a Taxpayer Identification Number: an ITIN, ATIN, or an SSN.

*Exception: A Child Who Is Born and Dies in the Same Tax Year

There is *one* narrow exception to the rule that requires all dependents to have a Social Security Number, ATIN, or an ITIN. If a child is born *and* dies within the same tax year and is not granted a Social Security Number, the taxpayer may still claim that child as a dependent.

The tax return must be filed on paper and the birth and death certificate attached to the return. The birth certificate must show that the child was born alive. The taxpayer enters "DIED" in the space for the dependent's Social Security Number on the tax return. A stillborn child does not qualify. The child must have been born alive, even if he only lived for a short time. This might seem like an obscure rule, but this question has showed up on prior exams, so try to remember it.

Example: Alice gave birth to a son on October 1, 2011. The baby had health problems and died within three days. The child was issued a death certificate and a birth certificate, but not a Social Security Number. Alice may claim her son as a qualifying child in 2011, even though he only lived a short time. She must file the return on paper and attach the death and birth certificate (**Publication 501**).

Filing Requirements and Thresholds

Not every person is required to file a tax return. A taxpayer is required to file a tax return if his 2011 income exceeds the *combined total* of the standard deduction and personal exemption amounts.[5] Sometimes, a taxpayer is required to though none of his income is taxable. To determine whether a person sho return, a tax preparer must check the taxpayer's **Form W-2**, and/or **Form(s) 1(**

There are different requirements for taxpayers who are self-employed. Generally, a taxpayer is required to file a tax return if he has self-employment earnings of $400 or more.

In order to determine whether someone must file a tax return, the tax practitioner must also determine if:

- The person can be claimed as a dependent on another's tax return
- Special taxes might be owed on different types of income
- Some of the taxpayer's income is excludable (or exempt)

The filing requirements listed below apply mainly to wage earners. There will be numerous examples at the end of the section in order to demonstrate different filing scenarios.

In the case of an individual taxpayer, filing requirements vary based on gross income, age, and filing status.

2011 Filing Requirements for Most Taxpayers

Here are the 2011 filing requirement thresholds:

- Single: $9,500
- Single, 65 or over: $10,950
- Head of Household (HOH): $12,200
- Head of Household, 65 or over: $13,650
- Married Filing Jointly (MFJ): $19,000
    - *Over 65, (MFJ): $20,150 (65 or over, one spouse)
    - *Over 65, (MFJ): $21,300 (65 or over, both spouses)
- Married Filing Separately (MFS): $3,700 (any age)
- Qualifying Widow/Widower: $15,300 ($16,450 if age 65 and older)

Example: Fredericka is 36 years old, single, and her gross income was $20,000 last year. She does not have any children. She is required to file a tax return status since her income was over $9,500. She will use the "Single" filing status.

Example: Frances and Javier are married and plan to file jointly. Frances is 64 and had a gross income of $11,000 for the tax year. Javier is 66 and his gross income was $5,000 for the year. Since their combined gross income was $16,000 (which is under $20,150), they are not required to file a tax return. The filing requirement threshold for joint filers when one spouse is over 65 is $21,150 in 2011.

---

[5] See the tables at the beginning of the book for the standard deduction and personal exemption amounts.

> **Example:** Albert is single and 67 years old. No one can claim him as a dependent. His gross income was $11,550 during the tax year. Based only on this information, Albert is required to file a return because his gross income was over the filing threshold for single taxpayers who are over 65.

There are special rules for dependents with taxable income, self-employed persons, and non-resident aliens.

A dependent is required to file when he has *any* of the following:
- "Unearned" income[6] of *more than* $950 (such as interest income)
- Earned income of *more than* $5,800 (such as wages)
- Gross income of *more than* the larger of:
    - $950 or
    - Earned income (up to $5,800) plus $300

> **Example:** Danny is a 16-year-old high school student who is claimed as a dependent on his parents' tax return. He works as a pizza delivery boy ten hours a week and in 2011 earned $3,200 in wages. He also had $1,100 of interest income from a Certificate of Deposit his grandmother gave him last year. Danny is required to file a tax return because his unearned income exceeds $950.

> **Example:** Taryn is 15. Her mother claims Taryn as a dependent on her tax return. Taryn worked part time on weekends during the school year and full time during the summer. She earned $5,900 in wages and did not have any other income. Taryn must file a tax return because her total "earned income" is more than $5,800.

> **Example:** Marc is 20, single, and a full-time college student. Marc's parents claim him on their joint income tax return. Marc received $200 in interest income and earned $2,750 in wages from a part-time job. Marc does NOT have to file a tax return because his total income of $2,950 ($200 interest plus $2,750 in wages) is below the filing threshold for dependents.

Generally, if a dependent child who must file a tax return cannot file it for any reason, such as age, then the parent (or other legal guardian) must file it on the child's behalf. If a child cannot sign his own tax return, the guardian must sign the child's name followed by the words "By (signature), parent for minor child."

Not all income is taxable. There are many types of income that are *reportable*, but not taxable, to the recipient. Even if a taxpayer is not legally required to file a tax return, he should—if eligible to receive a refund. Taxpayers should still file tax returns if any of the following are true:
- They had income tax withheld from their pay.

---

[6] "Unearned income" is all income that is not earned. Some common types of unearned income are prizes, inheritances, interest income, and dividends. "Earned income," on the other hand, is money that is earned by the taxpayer, such as wages or self-employment income.

- They made estimated tax payments or had a prior year overpayment.
- They qualify for the Earned Income Tax Credit (EITC).
- They qualify for any other refundable tax credits.

> **Example**: Rita is 65 years old, married, and has $9,500 of wage income in 2011. Her husband, Roger, has $10,000 in wage income. They have no dependents. Normally, Roger and Rita would not have a filing requirement. However, Rita has decided that she wants to file separately from her husband in 2011. Rita is therefore required to file a tax return because the filing threshold for MFS is $3,700. In this case, it is Rita's filing status that forces her to file a tax return. Roger must also file a tax return, because his filing status is also MFS by default. Roger cannot choose to file jointly with his wife unless she agrees, since both spouses are required to sign a joint return.

> **Example**: Holly is single with a dependent four-year-old child and qualifies for Head of Household filing status. Holly earns $8,500 in wages during 2011. She also earns $700 in self-employment income from cleaning houses on the side. Even though Holly makes less than the filing threshold for Head of Household filing status, Holly is required to file a tax return because her self-employment earnings exceed $400. Even if Holly did not have self-employment earnings, she should still file a tax return, because she likely qualifies for the Earned Income Credit, which is a refundable credit for low income wage earners. The Earned Income Credit will give her a nice refund in 2011.

Other Odd Filing Requirement Situations

Sometimes, the taxpayer is required to file a tax return in situations where the gross income threshold is not met. Here are examples where the taxpayer is required to file a tax return, even when gross income is below the regular filing requirement thresholds:

- If the taxpayer has self-employment earnings of $400 or more.
- **Church employees:** If a taxpayer is a church employee who is *exempt* from employers' Social Security and Medicare taxes and has wages of $108.28 or more. (***Note:** this seems like an odd exception; however, it has shown up on prior exams. Remember this special rule is for church employees only.)
- If the taxpayer owes Social Security tax or Medicare tax on unreported tips.
- If the taxpayer owes tax on an IRA, qualified retirement plan, Health Savings Account, Coverdell Education Savings Account, or Alternative Minimum Tax.
- If the taxpayer owes household employment taxes for a household worker such as a nanny.
- If the taxpayer is a non-resident alien with a U.S. business or tax liability not covered by tax withholding.
- If the taxpayer must *recapture* an education credit, investment credit, or other credit.

- If a non-resident alien has income from a trade or business in the U.S., or has passive income from a U.S. investment and not all the required U.S. tax was withheld from that income.

Unit 1: Questions

1. Generally, every taxpayer that files a tax return must use an identifying number. Which of the following is NOT a Taxpayer Identification Number for IRS purposes?

A. Social Security Number (SSN).
B. Adoption Taxpayer Identification Number (ATIN).
C. Individual Tax Identification Number (ITIN).
D. Preparer Tax Identification Number (PTIN).

The answer is D. A Preparer Tax Identification Number (PTIN) is used by preparers to identify themselves on a taxpayer's return. It is not an identifying number for taxpayer use. ###

2. Which IRS form is used to request an ATIN for an adopted child where the adoption is not yet final?

A. IRS **Form W-7A**.
B. IRS **Form W-2**.
C. IRS **Form SSA**.
D. IRS **Form 1099**.

The answer is A. An ATIN can be requested for an adopted child by using IRS **Form W-7A**. ###

3. Which of the following taxpayers is required to have an Individual Taxpayer Identification Number (ITIN)?

A. A non-resident alien with an SSN who moves outside the U.S.
B. A non-resident alien who must file a return and is not eligible for a valid SSN.
C. Anyone who doesn't have a Social Security Number.
D. All non-resident and resident aliens.

The answer is B. If a taxpayer must file a U.S. tax return or is listed on a tax return as a spouse or dependent and is not eligible for an SSN, he must apply for an ITIN. ###

4. The issuance of an ITIN does NOT:

A. Entitle the recipient to Social Security benefits or the Earned Income Tax Credit (EITC).
B. Create a presumption regarding the individual's immigration status.
C. Give the individual the right to work in the United States.
D. All of the above.

The answer is D. An ITIN is for reporting purposes only and does not entitle the taxpayer to the EITC or to Social Security benefits. An ITIN also does not create a presumption about the taxpayer's immigration or work status. ###

5. Which of the following statements regarding the ATIN is incorrect?

A. An ATIN may be used to claim the Earned Income Tax Credit.
B. The ATIN may NOT be used to claim the Earned Income Tax Credit.
C. An ATIN may be requested by a taxpayer who is unable to secure a Social Security Number for a child until his adoption is final.
D. An ATIN may be used by adults who wish to work in the U.S., but are not eligible for a Social Security Number.

The answer is A. An ATIN may NOT be used to claim the Earned Income Tax Credit. If the taxpayer is unable to secure a Social Security Number for a child until the adoption is final, he may request an Adoption Taxpayer Identification Number (ATIN).###

6. Steven and Rochelle had a child on December 2, 2011. The child only lived for an hour and died before midnight. What is the true statement regarding the child?

A. Steven and Rochelle may NOT claim the child as a dependent on their tax return, because the child did not live with them for the entire tax year.
B. Steven and Rochelle may NOT claim the child as a dependent on their tax return unless they get a Social Security Number for the child.
C. Steven and Rochelle MAY claim the child as a dependent on their tax return, even if they are unable to get a Social Security Number.
D. Steven and Rochelle may not claim the child as a dependent on their tax return for 2011, but they may claim the child for tax year 2012.

The answer is C. If a child is born and died in the same tax year, an SSN is not required in order to take the dependency exemption in that tax year. The tax return must be filed on paper, and the taxpayer must enter the word "DIED" in the space normally reserved for the SSN. ###

7. Larry and Zelda are married but they choose not to file jointly. Larry is 42 and Zelda is 36. Larry's gross income from wages was $30,150 and Zelda's was $3,900. Which of the following is true?

A. Only Larry is required to file.
B. Only Zelda is required to file.
C. Both Larry and Zelda are required to file.
D. Neither Larry nor Zelda are required to file.

The answer is C. Both Larry and Zelda must file tax returns. Taxpayers under 65 who use the "Married Filing Separately" status and earn more than $3,700 in 2011 must file a return. ###

8. Helen and Edward were married in 2011. They have no dependents. Edward wants to file jointly, but Helen does not want to file jointly with her husband. Helen is 65 and had a gross income of $2,000 for the tax year. Edward is 72. His gross income was $28,000 for the year. Which of the following statements is true?

A. Edward is required to file a tax return, and he must file MFS. Helen is not required to file a return.
B. Edward may still file jointly with Helen and sign on her behalf, so long as he notifies her in writing.
C. Edward and Helen are both required to file tax returns, and they must both file MFS.
D. Edward and Helen may both file SINGLE.

The answer is A. Since Edward and Helen are married, they must either file jointly or separately. Since Helen does not agree to file jointly with Edward, Edward is forced to file MFS. Helen is not required to file a tax return because her gross income in 2011 was $2,000. The filing requirement threshold for Married Filing Separately (MFS) is $3,700 (any age). ###

9. Janet and Harry are married and file jointly. During the tax year, Janet turned 67 and Harry turned 66. Janet's gross income was $19,000, and Harry's gross income from self-employment was $620. Harry had no other income. Based on this information, which of the following statements is true?

A. Janet and Harry are not required to file a tax return.
B. Janet and Harry are required to file a tax return.
C. Only Janet is required to file a tax return.
D. Only Harry is required to file a tax return.

The answer is B. Janet and Harry must both file a tax return. Normally, Janet and Harry would not be required to file because their combined gross income was less than $21,300 in 2011, and they are both over 65 (this threshold applies to taxpayers who are 65 or over, both spouses). However, they are required to file a tax return because they file jointly, and Harry's self-employment income exceeds $400. ###

10. Malik and Dorothy are married and ages 38 and 42, respectively. Malik earned $19,000 in wages, and Dorothy earned $3,500 in wages. Although they receive some assistance from friends and relatives, they cannot be claimed as dependents by anyone. Which of the following is correct?

A. They are both required to file a tax return, whether they file jointly or separately.
B. If they choose to file separately, Malik is required to file a return, but Dorothy is not.
C. They are both required to file a tax return only if either spouse chooses to file MFS.
D. If they choose to file separately, Dorothy is required to file a return, but Malik is not.

The answer is B. They may choose to file jointly, or they may file separately. If they choose to file separately, only Malik is required to file a return. Dorothy's wage income is less than the filing threshold for MFS ($3,700). ###

11. Trinity is a single, 22-year-old, full-time college student and is claimed as a dependent on her mother's tax return. In 2011, Trinity earned $5,900 in wages from her part-time job as an administrative assistant. Trinity has no other income. Is she required to file a tax return?

A. No, Trinity is not required to file a tax return.
B. Yes, Trinity is required to file a tax return.
C. Trinity is only required to file a tax return if she is a full-time student.
D. None of the above.

The answer is B. A single dependent whose earned income was over $5,700 in 2011 must file a return. ###

12. A person who is not required to file a tax return should still file a return for any of the following reasons except to _____.

A. Report self-employment net earnings of $400 or more.
B. Claim a refund of withheld taxes.
C. Claim the Earned Income Credit.
D. Claim the additional Child Tax Credit.

The answer is A. Even if the thresholds indicate that a return does not have to be filed, individuals who want to claim tax refunds, the EITC, or additional child tax credits should still file a return. A taxpayer with self-employment earnings of $400 or more is *required* to file a tax return. ###

13. Cecily is in the process of adopting an infant boy. She qualifies to take the child as a dependent, but she cannot obtain a Social Security Number for the child yet. What can you advise Cecily to do in order to claim the child?

A: Cecily may file a tax return on paper and put "adopted" in the line for the SSN.
B: Cecily must wait until a valid Social Security Number is issued in order to claim the child.
C. Cecily may apply for an ATIN in order to claim the baby.
D: Cecily may not claim the child until the adoption is final.

The answer is C. Cecily may request an ATIN and claim the child. An ATIN is an Adoption Taxpayer Identification Number issued by the IRS as a temporary Taxpayer Identification Number for the child in a domestic adoption where the taxpayers are unable to obtain the child's Social Security Number. The ATIN is to be used by the adopting taxpayers on their federal income tax return to identify the child while final domestic adoption is pending. ###

Unit 2: Filing Status

In order to file a tax return, a tax preparer must identify the taxpayer's filing status. There are five filing statuses, and you must clearly understand the rules governing each status.

There are also special rules that you must understand regarding annulled marriages and widows/widowers.

1. Single or "Considered Unmarried"

A taxpayer is considered SINGLE if, on the last day of the tax year, the taxpayer was:

- Unmarried
- Legally separated or divorced, or
- Widowed (and not remarried during the year).

Although a taxpayer is considered SINGLE, some taxpayers may qualify for another filing status that gives him a lower tax, such as Head of Household or Qualifying Widow(er).

A taxpayer who is single (or legally divorced) on the *last* day of the year is considered "single" for the *entire tax year*.

A taxpayer is also "considered unmarried" if, on the last day of the tax year, he is legally separated from his spouse under a divorce decree or separate maintenance decree.

Example: Jim and Jennifer legally divorced on December 31, 2011. Jim and Jennifer do not have any dependents. They each must file SINGLE for tax year 2011. They may NOT file a joint return for 2011.

State law governs whether a person is considered *married* or *legally separated*. If a taxpayer is legally divorced on the last day of the year, he is considered single for the whole year. Divorced taxpayers CANNOT choose "Married Filing Jointly" as their filing status.

*****Special Note: Annulled Marriages (Single):** If a marriage is annulled, then the marriage is considered *never to have existed*. Annulment is a legal procedure for declaring a marriage null and void. Unlike divorce, an annulment is *retroactive*. If a taxpayer obtains a court decree of annulment that holds that no valid marriage ever existed, the couple is considered unmarried even if they filed joint returns for earlier years.

Taxpayers who have annulled their marriage must file amended returns (**Form 1040X**) claiming Single (or Head of Household status, if applicable) for all the tax years affected by the annulment that are not closed by the statute of limitations. The statute of limitations for filing generally does not expire until *three years* after an original return was filed.

> **Example:** Sarah and Robert were granted an annulment on October 31, 2011. They were married for two years. They do not have any dependents. They each must file SINGLE for 2011, and the prior two years' tax returns must be amended to reflect "Single" as their filing status.

2. Married Filing Jointly (MFJ)

Married taxpayers may file jointly even if one spouse did not earn any income. Taxpayers MAY use the Married Filing Jointly (MFJ) status if they are married and:

- Live together as husband and wife
- Live apart but are not legally separated or divorced
- They are separated under an interlocutory (not final) divorce decree
- The taxpayer's spouse died during the year and the taxpayer has not remarried

For federal tax purposes, a "marriage" only qualifies for joint filing status if the marriage is between a man and a woman. Although many states now offer same-sex unions, they are not currently recognized for federal tax purposes.[7]

The IRS will also recognize a common law marriage if it is recognized by the state where the taxpayers now live or where the common law marriage began.[8] A U.S. resident or U.S. citizen who is married to a non-resident alien can elect to file a joint return as long as both spouses agree to be taxed on their worldwide income.

On a joint return, spouses report combined income and deduct combined allowable expenses. Spouses can file a joint return even if only one spouse had income. Both spouses must include all of their income, exemptions, and deductions on their joint return. Both husband and wife must agree to sign the return and are responsible for any tax owed. Both spouses may be held responsible for all the tax due, even if all the income was earned by only one spouse.

A subsequent divorce usually does not relieve either spouse of the liability associated with the original joint return.[9]

If a taxpayer files a separate return, he may elect to amend the filing status to "Married Filing Jointly" at any time within three years of the due date of the original

---

[7] The Defense of Marriage Act (DOMA) provides that the word "marriage" means only a legal union between one man and one woman as husband and wife. This tax issue is currently being litigated in several courts.

[8] Only nine U.S. states recognize common-law marriage (Alabama, Colorado, Kansas, Rhode Island, South Carolina, Iowa, Montana, Oklahoma, Texas, and the District of Columbia). You will not be required to memorize the states for the exam. Just realize and understand that common-law marriage exists and is a valid basis for the MFJ filing status.

[9] Married taxpayers are jointly responsible for the tax due on a joint return even if they later divorce. However, there are some cases where a taxpayer may request innocent spouse relief (covered extensively in Part 3 of the exam books) from a joint liability.

return. This does not include any extensions. A "separate return" includes a return filed claiming "Married Filing Separately," "Single," or "Head of Household" filing status.

Once a taxpayer files a joint return, he cannot choose to file a separate return (MFS) for the year *after* the due date of the return. So, for example, if a married couple filed their joint 2011 tax return on March 25, 2012, and one of the spouses decides to file MFS, then they only have until April 17,[10] 2012 to elect MFS filing status.

If a spouse dies during the year, the couple is still considered married for the whole year and can choose Married Filing Jointly as their filing status. In this case, the surviving spouse signs the joint return as the "surviving spouse" on the signature line of **Form 1040**.

*Exception: A personal representative for a decedent (deceased taxpayer) can change from a joint return elected by the surviving spouse to a separate return for the decedent, up to a year *after* the filing deadline.

Example: Kurt and his wife Susan have always filed jointly. Susan dies suddenly in 2011, and her will names Harriet, her daughter from a previous marriage, as the executor for her estate and all her legal affairs. Kurt files a joint return with Susan in 2011, but Harriet, as the executor, decides that it would be better for Susan's estate if her tax return was filed MFS. Harriet has the right to change Susan's filing status on her 2011 tax return to MFS. Harriet files an amended return for 2011 claiming MFS status for Susan, and signs the return as the executor.

3. Married Filing Separately (MFS)

The Married Filing Separately (MFS) status is for taxpayers who are married and either:
- Choose to file separate returns, or
- Do not agree to file a joint return.

Taxpayers who are married may choose the Married Filing Separately status, which means the husband and wife report their own incomes and deductions on separate returns, even if one spouse had no income. A married taxpayer who files separately must write the spouse's name and Social Security Number (or ITIN) on the front of the Form 1040 (see image).

If a taxpayer files a separate return, he generally reports only his own income, exemptions, credits, and deductions (although there are special rules in community property states). Special rules apply to Married Filing Separately taxpayers, which usually results in the taxpayer paying a higher tax. For example, when filing separately:
- The tax rate is generally higher than on a joint return, and
- Taxpayers cannot take credits for child and dependent care expenses, earned income, and certain adoption and education expenses.

---

[10] Don't forget that the due date for tax returns in the 2011 tax year is April 17, not April 15!

There are some rare instances when MFS might be a more beneficial filing status. There is a potential advantage of using MFS status whenever:
- Both spouses have taxable income, and
- At least one (usually the person with the lower income) has high itemized deductions that are limited by adjusted gross income (AGI). For example, it may happen that one spouse has very high medical expenses and the MFS filing status will give him a lower taxable income, because the medical expenses would have been "phased out" on a joint return.

One common reason taxpayers file as Married Filing Separately is to avoid an offset of their refund against their current spouse's outstanding prior debt. This includes past due child support, past due student loans, or a tax liability a spouse incurred before the marriage.

Example: Jerry and Danielle usually file jointly. However, Danielle has chosen to separate her finances from her husband. Jerry wishes to file jointly with Danielle, but she has refused. Danielle files using "Married Filing Separately" as her filing status; therefore, Jerry is forced to file MFS as well.

Example: Dinesh and Molly were married in 2011. Dinesh owes past due taxes from a prior year. Molly chooses to file separately from Dinesh, so her refund will not be offset by his overdue tax debt. If they were to file jointly, their refund would be retained in order to pay the debt.

There are special rules on MFS returns regarding itemized deductions. If a married couple files separately and one spouse itemizes deductions, the other spouse must either:
- Also itemize deductions, or
- Claim "0" (zero) as the standard deduction.

In other words, a taxpayer whose spouse itemizes deductions cannot take the standard deduction. The question of who is itemizing only becomes a consideration when *both* taxpayers are filing MFS. If one spouse qualifies for Head of Household, the fact that the other one is filing MFS and is itemizing doesn't apply.

Example: Tom and Judith always keep their finances separate. They want to file Married Filing Separately. Tom plans to itemize his casualty losses, so then Judith is forced to either itemize her deductions or claim a zero standard deduction.

The Basic Rules on an MFS Tax Return

1. The tax rate will generally be higher than it would be on a joint return.
2. The exemption amount for the Alternative Minimum Tax will be half that allowed to a joint return filer.
3. Neither spouse can take the credit for child and dependent care expenses.
4. Neither spouse can take the Earned Income Credit.

5. Taxpayers cannot take the exclusion or credit for adoption expenses in most cases.
6. Neither spouse can take education credits.
7. Neither spouse can exclude any interest from qualified U.S. savings bonds used for higher education expenses.
8. If one spouse itemizes deductions, the other spouse cannot claim the standard deduction, even if he does not have qualified expenses to itemize. If the taxpayers choose to claim the standard deduction, the basic standard deduction is half the amount allowed on a joint return.
9. A taxpayer's capital loss deduction for MFS is $1,500 instead of $3,000 when filing a joint return.
10. A taxpayer cannot roll over amounts from a traditional IRA into a Roth IRA on an MFS return.
11. For calculating the taxable portion of Social Security, the "provisional income amount" is zero (not $25,000 for Single or $32,000 for Married Filing Jointly).

4. Head of Household

Taxpayers may use the Head of Household (HOH) status if they meet three criteria:

- The taxpayer must be "considered unmarried" (single, divorced, or legally separated) on the last day of the year, or meet the tests for married persons living apart with dependent children.
- The taxpayer must have also paid more than half the cost of maintaining a main home.
- The taxpayer must have had a qualifying person living in his home *more* than half the year (an exception exists for a qualifying parent).

In general, the Head of Household status is for unmarried taxpayers who paid *more* than half the cost of keeping up a home for a qualified dependent relative who lived with them in the home more than half the tax year. Valid household expenses include:

- Rent, mortgage interest, real estate taxes
- Home insurance, repairs, utilities
- Domestic help, such as in-home cleaning services and lawn care
- Food eaten in the home

Welfare payments are not considered amounts that the taxpayer provides to maintain a home.

Special Rule for Dependent Parents: If a taxpayer's qualifying person is a dependent *parent*, the taxpayer may still file Head of Household even if the parent *does not live* with the taxpayer. The taxpayer must pay more than half the cost of keeping up a home that was the parent's main home for the entire year. A taxpayer also is considered "keeping up a main home" if he pays more than half the cost of keeping his parent in a rest home.

> **Example:** Sharon is 54 years old and single. She pays the monthly bill for Shady Pines Nursing Home, where her 75-year-old mother lives. Sharon's mother has lived at Shady Pines for two years and has no income. Since Sharon pays more than half of the cost of her mother's living expenses, Sharon qualifies to use the Head of Household filing status.

> **Example:** Tina is single and financially supports her mother, Rue, who lives in her own apartment. Rue dies suddenly on September 15, 2011. Tina may still claim her mother as a dependent and file Head of Household in 2011.

This rule also applies to parents, stepparents, grandparents, etc. who are related to the taxpayer by blood, marriage, or adoption (other examples include a stepmother or father-in-law).

*Special Rule for a Death or Birth during the Year: A taxpayer may still file as Head of Household if the qualifying individual is born (or dies) during the year. The taxpayer must have provided more than half of the cost of keeping up a home that was the individual's main home while the person was alive.

> **Example:** Tony and Velma have a child in 2011. The child only lives for one month. Tony and Velma may still claim the child on their tax return as a qualifying child. That is because a dependent can still be claimed, even though the child only lived for a short while.

For the purposes of the Head of Household filing status, a "qualifying person" is defined as:

- A qualifying child,
- A married child who can be claimed as a dependent, or
- A dependent parent.

The taxpayer's qualifying child includes the taxpayer's child or stepchild (whether by blood or adoption); foster child, sibling, or stepsibling; or a descendant of any of these. For example, a niece or nephew, stepbrother, foster child, or a grandchild may all be eligible as "qualifying persons" for the purpose of the Head of Household filing status.

> **Example:** Lewis's unmarried son, Lincoln, lived with him all year. Lincoln turned 18 at the end of the year. Lincoln does not have a job and did not provide any of his own support. Lincoln is not a dependent of anyone else. As a result, Lincoln is Lewis's qualifying child. Lewis may claim Head of Household filing status.

The "qualifying person" for Head of Household filing status must always be related to the taxpayer either by blood or marriage (with the exception of a foster child, who also qualifies if the child was legally placed in the home by a government agency or entity).

Example: Jeffrey has lived with his girlfriend, Patricia, and her son, Nolan, for five years. Jeffrey pays all of the costs of keeping up their home. Patricia is unemployed and does not contribute to the household costs. Jeffrey is not related to Nolan and cannot claim him as a dependent. No one else lives in the household. Jeffrey cannot file as Head of Household because neither Patricia nor Nolan is a "qualifying person" for Jeffrey.

An unrelated individual may still be considered a "qualifying relative" for a dependency exemption, but will NOT be a qualifying person for the Head of Household filing status. In the example below, the taxpayer lives with an unrelated person (a friend) who qualifies as his dependent, but since they are unrelated (either by blood or marriage), then the taxpayer cannot claim Head of Household filing status.

Example: Since her husband died five years ago, Joan has lived with her friend, Wilson. Joan is a U.S. citizen, is single, and lived with Wilson all year. Joan had no income and received all of her financial support from Wilson. Joan falls under the definition of a Qualifying Relative, and Wilson can claim Joan as a dependent on his return. However, Joan would not qualify Wilson to file as Head of Household.

In order for a taxpayer to file as Head of Household, a qualifying child does not have to be a dependent of the taxpayer (unless the qualifying person is married). So, to explain further, a taxpayer may still file as Head of Household and NOT claim the qualifying person as his dependent. This happens most often with divorced parents. The example below illustrates a common scenario.

Example: George and Elizabeth have been divorced for five years. They have one child, a 12-year-old daughter named Rebecca. Rebecca lives with her mother, Elizabeth, and only sees her father on weekends. Therefore, Elizabeth is the custodial parent. Elizabeth and George have an agreement with each other that allows George to claim the dependency exemption for Rebecca on his tax return. In 2011, George correctly files SINGLE and claims Rebecca as his dependent. Elizabeth may still file as Head of Household. There is an area on Form 1040 that allows Elizabeth to indicate Head of Household status and supply Rebecca's name and Social Security Number (see sample image below).

Taxpayers must always specify the qualifying person who makes them eligible for Head of Household filing status. If the qualifying person is also the taxpayer's dependent, then the dependent's name is entered on the Form 1040 Exemptions section, (line 6c). If the qualifying person is the taxpayer's child and is NOT a dependent, then the taxpayer must enter the child's name on the return's Filing Status section, (Form 1040, line 4).

Special Rules for HOH

Some married taxpayers who live apart from their spouses and provide for dependent children may be considered "unmarried" for Head of Household purposes. These taxpayers are permitted to file as Head of Household if they meet all the following criteria:

- The married taxpayer chooses to not file a joint return with his spouse.
- The taxpayer paid more than half the cost of keeping up the qualifying child's home for the year.
- The taxpayer's spouse *did not live in the home* during the last six months of the year.

Example: Luke and Laura separated in February 2011 and lived apart for the rest of the year. They do not have a written separation agreement and are not divorced yet. Their six-year-old daughter, Pauline, lived with Luke all year. Luke and Laura will not file a joint tax return. Luke paid more than half the cost of keeping up his home. Luke claims Pauline's exemption because he is the custodial parent. Luke can also claim Head of Household status for 2011. Although Luke is still legally married, he can file as Head of Household because he meets all the requirements to be "considered unmarried."

The taxpayer's home must be the *main home* of the taxpayer's qualifying child, stepchild, or eligible foster child for more than half the year in order to qualify under this special rule for married spouses who are living apart.

Example: Janine and Richard separated on July 10, but were not divorced at the end of the year. They have one minor child, Madeline, who is 10 years old. Even though Janine lived with Madeline and supported her for the remainder of the year, Janine does not qualify for Head of Household filing status because she and Richard **did not live apart** for the last six months of the year.

*Special Rule for Non-resident Alien Spouses: A taxpayer who is married to a *non-resident alien* spouse may elect to file as Head of Household even if both spouses lived together throughout the year.

Example: In 2010, Tim Jones met and married Maria Consuela, a non-resident alien. Maria is a citizen and resident of Spain. They lived together in Spain while Tim was on a sabbatical from his university teaching position. Tim and Maria have a child named Taylor, who was born in 2011. Tim may still file as Head of Household, even though Tim and Maria lived together all year, because Maria is a non-resident alien.

5. Qualifying Widow(er) With a Dependent Child

In actual practice, "Qualifying Widow(er)" is the least common filing status that you will encounter as a tax professional. However, because of its complexity, it is still heavily tested on the EA exam.

This filing status yields a tax rate *equal to* Married Filing Jointly. What this means is that surviving spouses receive the **same** standard deduction and tax rates as taxpayers who are Married Filing Jointly. In the year of the spouse's death, a taxpayer can file a joint return. For the following two years after death, the surviving spouse can use the "Qualifying Widow(er)" filing status as long as he or she has a qualifying dependent.

Basically, the favorable tax rates of the joint filing status are extended for a qualified widow or widower for two years following the date of death.

After two years, the taxpayer's filing status converts to Single or Head of Household, whichever applies.

For example, if the taxpayer's spouse died in 2009 and the surviving spouse did not remarry, he or she can use the "Qualifying Widow(er)" filing status for 2010 and 2011.

Example: Barbara and Kenneth are married. Kenneth dies on December 3, 2009. Barbara has one dependent child, a 15-year-old daughter named Hannah. Barbara does not remarry. Therefore, Barbara's filing status for 2009 is MFJ (the last year that Kenneth was alive). Barbara can file as a Qualifying Widow in 2010 and 2011, which is a more favorable filing status than Single or Head of Household.

However, if a surviving spouse *remarries* before the end of the year, "Married Filing Separately" must be used for the decedent's final return.

Example: Shelly lost her husband, Rodney, to cancer in January 2011. The couple has two infant daughters, Kylie and Penny. Shelly remarries in December 2011. Since Shelly remarried in the same year her former husband died, she no longer qualifies for the joint return filing status with her deceased husband. Shelly does qualify for Married Filing Jointly with her *new* spouse. It also means that Rodney's filing status for 2011 would be considered "Married Filing Separately."

To qualify for the Qualifying Widow(er) filing status, the taxpayer must:
- Not have remarried before the end of the tax year.

- Have been eligible to file a joint return for the year the spouse died; it does not matter if a joint return was actually filed.
- Have a child who qualifies as the taxpayer's qualifying child for the year.
- ==Have furnished over half the cost of keeping up the child's home for the entire year.==

> **Example:** Hazel's husband, Randy, died on July 20, 2009. Hazel has a dependent son who is three. Hazel files a joint return with Randy in 2009. In 2010, Hazel correctly files as a Qualifying Widow with Dependent Child. In 2011, however, Hazel remarries, so she no longer qualifies for the Qualifying Widow filing status. She must now file jointly with her new husband, or file MFS.

After a Spouse's Death

The chart shows which filing status to use for a widowed taxpayer who does not remarry and has a qualifying dependent.

Tax Year	Filing Status	Exemption for Deceased Spouse?
The year of death	Married Filing Jointly or Married Filing Separately	Yes
First year after death	Qualifying Widow(er)	No
Second year after death	Qualifying Widow(er)	No
After second year of death	Head of Household	No

Filing Status: Summary

Take a moment to review what you have covered in this lesson. The five filing statuses are:

- Single
- Married Filing Jointly
- Married Filing Separately
- Head of Household
- Qualifying Widow(er) With Dependent Child

Filing status is used to determine a taxpayer's filing requirements, standard deduction, eligibility for certain credits and deductions, and the correct tax.

If a taxpayer qualifies for more than one filing status, he may choose the one that produces a lower tax. If married taxpayers choose to file separately (MFS), they must show their spouse's name and Social Security Number on the return.

1. ==A person's marital status on the *last day of the year* determines the marital status for the entire year.==
2. SINGLE filing status generally applies to anyone who is unmarried, divorced, or legally separated according to state law.

3. A married couple may elect to file a joint return together. Both spouses must agree to file a joint return.
4. If one spouse died during the year, the taxpayer may file a joint return in the year of death.
5. Head of Household usually applies to taxpayers who are unmarried. A taxpayer must have paid more than half the cost of maintaining a home for a qualifying person in order to qualify for HOH.
6. A widow or widower with one or more dependent children may be able to use the Qualifying Widow(er) with Dependent Child filing status, which is only available for two years following the year of the spouse's death.

Unit 2: Questions

1. Which of the following statements is TRUE regarding the Head of Household filing status?

A. The taxpayer must be Single on the first day of the year in order to qualify for Head of Household filing status.
B. The taxpayer's spouse must live in the home during the tax year.
C. The taxpayer's dependent parent does not have to live with the taxpayer in order to qualify for Head of Household.
D. The taxpayer must have paid less than half of the cost of keeping up the house for the entire year.

The answer is C. Parents do not have to live with a taxpayer in order for the taxpayer to take the dependency exemption. This is a special rule for dependent parents. This rule also applies to parents or grandparents who are related to the taxpayer by blood, marriage, or adoption (examples include a stepmother or father-in-law). A taxpayer must pay over half of the household costs in order to qualify for this filing status. ###

2. The person who qualifies a taxpayer as Head of Household must be _____.

A. A minor child.
B. A blood relative.
C. The taxpayer's dependent OR the taxpayer's qualifying child.
D. A minor child or a full-time student.

The answer is C. The taxpayer must claim the person as a dependent unless the non-custodial parent claims the child as a dependent. Answer A is incorrect, because a qualifying dependent does not have to be a minor in many cases. Answer B is incorrect because a qualifying dependent may be related by blood, marriage, or adoption. ###

3. Gerald takes care of his grandson, Kyle, who is 10 years old. How long must Kyle live in the taxpayer's home in order for Gerald to qualify for Head of Household status?

A. At least three months.
B. More than half the year.
C. The entire year.
D. More than 12 months.

The answer is B. The relative must have lived with the taxpayer more than half the year (over six months) and be the taxpayer's dependent. The exception is that a taxpayer's dependent parent does not have to live with the taxpayer. ###

4. Dana's husband died on January 24, 2011. She has one dependent son who is eight years old. What is Dana's best filing status for tax year 2011?

A. Married Filing Jointly.
B. Single.
C. Qualifying Widow.
D. Head of Household

The answer is A. If a taxpayer's spouse died during the year, the taxpayer is considered married for the whole year for filing status purposes and may file as "MFJ." So Dana may file a joint return with her husband in 2011, which is the year he died. ###

5. A taxpayer may NEVER amend a joint tax return from "Married Filing Jointly" to "Married Filing Separately" after the filing deadline.

A. True.
B. False.

The answer is B, False. There is only one exception: The personal representative for a decedent (a deceased taxpayer) can change from a joint return elected by the surviving spouse to a separate return for the decedent. ###

6. Victor is 39 years old. He has been legally separated from his wife, Eleanor, since February 1, 2011. Their divorce was not yet final at the end of 2011. They have two minor children. One child lives with Victor and the other child lives with Eleanor. The children have been with their respective parents from February through December of 2011. Victor provides all of the support for the minor child living with him. Eleanor refuses to file jointly with Victor this year. Therefore, the most beneficial filing status that Victor qualifies for is:

A. Married Filing Separately.
B. Single.
C. Head of Household.
D. Qualifying Widower with a Dependent Child.

The answer is C. Victor qualifies for Head of Household filing status. His child lived with him for more than six months, and he did not live with his spouse the last half of the year. Victor may file as Head of Household because he is "considered unmarried" for tax purposes, and he paid more than half the cost of keeping up a home for the year for a qualifying child. Victor cannot file jointly with Eleanor, if she does not agree. ###

7. Lisa married Stuart in 2008. Stuart died in 2010. Lisa never remarried and has one dependent child. Which filing status should Lisa use for her **2011 tax return**?

A. Single.
B. Married Filing Jointly.
C. Head of Household.
D. Qualifying Widow(er).

The answer is D. In 2011, Lisa qualifies for "Qualifying Widow with Dependent Child" filing status. Lisa and Stuart qualified to file jointly in 2010, and Lisa would sign the tax return as a surviving spouse. The year of death is the last year for which a taxpayer can file jointly with a deceased spouse. Then, in 2011, Lisa would be eligible to file as a Qualifying Widow with Dependent Child. ###

8. Sean is single. His mother, Clara, lives in an assisted living facility. Sean provides all of Clara's support. Clara died on June 1, 2011. Clara had no income. Which of the following is true?

A. Sean may file as Head of Household and may also claim his mother as a dependent on his 2011 tax return.
B. Sean must file Single in 2011, and he cannot claim his mother as a dependent on his tax return.
C. Sean may claim his mother as a dependent on his tax return, but he cannot claim Head of Household status for 2011.
D. Sean may claim Head of Household status for 2011, but he cannot claim his mother as a dependent.

The answer is A. Because Sean paid more than half the cost of his mother's care in a care facility from the beginning of the year until her death, then he is entitled to claim an exemption for her, and he can also file as Head of Household. ###

9. Mary and Troy are married and live together. Mary earned $7,000 in 2011, and Troy earned $42,000. Mary wants to file a joint return, but Troy refuses to file with Mary and instead files a separate return. Which of the following statements is true?

A. Mary may file a joint amended tax return and sign Troy's name.
B. Mary and Troy must both file separate returns.
C. Mary may file as Single because Troy refuses to sign a joint return.
D. Mary does not have a filing requirement.

The answer is B. In this case, both spouses are required to file a tax return. Married couples must agree to file jointly. If one spouse does not agree to file jointly, they must file separately. ###

10. Kathy's marriage was annulled on February 25, 2012. She was married to her husband in 2009 and filed jointly with him in 2009 and 2010. She has not yet filed her 2011 return. Kathy has no dependents. Which of the following statements is true?

A. Kathy must file amended returns, claiming Single filing status for all open years affected by the annulment.
B. Kathy is not required to file amended returns, and she may file jointly with her husband in 2011.
C. Kathy is not required to file amended returns, and she must file Married Filing Separately on her 2011 tax return.
D. Kathy is not required to file amended returns, and she should file as "Single" on her 2011 tax return.

The answer is A. Kathy must file amended tax returns for 2009 and 2010. She cannot file jointly with her husband in 2011. If a couple obtains a court decree of annulment, the taxpayer must file amended returns (Form 1040X) claiming Single or Head of Household status for all tax years affected by the annulment that are not closed by the statute of limitations for filing a tax return. ###

11. The two filing statuses that generally result in the lowest tax amounts are Married Filing Jointly and _____.

A. Married Filing Separately.
B. Head of Household.
C. Qualifying Widow(er) with Dependent Child.
D. Single.

The answer is C. The Qualifying Widow(er) with Dependent Child filing status generally yields the same tax amount as Married Filing Jointly. ###

12. Dwight and Angela are married, but they choose to file separate tax returns for tax year 2011, because Dwight is being investigated by the IRS for a previous tax issue. Dwight and Angela file their separate tax returns on time. A few months later, after the investigation is over and Dwight is cleared of all wrongdoing, Dwight wishes to file amended returns and file jointly with his wife in order to claim the Earned Income Credit. Which of the following is TRUE?

A. Dwight is prohibited from changing his filing status in order to claim this credit.
B. Dwight and Angela may amend their MFS tax returns to Married Filing Jointly in order to claim the credit.
C. Dwight may amend his tax return to MFJ filing status, but he may not claim the credit.
D. Angela may not file jointly with Dwight after she has already filed a separate tax return.

The answer is B. Dwight and Angela are allowed to amend their separate returns to a joint return in order to claim the credit. If a taxpayer files a separate return, the taxpayer may elect to amend the filing status to "Married Filing Jointly" at any time within three years from the due date of the original return. This does not include any extensions. However, the same does not hold true in reverse. Once a taxpayer files a joint return, the taxpayer cannot choose to file a separate return for that year after the due date of the return (with a rare exception for deceased taxpayers). ###

13. Which of the following is NOT a valid filing status?

A. Married Filing Jointly.
B. Qualifying Widow(er) with Dependent Child.
C. Head of Household.
D. Annulled.

The answer is D. There is no such thing as an "annulled" filing status. There are five filing statuses: Married Filing Jointly, Qualifying Widow(er) with Dependent Child, Head of Household, Single, and Married Filing Separately. ###

14. Carol and Raul were married four years ago and have no children. They split up in 2010, but did not file for divorce. Although they lived apart during all of 2011, they are neither divorced nor legally separated. Which of the following filing statuses can they use?

A. Single or Married Filing Separately.
B. Married Filing Jointly or Married Filing Separately.
C. Married Filing Separately or Head of Household.
D. Single or Qualifying Widow(er).

The answer is B. As long as they are married and are neither divorced nor legally separated, Carol and Raul can file a joint return, or they can choose to file separately. They cannot file Single. ###

15. Which dependent relative may qualify a taxpayer for Head of Household filing status?

A. An adult stepdaughter supported by the taxpayer but who lives across town.
B. A family friend who lives with the taxpayer all year.
C. A parent who lives in his own home and not with the taxpayer.
D. A child who lived with the taxpayer for three months of the tax year.

The answer is C. A parent is the only dependent relative who does not have to live with the taxpayer in order for the taxpayer to claim Head of Household status. ###

16. Samantha is divorced and provided over half the cost of keeping up a home. Her five-year-old daughter, Pamela, lived with her for seven months last year. Samantha allows her ex-husband, Jim, to claim Pamela as a dependent. Which of the following statements is true?

A. Jim may take Pamela as his dependent and also file as Head of Household.
B. Jim may take Pamela as his dependent, and Samantha may still file as Head of Household.
C. Neither parent qualifies for Head of Household filing status because Pamela did not live with either parent for the entire year.
D. Samantha cannot release the dependency exemption to Jim, because their daughter did not live with Jim for over six months.

The answer is B. Samantha may use Head of Household status because she is not married and she provided over half the cost of keeping up the main home of her dependent child for more than six months. However, because Samantha's ex-husband claims Pamela as his dependent, the preparer must write Pamela's name on line 4 of the filing status section of **Form 1040** or **Form 1040A**. ###

17. Madison and Todd have a two-year-old daughter named Amanda. Madison and Todd are not married and do not live together. Madison and her daughter lived together all year. Todd lived alone in his own apartment. Madison earned $13,000 working as a clerk in a clothing store. Todd earned $48,000 as an assistant manager of a hardware store. He paid over half the cost of Madison's apartment for rent and utilities. He also gave Madison extra money for groceries. Todd does not pay any expenses or support for any other family member. All are U.S. citizens and have valid SSNs. Which of the following is true?

A. Todd may file as Head of Household.
B. Madison may file as Head of Household.
C. Todd and Madison may file jointly.
D. Neither may claim Head of Household filing status.

The answer is D. Todd provided over half the cost of maintaining a home for Madison and Amanda, but he cannot file Head of Household since Amanda did not live with him for over half the year. Madison cannot file HOH either, because she did not provide more than one-half the cost of keeping up the home for her daughter. However, either Todd or Madison may still claim Amanda as their dependent. ###

18. Iona has a 10-year-old child. Iona separated from her husband during the tax year. Which of the following would prevent Iona from filing as Head of Household?

A. Iona has maintained a separate residence from her husband since last year.
B. The qualifying child's principal home is with Iona.
C. Iona's parents assisted with 25% of the household costs.
D. The child lived with Iona starting in mid-July of the tax year.

The answer is D. For Iona to file as Head of Household, Iona's home must have been the main home of her qualifying child for *more than half* the tax year. If the child started living with Iona in July, then the child would not have been in the household sufficient time to qualify for this filing status. ###

19. Alexandra's younger brother, Sebastian, is seventeen years old. Sebastian lived with friends in January and February of 2011. From March through July of 2011, he lived with Alexandra. On August 1, Sebastian moved back in with his friends, with whom he stayed for the rest of the year. Since Sebastian did not have a job, Alexandra gave him money every month. Alexandra had no other dependents. Which of the following statements is true?

A. Alexandra may file as Head of Household for 2011.
B. Alexandra may file jointly with Sebastian in 2011.
C. Alexandra cannot file as Head of Household in 2011.
D. Sebastian may file as Head of Household in 2011.

The answer is C. Alexandra cannot claim Head of Household status because Sebastian lived with her for only five months, which is less than half the year. ###

20. Taxpayers are considered to be MARRIED for the entire year if:
A. One spouse died during the year and the surviving spouse has not remarried.
B. The spouses are legally separated under a separate maintenance decree.
C. The spouses are divorced on December 31 of the tax year.
D. The spouses had their marriage annulled December 31 of the tax year.

The answer is A. Generally, taxpayers are considered "married" for the entire year if:
- They were married on the last day of the tax year, or
- The spouse died during the year and the surviving spouse has not remarried ###

21. A U.S. resident or citizen who is married to a non-resident alien can file a joint return so long as both spouses _____.

A. Sign the return and agree to be taxed on their worldwide income.
B. Are living overseas.
C. Have valid Social Security Numbers
D. Are physically present in the United States.

The answer is A. A U.S. resident or citizen who is married to a non-resident alien can elect to file a joint return so long as both spouses agree to sign the return and be taxed on their worldwide income. A Social Security Number is not required, because a non-resident spouse that is ineligible for a Social Security Number may request an ITIN.###

22. The Married Filing Separately (MFS) status is for taxpayers who:

A. Are legally divorced on the last day of the year.
B. Are married and choose to file separate returns.
C. Are unmarried, but engaged to be married.
D. Are unmarried, but have a dependent child.

The answer is B. The Married Filing Separately (MFS) status is for taxpayers who are married and either:
- Choose to file separate returns, or
- Cannot agree to file a joint return.

Unit 3: Determining Residency and Tax Home

> **More Reading:**
> Publication 17, *Your Federal Income Tax*
> Publication 587, *Business Use of Your Home*
> Publication 519, *U.S. Tax Guide for Aliens*

Tax Home and Work Location

A taxpayer's "tax home" is his principal place of work, *regardless of where he actually lives*. A taxpayer's tax home is used for tax purposes, including determining if travel expenses are deductible.

Travel and meal expenses are considered deductible if the taxpayer is traveling away from his *tax home*. These rules are also used in determining if the taxpayer qualifies for the foreign earned income exclusion.

Multiple work locations: If a taxpayer has *more than one* place of business or work, the "tax home" must be determined using several factors. The following facts should be used to determine which one is the main place of business or work:

- The total time ordinarily spent in each place
- The level of business activity in each place
- Whether income from each place is significant

In determining which is the taxpayer's "main place of business," the most important consideration is the length of time spent at each location. If a taxpayer regularly works in more than one place, his tax home is the general area where the main place of business or work is located. If a taxpayer has more than one place of business, then his tax home is his main place of business.

> **Example:** Gary is a marketing consultant who lives with his family in Chicago, but works regularly (full-time) in Milwaukee where he stays in a hotel and eats in restaurants. Gary returns to Chicago every weekend. Gary may not deduct any of his travel, meals, or lodging expenses in Milwaukee because that is his tax home. Gary's travel on weekends to his family home in Chicago is not for work, so these expenses are also not deductible.

If a person does not have a regular place of business because of the nature of his work, then his tax home can be the place where he lives.

> **Example:** Seville is a truck driver. He and his family live in Tucson, Arizona. Seville is employed by a trucking firm that has its main terminal in Phoenix. At the end of his long trucking runs, Seville returns to his home terminal in Phoenix and spends one night there before returning home. Seville cannot deduct any expenses he has for meals and lodging in Phoenix or the cost of traveling from Phoenix to Tucson. This is because Phoenix is Seville's "tax home" (Publication 463).

There are special rules for temporary work assignments. When a taxpayer is working away from his main place of business and the job assignment is temporary, his *tax home* does not change. The taxpayer can also deduct his travel expenses because the job assignment is of a temporary nature, and therefore, the travel is considered business-related.

> ***Important Tip:** A temporary work assignment is any work assignment that is expected to last for *one year or less*. Travel expenses paid or incurred in connection with a temporary work assignment away from home are deductible. However, travel expenses paid in connection with an *indefinite* work assignment are *not deductible*. Any work assignment over one year in duration is considered *indefinite*.[11] A taxpayer cannot deduct travel expenses at a work location if it is realistically expected that he will work there for more than one year.

There is a special rule for military personnel. Members of the armed forces on a permanent duty assignment overseas are not considered to be "traveling away from home."

Therefore, members of the military cannot deduct their travel expenses for meals and lodging while on permanent duty assignment. However, military personnel that are permanently transferred from one duty station to another may be able to deduct their *moving expenses* as an adjustment to income (which will be explained in a later unit under Moving Expenses).

> **Example**: Terry is a construction worker who lives and works primarily in Los Angeles. Terry is also a member of a trade union in Los Angeles that helps him get work in the Los Angeles area. Because of a shortage of work, Terry agrees to take a job on a construction site in Fresno. The Fresno job lasts ten months. Since the job lasts less than one year, the Fresno job is considered *temporary* and Terry's tax home is still in Los Angeles. Therefore, Terry's travel expenses are deductible since he was traveling away from his "tax home" for business or work. Terry can deduct travel expenses, *including* meals and lodging, while traveling between his temporary place of work and his tax home in Los Angeles.

Once a taxpayer has determined that he is traveling away from his *tax home*, he can deduct "ordinary and necessary" expenses incurred while traveling on business.

Lodging, airline tickets, parking, tolls, and meals are all examples of deductible travel expenses.

Office in the Home

If a taxpayer has an office in his home that qualifies as a principal place of business, he can deduct daily transportation costs between the home office and another work location in the same trade or business. These are not commuting ex-

---

[11] There is an exception for federal crime investigations or prosecutions. If a taxpayer is a federal employee participating in a federal crime investigation or prosecution, he is not subject to the one-year rule and may deduct travel expenses as long as the investigation takes place.

penses, because commuting expenses are never deductible. However, the travel between a home office to a business location would be considered deductible travel.

In order to qualify as a home office, the space must be used **exclusively and regularly**:

- As the taxpayer's principal place of business, OR
- As a place to meet with patients or clients in the normal course of your business, OR
- In any connection with a business where the business portion of the home is a separate structure not attached to the home.

The rules regarding home office expenses are also covered in Part 2 of the EA exam. Exam candidates may be tested on the concept of a home office as it relates to employees, self-employed taxpayers, or business owners.

Example: Vince is a self-employed bookkeeper who works exclusively out of his home office. He has many clients. Vince travels from his home office directly to the client's business and performs his bookkeeping services on-site. Vince does not have any other office. In this case, the travel from his home office to the client's location is deductible as business mileage.

Example: Martha is a part-time tax preparer. During tax season, she uses her study to prepare tax returns during tax season. She also uses the study to exercise on her treadmill. The room is not used exclusively in Martha's profession, so she cannot claim a deduction for the business use. Also, since the space does not qualify as a bona-fide home office, then the travel from her home office to another business location (such as a client's office or home) would therefore not be deductible.

Nonresidents and Form 1040NR

Taxpayers who are not citizens or legal residents (green card holders) are generally considered non-residents for income tax purposes. Legal resident aliens (green card holders) are taxed in the same way as U.S. citizens.

"Residency" for IRS purposes is not the same as legal residency for green card status. This is an important concept to understand. An individual may still be considered a "U.S. resident" for tax purposes based on the *physical* time he spends in the United States, regardless of immigration status.

A non-resident can be someone who lives outside the U.S. and simply invests in U.S. property or stocks, and is therefore required to file a tax return in order to correctly report his earnings.

Each year, thousands of non-resident aliens are also gainfully employed in the United States. Thousands more own rental property or earn interest or dividends from U.S. investments, and are therefore required to file U.S. tax returns.

How to Determine Alien Tax Status

Taxpayers that qualify as U.S. residents (including all U.S. citizens and green card holders) must file a U.S. tax return (unless they are exempt, such as taxpayers who are below the income requirements), and ALL their worldwide income is subject to U.S. tax and must be reported on their U.S. tax return (**Form 1040**, *U.S. Individual Income Tax Return*).

If the taxpayer is an alien (not a U.S. citizen or green card holder), he is considered a *non-resident* for tax purposes *unless* he meets at least ONE of two tests:

1. **The Green Card Test, OR**
2. **The "Substantial Presence" Test.**

The "Green Card" Test: A taxpayer is considered a U.S. resident if he is a "Lawful Permanent Resident" of the United States (if the taxpayer has a "green card"). Green card holders are taxed just like U.S. citizens, regardless of where they live. If a taxpayer has a green card, he generally does not file **Form 1040NR.** Instead, green card holders must file **Form 1040,** regardless of where they live. An alien who has been present in the United States at *any time* during a calendar year as a Lawful Permanent Resident (green card holder) may choose to be treated as a resident alien for the entire calendar year.[12]

The "Substantial Presence" Test: The "Substantial Presence" test is based on a calendar year (January 1 – December 31). A taxpayer will be considered a U.S. resident for tax purposes only if he meets the "substantial presence" test for the calendar year.

To meet this test, the taxpayer must be physically present in the United States on at least:

- 31 days during the current year, and
- 183 days during the 3-year period that includes the current year (2011) and the two years immediately before that, counting:

All the days he or she was present in 2011 (current year) and

- 1/3 of the days he or she was present in 2010 (first year before current year) and
- 1/6 of the days he or she was present in 2009 (second year before current year)

---

[12] In some cases, an alien taxpayer can choose to be treated as both a non-resident alien and a resident alien during the same tax year. This usually occurs in the year the person arrives or departs from the United States. If so, some taxpayers may elect to be treated as a dual-status alien for this taxable year and a resident alien for the next taxable year if they meet certain tests. (For more information, refer to section Dual-Status Aliens – "First Year Choice" in Publication 519, *U.S. Tax Guide for Aliens*.)

If the taxpayer does *not* meet either the "Green Card Test" or the "Substantial Presence Test," then the taxpayer is considered a non-resident for tax purposes.

> **Note:** An individual who meets the requirements of the Substantial Presence Test is, for tax purposes, a resident alien of the United States. This status applies even though the person may be an undocumented alien. Remember: filing a tax return as a resident does **not affect** or alter immigration status.

Unlike U.S. citizens and U.S. residents, non-resident aliens are subject to U.S. income tax *only* on their U.S. source income.

> **Example:** Gertie is a German citizen who was physically present in the United States for 15 days in each of the years 2009, 2010, and 2011. She is not a green card holder. Gertie earned $28,000 in 2011 as a German translator for the U.S. government. Since the total days she was present in the U.S. for the three-year period does not meet the "substantial presence" test, Gertie is not considered a resident for tax purposes for 2011. Therefore, her earnings are taxed as a non-resident. Gertie is required to file a non-resident tax return in 2011 (**Form 1040NR**, *U.S. Non-resident Alien Income Tax Return*). If she does NOT file a U.S. tax return, then income tax will be withheld at the highest rate. This is called "backup" withholding.[13]

Non-residents are subject to *two different tax rates*, one for Effectively Connected Income (ECI), and one for Fixed, Determinable, Annual, or Periodic income (FDAP).

- **Effectively Connected Income (ECI)** is earned from the operation of a business in the U.S. or from personal service income earned in the U.S. (such as wages or self-employment income). It is taxed for a non-resident at the same rates as for a U.S. citizen.
- **FDAP income** is passive income (such as interest, dividends, rents, or royalties). This income is taxed at a flat 30% rate, unless a tax treaty specifies a lower rate. Most allied nations have beneficial tax treaties with the U.S. This includes most of Europe, Canada, and Mexico.

Tax Treaties

The United States has income tax treaties with a number of foreign countries. For non-resident aliens, these treaties can often reduce or even eliminate U.S. tax on various types of personal services and other income, such as pensions, interest, dividends, royalties, and capital gains.

---

[13] In most cases, a foreign person is subject to tax on his U.S. source income. Most types of U.S. source income received by a foreign person are subject to U.S. tax of 30%. A reduced rate, including exemption, may apply if there is a tax treaty between the foreign person's country of residence and the United States. Non-residents who do not provide a TIN (either an SSN or ITIN) are generally subject to automatic backup withholding on their U.S. source income.

When preparing actual tax returns for a foreign client, each individual treaty must be reviewed to determine whether specific types of income are exempt from U.S. tax or taxed at a reduced rate. More details about tax treaties can be found in **Publication 901**, *U.S. Tax Treaties*. Tax treaties are generally not tested on the Enrolled Agent exam; however, you must know that they exist.

Example: Gérard is a Philippine citizen living in the Philippines. In 2011, Gérard earned $150,000 in royalty income from his U.S. investments. This income is FDAP income and is taxed at a flat 30% rate (unless a tax treaty applies). He is required to file a Form 1040NR.

Example: Benita is a Brazilian citizen. Benita earned $45,000 of wage income in 2011 working as a translator for the Brazilian consulate. She worked in the United States for 70 days and then returned home to Brazil. She does not meet the Substantial Presence Test or the Green Card Test; therefore, she is a non-resident for tax purposes. Her income is ECI income and is taxed at the same rate as a U.S. citizen. Benita is required to file a Form 1040NR.

Special rule for non-resident spouses: Non-resident alien individuals who are married to U.S. citizens or green card holders (legal residents) may choose to be treated as resident aliens for income tax purposes.

Example: Lola and Bruno are married and both are non-resident aliens at the beginning of the year. In January, Bruno became a legal U.S. resident alien and obtained a green card and a Social Security Number. Lola and Bruno may both choose to be treated as resident aliens (for tax purposes) by attaching a statement to their joint return. Lola is not eligible for a Social Security Number, so she must apply for an Individual Tax Identification Number (ITIN). Lola and Bruno must file a joint return for the year they make the election, but they can file either joint or separate returns for later years.

Due Dates for Non-resident Aliens

Non-resident aliens who have income that is not subject to U.S. withholding are required to file an income tax return by June 15, two months *after* the regular filing deadline for individuals.

However, non-resident employees (such as a non-resident alien that earns wages while living or visiting the U.S.) who received wages that are subject to U.S. income tax withholding must file **Form 1040NR** by the due date.

> *****Basic Rule: Due Dates for Non-resident Tax Returns:** If the alien is a[n]
> receives wages or non-employee compensation that IS SUBJECT to U.[S.]
> withholding, or if he has a place of business in the United States, he must [file]
> by April 15[14].

If the alien is an employee or self-employed person whose income [is not] SUBJECT to U.S. income tax withholding, AND if he DOES NOT have a place of bu[si]ness in the United States, he must file by June 15.

Recordkeeping for Individuals

Taxpayers should keep copies of tax returns and records until the statute of limitations runs out for their return. Usually, this is three years from the date the return was filed, or two years from the date the tax was paid, whichever is later.

For example, if a taxpayer files his return one year late, then he should retain the records pertaining to that tax year at least three years after the date he filed the return.

Basic Tax Forms for Individuals: A Summary

Form 1040EZ

Of the tax return forms, Form 1040EZ is the simplest. The one-page form is designed for single and joint filers with *no dependents*. It shows the taxpayer's filing status, income, adjusted gross income, standard deduction, taxable income, tax, Earned Income Tax Credit (EITC), amount owed or refund, and signature. A taxpayer may use the 1040EZ under the following conditions (this list is not exhaustive):

- Taxable income is below $100,000
- The filing status is Single or Married Filing Jointly
- The taxpayer is under age 65 and not blind
- The taxpayer is not claiming any dependents
- Interest income is $1,500 or less

Form 1040A

Form 1040A is a two-page form. Page one shows the filing status, exemptions, income, and adjusted gross income. Page two shows standard deduction, exemption amount, taxable income, tax, credits, payments, amount owed or refund, and signature.

A taxpayer may use the 1040A under the following conditions:

- Taxable income is below $100,000
- The taxpayer may have capital gain distributions

---

[14] In 2012, the individual tax return due date for 2011 tax year returns is April 17, 2012, because of a holiday.

The taxpayer is entitled to claim *only* the following tax credits:
- The Credit for Child and Dependent Care expenses
- The Credit for the Elderly or the Disabled
- The Child Tax Credit
- The Additional Child Tax Credit
- The Education Credits
- The Retirement Savings Contributions Credit (The Saver's Credit)
- The Earned Income Credit

- The taxpayer claims an adjustment to income for IRA contributions and student loan interest

Form 1040

This form is also called the "long form." It is a two-page form that contains all specialized entries for additional types of income, itemized deductions, and other taxes. If a taxpayer cannot use Form 1040EZ or Form 1040A, he must use Form 1040. Form 1040 is designed to report all types of income, deductions, and credits.

Taxpayers who plan to itemize their deductions are required to use Form 1040. Also, when a married couple chooses to file separate returns and one spouse itemizes deductions, the other spouse cannot claim the standard deduction and therefore is forced to itemize as well.

Among the most common reasons why taxpayers must use Form 1040 are:
- Their taxable income exceeds $100,000.
- They want to itemize their deductions.
- They are reporting self-employment income.
- They are reporting income from the sale of property (such as the sale of stock or rental property).

Form 1040NR

This is the form used by non-resident aliens to report their U.S. source income. It is used by investors overseas, as well as non-resident taxpayers who earn money while in the U.S. The **1040NR** is NOT used by U.S. citizens or U.S. residents.

Example: Cisco Ramos is a boxing champion, and a legal citizen and resident of Mexico. Cisco receives a non-immigrant visa in order to attend and participate in a boxing match in the United States, where he earns $500,000 for his appearance. After his appearance, he returns to Mexico. Cisco is not eligible for an SSN and must request an ITIN in order to report his U.S. income. Without the ITIN, Cisco would be subject to automatic backup withholding on his U.S. earnings. Cisco's income is subject to a special treaty provision and his tax accountant reports his income and his tax on **Form 1040NR**.

Example: Yao Lee is a Chinese citizen. He has never been to the United States. Yao owns various U.S. investments, on which he earns dividends and capital gains income. He is not eligible for an SSN. In order to prevent backup withholding on his earnings, Yao requests an ITIN. His tax preparer files **Form 1040NR** every year to report Yao's U.S.-source income.

Unit 3: Questions

1. Cynthia is divorced and files as Head of Household. She has two children she will claim as dependents. She works as a secretary and earned $35,000 in wages for the tax year. She plans to itemize her deductions. Which tax form should Cynthia use?

A. Form 1040.
B. Form 1040A.
C. Form 1040EZ.
D. Form 1040NR.

The answer is A. Since Cynthia plans to itemize her deductions, she must file **Form 1040**. ###

2. Alfred lives in Cincinnati where he has a seasonal job for eight months each year and earns $25,000. He works the other four months in Miami, also at a seasonal job, and earns $9,000. Where is Alfred's tax home?

A. Miami.
B. Cincinnati.
C. Alfred is a transient for tax purposes.
D. Alfred has no tax home.

The answer is B. Cincinnati is Alfred's main place of work because he spends most of his time there and earns most of his income there. Therefore, Cincinnati is Alfred's tax home for IRS purposes. ###

3. A taxpayer who claims a dependent can use any form EXCEPT _____.

A. Form 1040.
B. Form 1040A.
C. Form 1040EZ.
D. A taxpayer who is claiming a dependent can use any of the forms listed above.

The answer is C. A taxpayer who is claiming a dependent cannot use **Form 1040EZ**. ###

4. Ray and Maggie are married, but he and his wife are filing MFS. Their combined income was $100,000. Ray earned $60,000 in wage income and plans to itemize his deductions. Maggie has $40,000 in self-employment income and she does not have anything to itemize. Which is the simplest form that Maggie can use for her tax return?

A. Form 1040.
B. Form 1040A.
C. Form 1040EZ.
D. Either Form 1040 or Form 1040A.

The answer is A. Maggie will be forced to file **Form 1040** for two reasons: she had self-employment income and because Ray plans to itemize deductions. When a married couple files separate returns and one spouse chooses to itemize deductions, the other spouse cannot claim the standard deduction and therefore must itemize. If Maggie has no itemized deductions, then her deduction would be zero. ###

5. Brad is working on a temporary work assignment in another city. He's not sure how long the assignment will last. He travels overnight every week. So far, the work assignment has lasted 11 months in 2011, and Brad has incurred $800 in travel expenses and $300 in meal expenses. What is his deductible expense for this activity in 2011?

A. $0.
B. $800.
C. $950.
D. $1,100.

The answer is A. Brad cannot deduct any of the expenses, because travel expenses paid in connection with an *indefinite* work assignment are not deductible. ###

6. Generally, how long should taxpayers keep the supporting documents for their tax returns?

A. Five years.
B. Three years.
C. Two years.
D. One year.

The answer is B. Taxpayers should keep the supporting documentation for their tax returns for at least three years from the date the return was filed, or two years from the date the tax was paid, whichever is later. This includes applicable worksheets and forms. ###

7. Felicity is a self-employed midwife who has a home office. Felicity's principal place of business is in her home, although she does not meet with clients in her home. Instead, she goes out to her clients' homes and performs her duties on-site. Which of the following statements is true?

A. Felicity can deduct the cost of round-trip transportation between her home office and her clients' place of business.
B. Felicity can NOT deduct the cost of round-trip transportation between her home office and her clients' homes, but she may deduct the transportation costs from her client's homes to other business locations.
C. Felicity does not have a qualified home office, because she does not meet clients in her home.
D. None of the above.

The answer is A. Felicity can deduct daily transportation costs between her home office and a client's location. Felicity does not have to meet with clients in her home in order for her home office to qualify as her principal place of business. The transportation costs between two work locations are considered a deductible travel expense. ###

8. Clark and Christy are both age 34 and will be filing jointly. They have no dependents. Their combined income was $31,000, which included $35 in interest income. The remainder of their income was from wages. They want to take the standard deduction. Which is the simplest form that Clark and Christy can use for their tax return?

A. Form 1040.
B. Form 1040A.
C. Form 1040EZ.
D. Form 1040NR.

The answer is C. Clark and Christy have no dependents, their combined income was less than $100,000, and they do not plan to itemize. Their interest income was also less than $1,500, so they may use Form 1040EZ to file their tax return. ###

9. Megan, an engineer, maintains a residence in Denver, Colorado where her employer has a permanent satellite office. In 2011, Megan's employer enrolls her in a ten-month executive training program at their corporate offices in Santa Clara, California. Megan will attend classroom training in Santa Clara and do temporary work assignments throughout the United States, but she does expect to return to work in Denver after she completes her training.

Every Monday she flies to Santa Clara and stays in the city the entire week. She maintains a small, one-bedroom apartment in Santa Clara and incurs all the ordinary and necessary expenses in the upkeep of the apartment. She returns to Denver on the weekends to spend time with family and attend to her personal affairs from her Denver residence. Where can Megan consider her "tax home" to be for the year 2011?

A. Santa Clara, California.
B. Denver, Colorado.
C. Neither, because Megan is a transient for tax purposes.
D. Both, because Megan spends time in both places.

The answer is B. Her tax home is still in Denver, because her work assignment is temporary. For IRS purposes, a "temporary work assignment" is any work assignment that is expected to last for one year or less. Since Megan is going to be away for only ten months, her tax home remains in Denver. Travel expenses paid or incurred in connection with a temporary work assignment away from home are deductible. ###

10. Munir is a citizen of Pakistan. In 2011, Munir is granted a U.S. green card and comes to the U.S. to work as a physician. Munir arrives in the U.S. on November 1, 2011. He earns $26,000 in U.S. wages in November and December. Which of the following is TRUE?

A. Munir is not required to file a U.S. tax return.
B. Munir is required to file a U.S. tax return, and he must file using Form 1040NR.
C. Munir is required to file a U.S. tax return, and he may file using Form 1040.
D. Munir is not required to file a U.S. tax return in 2011, but he will be required to file a return in 2012.

The answer is C. Munir is required to file a U.S. tax return, and he may file using **Form 1040.** Munir is a green card holder, and therefore he may choose to be treated as a U.S. resident for tax purposes, regardless of how much time he has been present in the United States. An alien who has been present in the United States at *any time* during a calendar year as a "Lawful Permanent Resident" (green card holder) may choose to be treated as a resident alien for the entire calendar year. Since Munir chooses to be taxed as a resident alien, he will be taxed on income from worldwide sources, including any income he earned while he was in Pakistan. ###

11. To meet the "substantial presence test," an individual must be physically present in the United States for a total of at least _____ days over a 3-year period.

A. 214
B. 183
C. 120
D. 31

The answer is B. Individuals who have been physically present for at least 183 days over a 3-year period, (including the current year), meet the requirements of the substantial presence test. This includes 183 days over a 3-year period comprising the current year (must be at least 31 days); 1/3 of the days in the first year before the current year; and 1/6 of the days in the second year before the current year. ###

12. Angela's husband, Brunson, has neither a green card nor a visa, and he does not have a tax home in another country. He was physically present in the United States for 150 days in each of the years 2009, 2010, and 2011. Is Dante a resident alien under the substantial presence test?

A. Yes, he is a resident for tax purposes
B. No, he is a nonresident for tax purposes
C. Brunson is a nonresident for tax purposes, but he may elect to file as a resident with his spouse.
D. None of the above answers are correct.

The answer is A. Brunson is a resident for tax purposes. He was present in the United States a total of 225 days. He meets the substantial presence test and is considered a resident alien for tax purposes. 150 days are counted for 2011; 50 days for 2010 (1/3 of 150); and 25 days for 2009 (1/6 of 150). ###

Unit 4: Exemptions and Dependents

> **More Reading:**
> Publication 501, *Exemptions, Standard Deduction, and Filing Information*

Taxpayers are allowed to take an exemption for themselves and also for their dependents. The 2011 exemption amount is $3,700 per person. The personal exemption is just like a tax deduction. It can reduce a person's taxable income to zero.

In prior years, the exemption was phased out for high income taxpayers. Not so in 2011—the personal exemption phase-out was eliminated; even the highest income taxpayers are still allowed to claim their personal exemptions.

A *dependency* exemption is not the same thing as a *personal* exemption. Taxpayers may qualify to claim two kinds of exemptions:

- Personal exemptions, which taxpayers can generally claim for themselves (and their spouses)
- Dependency exemptions, which taxpayers claim for their dependents

On a joint tax return, a married couple is allowed *two* personal exemptions, one for each spouse. A spouse is never considered the "dependent" of the other spouse. However, taxpayers may claim a personal exemption for their spouse simply because they are married. If a taxpayer's spouse dies during the year and the surviving spouse files a joint return, the surviving spouse can claim an exemption for the deceased spouse.

This is true even if only one spouse has income during the year. Only one exemption is allowed per person. So, for example, a married couple with one child would claim three exemptions on a jointly filed return.

Example: Jenny married Rick in April of 2011. Neither Jenny or Rick can be claimed as a dependent on another taxpayer's return. Both worked full-time and earned wage income in 2011. Jenny and Rick may claim two personal exemptions on their jointly filed return.

Example: Ho and Bình are married and have four dependent children. They file jointly. On their jointly filed return, they may claim a total of six exemptions: four dependency exemptions for their children and two personal exemptions for themselves.

Basic Rules for Dependents

A taxpayer can claim one dependency exemption for each qualified dependent, thereby reducing his taxable income. Some examples of dependents include a child, stepchild, brother, sister, or parent.

If a taxpayer can claim another person as a dependent—even if the taxpayer does not actually do so—the dependent cannot take a personal exemption on his own tax return.

Again, a dependent claimed on another taxpayer's return *cannot* claim a personal exemption on his own return. The dependent is only entitled to one personal exemption, whether he files his own return or is listed as a dependent on someone else's return.

> **Example:** Stacy is 20 and a full-time college student. Her parents provide all her financial support. She has a small part-time job where she earns $6,200 in 2011. Stacy cannot file a tax return and claim a dependency exemption for herself because her parents have claimed her on their own return. Stacy may file a tax return in order to obtain a refund of federal income tax withheld (if applicable). She may do so without claiming a personal exemption for herself.

A dependent may still be required to file a tax return. This happens most often with teenagers who also have jobs. They are usually claimed as dependents on their parents' tax return, but they also file their own return to report their wage income and receive a refund of income tax withheld.

> **Example:** Cole is a 15-year-old high school student who also works part-time at a supermarket. In 2011, he earned $4,210 from his part-time job. Cole still lives with his parents, who file jointly and claim him as a dependent on their return. Although his income is below the 2011 filing requirement, Cole files his own tax return in order to obtain a refund of the income taxes that were withheld at his job. He does not claim a personal exemption for himself (because his parents already claimed Cole's exemption on their joint return). However, Cole is still entitled to the standard deduction for single taxpayers. This wipes out all of his taxable income, and he receives a refund of the income tax that was withheld on his **Form W-2.**

Whether or not a dependent is required to file is determined by the amount of the dependent's earned income, unearned income, and gross income. Even though a dependent child may lose a personal exemption, most dependent children usually owe little or no tax on their individual returns because they can still offset a small amount of income with the standard deduction. In actual practice, it is rare to see a dependent who owes a large amount of tax.

Taxpayers may not claim a dependency exemption for an individual if they are themselves dependents of another taxpayer. (This is true even if the taxpayer has a qualifying child or relative).

> **Example:** Ava is unmarried, 17, and lives at home with her mother, Rose. Ava has a six-month-old baby named Vincent. Ava has $2,100 in wage income from a part-time job in 2011. Rose provides all of the financial support for her daughter, Ava, and her grandson, Vincent. Therefore, Ava and Vincent are both Rose's dependents. Ava allows Rose to claim her as a dependent. Ava cannot file a tax return claiming Vincent as her dependent, because she has already been claimed as a dependent on Rose's tax return.

There are certain rules that must be followed in order to claim a tax return. Dependency rules are extremely complex and heavily t exam. A dependent is always defined as either a:
- Qualifying child, or a
- Qualifying relative

The following sections discuss these rules in detail.

The Primary Tests for Dependency

In order to determine if a taxpayer may claim a dependency exemption for another person, you must FIRST determine if the dependent can legally be claimed on the taxpayer's return. There are four main tests to determine whether or not a dependent may be claimed on a taxpayer's return:

- **Citizenship or Residency Test**
- **Joint Return Test**
- **Qualifying Child of More Than One Person Test**
- **Dependent Taxpayer Test**

Next, we will explain each of these tests in detail.

1. Citizenship or Residency Test

In order for a taxpayer to claim a dependency exemption for someone, a residency test must be met. To meet the *"citizen, national, or resident test,"* an individual must be a citizen of the United States, a resident of the United States, or a citizen or resident of Canada or Mexico. There is also an exception for foreign-born adopted children.

Example: Horatio is an American citizen. He provides all of the financial support for his mother, who is a resident of Canada. Horatio may claim his mother as a dependent (***Note:** She does not have to live with him, since she is a dependent parent). Horatio may need to request an ITIN number for his mother if she does not have a valid Social Security Number.

2. Joint Return Test

A dependent cannot file a joint return with his spouse. In other words, once an individual files a joint return, that individual cannot be taken as a dependent by another taxpayer.

Example: Ellen is 18 years old and had no income in 2011. She got married on November 1, 2011. Ellen's new husband had $26,700 income and they file jointly, claiming two personal exemptions on their tax return. Ellen's father, Joseph, supported her throughout the year and even paid for their wedding. However, Ellen's father cannot claim Ellen as his dependent because she already filed a joint return with her new husband.

However, the **Joint Return Test** does *not apply* if the joint return is filed by the dependent only to claim a refund and no tax liability exists for either spouse, even if they filed separate returns.

> **Example:** Greg and Sandy are both 18 and married. They live with Sandy's mother, Michelle. In 2011, Greg had $1,800 of wage income from a part-time job and no other income. Neither Greg nor Sandy is required to file a tax return. Taxes were taken out of Greg's wages due to regular withholding so they file a joint return only to get a refund of the withheld taxes. The exception to the Joint Return Test applies, so Michelle may claim exemptions for both Greg and Sandy on her tax return, as long as all the other tests for dependency are met.

3. Qualifying Child of More Than One Person Test

Sometimes a child meets the rules to be a qualifying child of more than one person. However, only one person can claim that dependent on his tax return.

> **Example:** Dan and Linda live together with their daughter, Savannah. They are not married. Savannah is a qualifying child for both Dan and Linda, but only one of them can claim her as a dependent on their tax return.

4. Dependent Taxpayer Test

If a person can be claimed as a dependent by another taxpayer, that person cannot claim *anyone else* as a dependent. A person who is claimed as a dependent on *someone else's* return cannot claim a dependency exemption on *his own* return.

> **Example:** Eva is a 17-year-old single mother who has an infant son. Eva is claimed as a dependent by her parents. Therefore, since Eva is a dependent of her parents, she is prohibited from claiming her infant son as a dependent on her own tax return.

Qualifying Child or Qualifying Relative?

Once the preparer determines that a dependent may be claimed on a taxpayer's return, then he must decide the type of dependency relationship the dependent has with the taxpayer.

There are only two types of dependents, a ***qualifying child*** and a ***qualifying relative***. There are very specific tests for identifying the difference between a qualifying child and a qualifying relative, and these are heavily tested.

For the Enrolled Agent exam, you must understand the differences between these two types of dependency relationships.

Tests for a Qualifying Child

The tests for a qualifying child are more stringent than the tests for a qualifying relative. A qualifying child entitles a taxpayer to numerous tax credits, including the Earned Income Tax Credit and the Child Tax Credit. A "qualifying relative," on the other hand, does not qualify a taxpayer for the EITC.

To determine if a taxpayer may claim a dependency exemption for another person, begin with the five tests for a qualifying child:

- **Relationship test**
- **Age test**
- **Residency test**
- **Support test**
- **Tie-breaker test (for a qualifying child of more than one person)**

1. Relationship test

The qualifying child must be related to the taxpayer by blood, marriage, or legal adoption. Qualifying children include:

a. A child or stepchild
b. An adopted child
c. A sibling or stepsibling
d. A descendant of one of the above (such as a grandchild, niece, or nephew)
e. An eligible foster child

2. Age test

In order to be a qualifying child, the dependent must be:

- Under the age of 19 at the end of the tax year, OR
- Under the age of 24 *and* a full-time student, OR
- Permanently and totally disabled at any time during the year (of any age).

A child is considered a full-time student if he attends a qualified educational institution full-time at least five months out of the year.

Example: Andrew is 45 years old and totally disabled. Karen, his 37-year-old sister, provides all of Andrew's support and cares for him in her home, where he lives with her full-time. Although Andrew does not meet the age test, since he is **completely disabled,** he is still considered a *qualifying child* and a dependent for tax purposes. Karen may claim Andrew as her "qualifying child," and also file as Head of Household. (***Note:** Watch out for "trick" questions about disabled dependents!)

Also, a child who is claimed as a dependent must be *younger than* the taxpayer who is claiming him. There is an exception for dependents who are disabled. For taxpayers filing jointly, the child must be *younger* than *one spouse* listed on the return, but does NOT have to be younger than both spouses.

Example #1: Owen and Sydney are both 22 years old and file jointly. Sydney's 23-year-old brother, Parker, is a full-time student, unmarried, and lives with Owen and Sydney. Parker is not disabled. Owen and Sydney are both younger than Parker. Therefore, Parker is not their qualifying child, even though he is a full-time student.

Example #2: Lucius, age 34, and Paige, age 20, are married and file jointly. Paige's 23-year-old nephew, Jason, is a full-time student, unmarried, and lives with Lucius and Paige. Lucius and Paige provide all of Jason's support. In this case, Lucius and Paige may claim Jason as a qualifying child on their joint tax return because he is *younger than* Lucius. Jason is a full-time student, so he is a qualifying child for tax purposes.

3. Support test

A qualifying child cannot provide more than one-half of his own support. A full-time student does not take scholarships (whether taxable or non-taxable) into account when calculating the support test.

Example #1: Samuel has an 18-year-old daughter named Tiffany. Samuel provided $4,000 toward his teenage daughter's support for the year. Tiffany also has a part-time job and provided $13,000 of her own support. Therefore, Tiffany provided over half of *her own support* for the year. Tiffany does not pass the support test, and consequently, she is not Samuel's qualifying child. Tiffany can file a tax return as "Single" and claim her own exemption.

Example #2: Penelope is 15 years old and had a small role in a television series. She earned $40,000 as a child actor, but her parents put all the money in a trust fund to pay for college. She lived at home all year. Penelope meets the support test since her earnings were not used for her own support. Since she meets the tests for a qualifying child, Penelope can be claimed as a dependent by her parents.

Multiple Support Agreements: There are special rules for *multiple support* agreements. A *multiple support agreement* is when two or more people agree to join together to provide a person's support. This happens commonly with adult children who are taking care of their parents. There are special rules for claiming a dependency exemption when a taxpayer has a multiple support agreement. IRS **Form 2120** is used to declare a *multiple support agreement*.

Example: Benjamin and Matthew are two brothers who support their disabled mother, Abigail. Abigail is 83 and lives with Benjamin. In 2011, Abigail receives 20% of her financial support from Social Security, 40% from Benjamin, and 60% from Matthew. Under IRS rules for multiple support agreements, either Matthew or Benjamin can take the exemption for their mother if the other signs a statement agreeing not to do so. The one who takes the exemption must attach **Form 2120** (or a similar declaration) to his tax return.

In order for a *multiple support agreement* to be valid, the taxpayer who claims the dependent must provide over 10% of the person's support, at a minimum.

Example: Olivia, Sophia, and Emily are sisters who help support their 72-year-old father, Eugene. Olivia provides 80% percent support, Sophia provides 15%, and Emily provides 5%. Under a multiple support agreement, either Olivia or Sophia can claim an exemption for their father. Emily did not provide over 10% of her father's support, so she is not eligible to claim him as a dependent. The one who claims the exemption must attach **Form 2120** to her return. Emily does not have to sign the form.

Foster Care Payments

Payments received for the support of a foster child from a child placement agency are considered support provided by the agency (not support provided by the child).

Example: Gina is a foster parent. Gina provided $3,000 toward her 10-year-old foster child's support for the year. The state government provided $4,000, which was considered support provided by the state, not by the child. Gina's foster child did not provide more than half of her own support for the year. Therefore, the child may be claimed as a qualifying child by Gina if all the other tests are met.

4. Residence (or Abode) Test

In general, a *qualifying child* must live with the taxpayer for more than half the tax year (over six months). Exceptions apply for children of divorced parents, kidnapped children, temporary absences, and for children who were born or died during the year.[15]

A *temporary absence* includes illness, college, vacation, military service, and incarceration in a juvenile facility. It must be reasonable to assume that the absent child will return to the home after the temporary absence.

The taxpayer must continue to maintain the home during the absence.

Example: Douglas and Andrea file jointly. They have one daughter named Isabella who is 29 years old. In March of 2011, Isabella lost her job and moved back in with her parents. Isabella earned $4,000 at the beginning of 2011 before she was laid off. Douglas and Andrea therefore provided the majority of Isabella's support for the rest of the year. Isabella got a new job in December and moved out. Isabella is not a qualifying child for federal tax purposes. Although Isabella meets the relationship, residence, and support test, she *does not* meet the age test.

---

[15] A taxpayer cannot claim an exemption for a stillborn child.

> **Example**: Scott is unmarried and lives with his 10-year-old son, Elijah. Scott provides all of Elijah's support. In 2011, Elijah became very ill and was hospitalized for seven months. Elijah is still considered Scott's qualifying child, because the illness and hospitalization count as a temporary absence from home. Scott may claim Elijah as his qualifying child and also file for Head of Household status.

*Special rules: Kidnapped child

A taxpayer can treat a kidnapped child as meeting the residency test, but both of the following must be true:

- The child is presumed to have been kidnapped by someone who is not a family member.
- In the year the kidnapping occurred, the child lived with the taxpayer for more than half of the year before the kidnapping.

This special tax treatment applies for all years until the child is returned. However, the last year this treatment can apply is the earlier of:

- The year there is a determination that the child is dead, or
- The year the child would have reached age 18.

5. The Tie-Breaker Test

Only one person can claim the same qualifying child. If a child is the qualifying child of more than one person, only one person can claim the child as a qualifying child on his tax return.

If two taxpayers disagree on who gets to claim a child as their qualifying child, and more than one person attempts to claim the same child, then the tie-breaker rules apply.

Under the tie-breaker rule, the child is treated as a qualifying child only by:

- The parents, if they file a joint return.
- The parent, if only one of the persons is the child's parent.
- The parent with whom the child lived the longest during the year.
- The parent with the highest AGI if the child lived with each parent for the same amount of time during the tax year, and they do not file a joint return together.
- The person with the highest AGI, if no parent can claim the child as a qualifying child.
- A person with the higher AGI than any parent who can also claim the child as a qualifying child but does not.

Example: Jaime has a three-year-old son named Orlando. Jaime is not married. Jaime and Orlando live with Jaime's father, Theodore. Jaime claims Orlando as her qualifying child. Because Jaime claims Orlando as a qualifying child, the child may not be treated as a qualifying child of the grandfather, Theodore, for any purpose.

Example: Olga and her sister, Rosa, live together. They also live and take care of their seven-year-old niece, Brianna, who lived with Olga and Rosa all year. Brianna's biological mother is incarcerated and unable to claim Samantha. Olga is 25 years old, and her AGI is $9,300. Olga's only income was from a part-time job. Rosa's AGI is $15,000. Rosa's only income was from her job. Brianna is a qualifying child of both Olga and Rosa because she meets the relationship, age, residency, and joint return tests for both aunts. However, Rosa has the right to claim Brianna as her qualifying child. This is because Rosa's AGI, $15,000, is more than Olga's AGI, $9,300.

Tests for "Qualifying Relatives"

A person who is not a "qualifying child" may still qualify as a dependent under the rules for "qualifying relatives."

There is a six-part test for *qualifying relatives*. Under these tests, even an individual who is *not a family member* can still be a "qualifying relative." Unlike a qualifying child, a *qualifying relative* can be any age.

*****Note:** There is no "age test" for a qualifying relative, and the support test and relationship test have different criteria.

In order to be claimed as a "qualifying relative," the dependent must meet all of the following criteria:

- **Relationship (or Member of Household) Test**
- **Gross Income Test**
- **Total Support Test**
- **Joint Return Test**
- **Citizenship or Residency Test**

1. Relationship Test (or Member of Household)

The dependent must be related to the taxpayer in certain ways. A family member who is related to the taxpayer in any of the following ways ***does not*** have to live with the taxpayer to meet this test:

- A child, stepchild, foster child, or a descendant of any of them (for example, a grandchild).
- A sibling, stepsibling, or a half sibling.

- A parent, grandparent, stepparent, or other direct ancestor (but this does not include foster parents).
- A niece or nephew, a son-in-law, daughter-in-law, father-in-law, mother-in-law, brother-in-law, or sister-in-law[16].
- ***OR** the dependent **must have lived with** the taxpayer the ENTIRE tax year, and the individual cannot have earned more than the personal exemption amount (in 2011, the amount is $3,700).

This means that an unrelated person who lived with the taxpayer for the entire year can also meet the member of household or relationship test.

> ***Note:** If a relationship violates local laws, this test is not met. For example, if a taxpayer's state prohibits cohabitation, then that person cannot be claimed as a dependent, even if all other criteria are met.

> **Example:** Isaac's 12-year-old grandson, Josh, lived with him for three months in 2011. For the rest of the year, Josh lived with his mother, Natalie, in another state. Natalie is Isaac's 32-year-old daughter. Even though Josh and Natalie lived in another state, Isaac still provided all of their financial support. Josh is not Isaac's *qualifying child* because he does not meet the residency test (Josh did not live with Isaac for more than half the year). However, Josh is Isaac's *qualifying relative*. Natalie can also be Isaac's qualifying relative if the *gross income test* is met.

*Note: Any of these relationships that are established by marriage are *not ended* by death or divorce. So, for example, if a taxpayer supports a mother-in-law, he can continue to claim her as a dependent even if he and his ex-spouse are divorced or if he becomes widowed.

> **Example #1**: Mia and Caleb have always financially supported Mia's elderly mother, Gertrude, and claim her as their dependent on their jointly filed returns. However, in 2010, Mia dies and Caleb becomes a widower. Caleb remarries in 2011, but continues to support his former mother-in-law, Gertrude. Caleb can continue to claim Gertrude on his tax returns, even though he has remarried. This is because of the special rule that dependency relationships established by marriage do not end by death or divorce.

---

[16] ***Note:** The listing of family members for the "relationship test" does NOT include COUSINS. A cousin must live with the taxpayer for the entire year and also meet the *gross income test* in order to qualify as a dependent. In that respect, they are treated by the IRS just like an unrelated person.

Example #2: Bella and Dean are married. Together they are raising Dean's 16-year-old daughter, Sarah, from Dean's first marriage. Dean dies suddenly in 2010, and Bella becomes a widow. In 2011, Bella remarries, but she continues to raise and support her stepdaughter, Sarah. Bella may continue to claim Sarah as her dependent since dependency relationships established by marriage do not end with death or divorce.

Example #3: Todd has lived all year with his girlfriend, Eva, and her two children in his home. Their cohabitation does not violate local laws. Eva does not work and is not required to file a 2011 tax return. Eva and her two children pass the "not a qualifying child test" to be Todd's qualifying relatives. Todd can claim them as dependents if he meets all the other tests.

2. Gross Income Test

A *qualifying relative* cannot earn more than the personal exemption amount. In 2011, the personal exemption amount is $3,700. For the purposes of this test, "gross income" includes:

- All taxable income in the form of money, property, or services
- Gross receipts from rental property
- A partner's share of gross partnership income (not net)
- Unemployment compensation
- Taxable scholarships and grants

For the purposes of this test, "gross income" does NOT include:

- Tax-exempt income
- Income earned by a disabled person at a sheltered workshop

3. Total Support Test

In order to claim an individual as a "qualifying relative" the taxpayer must provide over half of the dependent's total support during the year. "Support" includes amounts from Social Security and welfare payments, even if that support is non-taxable.

"Support" does not include amounts received from non-taxable scholarships. Support can include the fair market value of lodging.

Example #1: Ella is 78 and lives in her own apartment. She received $7,000 in Social Security benefits in 2011, which she used to pay for her apartment. Ella's daughter, Laurie, provided $2,200 in support to her mother by paying her utility bills and buying her groceries. Even though Ella's Social Security benefits are not taxable and she does not have a filing requirement, Laurie cannot claim her mother as a dependent because Ella provided over one-half of her own support.

Example #2: Nicholas lives with Gavin, who is an old army buddy of his. Nicholas provided all of the support for Gavin, who lived with Nicholas all year in his home. Gavin has no income and does not file a 2011 tax return. Nicholas can claim Gavin as his qualifying relative if all of the other tests are met.

Example #3: Morgan provided $4,000 toward her father's support during the year. In 2011, Morgan's father earned income of $600, had non-taxable Social Security benefits of $4,800, and tax-exempt interest of $200. He uses all these for his support. Morgan cannot claim an exemption for her father because the $4,000 she provides is not more than half of her father's total support of $9,600 ($4,000 + $600 + $4,800 + $200).

4. Joint Return Test

If the dependent is married, he cannot file a joint return with his spouse, unless the return is filed solely to obtain a refund of withheld income taxes. (With the "Joint Return Test," the same exceptions apply for a qualifying relative as for qualifying children.)

5. Citizenship or Residency Test

A "qualifying relative" must be either a citizen or resident alien of:
- The United States, or
- Canada, or
- Mexico.

This means that a child who lives in Canada or Mexico may still be a *qualifying relative* of a U.S. taxpayer.

Even If the child does not live with the taxpayer at all during the tax year, the child may still be eligible to be claimed as a *qualifying relative*.

Example: Manuel provides all the financial support of his children, ages 6 and 12, who live in Mexico with Manuel's mother, their grandmother. Manuel is unmarried and lives in the United States. He is a legal U.S. resident alien (green card holder) and has a valid Social Security Number. However, Manuel's children are citizens of Mexico and do not have SSNs. Regardless, both his children are still "qualifying relatives" for tax purposes. Manuel may claim them as dependents if all the tests are met. Manuel may also be able to claim his mother as a dependent if all the tests are met. He will be required to request ITINs for his children and his mother using **Form W-7**.

Special Rules for Children of Divorced or Separated Parents

Generally, to claim a child as a dependent, the child must live with the taxpayer for over half the year (over six months). There is an exception to this rule for divorced/separated parents.

If the child did not live with the taxpayer, the custodial parent may still allow the non-custodial parent to claim the dependency exemption.

A non-custodial parent may still qualify to take the dependency exemption for a child if the custodial parent agrees in writing. The non-custodial parent must attach IRS **Form 8332** in order to claim the dependency exemption. A copy of a divorce decree is not sufficient.[17]

Regardless of the language of a divorce agreement, without **Form 8332** signed and attached to the return, the IRS will not recognize the deduction by a non-custodial parent.

```
Form 8332              Release/Revocation of Release of Claim           OMB No. 1545-0074
(Rev. January 2010)    to Exemption for Child by Custodial Parent
Department of the Treasury                                              Attachment
Internal Revenue Service    ▶ Attach a separate form for each child.   Sequence No. 115

Name of noncustodial parent                    Noncustodial parent's
                                               social security number (SSN) ▶

Part I   Release of Claim to Exemption for Current Year

I agree not to claim an exemption for _____
                                          Name of child
for the tax year 20____
```

If a divorce decree does not specify which parent is the custodial parent or which parent receives the dependency exemption, the exemption will automatically go to the parent who has physical custody for the majority of the year.

Example: Alexis and Nathan are divorced. They have one child named Dylan. In 2011, Dylan lived with Alexis for 300 nights and with Nathan for 65 nights. Therefore, Alexis is the custodial parent. Alexis has the right to claim Dylan on her tax return as her qualifying child. However, Alexis may choose to release the exemption to Nathan by signing **Form 8332**.

Note: Even if the custodial parent releases the dependency exemption to the non-custodial parent, the custodial parent still has the right to claim Head of Household status, the Earned Income Credit, and Dependent Care Credit.

Example: Gary and Frieda are divorced, and have one minor child named Sunny. Frieda is the custodial parent, but she agrees to release the dependency exemption for their child over to Gary by signing **Form 8332.** Gary will file "Single" and claim Sunny as his dependent. Frieda may still file as "Head of Household" even though she does not claim the dependency exemption for Sunny. That is because Frieda is the parent who lived with Sunny and maintained the home in which her child lived for most of the year.

If the custodial parent waives his dependency exemption, the non-custodial parent may claim the Child Tax Credit along with the dependency exemption.

A child will be treated as the qualifying child (or qualifying relative) of the non-custodial parent if ALL of the following apply:

---

[17] A non-custodial parent claiming an exemption for a child can no longer attach pages from a divorce decree or separation agreement instead of Form 8332 if the decree or agreement was executed after 2008.

- The parents are divorced or legally separated
- The parents are separated under a written separation agreement
- The parents lived apart at all times during the last six months of the year
- The child received over half of his support from the parents
- The child is in the custody of either of the parents for more than half of the year

A taxpayer *may not* claim a dependency exemption for a household employee (such as a housekeeper), even if the employee lived with the taxpayer.

The Kiddie Tax

The "Kiddie Tax" deals with the taxation of unearned income of children (such as interest income). Years ago, wealthy families would transfer investments to their minor children and save thousands of dollars in investment income because the money would be taxed at a lower rate. This was completely legal until Congress closed this tax loophole, and now, investment income earned by dependent children is taxed at the parents' marginal rate.

This new law became known as the "Kiddie Tax." The Kiddie Tax does not apply to wages or self-employment income—it applies to *investment income* only. Examples of unearned income include bank interest, dividends, and capital gains distributions.

Originally, this tax only applied to children under age 14. In 2006, the age limit was increased to 18. In 2008, the Kiddie Tax was extended to apply to dependent students until they reach age 24.

The Kiddie Tax does not kick in until the dependent has a certain amount of investment income. In 2011, the threshold is $1,900 in investment income.

A child may still owe income tax, even with less than $1,900 in income. But this is rare. This $1,900 threshold only applies to investment income.

Until the child turns 18 (or is a full-time student up to age 24), the Kiddie Tax will be applied automatically if the child's investment income exceeds $1,900.

The Kiddie Tax rules allow children under 19 (24 if a student) to have unearned income (interest, rental, capital gain, dividends, etc.) up to $950 in 2011 and to use their standard deduction to shelter it from tax. The next $950 in 2011 of income is taxed at the child's tax rate. Any additional unearned income will be taxed at the marginal tax rate of the parents. If the parents are divorced or single, the rate taxed to the child (above $1,900) will be the higher of the two parents'.

Any additional investment income would then be taxed at the parents' rate. (*Remember, the Kiddie Tax rules apply to unearned income, not to wages!)

For 2011, a person who is claimed as a dependent is entitled to a standard deduction amount of the **larger** of:

- Earned income (such as wages) + $300, or

- $950 (unearned income).

> **Example:** Bill and Donna have one 14-year-old son named Jack. In 2011, Jack has $2,900 of interest income from a CD that his grandfather gave him. He does not have any other income. The first $950 of investment income is not taxable, because the standard deduction for dependents is $950. The next $950 will be taxed at the 10% income tax rate. The remainder, $1,000, will be taxed at the parents' tax rate.

After the child turns 18, the Kiddie Tax applies *unless* the child's earned income is more than half his overall support. In this case, "earned income" could be income from wages or self-employment. For dependents that are 19 to 23 years old, the Kiddie Tax applies to a dependent child who is a full-time student *unless* the child's earned income is more than half his overall support.

The Kiddie Tax does not apply if the child is Married Filing Jointly.

There are two ways to report investment income for a child and the resulting Kiddie Tax. A taxpayer may choose to file either:

- **Form 8814,** *Parents' Election to Report Child's Interest and Dividends*, which allows the parents to include the child's investment income on their return or,
- Have the child file a separate return, and report the Kiddie Tax using **Form 8615,** *Tax for Certain Children Who Have Investment Income of More Than $1,900.*

The tax on the child's income will be the same either way.

In order to use **Form 8814** to report a dependent's income, the child's investment income must be *more than* $950 and less than $9,500.

If the parent reports his child's investment income on a separate return, the child must report the income on **Form 1040** and include **Form 8615**. This form automatically figures the tax using the parent's highest marginal rate.

Dependency Tests (Snapshot)

Tests for a Qualifying Child

The child must be a son, daughter, stepchild, foster child, brother, sister, half-brother, half-sister, stepbrother, stepsister, or a descendant of any of these.
The child must be: • Under age 19 at the end of the year and younger than the taxpayer (or his spouse, if filing jointly), • Under age 24 at the end of the year, a full-time student, and younger than the taxpayer (or his spouse, if filing jointly), or • Any age if disabled.
The child must have lived with the taxpayer for more than half of the year (over six months). Exceptions exist for temporary absences, kidnapped children, and dependents that died/were born during the year.
The child must not have provided more than half of his own support for the year.
The child cannot file a joint return for the year (unless that joint return is filed only as a claim for refund).
If the child meets the rules to be a qualifying child of more than one person, only one taxpayer can claim the child.

Tests for a Qualifying Relative

The person cannot be the qualifying child of anyone else.
The person either (a) must be related to the taxpayer in certain ways OR (b) must live with the taxpayer all year as a member of the household. There is no age test for a qualifying relative.
The person's gross income for the year must be less than $3,700 in 2011.
The taxpayer must provide more than half of the person's total support for the year.

Unit 4: Questions

1. Dan is unmarried and lives alone. Dan's mother received $5,600 in Social Security benefits and $100 in taxable interest income in 2011. She paid $4,000 for living expenses and $400 for recreation. She also put $1,300 in a savings account. Dan also spent $4,800 of his own money on his mother's support in 2011, which paid her rent for the entire year. Dan and his mother did not live together. Which of the following is true?

A. Dan may claim his mother as a dependent, and also file as Head of Household.
B. Dan may not claim his mother as a dependent, but he may file as Head of Household.
C. Dan may claim his mother as a dependent, but he may not file as Head of Household.
D. Dan may not claim his mother as a dependent, and he cannot file as Head of Household.

The answer is A. Dan may claim his mother as a dependent, and also file as Head of Household. Even though Dan's mother received a total of $5,700 ($5,600 + $100), she spent only $4,400 ($4,000 + $400) for her own support. Since Dan spent more than $4,400 for her support and no other support was received, Dan has provided more than half of her support. Also, Dan paid for all her lodging costs, so he paid more than half the cost of keeping up a home that was the main home for the entire year for his parent. Therefore, Dan is also eligible to file as Head of Household. ###

2. Roy is a client who tells you that his wife died in February 2011. Based on this information, Roy can claim _____.

A. Only the personal exemption for himself.
B. Only the personal exemption for his wife.
C. Personal exemptions for both himself and for his wife.
D. A personal exemption for himself and a partial exemption for his wife.

The answer is C. In 2011, Roy can claim a personal exemption for his deceased wife, along with a personal exemption for himself. A taxpayer whose spouse dies during the year may file jointly in the year of death. ###

3. Alyssa is 18 years old and a full-time student. She comes into your office with some questions about her tax return. She says that she is claimed as a dependent on her parents' tax return. Over the summer, she worked in a clothing boutique and earned $7,000. Alyssa wants to file a tax return to report her wage income and get a refund. How many exemptions may she claim on her tax return?

A. Zero.
B. One.
C. Two.
D. Three.

The answer is A. Since Alyssa is claimed as a dependent on her parents' tax return, she cannot claim an exemption for herself. Therefore, her total number of exemptions is zero. She can still file a tax return in order to claim a refund of taxes withheld. ###

4. John is the sole support of his mother. To claim her as a dependent on his **Form 1040,** John's mother must be a resident or citizen of which of the following countries?

A. United States.
B. Mexico.
C. Canada.
D. Any of the above.

The answer is D. To qualify as a dependent, the dependent must be a citizen or resident alien of the United States, Canada, or Mexico. ###

5. In a multiple support agreement, what is the minimum amount of support that a taxpayer can provide and still claim the dependent?

A. 10% support.
B. 15% support.
C. 50% support.
D. 75% support.

The answer is A. The law provides for multiple support agreements. These multiple support agreements usually exist when family members collectively support a relative, oftentimes a parent. The taxpayer can claim the dependent if he paid more than 10% of the support. ###

6. Avery, 52, is a single father with one adopted son named Wyatt who has Down syndrome. Wyatt is 32 years old and permanently disabled. Wyatt lives with his father. Wyatt had $800 in interest income and $5,000 in wages from a part-time job in 2011. Which of the following statements is true?

A. Avery can file as Head of Household, with Wyatt as his qualifying child.
B. Avery does not qualify for Head of Household, but he could still claim Wyatt as his qualifying relative, because Wyatt does not meet the age test for a qualifying child.
C. Avery can file as Head of Household, with Wyatt as his qualifying relative.
D. Avery must file Single and he cannot claim Wyatt, because Wyatt earned more than the standard deduction amount.

The answer is A. Even though Wyatt is over the normal age threshold for a qualifying child, he is still considered a qualifying child for tax purposes. This is because Wyatt is permanently disabled and Avery provides his financial support and care. Since Wyatt is disabled, he is therefore also a "qualifying child" for the purposes of Head of Household filing status. ###

7. Clifford and Lily divorced in 2010 and they have one child together. Clifford's child lived with him for ten months of the year in 2011. The child lived with Lily for the other two months. The divorce decree states that Lily is supposed to be the custodial parent, not Clifford. Who is considered the custodial parent for IRS purposes?

A. Clifford.
B. Lily.
C. Neither.
D. Both.

The answer is A. For IRS purposes, the "custodial parent" is the parent with whom the child lived for the greater part of the year. The other parent is the non-custodial parent. If the parents divorced or separated during the year and the child lived with both parents before the separation, the custodial parent is the one with whom the child lived for the greater part of the rest of the year. ###

8. Haley is 23 and a full-time college student. During the year, Haley lived at home with her parents for four months and lived in the dorm for the remainder of the year. During the tax year, Haley worked part-time and earned $6,000, but that income did not amount to half of her total support. Can Haley's parents still claim her as a dependent?

A. No, because Haley earned more than the personal exemption amount.
B. No, because Haley did not live with her parents for more than half the year, and she does not meet the age test.
C. Yes, Haley's parents can claim her as a qualifying child.
D. Yes, Haley's parents can claim her as a dependent, but only as a qualifying relative, not as a qualifying child.

The answer is C. Haley meets all the qualifying child tests: the relationship test; the age test (because she is under 24 and was a full-time student); the residence test (because the time spent at college is a legitimate temporary absence); and the support test (because she did not provide over half of her own support). ###

9. Carson has a 12-year-old daughter named Emma. In 2011, Emma had $950 in interest income from a bank account. Which of the following statements regarding Emma's unearned income is correct?

A. Tax will be assessed to Carson and is calculated using Emma's tax rate.
B. Emma is not required to file a return, and Carson is not required to report his daughter's income on his own tax return.
C. Emma is required to file a tax return, and income tax will be assessed at a flat rate of 10%.
D. Carson may elect to report Emma's interest income on his own tax return. Her income will be taxed at the parents' highest marginal rate.

The answer is B. Emma is not required to file a tax return, because her unearned income is less than the standard deduction amount for dependents. The first $950 of investment income (which is equal to the dependent's standard deduction) escapes income tax. Emma has no filing requirement, and her father is not required to report the income on his own return. ###

10. Anthony's daughter, Violet, age sixteen, lived with him for six months of the year. Anthony also paid for Violet to go to summer camp for two months. Violet then lived with Anthony's ex-wife for the rest of the year. Who is considered the custodial parent for tax purposes?

A. Anthony.
B. Anthony's ex-wife.
C. Neither.
D. The summer camp.

The answer is A. The time at summer camp would be considered a temporary absence. The custodial parent is the parent with whom the child lived for the greater part of the year. Therefore, Anthony is allowed to claim Violet as his qualifying child. ###

11. Cheryl is 46 and unmarried. Her nephew, Bradley, lived with her all year and was 18 years old at the end of the year. Bradley did not provide more than half of his own support. He had $4,200 in income from wages and $1,000 in investment income. Which of the following is true?
A. Bradley qualifies as Cheryl's "qualifying child" for tax purposes.
B. Bradley is not a qualifying child; however, he can be claimed by Cheryl as a qualifying relative.
C. Bradley is not a qualifying child or qualifying relative, because he had income that exceeded the personal exemption amount.
D. Cheryl can claim Bradley only if he is a full-time student, since he is no longer a minor child.

The answer is A. Bradley is Cheryl's qualifying child because he meets the age test, support test, and relationship test. Also, because Bradley is single, he is a qualifying person for Cheryl to claim Head of Household filing status. Bradley is not required to be a full-time student, because the IRS says that any child under the age of 19 at the end of the tax year will be treated as a qualifying child if all the other tests are met. Bradley is only 18 years old, and therefore, he passes the age test. ###

12. There are many tests which must be met for a taxpayer to claim an exemption for a dependent as a qualifying relative. Which of the following is NOT a requirement?
A. Citizen or Resident Test.
B. Member of Household or Relationship Test.
C. Disability Test.
D. Joint Return Test.

The answer is C. There is no such thing as a "Disability Test" for a qualifying relative. ###

13. Tony and Isabelle are the sole support of all the following individuals (All are U.S. citizens but none lives with them, files a tax return, or has any income):

1. Jennie, Tony's grandmother.
2. Julie, Isabelle's stepmother.
3. Jon, father of Tony's first wife.
4. Timothy, Isabelle's cousin.

How many exemptions may Tony and Isabelle claim on their joint return?

A. 2.
B. 3.
C. 4.
D. 5.

The answer is D. They may take three dependency exemptions on their tax return, and two personal exemptions for themselves. The taxpayers may take dependency exemptions for all the dependents listed, except for Timothy. Timothy would have to live with Tony and Isabelle all year in order for them to claim him as their dependent. Parents (or grandparents, in-laws, stepparents, etc.) do not have to live with a taxpayer in order to qualify as dependents. Tony can claim Jonathan, because Jonathan was once his father-in-law. ###

14. Ted and Sharon are married and are the sole support of their 23-year-old son, Ashton, who lives with them. Ashton is not a student and not disabled. Ashton was unable to find steady work in 2011, but received $4,900 from a charitable foundation for painting a mural. Which of the following statements is true?

A. Ted and Sharon may claim Ashton as a qualifying child on their federal income tax return.
B. Ted and Sharon may claim Ashton as a qualifying relative on their federal income tax return.
C. Ted and Sharon may not claim Ashton as a dependent.
D. Ted and Sharon may only claim Ashton if they file MFS.

The answer is C. Ashton is not a minor, not a student, and not disabled. Therefore, he does not qualify as a "qualifying child." He does not qualify as a "qualifying relative," either, because he fails the "Gross Income Test." A qualifying relative cannot earn more than the personal exemption amount. In 2011, the personal exemption amount is $3,700. Since Ashton earned $4,900 in 2011, he cannot be claimed as a dependent. ###

15. If a child being adopted is eligible to be claimed as a dependent by the adoptive parents, what must occur in order for the child to be taken as a dependent on the adoptive parents' tax return?

A. An identifying number must be obtained for the child (an ATIN, ITIN, or Social Security Number).
B. The adoption must become final first.
C. The child must be related to the taxpayer by blood.
D. Only domestic adoptions qualify; a taxpayer cannot claim a dependency exemption for a foreign-born child.

The answer is A. A Tax Identification Number must be obtained for the child. The adoption does not have to be final. Parents in the process of a U.S. adoption who are unable to obtain the child's Social Security Number should request an Adoption Taxpayer Identification Number (ATIN) in order to claim the child as a dependent. The term "adopted child" includes a child who was lawfully placed with the taxpayer for legal adoption. The adoption does not have to be final for the parents to take a dependency exemption if the child has been lawfully placed by a government authority or U.S. court. ###

16. Peter filed for divorce in 2011. He and his wife moved into separate residences on April 20, 2011. Peter's 10-year-old daughter lived with him for the entire year in 2011. Peter owns the home and pays all the costs of upkeep for it. His ex-wife did not live in the home at any time during the year. Which of the following is true?

A. Peter must file jointly with his wife in 2011, since they are still legally married. They may claim their daughter as a dependent on their jointly filed return.
B. Peter must file Single in 2011.
C. Peter must file MFS in 2011.
D. Peter qualifies for HOH filing status.

The answer is D. Peter qualifies for Head of Household filing status. Since Peter and his wife lived in separate residences for the last six months of the year and Peter had a qualifying child, he may file as Head of Household. ###

17. Tyler is single and 17 years old. He works a part-time job at night and is going to school full-time. His total income for 2011 was $10,500. Tyler lives with his parents, who provided the majority of Tyler's support. Tyler's parents are claiming him as a dependent on their 2011 tax return. Which of the following statements is true?

A. Tyler is required file his own return, and he may also take an exemption for himself.
B. Tyler is not required to file his own return.
C. Tyler's parents may not claim him as a dependent because Tyler earned more than the standard deduction amount for 2011.
D. His parents may claim Tyler as their qualifying child. Tyler is required to file a tax return, but he cannot claim a personal exemption for himself. He is still entitled to the standard deduction for SINGLE filers.

The answer is D. Tyler's parents may claim him as their qualifying child because he is a child under the age of 19 and does not provide more than half of his own support. Tyler is required to file a tax return but cannot claim an exemption for himself. ###

18. A child has investment income. What is the income limit threshold for when the Kiddie Tax kicks in?

A. $0.
B. $950.
C. $1,900.
D. $3,700.

The answer is C. In 2011, a child's unearned income in excess of $1,900 is subject to the Kiddie Tax rules. ###

19. Grant is 16 and has $4,000 in investment income. How should he report the Kiddie Tax?

A. Grant can file his own tax return (including IRS Form 8615).
B. The income can be added to Grant's parents' return (using Form 8814).
C. Grant is not required to file a return to report the income, because it is under the personal exemption amount for 2011.
D. Both A and B.

The answer is D. With the Kiddie Tax, there are two ways you can satisfy a child's filing requirement. Grant may file his own tax return (including IRS **Form 8615**), or the income can be added to Grant's parents' return (using **Form 8814**). ###

20. Frank provided $4,000 toward his 17-year-old son's support for the year. Frank's son has a part-time job and provided $16,000 to his own support. Which of the following is TRUE?

A. Frank may claim his son as a qualifying child on his return.
B. Frank may claim his son as his business partner on his return.
C. Frank may not claim his son as a dependent on his return.
D. None of the above is correct.

The answer is C. Frank's son provided more than half of his *own support* for the year. Therefore, he is not Frank's qualifying child. ###

21. Ben lives with his brother, Steven. Ben received $3,200 in wages in 2011. Steven provided $2,900 in monetary support to Ben in 2011 by paying his medical bills and groceries. However, Steven also provided a home for Ben, of which the Fair Rental Value was approximately $500 per month. Which of the following is true?

A. Steven can claim his brother Ben as a dependent because Steven provided more than one-half of Ben's support.
B. The value of the lodging cannot be considered as part of the calculation of support.
C. Steven cannot claim his brother as a dependent under any circumstances.
D. Steven can only claim his brother as a dependent if he is disabled.

The answer is A. Steven can claim his brother, Ben, as a dependent because Steven provided more than one-half of Ben's support. The value of the lodging can be considered as part of the calculation of support. ###

22. Persons who can be claimed as a dependent may file a tax return, but they cannot:

A. Claim any deductions.
B. Claim any exemptions.
C. File a claim for a refund.
D. File an amended return.

The answer is B. Persons who can be claimed as a dependent may file a tax return, but they cannot claim any exemptions. If a taxpayer can claim another person as a dependent—even if the taxpayer does not actually do so—the dependent cannot take a personal exemption on *his* tax return. ###

23. Mateo is a U.S. resident. He has a 10-year-old child named Rey, who is a legal resident of Mexico. Rey does not have an SSN. Mateo would like to claim Rey as a dependent on his tax return. Rey lived with Mateo for eight months and with his grandmother in Mexico for the remaining part of the year. Does Rey meet the requirements of the "citizen or resident" test?

A. No, because Rey does not have a valid SSN.
B. No, because Rey is a resident of Mexico.
C. Yes, Rey meets the requirements of the "citizen or resident" test.
D. None of the above.

The answer is C. Rey meets the requirements of the "citizen or resident" test. In order to meet the "citizen or resident" test, a person must be a U.S. citizen or resident, OR a resident of Canada or Mexico for at least some part of the year. ###

24. Donna Wiley has three children, Noel, Tim, and Mary. Each child contributes toward Mrs. Wiley's support. Mark needs assistance in determining which of them should claim Mrs. Wiley as a dependent. Noel provides 65%, Tim, 25%, and Mary, 10%. Which of Mrs. Wiley's children would be eligible to claim a dependency exemption for Mrs. Wiley under a multiple support agreement?

A. Noel or Tim
B. Tim
C. Mary
D. Noel

The answer is A. Either Noel or Tim may claim the exemption because both provide more than 10% of Mrs. Wiley's support. Mary is not eligible because she does not provide more than 10%. Noel and Tim must decide which one will claim Mrs. Wiley on their tax return. ###

Unit 5: Due Dates, Estimates, and Extensions

> **More Reading:**
> Publication 505, *Tax Withholding and Estimated Tax*
> Publication 594, *Understanding the Collection Process*
> Publication 3, *Armed Forces' Tax Guide*

Due Dates and Extensions

The regular due date for individual tax returns is *usually* April 15. If April 15 falls on a Saturday, Sunday, or legal holiday, the due date will be delayed until the next business day.

In 2012, April 15 falls on a Sunday and April 16, 2012 falls on Emancipation Day, which is a federal holiday in the District of Columbia (Washington, D.C.) Therefore, the IRS has extended the due date for 2011 individual tax returns to Tuesday, **April 17, 2012.**

If a taxpayer cannot file his tax return by the due date, he may request an extension by filing IRS **Form 4868**, *Application for Automatic Extension of Time to File*. Extended individual tax returns are due by **October 15, 2012.**

An extension will grant a taxpayer an additional six months to file his individual tax return. **Form 4868** may be filed electronically. An extension will give a taxpayer extra time to file his return, but it does NOT extend the time to pay any tax due.

A taxpayer will owe interest on any unpaid amount that is not paid by the filing deadline, plus a late payment penalty if he has not paid at least 90% of his total tax due by that date. Taxpayers are expected to estimate and pay the amount of tax due by the filing deadline.

The IRS will accept a postmark as proof of a timely-filed return. For example, if the tax return is postmarked on April 10 but does not arrive at the IRS Service Center until April 30, the IRS will accept the tax return as having been filed on time. E-filed tax returns are also given an "electronic postmark" to indicate the day that they are transmitted. You should memorize the due dates for tax returns and extensions for the EA exam.

Penalties and Interest on Late Filing

An extension only grants a taxpayer additional time to file, NOT additional time to pay. Interest and penalties will continue to accrue on any unpaid balance until the taxpayer finally files his tax return and pays any amounts that are owed. There are three separate penalties:

- Failure-to-file penalty (the failure to file on time)
- Failure-to-pay penalty (the failure to pay on time)
- Interest on the delinquent amount due

> *Note:* Penalties are tested on all three sections of the EA exam. Be sure you understand the most common types of taxpayer and preparer penalties.

IRS Penalties In General

If a taxpayer does not FILE on time, he will face a *failure-to-file* penalty.

If a taxpayer does not PAY on time, he will face a *failure-to-pay* penalty.

Failure to File

In terms of percentages, the "failure-to-file" penalty is much higher than the "failure-to-pay" penalty. So, even if a taxpayer cannot pay all the taxes he owes, he should still file his tax return on time. The penalty for late filing is usually 5% of the unpaid taxes for each month (or part of a month) that a return is late. This penalty will not exceed 25% of the unpaid tax on the return.

The failure-to-file penalty is calculated based on the time from the due date of the return to the date the taxpayer actually files. This penalty is calculated on the amount due on the return, so if the taxpayer is due a refund or has no tax liability, then this penalty will not be assessed.[18]

However, if a taxpayer files his return more than 60 days after the due date (or extended due date), the *minimum* penalty is the smaller of:

- $135, OR
- 100% of the unpaid tax.

Failure to Pay

If the taxpayer does not pay his taxes by the due date, he will have to pay a failure-to-pay penalty. This is 0.5% (½ of 1 percent) of the unpaid tax for each month after the due date that the taxes are not paid. This penalty will not exceed 25% of the unpaid tax.

If a taxpayer files a request for an extension of time to file and pays *at least* 90% of the actual tax liability by the original due date, he will not be faced with a failure-to-pay penalty if the remaining balance is paid by the *extended* due date.

If both of these penalties apply in any month, the 5% failure-to-file penalty is reduced by the failure-to-pay penalty.

A taxpayer will not be assessed either penalty if he can show that he failed to file or pay on time because of reasonable cause and not because of willful neglect.[19]

---

[18] We are only talking about penalties for individual taxpayers at this point. The penalties for entities are different and will be covered in Part 2.

[19] There are exceptions to the general deadlines for filing a return and paying tax. One exception is for armed forces personnel serving in a combat zone. The second is for citizens or resident aliens working abroad.

Penalty	Dollar Amount
Failure to file	• 5% of unpaid balance per month, up to a m 25%. • More than 60 days late, the smaller of $135 or of the tax due on the return. • No penalty if the taxpayer is due a refund. • The failure-to-file penalty is reduced by the failure-to-pay penalty if both apply to the same tax return.
Failure to pay	• 0.5% of unpaid balance per month, up to a maximum of 25%. • 0.25% of the unpaid balance while an installment agreement is in place.
Interest on the amount due	• Interest is charged on any unpaid tax from the due date of the return until the date of payment. The interest rate is determined quarterly and is the federal short-term rate[20] plus 3%, compounded daily.

Estimated Tax Payments

The federal income tax is a "pay-as-you-go" tax. A taxpayer must pay taxes as he earns or receives income throughout the year. If a taxpayer earns income that is not subject to withholding (such as self-employment income, rents, alimony, etc.), he will often be required to make estimated tax payments each quarter of the tax year. Estimated tax is used to pay not only income tax, but self-employment tax and Alternative Minimum Tax as well.

Taxes are generally not withheld from payments that are made to independent contractors (1099 income). Taxes are withheld from wages, salaries, and pensions. Taxpayers can avoid making estimated tax payments by ensuring they have enough tax withheld from their income. A taxpayer must make estimated tax payments if:

- He expects to owe at least $1,000 in tax (after subtracting withholding and tax credits)
- He expects the total amount of withholding and tax credits to be less than the smaller of:
  - 100% of the tax shown on the taxpayer's prior year return
  - 90% of the tax shown on the taxpayer's current year return

A U.S. citizen or U.S. resident is not required to make estimated tax payments if he had zero tax liability in the prior year.[21]

---

[20] You will not have to memorize the interest rate. If you need to calculate interest on a problem for the EA exam, you'll be given the rate.
[21] This rule only applies to U.S. citizens or residents; it does not apply to non-resident aliens.

> **Example**: Cassius, who is single and 25 years old, was unemployed for most of 2010. He earned $2,700 in wages before he was laid off, and he received $1,500 in unemployment compensation afterward. He had no other income. Even though he had gross income of $4,200, he did not have to pay income tax because his gross income was less than the filing requirement. In 2011, Cassius began working as a carpenter. He made no estimated tax payments in 2011. Even though he owed $3,000 in tax at the end of the year, Cassius does not owe the underpayment penalty for 2011 because he had zero tax liability in the prior year.

Generally, a taxpayer will not have an underpayment penalty if either:
- Total estimated tax is less than $1,000, or
- The taxpayer had zero tax liability for the prior year.

Safe Harbor Rule for Estimated Payments

The majority of taxpayers who pay estimated tax rely on the "Safe Harbor Rule" in order to avoid any potential penalties.

There will be no underpayment penalty if the taxpayer pays at least 90% of whatever the current year's tax bill turns out to be. Since it is often difficult to guess what a person or business will earn during the year, most taxpayers find it easier to use the Safe Harbor Rule.

The first "safe harbor" applies to taxpayers whose adjusted gross income is $150,000 or less.[22] The taxpayer will not be assessed penalties in 2012 if the taxpayer pays *at least* the amount of the tax liability on his 2011 tax return (the amount on line 60 of Form 1040 reduced by any tax credits).

> **Example:** Gerald earned $95,000 in 2011. His overall tax liability for the tax year was $8,200, after taking into account his deductions and credits. Although Gerald expects his income to increase in 2012, he will not be assessed a penalty for underpayment of estimated taxes so long as he pays at least $8,200 in estimated tax during the year.

> ***Note:*** For high income taxpayers with adjusted gross income of over $150,000 ($75,000 if MFS), the safe harbor amount is 110% of the previous year's tax liability.

Less Than $1,000 Due

A taxpayer will not face an underpayment penalty if the total tax shown on his return (minus the amount paid through withholding) is less than $1,000. This "safe harbor" only applies to individual taxpayers (not to entities).

---

[22] No underpayment penalty will apply if the balance on the 2011 tax return is $1,000 or less.

Example: Dominique has a full-time job as a secretary. She also earns money part-time as a self-employed manicurist. In 2011, she did not make estimated payments. However, Dominique made sure to increase her withholding at her job in order to cover any amounts that she would have to pay on her self-employment earnings. When she files her tax return, she discovers that she owes $750. She will not owe an underpayment penalty, because the total tax shown on her return was less than $1,000.

Estimated Payment Due Dates (Quarterly Payments)

For estimated tax purposes, the year is divided into four payment periods. Each period has a specific payment due date. Taxpayers generally must have made their first estimated tax payment for the year by April 15.

If the due date falls on a Saturday, Sunday, or legal holiday, the due date is the next business day. If a payment is mailed, the date of the U.S. postmark is considered the date of payment.

> First Payment Due: April 15
> Second Payment Due: June 15
> Third Payment Due: September 15
> Fourth Payment Due: January 15 (of the following year)

Special Exception for Farmers and Fishermen

Estimated tax requirements are different for farmers and fishermen. Farmers and fishermen are not required to pay estimated taxes throughout the year. Unlike other taxpayers, farmers and fishermen may choose to pay all their estimated tax in one installment.

Qualified farmers and fishermen only have one due date for estimated taxes (if they choose). They have two choices:

- They may pay all of their 2011 estimated taxes by January 15, 2012, OR
- If they are able to file their 2011 tax return by March 1, 2012 and pay all the tax they owe, they do not need to make an estimated tax payment. They may file and pay their tax along with the return.

Example #1: Jay is the self-employed owner of a commercial fishing vessel. One hundred percent of his income is from commercial fishing. Therefore, Jay is not required to pay quarterly estimated taxes. Jay's records are incomplete, so he asks his tax accountant to file an extension on his behalf. Since Jay is unable to file his tax return by March 1, 2012, his Enrolled Agent notifies Jay that he is required to pay his estimated taxes in a lump sum by January 15, 2012.

Example #2: Karla owns a farm, and 100 percent of her income is from farming. She is not required to pay quarterly estimated taxes. Karla filed her tax return on February 20, 2012 and enclosed a check for her entire balance due, which was $4,900. Since Karla filed before the March 1 deadline, she will not be subject to any penalty.

In order to qualify for this special treatment, the farmer (or fisherman) must have at least two-thirds of his total gross income from farming or fishing. For the purpose of this rule, qualified "farming" income includes:

- Gross farming income from **Schedule F**, *Profit or Loss From Farming*
- Gross farming rental income from **Form 4835**, *Farm Rental Income and Expenses*
- Gains from the sale of livestock used for draft, breeding, sport, or dairy purposes reported on **Form 4797**
- Crop shares for the use of a farmer's land

Qualifying gross income from farming does NOT include:

- Gains from sales of farmland and/or depreciable farm equipment
- Income received from contract harvesting and hauling with workers and machines furnished by the taxpayer

*****Note:** Income from wages received as a farm employee are not considered farm income for the purposes of this special estimated tax treatment.

Example: Fernando owns a dairy farm and files a **Schedule F**. In 2011, his farm income from **Schedule F** was $95,000. He also had $3,500 in interest income and $41,500 in rental income from an unrelated business. Fernando's total gross income for the year was $140,000 ($3,500 + $41,500 + $95,000). Fernando qualifies to use the special estimated tax rules for qualified farmers, since 67.9% (at least two-thirds) of his gross income is from farming ($95,000 ÷ $140,000 = .679).

Backup Withholding

Sometimes, individuals will be subject to "backup withholding." This is when an entity is required to "withhold" certain amounts from a payment and remit the amounts to the IRS. Most U.S. taxpayers are exempt from backup withholding. However, the IRS requires backup withholding if a taxpayer's name and Social Security Number on **Form W-9,** *Request for Taxpayer Identification Number and Certification*, does not match its records.

Example: Heath owns a number of investments through the Big Corp Investment Company. In 2011, the IRS notifies Big Corp that Heath's Social Security Number is incorrect. Big Corp notifies Heath by mail that they need his correct Social Security Number, or they will have to start automatic backup withholding on his investment income. Heath ignores the notice and never updates his SSN. Big Corp is forced to begin backup withholding on Heath's investment income.

The IRS will sometimes require mandatory backup withholding if a taxpayer has a delinquent tax debt, or if a taxpayer fails to report all his interest, dividends, and other income.

Payments that may be subject to backup withholding include interest, dividends, rents, and royalties, payments to independent contractors for services, and broker payments. The current backup withholding rate is 28%. Under the backup withholding rules, the business or bank must withhold on a payment if:

- The individual did not provide the payer with a valid Taxpayer Identification Number or Social Security Number.
- The IRS notified the payer that the Taxpayer Identification Number (or SSN) is incorrect.
- The IRS has notified the payer to start withholding on interest and dividends because the payee failed to report income in prior years.
- The payee failed to certify that it was not subject to backup withholding for underreporting of interest and dividends.

If a taxpayer wishes to change his withholding amounts, **Form W4**, *Employee's Withholding Allowance Certificate,* is used to change withholding from wages. The employee must submit this form to his employer, NOT to the IRS.

Oddball Situations: Exceptions to the Normal Deadlines

There are special rules that are favorable for taxpayers who live outside the United States. A taxpayer will be granted an automatic two-month extension to file **and pay any tax due** if the taxpayer is a U.S. citizen or legal U.S. resident, AND

- The taxpayer is living outside the United States and his main place of business is outside the United States; OR
- The taxpayer is on active military service duty outside the U.S.

Taxpayers Serving in a Combat Zone

Additionally, the deadline for filing a tax return, claim for refund, AND deadline for tax owed will be automatically extended for any service member, Red Cross personnel, accredited correspondents, or contracted civilians serving in a combat zone. In fact, taxpayers serving in a combat zone have all of their tax deadlines suspended until they leave the combat zone.

Example: Philip is a member of the U.S. Armed Forces who has been serving in a combat zone since March 1. Philip is entitled to an extension of time for filing and paying his federal income taxes. In addition, IRS deadlines for filing, collections, etc., are suspended while Philip is serving in the combat zone, **plus** another 180 days after his last day in the combat zone. During this period, assessment and collection deadlines are extended, and Philip will not be charged interest or penalties attributable to the extension period.

The deadline extension provisions apply not only to members serving in the U.S. Armed Forces in combat zones, but to their spouses as well.

Statute of Limitations

Generally, the taxpayer must file a claim for a credit or refund within three years from the date the original return was filed or two years from the date the taxpayer paid the tax, whichever is later.[23]

There is no penalty for failure to file if the taxpayer is due a refund. However, the taxpayer may have many legal deductions that the IRS doesn't know about. In order to claim a refund and avoid possible collection action, a tax return must be filed. If the taxpayer does not file a claim for a refund within this three-year period, he usually won't be entitled to the refund.

> **Example:** Juan hasn't filed in a long time, and now he wants to file six years of delinquent tax returns: 2006 through 2011. Juan files the returns and realizes that he had refunds for each year. If Juan files all the back tax returns by April 17, 2012, Juan will receive the refunds for his 2008, 2009, 2010, and 2011 tax returns. His refunds for 2006 and 2007, however, have expired.

The same statute of limitations applies on refunds being claimed on amended returns. In general, if a refund is expected on an amended return, taxpayers must file the return within three years from the due date of the original return, or within two years after the date they paid the tax, whichever is later.

> **Example:** David made estimated tax payments of $1,000 and filed an extension to file his 2008 income tax return. When David filed his return on August 15, 2009, he paid an additional $200 tax due. He later finds an error on the return and files an amendment. Three years later, on August 15, 2012, David files an amended return and claims a refund of $700.

> **Example:** Aisha's 2008 tax return was due April 15, 2009. She filed it on March 20, 2009. In 2011, Aisha discovered that she missed a big deduction on her 2008 return. Now she wants to amend her 2008 return, expecting the correction to result in a large refund. If she gets it postmarked on or before April 17, 2012, it will be within the three-year limit and the return will be accepted. But if the amended 2008 return is received by the IRS after that date, it will fall outside the three-year period and Aisha will not receive the refund.

Special Cases (Extended Statute for Claiming Refunds)

In some cases, a request for a tax refund will be honored past the normal three-year deadline. These special cases are:
- A bad debt from a worthless security (up to **seven years** prior)

---

[23] Section 6511 (3-year refund statute)

- A payment or accrual of foreign tax
- A net operating loss carryback
- A carryback of certain tax credits
- An injured spouse claim (up to seven years prior)
- Exceptions for military personnel

Time periods for claiming a refund are also extended when a taxpayer is "financially disabled." This usually requires that the taxpayer be mentally or physically disabled to the point that he is unable to manage his financial affairs. If the taxpayer qualifies, he may file a refund after the three-year period of limitations.

Statute of Limitations for IRS Assessment

The IRS is required to assess tax or audit a taxpayer's return within three years after the return is filed.[24] If a taxpayer files his tax return late, then the IRS has the later of three years from:

- The due date of the return, or
- The date the return was actually filed.

If a taxpayer never files a return, the statute remains open. If a taxpayer files his return prior to the return deadline, the time is measured from the April 15 deadline.

Generally, the IRS will select returns filed within the last three years for examination. Additional years can be added if a "substantial understatement" is identified. A "substantial understatement" is defined as 25% (or more) of the income shown on the return. If a taxpayer omitted 25% of his income or more, the IRS has up to six years to assess a deficiency.

There is an exception for outright fraud; if the taxpayer files a fraudulent tax return, the statute for IRS audit never expires. However, the burden of proof switches to the IRS in cases where the statute has expired.

Example: Caroline filed her 2008 tax return on February 27, 2009. The three-year statute period for an audit began April 15, 2009 (the filing deadline) and will stop on April 15, 2012. After that date, the IRS must be able to prove fraud or a substantial understatement of income (25% or more) in order to audit the tax return.

Statute of Limitations for IRS Collections

The statute of limitations for IRS collection is ten years.[25] However, the clock only starts ticking when the tax return is filed. The statute of limitations on a tax assessment begins on the day *after* the taxpayer files his tax return. So, if a taxpayer never files a return, the IRS can attempt to collect indefinitely. In other words, there is no statute of limitations for assessing and collecting tax if no return has been filed.

---

[24] Internal Revenue Code, Section 6501 (3-year audit statute)
[25] Section 6502 (10-year debt collection statute)

The ten-year period begins on the day after the date of assessment; that is, the date of assessment is excluded from the computation of the ten-year period.

Statute of Limitations: Snapshot	
Claims for a refund	Three years from the time the original return was filed, or two years from the time the tax was paid, whichever is later.
IRS assessment	Three years after the return is considered filed. Exceptions apply in cases of fraud, failure to file, and substantial understatement.
Substantial understatement	If a substantial understatement is discovered (25% or more income is omitted on the return), the statute for IRS assessment is six years.
Fraud	No limit.
Unfiled returns	No limit.
Collections	The statute of limitations for IRS collections is 10 years from the date of assessment.

Unit 5: Questions

1. Theo forgot to file his tax return, and his return was mailed over 60 days late. He did not file an extension. Theo owed $120 with his return. What is his minimum penalty for late filing?

A. $0.
B. $120.
C. $135.
D. $220.

The answer is B. If a return is filed over 60 days late, the minimum penalty for late filing is the smaller of $135 or 100% of the tax owed. Since he owed $120 with the return, his penalty is 100% of the amount due. ###

2. Which statement about estimated tax payments is NOT correct?

A. An individual whose only income is from self-employment will have to pay estimated payments.
B. If insufficient tax is paid through withholding, estimated payments may still be necessary.
C. Estimated tax payments are required when the withholding taxes are greater than the overall tax liability.
D. Estimated tax is used to pay not only income tax, but self-employment tax and Alternative Minimum Tax as well.

The answer is C. If a taxpayer's withholding exceeds his tax liability, no estimated payments would be required. The taxpayer would get a refund of the overpaid tax when he files his tax return. ###

3. Which of the following is NOT an acceptable reason for extending the statute of limitations for a refund past the normal deadline?

A. A bad debt from a worthless security.
B. Living outside the country for three years.
C. Exceptions for military personnel.
D. An injured spouse claim.

The answer is B. Living outside the country is not a valid excuse for extending the statute of limitations for claiming a refund. In some cases, a request for a tax refund will be honored past the normal three-year deadline. Exceptions exist for military personnel, injured spouse claims, and bad debts from worthless securities. ###

4. Dottie is a U.S. resident who paid estimated tax in 2011 totaling $2,500. In 2012, Dottie quit her business as a self-employed contractor and is now unemployed. She expects to have zero tax liability in 2012. Which of the following statements is true?

A. Dottie is still required to make estimated tax payments in 2012.
B. Dottie is not required to make estimated tax payments in 2012.
C. Dottie must pay a minimum of $2,500 in estimated tax in 2012, or she will be subject to a failure-to-pay penalty.
D. Dottie must make a minimum of $2,250 (90% X $2,500) in estimated tax payments in 2012, or she will be subject to an underpayment penalty.

The answer is B. A taxpayer is not required to pay estimated tax if she expects to have zero tax liability. ###

5. Charles had a $4,500 tax liability in 2011. In 2012, Charles expects to owe approximately $3,200 in federal taxes. In 2012 he has $1,200 in income tax withheld from his paycheck. Which of the following statements is true?

A. Charles does not need to pay estimated taxes in 2012.
B. Charles is required to make estimated tax payments in 2012.
C. Charles is required to adjust his withholding. He cannot make estimated tax payments because he is an employee.
D. None of the above.

The answer is B. Charles is required to make estimated tax payments because his expected tax liability for 2012 exceeds $1,000. His withholding is insufficient to cover his tax liability. Charles could elect to adjust his withholding with his employer so the taxes are taken out of his pay automatically. If Charles does not adjust his withholding, he will be required to make estimated tax payments. If he does not make estimated tax payments, then he will be subject to a penalty. ###

6. Audrey is self-employed and expects to owe $2,500 in taxes for 2012. Her tax liability for her prior tax year was zero, because her business had a loss. Which of the following is true?

A. Audrey is required to pay estimated tax in 2012.
B. Audrey is NOT required to pay estimated tax for 2012.
C. Audrey must pay at least $1,500 in estimated tax for 2012.
D. None of the above.

The answer is B. Since Audrey had no tax due on her prior year return, she is not required to pay estimated tax. The taxpayer must pay estimated tax only if both of the following apply:
1. The taxpayer expects to owe at least $1,000 in tax after subtracting withholding and credits.
2. The taxpayer expects withholding and credits to be less than the smaller of (1) 90% of the tax to be shown on the current year tax return, or (2) 100% of the tax shown on the prior year tax return. ###

7. Which of the following statements is TRUE regarding the filing of **Form 4868**, *Application for an Automatic Extension of Time to File U.S. Individual Income Tax Return?*

A. Interest is not assessed on any income tax due if Form 4868 is filed.
B. Form 4868 provides the taxpayer with an automatic six-month extension to file and pay.
C. Even though a taxpayer files Form 4868, he will owe interest and may be charged a late payment penalty on the amount owed if the tax is not paid by the due date.
D. A U.S. citizen, who is out of the country on vacation on the due date, will be allowed an additional twelve months to file as long as "Out of the Country" is written across the top of Form 1040.

The answer is C. Even though a taxpayer files **Form 4868**, he will owe interest and a late payment penalty on the amount owed if he does not pay the tax due by the regular due date.
###

8. What is the statute of limitations for IRS assessment on a tax return where over 25% of the taxpayer's income was omitted?

A. There is no statute of limitations on a return where income was omitted.
B. Three years from the date the return was filed.
C. Six years from the date the return was filed.
D. Ten years from the date the return was filed.

The answer is C. If a taxpayer omitted 25% of his income or more, the IRS has up to six years to assess a deficiency.
###

9. **Form 4868,** *Application for Automatic Extension of Time to File U.S. Individual Income Tax Return*, will provide an individual taxpayer with the following:

A. An automatic extension of five months to file.
B. An automatic extension of six months to pay taxes due.
C. An automatic extension of eight months to file the return, but not to pay taxes due.
D. An automatic extension of six months to file the return.

The answer is D. IRS **Form 4868** will give a taxpayer an additional six months to file his tax return. It does not give the taxpayer an additional six months to pay his taxes due. Even though a taxpayer may file **Form 4868,** he will owe interest and may be charged a late payment penalty on the amount owed if he does not pay the tax due by the regular due date. ###

10. Todd is a self-employed architect and must make estimated tax payments. What is the due date for his third estimated tax payment for tax year 2011?

A. September 15, 2011.
B. January 15, 2012.
C. September 1, 2012.
D. July 15, 2011.

The answer is A. The third-quarter payment for estimated tax is due September 15, 2011. For estimated tax payments, a year is divided into four quarterly payment periods. Each period has a due date. The payments are due as follows:

Periods	Due Date
Jan. 1–March 31	April 15
April 1–May 31	June 15
June 1–Aug. 31	September 15
Sept. 1–Dec. 31	January 15 (following year)

###

11. Logan had the following gross income amounts in 2011:

- Taxable interest: $3,000
- Dividends: $42,000
- Farm income (Schedule F): $80,000

Is Logan allowed to use the special estimated tax rules for farmers and fishermen?

A. Yes, Logan is a qualified farmer.
B. No, Logan is not a qualified farmer, and he must make quarterly estimated tax payments.
C. Unable to determine based on the information given.
D. Logan is a farm employee.

The answer is B. Based on his income, Logan does not qualify to use the special estimated tax rules for qualified farmers. At least **two-thirds** of his gross income (66.6%) must be from farming in order to qualify. Logan's gross farm income is 64% of his total gross income ($80,000 ÷ $125,000 = 0.64). Therefore, Logan is not a qualified farmer. ###

Unit 6: Taxable and Non-taxable Income

More Reading:
Publication 525, *Taxable and Non-taxable Income*
Publication 504, *Divorced or Separated Individuals*
Publication 4681, *Canceled Debts, Foreclosures, Repossessions, and Abandonments*
Publication 514, *Foreign Tax Credit for Individuals*
Publication 544, *Sales and Other Dispositions of Assets*
Publication 550, *Investment Income and Expenses*
Publication 529, *Miscellaneous Deductions*

Gross income includes all money, goods, property, and services that are not exempt from tax. In addition to wages, salaries, commissions, fees, and tips, this includes other forms of compensation such as fringe benefits and stock options.

Basically, all income is taxable unless otherwise exempt. The IRS's position is that all income is taxable unless it is specifically excluded.

A "deduction" is an expense that is deductible from a taxpayer's gross income. An "exclusion" is a type of income that is not taxable. It is important to understand the difference between an "exclusion" and a "deduction," because many deductions are phased out as the taxpayer's gross income increases. However, excluded income retains its character as excluded income, no matter what the taxpayer's gross income is.

Most of the time, excluded income does not have to be reported. There are some instances where excluded income must be reported on a tax return, but it is still not taxable to the recipient. An example of this is non-taxable combat pay. Combat pay must be reported on a taxpayer's return, but it is not subject to income tax.

Example: Brock is a popular recording artist and makes over $600,000 in wages per year. Because of his high income, Brock is phased out for many deductions. However, in 2011 Brock is involved in an auto accident where he sustains major injuries. Brock sues the other driver and receives a settlement of $80,000 from the insurance company. The insurance settlement is excluded income, because compensation for physical injuries is not taxable to the recipient.

Sources of All Income

When taxpayers prepare a federal income tax return such as IRS Form 1040, they must calculate three levels of income:

1. **Gross Income:** To calculate a taxpayer's liability, the IRS requires that he first calculate "total income" or "gross income." This is the sum of all sources of taxable income that the taxpayer receives during the year.
2. **Adjusted Gross Income (AGI):** AGI is total income minus certain allowable deductions. These deductions include, but are not limited to, IRA contributions, qualified

student loan interest, some expenses if self-employed, alimony payments, and moving expenses.
3. **Taxable Income:** This is the amount of income on which a taxpayer owes income taxes (calculated by subtracting any deductions and exemptions from adjusted gross income).

How to Calculate Gross Individual Income (Tax Formula)

Start with GROSS INCOME
MINUS- Adjustments to Income ("Above the Line" Deductions)
= ADJUSTED GROSS INCOME
MINUS- Greater of Itemized Deductions (or Standard Deduction)
MINUS- Personal Exemptions
= TAXABLE INCOME
X Tax Rate
= GROSS TAX Liability
MINUS- Credits
= NET TAX Liability or Refund Receivable

The Internal Revenue Code (IRC) describes types of income that are taxable and non-taxable. In this unit, we will cover the most common types of taxable and non-taxable income.

Earned Income vs. Unearned Income

Earned income is received for services performed, such as wages, salaries, tips, or professional fees. *Unearned* income is also called "passive income," or investment income. Earned income (such as wages) is treated differently from passive income (such as dividends).

Earned income is generally subject to Social Security tax and Medicare tax (also called the FICA tax). Investment income and other passive income is generally NOT subject to FICA tax.

Some income is considered variable, which means it is considered earned income for some taxpayers and unearned income for others.

The Doctrine of Constructive Receipt

The doctrine of "constructive receipt" is very important. This concept is often tested on the Enrolled Agent exam. It means that the IRS believes that taxpayers should be taxed on their income when it becomes available, regardless of whether it is actually in their physical possession.

For example, a check that a taxpayer receives before the end of the tax year is considered income constructively received in that year, even if the taxpayer does not deposit the check into his bank account until the next year. Taxpayers must include in income any amounts that are constructively received during the tax year.

Example: Gerardo is on vacation in Las Vegas. The postal service tries to deliver a check to Gerardo on December 30, but he is not at home to receive it, so it's left in his mailbox. Even though he did not have the check in his physical possession, it is still considered to have been constructively received by the taxpayer. Gerardo must still include the amount in gross income for that tax year.

If a taxpayer refuses income, such as a prize or an award, then the income is not considered to have been "constructively received."

Also, if there are significant restrictions on the income, or if the income is not accessible to the taxpayer, then it is not considered to have been "constructively received."

Example: Opal won a big prize for concert tickets from a local radio station. The front-row concert tickets were valued at $1,200. This was a taxable award for Opal, and she is required to pay taxes on the fair market value (FMV) of the tickets. However, on the day of the concert, the radio station does not receive the tickets in time from the promoter. Opal is not able to attend the concert. Since Opal never actually received the proceeds, the prize is not taxable to her. She never had "constructive receipt" of her prize.

"Claim of Right" Doctrine

Under the claim of right doctrine, income received without restriction—income the taxpayer has complete control over—must be reported in the year received, even if there's a possibility it may have to be repaid in a later year.

If there is a dispute and income is later repaid, the repayment is deductible in the year paid. As a result, taxpayers are not required to amend their federal gross income for an earlier year based on a subsequent repayment of amounts held under a claim of right by filing an amended return.

Example: In 2011, a gallery owner named Courtney receives $25,000 from the sale of a painting. She properly includes $25,000 in her gross income and pays taxes on the income for the 2011 tax year. On March 1, 2012, the customer discovers that the painting is a forgery and returns it for a full refund of $25,000. Since Courtney pays back the $25,000 in tax year 2012, she is entitled to deduct the amount from her gross income. No further claim of right deduction is allowed.

However, this does not include income that has substantial restrictions applied to it. The issue usually lies with control over the income. Income received by an agent for a taxpayer is income constructively received in the year the agent received it. If a taxpayer agrees by contract that a third party is to receive income for him, he must include the amount in his own income when the third party receives it.

Example: Holden's wages are being garnished for back child support. Holden's employer garnishes part of Holden's salary. Since the amount would have normally been included in Holden's paycheck, he must still recognize the income as if he had received it himself. Holden must include that amount in his gross income, even though he never actually received it.

Prizes and Awards

Prizes and awards are usually taxable. If the prize or award is in a form other than cash, the FMV of the property is treated as the taxable amount. The winner may avoid taxation of the award by rejecting the prize. The taxpayer may also choose to transfer the prize to a charity or other non-profit.

Example: Jerry is a college instructor. He is chosen as *teacher of the year* by a national education association. He is awarded $3,000, but Jerry does not accept the prize. Instead, Jerry directs the association to transfer his winnings to a college scholarship fund. Jerry never receives a check or has control over the funds. Therefore, the award is not taxable to Jerry.

Some prizes and awards are excludable from income. An award recipient may exclude the FMV of the prize from gross income if:

- The amount received is in recognition of religious, scientific, charitable, or similar meritorious achievement (**Example**: a non-profit charity awards a Christmas gift to a needy individual);
- The recipient is selected without action on his part;
- The receipt of the award is not conditioned on substantial future services; and
- The amount is paid by the organization making the award to a tax-exempt organization (including a governmental unit) designated by the recipient.

Employee Awards (Exclusion from Income)

There is also an exclusion for awards given to employees. Certain employee awards may qualify for exclusion from the employee's gross income as a *non-taxable fringe benefit*. A prize may also qualify for exclusion from income if it is a scholarship.

Amounts paid for employee awards are still deductible to the employer and not taxable to the employee if certain rules are followed.[26] A cash award is always taxable to the employee. An achievement award in the form of property, if given to

---

[26] Employee awards and fringe benefits are covered in more detail in Part 2. For Part 1 of the EA exam, you must understand the tax implications of how an employee award would be reported by an individual who receives the award (the employee). For Part 2 of the exam, you would need to understand the tax implications of employee awards from the perspective of the *employer* or business.

the employee for length of service or as a safety achievement, is not taxable to the employee and is still deductible by the employer.

Employers can exclude from wages the value of achievement awards given to an employee from the employee's wages if the cost is not more than the amount the employer can deduct as a business expense for the year. The excludable annual amount is $1,600 for qualified plan awards (per employee).

The limit is $400 for awards that are not "qualified plan awards." A "qualified plan award" is an award that does not favor highly compensated employees (HCE). Basically, a non-qualified award is an award that is given to highly compensated executives, but not to rank-and-file employees.

> **Example:** Space Corporation awards a set of golf clubs to an employee as a non-qualified plan employee achievement award. The fair market value of the golf clubs is $750. The amount included in taxable wages to the employee is $350 ($750 – $400). If the award had been a *qualified plan award*, the employee would not have been taxed on the FMV of the award.

> **Example:** Rowan received three employee achievement awards during the year: a watch valued at $250, a stereo valued at $1,000, and a set of golf clubs valued at $500. She received each of the awards for length of service and exceptional safety achievement. They are all qualified plan awards and would normally be excluded from her income, assuming that the other requirements for qualified plan awards are satisfied. However, because the $1,750 total value of the awards is more than $1,600, Rowan must include $150 ($1,750 – $1,600) in her income.

The employer must make the award as part of a meaningful presentation, and it should not simply be disguised pay.

Income from Canceled Debt

Generally, if a taxpayer's debt is canceled or forgiven, the taxpayer must include the canceled debt in his gross income. Cancellation of debt can involve auto loans, credit card debt, medical care, professional services, installment purchases of furniture or other personal property, mortgages, and home equity loans.

A debt includes any indebtedness for which a taxpayer is liable or which attaches to the taxpayer's property. Generally, if a debt for which a taxpayer is personally liable is canceled or forgiven, (other than as a gift), the taxpayer must include the canceled amount in income.

Taxpayers often question the taxability of canceled debt because they did not receive any actual money. In situations where property is surrendered or repossessed (such as a foreclosure), taxpayers may feel that by giving up the property, they should be relieved from any further obligation.

However, cancelled debt is taxable because the benefit to the taxpayer is the relief from personal liability to pay the debt.

Canceled debt should be reported on **Schedule C** if the debt was incurred in a business. If the debt is a *non-business* debt, the canceled debt amount should be reported as "other income" on line 21 of a taxpayer's **Form 1040.**

If property securing the debt was foreclosed on or abandoned, the taxpayer may need to report the disposition (sale) on **Form 8949**, *Sales and Other Dispositions of Capital Assets*, and **Schedule D**, *Capital Gains and Losses*.

When an entity cancels a debt of $600 or more, the taxpayer generally receives a **Form 1099-C**, *Cancellation of Debt*.

Example: Phoebe borrows $10,000 to take a vacation and defaults on the loan after paying back only $2,000. She spends all the money and is unwilling to make payments on the loan. The lender is unable to collect the remaining amount of the loan. Phoebe is not insolvent. Therefore, there is a cancellation of debt of $8,000, which is taxable income to Phoebe. She must include it on her tax return as "other income."

There are some exceptions to this rule, most notably the exception for the debt forgiveness from the foreclosure or sale of a primary residence (covered in detail next). There is also an exception for taxpayers who are insolvent. If a debt is forgiven as a gift, then the canceled debt does not have to be included in income.

If a financial institution offers a discount for the early payment of a mortgage loan, the amount of the discount is taxable as cancelled debt. This occurs when a lender discounts or reduces the principal balance of a loan to reward an early payoff.

Recourse and Nonrecourse Debt in General

Knowing whether a loan is recourse or nonrecourse will often determine the taxability of the cancelled debt.

Recourse debt holds the borrower personally liable for any amount not satisfied by the surrender of secured property. If a lender forecloses on property subject to a recourse debt and cancels the portion of the debt in excess of the fair market value (FMV) of the property, the canceled portion of the debt is treated as ordinary income. This amount must be included in gross income unless it qualifies for an exception or exclusion.

With a recourse loan, the cancelled portion of debt is generally treated as ordinary income and included in gross income (unless it qualifies as an exception or exclusion). When a residence that is security for a mortgage is abandoned or foreclosed upon, it is treated as having been sold. This results in the foreclosure being reported on **Form 8949** and **Schedule D** as sale of home.

If the loan is a recourse loan, then the canceled debt is taxable unless an exception applies. If a loan is "recourse," then the taxpayer must generally report two transactions:

1. The cancellation of debt income
2. Gain or loss on the sale or repossession

In addition to this cancellation of indebtedness income, the taxpayer may realize a gain or loss on the disposition of the property; this amount is generally the difference between the FMV of the property at the time of the foreclosure and the taxpayer's adjusted basis in the property.

Generally, if the taxpayer abandons property that secures debt for which the taxpayer is personally liable, (such as a home that he abandons) the taxpayer will not have a recognized gain or loss until the later foreclosure is completed.

A *non-recourse debt* is a type of loan that is secured by collateral, and where the borrower does not have liability for the loan. Many mortgages are non-recourse. This means that if the borrower defaults, the lender can seize the home, but cannot seek out the borrower for any further compensation, even if the FMV of the home does not cover the full value of the loan amount.

If the taxpayer abandons property that secures debt for which the taxpayer is NOT personally liable, (a nonrecourse loan) the abandonment is treated as a sale or exchange. If a loan is non-recourse and the borrower does not retain the asset, then the borrower does not have to recognize cancellation of debt income.

Example: Cain lost his yacht to because he could no longer make his payments. At the time of repossession, he owed a balance of $170,000 to the lender and the FMV of the yacht was $140,000. Cain is personally liable for the debt (it is a recourse loan), so the abandonment is treated as a sale. The "selling price" from the repossession is $140,000.

Example: Doreen bought a new car for $15,000. She made a $2,000 down payment and borrowed the remaining $13,000 from her bank. Doreen is personally liable for the car loan (recourse debt). The bank repossessed her car because she stopped making payments. The balance due on the loan at the time of the repossession was $10,000. The fair market value of the car when repossessed was only $9,000. Since a repossession is treated as a sale, the gain or loss must be computed. The amount she realizes is $9,000. This is the amount of the canceled debt ($10,000) up to the car's FMV ($9,000). Doreen figures her gain on the repossession by comparing the amount realized ($9,000) with her adjusted basis ($15,000). Doreen has a $6,000 non-deductible loss. She also has ordinary income from cancellation of debt. That income is $1,000 ($10,000 canceled debt − $9,000 FMV). Doreen must report the canceled debt as income on line 21 of her **Form 1040**.

*Note: If a personal vehicle is repossessed, then the repossession is treated as a sale, and the gain or loss must be computed.

Qualified Principal Residence Indebtedness (QPRI)

This is the exception created by the *Mortgage Debt Relief Act of 2007* and applies to most homeowners. The provisions in the act were extended by Congress through 2012.

The IRS generally allows taxpayers to exclude income from the discharge of debt on their principal residence. A *qualified* "principal residence" does NOT include rentals or vacation homes.

Debt reduced through mortgage restructuring, as well as mortgage debt forgiven in foreclosure, may also qualify for exclusion.

When a bank forecloses on a home and then sells the home for *less than* the borrower's outstanding mortgage and forgives the unpaid mortgage debt, the canceled debt previously would have been taxable income to the homeowner. The basis of the principal residence must be reduced (but not below zero) by the amount excluded from gross income. Debt reduced through mortgage restructuring (as well as mortgage debt forgiven in connection with a foreclosure) qualifies for this relief.

The amount excluded reduces the taxpayer's basis in the home. To claim the exclusion, the taxpayer must file **Form 982,** *Reduction of Tax Attributes Due to Discharge of Indebtedness*, with his individual income tax return.

Up to $2 million of forgiven debt is eligible for this exclusion ($1 million if Married Filing Separately). The exclusion doesn't apply if the discharge is due to services performed for the lender or any other reason not directly related to a decline in the home's value or the taxpayer's financial condition. A taxpayer can exclude canceled debt if it is qualified principal residence indebtedness.

Qualified Principal Residence Indebtedness is debt incurred in:
- Acquiring,
- Constructing, or
- Substantially improving the taxpayer's principal residence.

The qualified debt also includes debt secured by the residence from refinancing, so long as the refinancing was incurred to acquire, construct, or substantially improve the home.

*Note: A loss on the sale or disposition of a personal residence is NOT deductible.

Example: Adam's home is subject to a $320,000 mortgage debt. Adam's creditor forecloses in April 2011. Due to declining real estate values, the residence is sold for $280,000 in December 2011. Adam has $40,000 of income from discharge of indebtedness. Before the new law, the $40,000 would have been includable in Adam's gross income. However, Adam may claim the exclusion by filing **Form 982** with his 2011 tax return.

"Ordering Rule" for Principal Residence Indebtedness

If only a *part* of a loan is qualified principal residence indebtedness, the exclusion from income for QPRI applies only to the extent the amount canceled exceeds the amount of the loan that is NOT qualified principal residence indebtedness. However, the remaining part of the loan may qualify for a different exclusion (such as the exclusion for insolvency).

> **Example:** Ken incurred debt of $800,000 when he purchased his home for $880,000. Ken made a down payment of $80,000 and financed the rest. When the FMV of the property was $1 million, Ken refinanced the debt for $850,000. At the time of the refinancing, the balance of the original loan was $740,000. Ken used the $110,000 he obtained from the refinancing ($850,000 minus $740,000) to buy a luxury car and take a vacation to the Bahamas. About two years after the refinancing, Ken lost his job. Ken's home declined in value to $750,000. Based on Ken's circumstances, the lender agreed to a short sale of the property for $735,000 and to cancel the remaining $115,000 of the $850,000 debt. Under the "ordering rule," Ken can exclude only $5,000 of the canceled debt from his income using the exclusion for canceled qualified principal residence indebtedness ($115,000 canceled debt minus the $110,000 amount of the debt that was not qualified principal residence indebtedness—basically the money he spent on personal purchases, such as a car). Ken must include the remaining $110,000 of canceled debt in income (unless another exception or exclusion applies).

If the taxpayer is personally liable for the debt (recourse debt), and the amount of outstanding debt (mortgage) exceeds the home's FMV, the difference is treated as cancellation of debt income.

- If the canceled debt qualifies as excludable from gross income, the exclusion is reported on **Form 982**
- Otherwise, the canceled debt is reportable as ordinary income on **Form 1040, line 21**

Canceled Debt that is Otherwise Deductible

If a taxpayer uses the cash method of accounting, he should NOT recognize canceled debt income if payment of the debt would have otherwise been a deductible expense.

> **Example:** Warren is a cash-basis, self-employed farmer who reports his income on **Schedule F.** Warren gets $2,200 in accounting services for his farm on credit. Later, Warren has trouble paying his farm debts and his accountant forgives the amount he owes. Warren does not include the canceled debt in his gross income because payment of the debt would have been deductible as a business expense anyway.

Non-taxable Canceled Debt

There are examples where canceled debt is not included in income (not taxable), but may still have to be reported on the taxpayer's return. Canceled debts that meet the requirements for any of the following exceptions or exclusions are not taxable:

Canceled Debt that Qualifies for **EXCEPTION** to Inclusion in Gross Income:
- Amounts specifically excluded from income by law (such as gifts, bequests, or inheritances)
- Cancellation of certain qualified student loans
- Canceled debt that if paid by a taxpayer is otherwise deductible
- A purchase price reduction given by a vendor (a discount on a purchase, like a rebate on a printer, for example)

Canceled Debt that Qualifies for **EXCLUSION** from Gross Income:
- Cancellation of Qualified Principal Residence Indebtedness
- Cancellation of debt when the loan is a non-recourse loan
- Debt canceled in a Title 11 bankruptcy case
- Debt canceled during insolvency
- Cancellation of qualified farm indebtedness
- Cancellation of qualified real property business indebtedness

Bankruptcy

Debts discharged through bankruptcy court in a Title 11 bankruptcy case are not considered taxable income. The taxpayer must attach **Form 982** to his federal income tax return to report debt that is canceled in bankruptcy.

Insolvency

If a taxpayer is insolvent when the debt is canceled, the canceled debt is not taxable. A taxpayer is "insolvent" when total debts are more than the fair market value of his total assets. For purposes of determining insolvency, assets include the value of everything the taxpayer owns (*including* the value of pensions and retirement accounts).

> **Example:** In 2011, Darla had $5,000 in credit card debt, which she did not pay. Darla received a **Form 1099-C** from her credit card company showing canceled debt of $5,000. Darla's total liabilities immediately before the cancellation were $15,000, and the FMV of her total assets immediately before the cancellation was $7,000. This means that at the time the debt was canceled, Darla was insolvent to the extent of $8,000 ($15,000 total liabilities minus $7,000 FMV of her total assets). Therefore, Darla can exclude the entire $5,000 canceled debt from income.

Qualifying Farm Debts

If a taxpayer incurred the canceled debt in farming, the canceled debt is generally not considered taxable income.

Non-recourse Loans

A non-recourse loan (covered earlier) is a loan for which the lender's only remedy in case of default is to repossess the property being financed or used as collateral. That is, the lender cannot pursue the taxpayer personally in case of default. Forgiveness of a non-recourse loan resulting from a foreclosure does not result in cancellation of debt income.

Certain Canceled Student Loans are Not Taxable

Some student loans contain a provision that the debt will be canceled if the student eventually works for a certain period of time in certain professions. The taxpayer does not have to recognize canceled debt income if the student loan is later canceled after he performs the agreed-upon services. To qualify, the loan must have been made by:
- The federal government,
- A state or local government, or government agency,
- A tax-exempt public benefit corporation that has assumed control of a state, county, or municipal hospital, and whose employees are considered public employees under state law, or
- An educational institution, as part of a program of the institution designed to encourage students to serve in occupations or areas with unmet needs and under which the services provided are for or under the direction of a governmental unit or a tax-exempt section 501(c)(3) organization.

Example: Tatum is a medical student completing her residency. She agrees to work as a doctor in a state program in Minnesota serving rural and poor communities. Tatum agreed to take a job as a pediatrician in the state's rural towns for four years in return for the forgiveness of her student loans. The canceled debt qualifies for non-recognition treatment, and the canceled debt does not have to be recognized as income.

All of these exceptions are discussed in detail in IRS **Publication 4681**, *Canceled Debts, Foreclosures, Repossessions, and Abandonments.*

Canceled Debt: Summary

*Canceled Debt that is Excludable from Gross Income

These amounts are not reported on the tax return:
- Gifts, inheritances, or bequests
- Cancellation of qualified student loans

- Canceled debt that if paid by a cash basis taxpayer is otherwise deductible
- A purchase price reduction given by a seller (such as a discount on a car purchase from a car dealer)

*Canceled Debt that Qualifies for Exclusion from Gross Income

These amounts must be reported on the tax return, but are excludable from gross income:

- Cancellation of qualified principal residence indebtedness
- Debt canceled in a Title 11 bankruptcy case
- Debt canceled due to insolvency
- Cancellation of qualified farm indebtedness
- Cancellation of qualified real property business indebtedness

The exclusion for *"qualified principal residence indebtedness"* allows taxpayers to exclude up to $2 million ($1 million if Married Filing Separately) of "qualified principal residence indebtedness."

On the Enrolled Agent exam, the principal residence exclusion is the exclusion most commonly tested on the subject of canceled debt.

Gambling Winnings

Gambling winnings are fully taxable and must be reported on the tax return. Gambling winnings are reported to the taxpayer on IRS **Form W-2G**. A taxpayer will receive a **Form W-2G** if he wins:

- $600 or more in winnings from gambling;
- $1,200 or more in winnings from bingo or slot machines;
- $1,500 or more in proceeds from keno; or
- Any gambling winnings subject to federal income tax withholding.

A taxpayer must report and pay tax on all gambling winnings, even if he does not receive **Form W-2G** for the winnings. Gambling income includes winnings from lotteries, raffles, horse races, and casinos. It includes cash winnings and also the fair market value of prizes such as cars and trips.

Gambling losses are deductible, but only on **Schedule A** as an itemized deduction. The amount of the deduction is limited to the amount of gambling winnings. So, for example, if a taxpayer wins $11,000 in 2011 but has $15,000 in gambling losses, the taxpayer can only deduct $11,000 (the amount of his gambling winnings) on **Schedule A**.

Taxpayers may only deduct gambling losses if they itemize.

Example: Yolanda had $1,000 in gambling winnings for the year. She had $3,000 in gambling losses. Her deduction for gambling losses cannot exceed $1,000, the amount of her gambling winnings. Yolanda must itemize and list her gambling losses on **Schedule A, Form 1040**. Yolanda's gambling winnings are reported to her on IRS **Form W-2G**.

An accurate diary or similar record of gambling winnings and losses must be kept along with tickets, receipts, canceled checks, and other documentation. These supporting records need not be sent in with the tax return, but should be retained in case of an audit.

Gambling winnings are reported as "other income" on line 21 of **Form 1040**.

Self-Employment Income and SE Tax

Self-employment income is earned by taxpayers who work for themselves. Generally, these are small business owners. Self-employed taxpayers must include this type of income on their tax returns.

Most self-employed people report their income (and loss) on **Schedule C, Form 1040**. However, self-employed farmers or fishermen report their earnings on **Schedule F, Form 1040**. Self-employment income also includes:

- Income of ministers, priests, and rabbis for the performance of services such as baptisms and marriages;
- The distributive share of partnership income allocated to general partners or managers of a Limited Liability Company (the income is reported to the partner on IRS **Form K-1**).

Any taxpayer who has self-employment income of $400 or more in a year must file a tax return and report the earnings to the IRS.

Self-employment tax (also called *SE Tax*) is a tax consisting of Social Security and Medicare taxes primarily for self-employed individuals. It is similar to the Social Security and Medicare taxes withheld from the pay of wage earners. Self-employment tax is calculated on IRS **Schedule SE**. If a taxpayer operates more than one business, he may combine the net incomes together and use only one **Schedule SE.**

Taxpayers are required to pay their income tax liabilities as they earn or receive income during the year, and this includes self-employed taxpayers. Self-employed individuals must generally make estimated tax payments.

Payroll tax and self-employment tax are very confusing concepts for most exam candidates, especially those who do not have payroll tax experience. A person who is self-employed must pay his own Social Security and Medicare taxes. If an employee is working for an employer, the employer pays half of these taxes and the employee pays the other half. But self-employed people are responsible for paying the entire amount.

The Social Security tax rate for 2011 is 13.3% on self-employment income up to $106,800. If net earnings exceed $106,800, the taxpayer will continue to pay only the Medicare portion of the Social Security tax, which is 2.9%, on the rest of their earnings.

This tax law change is a temporary decrease in the *employee's* share of payroll tax. In 2011, Social Security tax was withheld from an employee's wages at the rate of

4.2% (down from 6.2%), up to the Social Security wage limit of $106,800. There was no change to Medicare withholding.

The same reduction applies to net earnings from self-employment—the temporary rate is 10.4% (down from 12.4%), up to the Social Security wage limit of $106,800. As a result of this change, the overall self-employment tax is reduced from 15.3% to 13.3%. See Schedule SE Instructions for more information.

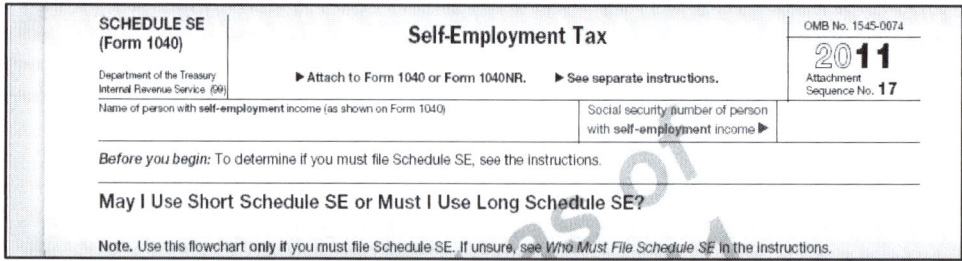

The part that may be confusing is the fact that there is a "cap" on Social Security tax, but there is NO "cap" on Medicare tax. Incidentally, this cap also applies to people who are regular wage earners.

If a taxpayer has wages in addition to self-employment earnings, then the tax on the wages is paid first.

Example: Kendall has a job where she earns a salary. She also earns extra money as a self-employed web designer. She will pay the appropriate Social Security taxes on both her wages and her business earnings. In 2011, Kendall has $30,000 in wages and $40,000 in self-employment income from her web design business. In 2011, she will pay the appropriate Social Security taxes on both her wages and business earnings, since her combined income did not exceed $106,800.

Example #2: In 2011, Devon has a full-time job and also makes money on weekends as a self-employed musician. In 2011, Devon's wages from his job are $77,500. He also has $30,000 in net earnings from his music business for total income of $107,500. Devon does not pay dual Social Security taxes on his earnings that exceed $106,800. His employer will withhold 5.65% in Social Security and Medicare taxes on his $77,500 in earnings. Devon must pay 13.3% in Social Security and Medicare taxes on his first $29,300 in self-employment earnings and 2.9% in Medicare tax on the remaining $700 in earnings (example from SSA.gov).

Remember, taxpayers are required to pay Social Security tax on their wages ONLY up to $106,800—but they must continue to pay Medicare taxes on any additional amount they make, even if they earn a million dollars.

There are two income tax deductions related to the self-employment tax that reduce overall taxes on a taxpayer with self-employment income.

- First, net earnings from self-employment are reduced by half of the total Social Security tax. This is similar to the way employees are treated under the tax

laws, because the employer's share of the Social Security tax is not considered wages to the employee.
- Second, the taxpayer can deduct half of the Social Security tax on IRS **Form 1040** as an *adjustment* to gross income. The amount is not an itemized deduction or a business deduction, and must not be listed on **Schedule A** or **Schedule C**.

More than One Business

If a taxpayer runs more than one business, then he will "net" the profit (or loss) from each to determine the *total earnings* subject to SE tax. This only applies to taxpayers who have more than one business. Taxpayers cannot "combine" a spouse's income (or loss) to determine their individual earnings subject to SE tax. However, a single person with two sole proprietorships may combine income and losses from both businesses to figure self-employment tax.

Example: Tanner is a sole proprietor who owns a barbershop. Tanner has $19,000 in net income for 2011. His wife, Erin, has a candle-making business, and she has a business LOSS of ($12,000) for 2011. Tanner must pay self-employment tax on $19,000, regardless of how he and Erin choose to file. That is because married couples cannot "offset" each other's self-employment tax. The income of each business is allocated to the individual—not the gross amount shown on a joint tax return.

Example: Darren is a single taxpayer and has two small businesses. He owns a computer repair shop and he also runs a car wash. Both businesses are sole proprietorships. The computer repair business has net income of $45,000 in 2011. The car wash, however, is doing poorly. It has a net LOSS of ($23,000) in 2011. Darren only has to pay self-employment tax on $22,000 ($45,000-$23,000) of income, because he may "net" the income and losses from both his businesses.

Employee Fringe Benefits (Taxable and Non-taxable)

Fringe benefits are offered to employees by employers as a condition of their employment. Some fringe benefits are taxable and some are not. This next section will cover each type of fringe benefit, which are frequently tested on Part 1 and Part 2 of the EA exam, both from the perspective of the individual (the employee receiving the benefits) and the business owner (the entity providing the benefits.

Common fringe benefits include health benefits, vacation pay, and parking passes. Although most employee fringe benefits are non-taxable, some benefits must be included in an employee's taxable income. This is usually reported on the taxpayer's **Form W-2.** Examples of *taxable* fringe benefits include:
- OFF-SITE athletic facilities and health club memberships.
- The value of employer-provided life insurance over $50,000.
- Any cash benefit or benefit in the form of a credit card or gift card.

- Season tickets to sporting events, although single tickets can be excluded in certain cases.
- Transportation benefits, if the value of a benefit for any month is more than the non-taxable limit. Employers cannot exclude the excess from the employee's wages as a de minimis transportation benefit.
- Employer-provided vehicles, if they are used for personal purposes.

> **Example:** Tanning Town Inc. owns a tropical resort employees can use free of charge. Sam decides to visit the resort with his family. The fair market value of the stay is $5,000. Sam must include the FMV of the accommodations in his taxable income. The employer usually figures the taxable amount. If the FMV is $5,000 for Sam's two-week stay, then $5,000 will be included in his taxable wages.

Non-taxable Employee Fringe Benefits

Most fringe benefits are not taxable and may be excluded from an employee's income. The following are some common types of non-taxable employee fringe benefit.

Cafeteria Plans

A *cafeteria plan* provides employees an opportunity to receive certain benefits on a pretax basis. The plan may make benefits available to employees, their spouses, and dependents. The most common type of cafeteria plan offers health benefits to an employee and his family. Some cafeteria plans may also offer coverage to former employees and their spouses. Generally, qualified benefits under a cafeteria plan are not subject to FICA, FUTA, Medicare tax, or income tax withholding.

Employee contributions to the cafeteria plan are usually made via salary reduction agreements, taken directly out of the employee's paycheck. The employee usually agrees to contribute a portion of his salary on a pretax basis to pay for a portion of the qualified benefits.

Participants in a cafeteria plan must be permitted to choose among at least one taxable benefit (such as cash) and one *qualified* benefit. A *qualified* benefit is a benefit that is non-taxable. Qualified benefits include:

- Accident, dental, vision, and medical benefits (but NOT Archer medical savings accounts or long-term care insurance)
- Adoption assistance
- Dependent care assistance
- Group-term life insurance coverage (up to $50,000 of life insurance coverage may be provided as a non-taxable benefit to an employee, covered in more detail later)
- Health Savings Accounts

Note: If an employer pays the cost of an accident insurance plan for an employee, then the amounts received under the plan are taxable to the employee. If a taxpayer pays the cost of an accident insurance plan *for himself*, then the benefits received under the plan are not taxable.

FSA: A Flexible Spending Arrangement

An FSA is a form of cafeteria plan benefit, funded by salary reduction, which reimburses employees for expenses incurred for certain qualified benefits. An FSA may be offered for dependent care assistance, adoption assistance, and medical care reimbursements. The benefits are subject to an annual maximum and an annual "use-or-lose" rule. An FSA cannot provide a cumulative benefit to the employee beyond the plan year. The employee must substantiate his expenses, and then the distributions to the employee are tax-free.

Dependent Care Assistance

An employee can generally exclude from gross income up to $5,000 in 2011 ($2,500 if MFS) of benefits received under a dependent care assistance program each year. Amounts paid directly to the taxpayer or to a daycare provider qualify for exclusion. IRS **Form 2441**, *Child and Dependent Care Expenses,* must be filed in order to claim the exclusion. The amount that qualifies for exclusion is limited to:

- The total amount of the dependent care benefits received
- The employee's earned income
- The spouse's earned income
- $5,000 ($2,500 if Married Filing Separately)

Example: John's employer offers a cafeteria plan that allows for dependent care assistance. John files jointly with his wife, Cindy. Cindy works part-time as a bookkeeper. John makes $50,000 in 2011. Cindy earns $4,500 as a part-time bookkeeper. They have $5,500 in daycare costs for 2011. The maximum amount that can be excluded in 2011 is $4,500, the amount of Cindy's earned income.

Example: Tina's employer provides a dependent care assistance flexible spending plan to its employees through a cafeteria plan. In addition, it provides occasional on-site dependent care to its employees at no cost. Tina had $4,500 deducted from her pay for the dependent care flexible spending arrangement. In addition, she used the on-site dependent care several times. The fair market value of the on-site care was $700. Tina's **Form W-2** will report $5,200 of dependent care assistance ($4,500 flexible spending + $700 FMV of on-site dependent care.) Since the IRS only allows an exclusion of $5,000 in dependent care assistance per year, Boxes 1, 3, and 5 of her **Form W-2** should include $200 (the amount in excess of the non-taxable assistance), and applicable taxes should be withheld on that amount.

De Minimis Employee Benefits

Some employee benefits are so small that it would be impractical for the employer to account for them. These are called *de minimis* benefits. The exclusion applies, for example, to the following items:

- Coffee, doughnuts, or soft drinks provided to employees.
- Occasional meals while employees work overtime (100% of the cost).
- Occasional company picnics for employees.
- Occasional use of the employer's copy machine.
- Holiday gifts, other than cash, such as a gift basket or holiday ham.
- An employer-provided cell phone: The value of an employer-provided cell phone is excludable from an employee's income as a working condition fringe benefit. Personal use of the phone is excludable from an employee's income as a *de minimis* fringe benefit.

De Minimis Meals: An exclusion for 100% of the cost of meals provided to employees on the employer's premises *for the employer's convenience* are not taxable to the employee and *not subject* to the 50% limit.[27] Meals employers furnish to a restaurant employee during, immediately before, or after, the employee's working hours are considered furnished for the employer's convenience.

Example: Ellen is a registered nurse who is not allowed to leave the hospital premises during her long shifts. She works in the emergency room, and she must always be available to help patients immediately. So the hospital provides meals and a place for Ellen to sleep during her shift. Ellen does not have to recognize the value of the meals as income. The hospital also does not have to add the FMV of Ellen's meals to her wages. In addition, the meals are 100% deductible by the employer and not subject to the 50% limit, because the meals are provided as a condition of her employment and are for the convenience of her employer.

*NOTE: Most *cash* benefits or their equivalent (such as gift cards or credit cards) cannot be excluded as de *minimis* fringe benefits under any circumstances. Season tickets to sporting events, commuting use of an employer-provided car more than once a month, and membership to a private country club or athletic facility are never excludable as *de minimis* fringe benefits. There is an exception for unusual or emergency circumstances (explained next).

---

[27] Meals are generally 50% deductible. This means when a business pays for a meal, only 50% of its cost is deductible by the employer. There are some exceptions for employer-provided meals during company parties and picnics, and if the meal is given to the employee for the convenience of the employer.

Example: A commuter ferry breaks down unexpectedly, and the engineers are required to work overtime to make repairs. After working eight hours, the engineers break for dinner because they will be working overtime until the engine is repaired. The supervisor gives each employee $10 for a meal. The meal is not taxable to the engineers because it was provided to permit them to work overtime in a situation that is not routine.

No-Additional-Cost Services

Non-taxable fringe benefits include services provided to employees that do not impose any substantial additional cost. They may be excludable as a no-additional-cost fringe benefit.

A "no-additional-cost service" is a service offered by the employer to its customers in the ordinary course of the line of business of the employer in which the employee performs substantial services, and the employer incurs no substantial additional cost (including foregone revenue) in providing the service to the employee: IRC 132(b).

An employer can offer discounts, as well as on-site benefits, such as an on-site gym.[28]

Example: Trey works for a local fitness club. He is allowed to work out for free as a condition of his employment. This is because this fringe benefit is a "no-additional cost" service. It doesn't cost the employer anything to allow this employee benefit. Trey is also allowed a 10% discount on vitamins that the gym sells to patrons, so long as the vitamins are for his own use (**Publication 15-B**).

Other examples include transportation tickets, free flights, hotel rooms, entertainment facilities, etc.; however, these services may occur in connection with governmental facilities as well (for example, the use of a municipal golf course or recreation center).

Transportation fringe benefits also include the FMV of flights that are offered to airline employees.

Example: Henrietta is a flight attendant with Jet Way Airlines. She is allowed to fly for free on stand-by flights when there is an extra seat. This is an example of a fringe benefit that is allowed for no additional cost to the employer and is therefore non-taxable to the employee.

---

[28] If the employer provides employees with the free or low cost use of an employer-operated gym or other athletic club on the employer's premises, the value is not included in the employee's compensation. The gym must be used primarily by employees, their spouses, and their dependent children. If the employer pays for a fitness program provided to the employee at an off-site resort hotel, country club, or athletic club, the value of the program is included in the employee's compensation (*frequently tested).

Employer-Provided Educational Assistance

An employer-provided educational assistance program can be excluded up to a certain amount. (The amounts must be for tuition, books, required fees, and supplies). Room and board do not qualify as educational expenses for the purposes of an employer-sponsored educational assistance plan. The maximum excluded educational benefit is $5,250 in 2011.

Transportation Fringe Benefits

Employers may provide transportation benefits to their employees up to certain amounts without having to include the benefit in the employee's income. Qualified transportation benefits include transit passes, paid parking, and transportation in a commuter highway vehicle (shuttle).

The employer may also offer cash reimbursement under a qualified reimbursement arrangement (also called an "accountable plan," which is explained later).

In 2011, employees may exclude:

- $230 per month in transit benefits (vehicle and transit passes), and
- $230 per month in parking benefits.

This is up to a combined maximum of $460 per month in 2011. Employees may receive transit passes and benefits for parking during the same month; they are not mutually exclusive. An employer may also reimburse an employee for a bicycle[29] that is used for commuting purposes. A qualified bicycle commuting reimbursement is a reimbursement of up to $20 per month for reasonable expenses incurred by the employee in conjunction with his commute to work by bike.

However, the use of a company car for commuting purposes is a taxable benefit. So, if an employer allows an employee to use a company vehicle for commuting, then the value of the vehicle's use is taxable to the employee. Personal use of an employer's vehicle is considered "taxable wages" to the employee.

Example: Joe, an employee of Blue-Blood Corp., uses an employer-provided car. In 2011, Joe drives the car 20,000 miles, of which 4,000 were personal miles or 20% (4,000/20,000 = 20%). The car has an annual lease value of $4,100. Personal use is therefore valued at $820 and is included in Joe's wages.

Accountable Plans

An *accountable plan* is a plan where an employer reimburses employees for business-related expenses such as mileage, meals, and travel expenses. For expenses to qualify under an accountable plan, the employee must follow certain rules in order to have the expenses reimbursed. An accountable plan requires employees to meet all of the following requirements. Employees must:

- Have incurred the expenses while performing services as employees

---

[29] Section 132 (f) of the Internal Revenue Code

- Adequately account for the expenses within a reasonable period of time
- Adequately account for their travel, meals, and entertainment expenses
- Provide evidence of their employee business expenses, such as receipts or other records
- Return any excess reimbursement or allowance within a reasonable period of time

Under an accountable plan, a business may advance money to employees; however, certain conditions must be met. The cash advance must be reasonably calculated to equal the anticipated expenses. The business owner must make the advance within a reasonable period of time. If any expenses reimbursed under this arrangement are not substantiated, a business is not allowed to deduct them under an accountable plan.

Instead, the reimbursed expenses are considered a non-accountable plan and become taxable to the employee.

Example: Donna is an Enrolled Agent who runs a tax preparation business. She advances $250 to her employee, Ayden, so that he can become a Notary. Ayden spends $90 on a Notary course and then another $100 to take the Notary exam, which he passes. Ayden returns the unused funds ($60) as well as copies of his receipts to Donna, his boss. The expenses are qualified expenses under an accountable plan. Donna may deduct the $190 ($90 + $100) as a business expense, and the amounts are not taxable to Ayden.

Cash reimbursements are excludable if an employer establishes a bona fide reimbursement plan. This means there must be reasonable procedures to verify reimbursements and employees must substantiate the expenses using receipts or other substantiation.

Example: Mai Ling buys a transit pass for $120 each month in 2011. At the end of each month, she presents her used transit pass to her employer and certifies that she purchased and used it during the month. The employer reimburses her $120 in cash. The employer has established a bona fide reimbursement arrangement for purposes of excluding the $120 reimbursement from the employee's gross income in 2011. The reimbursement is not taxable to Mai Ling, and it is deductible by the employer.

Accountable Plans: Travel Reimbursements

Qualifying expenses for travel are excludable from an employee's income if they are incurred for *temporary* travel on business away from the area of the employee's tax home. Travel expenses paid in connection with an indefinite work assignment are not excludable. Any work assignment in excess of one year is considered "indefinite."

Travel expense reimbursements include:

- Costs to travel to and from the business destination (flights, mileage reimbursements)
- Transportation costs while at the business destination (taxi fare, shuttles)

- Lodging, meals, and incidental expenses
- Cleaning, laundry, and other miscellaneous expenses

> **Example:** Woody works for a travel agency in Detroit. He flies to Denver to conduct business for an entire week. His employer pays the cost of transportation to and from Denver, as well as lodging and meals while there. The reimbursements for substantiated travel expenses are excludable from Woody's income, and the reimbursements are deductible by his employer.

Employer-Provided Life Insurance as a Fringe Benefit

Employers may deduct the cost of life insurance premiums provided to employees. Employer-provided life insurance is a non-taxable fringe benefit only up to $50,000. Coverage amounts over $50,000 are taxable to the employee. The employer must calculate the taxable portion of the premiums for coverage that exceeds $50,000.

> **Example:** Carol, a 47-year-old employee, receives $40,000 of life insurance coverage per year under a policy carried by her employer. Her employer agrees to pay the premiums on the first $40,000 of coverage as part of Carol's cafeteria plan. She may also elect another $100,000 of additional life insurance coverage. This optional coverage is also carried by her employer. The cost of $10,000 of this additional amount is excludable; the cost of the remaining $90,000 of coverage is included in income. Since only $50,000 of life insurance coverage can be non-taxable to the employee, Carol will be taxed on the difference between the premiums.

Employer-Provided Retirement Plan Contributions

Many employers contribute to their employees' retirement plans. This contribution is not taxable to the employee when it is made. The contribution only becomes taxable when the employee finally withdraws the funds from his retirement account.

This rule also applies to elected deferrals. Employees may elect to have part of their pretax compensation contributed to a retirement fund. An elective deferral is excluded from wages, but is still subject to Social Security and Medicare tax. Elective deferrals include contributions into the following retirement plans:

- 401(k) plans, 403(B) plans, Section 457 plans
- SIMPLE plans
- Thrift Savings Plans for federal employees

Elective deferrals to a **Roth** retirement plan are taxable to the employee. That is because a Roth plan is always funded with post-tax income.

Special Rules for Highly Compensated Employees (HCEs)

Highly compensated employees cannot exclude the value of employer-provided benefits from income unless certain specific requirements are met. This is to discourage companies from offering spectacular tax-free benefits to their highly compensated executives, while ignoring the needs of lower-paid employees.

A highly compensated employee (HCE) is defined as anyone who:
- Is an officer of the corporation, OR
- Was at least a "5% shareholder," OR
- Received over $160,000 in compensation during 2011 and is in the top 20% of employees based upon compensation, OR
- Is a spouse or dependent of any of the individuals listed above.

The law for highly compensated employees includes a "look-back provision," so employees who were previously considered HCEs are generally still considered HCEs for 2011 plan year testing (Publication 15-B).

> **Example:** Fengrew Inc. is a C Corporation. Fengrew Inc. has 300 employees, 45 of which are considered "highly compensated employees." Fengrew Inc.'s cafeteria plan is available to all the employees; therefore, the discrimination rules do not apply, and the employee's benefits are not taxable.

If a plan favors key (HCE) employees, the employer is required to include the value of the benefits they could have selected in their wages. A plan is considered to have "favored" HCEs if over 25% of all the benefits are given to HCEs.

However, a benefits plan that covers union employees under a collective bargaining agreement is not included in this rule.

Interest Income

Interest is a passive form of income. Taxable interest includes interest received from bank accounts and other sources. Certain distributions commonly called "dividends" are actually interest. Credit unions, for instance, commonly call their distributions "dividends." The IRS considers these credit union distributions to be interest income, rather than dividends.

Interest income is reported to the taxpayer on IRS **Form 1099-INT**. If interest income exceeds $1,500, the taxpayer must report the interest on **Schedule B, Form 1040**. A taxpayer cannot file **Form 1040EZ** if his interest income exceeds $1,500.

Tax-exempt interest is reported on page one (the front) of IRS **Form 1040**.

Dividends that are Actually Interest

Taxpayers must report these so-called "dividends" on deposits as interest income. The following are some other sources of taxable interest:
- Credit unions
- Domestic building and loan associations
- Domestic savings and loan associations
- Federal savings and loan associations
- Mutual savings banks
- Certificates of Deposits (CDs) and other deferred interest accounts

Taxpayers should report these earnings as interest on their **Form 1040**.

Gift for Opening a Bank Account

If a taxpayer receives non-cash gifts or services for making deposits or for opening an account in a savings institution, the value of the gift may have to be reported as interest. For deposits of less than $5,000, gifts or services valued at more than $10 must be reported as interest. For deposits of $5,000 or more, gifts or services valued at more than $20 must be reported as interest. The value of the gift is determined by the financial institution.

Interest on Insurance Dividends

Interest on insurance dividends left on deposit with an insurance company that can be withdrawn annually is taxable in the year it is credited to the taxpayer's account. However, if the taxpayer cannot withdraw the income except on a certain date (the anniversary date of the policy or other specified date), the income is considered restricted and not taxable when it is earned. The interest is taxable in the year that the withdrawal is allowed.

Interest Earned on U.S. Treasury Bills, Notes, & Bonds

Interest on U.S. obligations, such as U.S. Treasury bills, notes, and bonds issued by any agency of the United States, is taxable for federal income tax purposes.

*Special NOTE: Money borrowed to invest in Certificate of Deposits: The interest a taxpayer pays on loans borrowed from a bank to meet the minimum deposit required for a Certificate of Deposit (investment CD) from the institution and the interest a taxpayer earns on the certificate are *two separate things*.[30] The taxpayer must include the total interest earned on the certificate in income. If the taxpayer itemizes deductions, he can deduct the interest paid as investment interest paid, up to the amount of net investment income. (This is a concept frequently tested on the EA exam.)

> **Example:** Sienna wanted to invest in a $10,000 six-month CD. So she deposited $5,000 in a CD with a credit union and borrowed $5,000 from another bank to make up the $10,000 minimum deposit required to buy the six-month CD. The certificate earned $575 at maturity in 2011, but Sienna actually received NET $265 in interest income that year. This represented the $575 Sienna earned on the CD, minus $310 interest charged on the $5,000 loan. The credit union gives Sienna a **Form 1099-INT** for 2011 showing the $575 interest Sienna earned. The bank also gives Sienna a statement showing that Sienna paid $310 interest for 2011. Sienna must include the total interest amount earned, $575, in her interest income for 2011. Only if Sienna itemizes can she deduct the interest expense of $310. The investment interest paid is a deduction on **Schedule A (Form 1040).** Sienna can deduct $310 as investment interest.

---

[30] This concept has been tested on multiple prior exams.

Original Issue Discount (OID)

Original Issue Discount (OID) is a form of imputed income interest. OID income occurs when a debtor issues a debt instrument, such as a zero coupon bond, for less than the "issue price" of the debt instrument. If there is OID of at least $10 for the calendar year, the interest income must be reported to the taxpayer on **Form 1099-OID**. .

Wages and Employee Compensation

Wages are the most common type of employee compensation. Wages, salaries, bonuses, and commissions are compensation received by employees for services performed.

All income from wages, salaries, and tips is taxable to the employee and deductible by the employer. Wages paid by an employer are reported on IRS **Form W-2.** Employers are generally required to issue a **Form W-2** to their employees by January 31 of each year. Wages are reported by the employee as taxable income on **Form 1040.**

Employers are required by law to withhold Social Security and Medicare taxes. If the employer fails to withhold Social Security and Medicare, the employee is required to file IRS **Form 8919,** *Uncollected Social Security and Medicare Tax on Wages.*

Advance commissions and other advance earnings are all taxable in the year they are received. It doesn't matter whether or not the employee has earned the income. If the employee receives wages in advance, he must recognize the income in the year it is constructively received.

This is true even if the employee is forced to pay back some of the money at a later date. If the employee later pays back a portion of the earnings, that sum would be deducted from wages at that time.

> **Example:** Maddox requests a salary advance of $1,000 on December 18, 2011 in order to go on a two-week vacation. Maddox must recognize the income on his 2011 tax return, even though he will not actually earn the money until 2012, when he returns from his vacation.

"Supplemental wages" is compensation that is paid to an employee in addition to his regular pay. These amounts are listed on the employee's Form W-2 and are taxable just like regular wages, even if the pay is not actually for work performed. Vacation pay is an example of supplemental wages that is taxable just like any other wage income, even though the employee has not technically "worked" for the income. Supplemental wages include:

- Bonuses, commissions, prizes
- Severance pay, back pay, and holiday pay
- Accumulated vacation pay and sick leave
- Payment for non-deductible moving expenses

Severance pay is taxable as ordinary income, just like wages. Even though severance pay is usually issued to employees who are being terminated and is not actually for work performed, it is still taxable to the employee and still subject to Social Security and Medicare tax.

Reporting Tip Income

All tips are taxable as ordinary income. Individuals who receive $20 or more per month in tips must report their tip income to their employer. Employers must withhold Social Security, Medicare, and income taxes due on reported tips. The employer withholds FICA taxes due on tips from the employee's wages and pays both employer and employee portions of the tax in the same manner as the tax on the employee's regular wages.

Tips are received by food servers, baggage handlers, hairdressers, and others for performing services.

Taxpayers who do not report all of their tips to their employer must report the Social Security and Medicare taxes on their **Form 1040.** Employees use **Form 4137**, *Social Security and Medicare Tax on Unreported Tip Income,* to compute and report the additional tax.

Taxpayers who are *self-employed* and receive tips must include their tips in gross receipts on **Schedule C.** Examples of this type of taxpayer include self-employed hair stylists and manicurists.

> **Example:** Lydia works two jobs. She is an administrative assistant during the week and a bartender on the weekends. She reports all of her tip income ($3,000) to her employer. Her **Forms W-2** show wage income of $21,000 (assistant) and $8,250 (bartender). Lydia must report $29,250 on her **Form 1040,** which is the total amount earned at both jobs. Lydia reported the tip income to her employer, so her bartending tips are *already included* on her **Form W-2** for that job, so the amount she reports is $21,000 + $8,250.

Individuals who receive *less than* $20 per month in tips while working one job do not have to report their tip income to their employer. While all tips are subject to income tax, tips of less than $20 per month are:
- Exempt from Social Security and Medicare taxes
- Still subject to federal income tax and must be reported on Form 1040

Non-cash tips (for example, concert tickets or other items) do not have to be reported to the employer, but they must be reported and included in the taxpayer's income at their fair market value.

Garnished Wages

An employee may have his wages garnished for many different reasons. Sometimes the employee owes child support, back taxes due, or other debts. It doesn't matter how much is actually garnished from the employee's paycheck. The full amount (the gross wages) is taxable to the employee and must be included in the employee's wages at year end.

Disability Retirement Benefits

Disability retirement benefits are taxable as wages if a taxpayer retired on disability before reaching the minimum retirement age. These benefits are taxable as wages on the taxpayer's **Form 1040**. Once the taxpayer reaches retirement age, the payments are no longer taxable as wages. They are then taxable as pension income.

Disability Payments from an Insurance Policy

For payments made pursuant to an individual disability income insurance policy, benefits normally are free of income tax. Disability income benefits are excluded from income if the taxpayer pays the premiums for the policy. For health insurance paid for by the employer, the employer deducts the cost and the employee pays no tax on the premiums paid by the employer. The employee also does not pay any tax on the benefits received.

Sick pay is not the same thing as "disability pay." Sick pay is always taxable as wages, just like vacation pay.

Property In Lieu Of Wages

An employee who receives property instead of wages for services performed must generally recognize the fair market value of the property when it is received. However, if an employee receives stock or other property that is restricted, the property is not included in income until it is available without restriction to the employee.

> **Example:** Barry receives stock from his company as part of his promotion. He receives $5,000 worth of stock, a total of 500 shares. However, Barry cannot sell or exercise the shares for five years. If Barry quits his job, he forfeits the shares. He does not have to recognize this restricted stock as income in the year he received it. This is because the stock is subject to multiple restrictions. This stock will be taxable when Barry chooses to sell it or otherwise gains complete control over it.

Military Pay Exclusion-Combat Zone Wages

Wages earned by military personnel are generally taxable. However, there are special rules for military personnel regarding taxable income, including many exclusions for those on active duty.

Combat zone wages and hazardous duty pay are excludable for certain military personnel. Enlisted persons who serve in a combat zone for any part of a month may exclude their pay from tax. For officers, pay is excluded up to a certain amount, depending on the branch of service.

> **Example:** Lee is a Marine. He served in a combat zone from January 1, 2011 to November 3, 2011. He will only be required to report his income for December 2011, because all of the other income is excluded from taxation as combat zone pay. Even though Lee only served three days in November in a combat zone, his income for the entire month of November is excluded.

Special Deadlines for Military Personnel

Military personnel serving in a combat zone also have an automatic extension for most tax matters. Military personnel, unlike civilian taxpayers, are granted extensions for filing and also paying their income tax due. While a taxpayer is serving in a combat zone, he is granted extensions for requesting innocent spouse relief and collection due process hearing. A 90-day limit for filing a Tax Court petition also does not apply while the taxpayer is serving in a combat zone.

Substitute W-2 Form

If for some reason an employee does not receive his **Form W-2** (perhaps the employer went out of business), the employee may file his tax return on paper using IRS **Form 4852,** *Substitute for Form W-2, Wage and Tax Statement*. **Form** 4852 is a substitute wage and tax statement that taxpayers may use when it is impossible to get a W-2 from the employer.

Taxpayers should only use IRS **Form** 4852 as a last resort. IRS **Form** 4852 is used to essentially re-create the W-2 form that the employee would have received. Usually, an earnings statement or similar document is used as a basis to re-create the data required in order to complete and file the taxpayer's return.

> **Example:** Manny was working for a plumbing company in 2011. In December 2011, the owner died, and final payroll returns were not filed. The business was closed and Manny never got a **Form W-2** for the wages he earned in 2011. Manny may file a **Form 4852** as a substitute for the **Form W-2,** explaining the circumstances why he could not obtain a **Form W-2.** Then Manny may use his earnings statement or other records to attempt a re-creation on his taxable income and withholding.

Barter Exchanges and Barter Income

Bartering is an exchange of property or services. Usually there is no exchange of cash. Barter may take place on an informal, one-on-one basis between individuals and businesses, or it can take place on a third party basis through a barter exchange company.

While our ancestors may have exchanged eggs for corn, today a person can barter computer services for auto repair. Another example of a one-on-one exchange transaction is a plumber doing repair work for a dentist in exchange for dental services. The fair market value of the goods and services exchanged must be reported as income by both parties. Income from bartering is taxable in the year it is performed.

If a taxpayer agrees to exchange services with another person and both have agreed ahead of time as to the value of the services, the agreed-upon value will be accepted as fair market value.

Alimony (as Income to the Recipient)

This book will cover the concept of alimony from two perspectives: from the perspective of the payor and the payee. In this section, we will cover the concept of alimony as income.

Alimony is taxable *income* to the recipient and *deductible* by the payor.

Example: Mark and Sibba are divorced. Their divorce decree calls for Mark to pay Sibba $200 a month as child support and $150 a month as alimony. Mark makes all of his child support and alimony payments on time. Therefore, in 2011, Mark may deduct $1,800 ($150 X 12 months) as alimony paid and Sibba must report $1,800 as alimony received. The amount paid as child support, $2,400 ($200 X 12), is not deductible by Mark, and is not reported as income by Sibba.

Alimony "paid" is an adjustment to income. Spouses do not have to itemize in order to deduct their alimony payments. The alimony paid is listed on the first page of **Form 1040** as an adjustment to income. Taxpayers must claim the deduction on **Form 1040**.

They cannot use **Form 1040A** or **Form 1040EZ**. Taxpayers must provide the Social Security Number of the former spouse receiving the alimony payments. Alimony paid is an adjustment to income for the payor, and is taxable to the receiving spouse as ordinary income.

If a divorce agreement specifies payments of both alimony and child support and only partial payments are made by the payor, then the partial payments are considered to be child support until this obligation is fully paid, and any excess is then treated as alimony. Child support is not taxable income to the receiver and not deductible by the payor.

Example: Sandra and Jessie are divorced. Their divorce decree calls for Jessie to pay Sandra $2,000 a month ($24,000 ($2,000 x 12) a year) as child support and $1,500 a month ($18,000 ($1,500 x 12) a year) as alimony. Jessie falls behind on his payments and only manages to pay $36,000. In this case, $24,000 is considered child support and only the remaining amount is considered alimony. Jessie can deduct only $12,000 ($36,000 - $24,000) as alimony paid. Sandra would report $12,000 as alimony income received.

If the payment amount is to be reduced based on a contingency *relating to a child* (e.g., attaining a certain age, marrying), the amount of the reduction will be treated as child support.

Remember, child support is NOT alimony! The IRS treats alimony very differently from child support in the United States. Child support is never deductible because it is viewed as a payment that a parent is making simply for the support of his child.

Also, any alimony payments that continue after the receiving spouse has died will automatically be considered child support, not alimony.

> **Example:** Under Cary's divorce decree, he must pay his ex-wife, Jennifer, $30,000 per year. The payments will stop after 15 years (or upon Jennifer's death). Jennifer dies ten years later. The divorce decree provided that if Jennifer dies before the end of the 15-year period, Cary must still pay Jennifer's estate the difference between $450,000 ($30,000 annually × 15 years) and the total amount paid up to that time. Jennifer dies at the end of the tenth year, and Cary must pay Jennifer's estate $150,000 ($450,000 − $300,000). Since the payment is required even after Jennifer's death, none of the annual payments are considered alimony for tax purposes. The payments are actually "disguised child support" and cannot be deducted by Cary as alimony.

Property Settlements Pursuant to Divorce are Not Alimony!

Property settlements, which are simply a division of property, are not treated as alimony. Property transferred to a former spouse incident to a divorce is treated as a gift. "Incident to a divorce" means a transfer of property within one year after the date of the divorce, or a transfer of property related to the cessation of the marriage, as determined by the courts.

Alimony payments made under a divorce agreement are deductible by the PAYOR if all of the following requirements are met:

- The spouses may not file joint returns with each other.
- Payments are made in cash or a cash equivalent (such as checks or money orders). Payments made to a third party can be considered alimony. For example, if one spouse pays the medical bills of his ex-wife, the cash payment to the hospital can count as alimony.

> **Example:** Ben is required to pay $1,000 per month in alimony to Karen, his former spouse. Karen has medical bills of $1,500, and Ben agrees to pay the medical bills in lieu of the regular alimony payment. The $1,500 would qualify as alimony payment to a third party, since it was made on Karen's behalf to her creditor.

In order for a payment to qualify as alimony:

- The divorce agreement may not include a clause indicating that the payment is something else (such as child support or repayment of a loan, etc.)
- If the spouses are legally separated, the spouses cannot live together when the payments are made.
- The payor must have no liability to make any payment (in cash or property) after the death of the former spouse.
- The alimony payment must not be treated as child support.

Qualifying Alimony (General Rules)

The following rules apply to alimony regardless of when the divorce or separation instrument was executed. Alimony does NOT include:
- Child support
- Non-cash property settlements
- Payments that are community income
- Payments to keep up the payor's property
- Free use of the payor's property

An Amended Divorce Decree

An amendment to a divorce decree may change the nature of the payments. Amendments are not ordinarily retroactive for federal tax purposes. However, a retroactive amendment to a divorce decree correcting a clerical error to reflect the original intent of the court will generally be effective retroactively for federal tax purposes.

> **Example:** A court order retroactively corrected a mathematical error on Pat's divorce decree to express the original intent to spread the alimony payments over more than ten years. This change also is effective retroactively for federal tax purposes, since it is a correction of an error by the courts.

Legal Fees and the Cost of Divorce

A taxpayer cannot deduct legal fees and court costs for getting a divorce. But he may deduct legal fees paid for tax advice in connection with a divorce and legal fees to obtain alimony. In order to be deductible, the tax advice fees must be separately stated on the attorney's bill. In addition, a taxpayer may deduct fees paid to appraisers, actuaries, and accountants for services in determining the correct tax or in helping to get alimony.

A taxpayer can deduct fees for legal advice on federal, state, and local taxes of all types, including income, estate, gift, inheritance, and property taxes, even if the advice is related to a divorce. If an attorney's legal fee includes amounts for tax advice and other tax services, the taxpayer must be able to prove the expense was incurred for tax advice and not for some other legal issue.

> **Example:** The lawyer handling Jenna's divorce consults another law firm, which handles only tax matters, to get information on how the divorce will affect her taxes. Since Jenna consulted with the second law firm specifically to discuss tax matters, Jenna can deduct the part of the fee paid to the second firm and separately stated on her bill, as an itemized deduction on **Schedule A,** subject to a 2% limit.

> **Example:** The lawyer handling Mack's divorce uses the firm's tax department for tax matters related to his divorce. Mack's statement from the firm shows the part of the total fee for tax matters. This is based on the time required, the difficulty of the tax questions, and the amount of tax involved. Mack can deduct this part of his bill as an itemized deduction on **Schedule A**, subject to a 2% limit.

Because a taxpayer must include alimony received in gross income, a taxpayer may deduct fees paid to an attorney to collect alimony.

The taxpayer can claim deductible legal fees only by itemizing deductions on **Schedule A (Form 1040)**. The fees must be claimed as miscellaneous itemized deductions subject to the 2%-of-adjusted-gross-income limit. (For more information on this issue, see IRS **Publication 529**, *Miscellaneous Deductions*.)

> **Example #1:** The lawyer handling Paul's divorce also works on the tax matters. The fee for tax advice and the fee for other services are shown separately on the lawyer's statement. They are based on the time spent on each service and the fees charged for similar services. Paul can deduct the fee charged for tax advice only, subject to a 2% limit.

> **Example #2:** Betty pays an attorney $4,500 for handling her divorce. Betty also pays an additional $1,500 fee for services in collecting alimony that her former husband refuses to pay. Betty can deduct the fee for collecting alimony ($1,500), subject to a 2% limit, if it is separately stated on the attorney's bill.

Securities Income (Dividends from Stocks & Bonds)

Investors typically buy and sell securities and then report income from dividends, interest, or capital appreciation. The income that is earned on these investments is reported on **Schedule B**. A taxpayer must file **Schedule B**, *Interest and Ordinary Dividends*, when any of the following apply:

- The taxpayer had over $1,500 of taxable interest or ordinary dividends.
- The taxpayer is claiming the education exclusion of interest from series EE savings bonds.
- The taxpayer received ordinary dividends as a nominee. "Nominee interest" occurs when a taxpayer receives a 1099-INT form, but the interest really belongs to another party. This is very common when taxpayers set up accounts for family members and minor children.
- The taxpayer had foreign accounts or received a distribution from a foreign trust.
- The taxpayer received interest as part of a seller-financed mortgage.

Sometimes, taxpayers will sell their stocks and bonds. The sale of securities results in capital gains and losses that must be reported on **Form 1040, Schedule D,**

Capital Gains and Losses. Capital gains, losses, and stock sales are discussed in more detail in a later unit.

Investors can deduct the expenses related to earning investment income. These include expenses for investment counseling and advice, legal and accounting fees, and investment newsletters. Investment expenses are deductible on **Form 1040, Schedule A,** *Itemized Deductions,* as miscellaneous deductions to the extent that they exceed 2% of adjusted gross income.

A. Ordinary Dividends

A "dividend" is a distribution of income made by a corporation to its shareholders, out of net earnings and profits. Ordinary dividends are corporate distributions in cash (as opposed to property or stock shares). Amounts received as dividends are taxed as ordinary income. Dividends are passive income, so they are not subject to self-employment tax.

Any distribution *in excess* of earnings and profits (both current and accumulated) is considered a recovery of capital and is therefore not taxable.

Capital gains and losses from the sale of securities (stock sales and trades) are covered in a later unit. Distributions in excess of earnings and profits reduce the taxpayer's basis. Once basis is reduced to zero, any additional distributions are capital gain and are taxed as such.

Ordinary dividends are reported on **Schedule B**. If the total dividend income is $1,500 or less, all of the income can be reported directly on page one of IRS **Form 1040**. Qualified dividends are reported on **Schedule B**.

Qualified dividends are dividends that are eligible for a lower tax rate than other ordinary income. Ordinary dividends and qualified dividends are reported to the taxpayer on **Form 1099-DIV**.

Capital gain distributions are also reported on **Form 1099-DIV**. Capital gain distributions from a mutual fund are always reported as long-term capital gains on **Schedule B**.

B. Qualified Dividends

Qualified dividends are given preferred tax treatment.

Qualified dividends are dividends that meet specific criteria in order to receive the lower 0% or 15% maximum tax rate that applies to capital gains. Qualified dividends are reported to the taxpayer on **Form 1099-DIV**.

Qualified dividends are subject to a 15% tax rate if the taxpayer's regular tax rate is 25% or higher. If the taxpayer's regular tax rate is under 25%, the qualified dividends are subject to a zero percent rate (they are essentially non-taxable). In order for the dividends to qualify for the lower rate, all of the following requirements must be met:

- The dividends must have been paid by a U.S. corporation or a qualified foreign corporation.
- The taxpayer must meet the holding period. The taxpayer must have held the stock for more than 60 days during the 121-day period that begins 60 days before the ex-dividend date. The ex-dividend date is the date *following* the declaration of a dividend.

When trying to figure the holding period for qualified dividends, the taxpayer may count the number of days he held the stock AND include the day he disposed of the stock. The date the taxpayer *acquires* the stock is not included in the holding period.

Example: Israel bought 5,000 shares of Sundowner Corp. stock on July 9, 2011. Sundowner Corp. paid a cash dividend of 10 cents per share. The ex-dividend date was July 17, 2011. Israel's **Form 1099-DIV** from Sundowner Corp. shows $500 in dividends. However, Israel sold the 5,000 shares on August 12, 2011. Israel held his shares of Sundowner Corp. for only 34 days of the 121-day required holding period (from July 10, 2011 through August 12, 2011). The 121-day period began on May 18, 2011 (60 days before the ex-dividend date) and ended on September 15, 2011. Israel has no qualified dividends from Sundowner Corp. because he held the Sundowner stock for less than the required 61 days. He does not qualify for the preferred tax treatment that is given to qualified dividends.

Example: Tim bought 10,000 shares of Greenway Mutual Fund stock on July 9, 2011. Greenway Mutual Fund paid a cash dividend of 10 cents a share. The ex-dividend date was July 17, 2011. The Greenway Mutual Fund advises Tim that the portion of the dividend eligible to be treated as qualified dividends equals 2 cents per share. Tim's **Form 1099-DIV** from Greenway Mutual Fund shows total ordinary dividends of $1,000 and qualified dividends of $200. However, Tim sold the 10,000 shares on August 12, 2011. Tim has no qualified dividends from Greenway Mutual Fund because Tim held the Greenway Mutual Fund stock for less than 61 days.

C. Mutual Fund Distributions/Capital Gain Distributions

Taxpayers who receive mutual fund distributions during the year will also receive IRS **Form 1099-DIV** identifying the type of distribution received. A distribution may be an ordinary dividend, a qualified dividend, a capital gain distribution, an exempt-interest dividend, or a non-dividend distribution. Mutual fund distributions can be reported on **Form 1040** or **Form 1040A**. Taxpayers cannot use **Form 1040EZ** to report mutual fund distributions.

Mutual fund distributions are reported depending upon the character of the income source. Capital gain distributions from a mutual fund are *always* treated as long-term *regardless* of the actual period the mutual fund investment is held.

Distributions from a mutual fund investing in tax-exempt securities will be tax-exempt interest. In some cases, a mutual fund may pay tax-exempt interest dividends, paid from tax-exempt interest earned by the fund. Since the exempt-interest dividends keep their tax-exempt character, they are not taxable. Even so, the taxpayer must report them on his tax return. This is an information reporting requirement only, and does not convert tax-exempt interest to taxable interest. However, this income is generally a "tax preference item" and may be subject to the Alternative Minimum Tax.

The mutual fund will supply the taxpayer with a **Form 1099-INT** showing the tax-exempt interest dividends.

If a mutual fund or Real Estate Investment Trust (REIT) declares a dividend in October, November, or December payable to shareholders but actually pays the dividend during January of the following year, the shareholder is still considered to have received the dividend on December 31 of the prior tax year. The taxpayer must report the dividend in the year it was declared.

D. Stock Dividends

A stock dividend is simply a distribution of stock by a corporation to its own shareholders. This happens when a corporation chooses to distribute stock rather than money. A stock dividend is also called a "stock grant" or a "stock distribution."

Generally, a stock dividend is not a taxable event. This is because the receiver of the stock (a shareholder) is not actually receiving any money. A non-taxable stock dividend does not affect a taxpayer's income in the year of distribution. A stock dividend will affect a shareholder's basis in his existing stock. The basis of the stockholder's existing shares is divided to include the new stock. So a stock dividend will essentially reduce basis.

Example: Razor Ball Corporation agrees to a year-end stock dividend. Scarlett is a shareholder in Razor Ball. She currently owns 100 shares, and her basis in the shares is $50 each, for a total of $5,000. Scarlett is granted a stock dividend of 100 shares. After the dividend, Scarlett owns 200 shares. Her new basis in each individual share is $25 per share. However, her overall basis in the shares does not change (it is still $5,000). Scarlett would recognize income when she decided to sell the shares.

Example: Fun Time Corporation agrees to issue a year-end stock dividend. Dale owns 1,000 shares in Fun Time, and his current basis in the shares is $10 each, for a total of $10,000. In 2011, Dale is granted a stock dividend of 100 shares, but Fun Time gives all the shareholders the option of receiving cash instead of stock. Therefore, the stock dividend becomes a taxable event. Dale decides to take the stock instead of the cash. The fair market value of the stock at the time of the distribution is $15 per share. Dale must recognize $1,500 in income ($15 FMV X 100 shares=$1,500). After the dividend, Dale owns 1,100 shares. Dale's basis in the new shares is $15 per share. Dale's basis in the old shares remains the same.

Exception: If the taxpayer (shareholder) has the option to receive *cash instead of stock*, then the stock dividend becomes taxable. The recipient of the stock include the fair market value of the stock in his gross income. That amount becomes the basis of the new shares received.

Security Benefits

Generally, if the taxpayer *only* has Social Security income, the income is not taxable and a taxpayer is not required to file a tax return.

Social Security benefits *become* taxable once the taxpayer starts to receive other types of income, such as wages or interest income. This usually happens when a retired person who is receiving Social Security benefits also has a job. The taxable portion of Social Security benefits is never more than 85%. In most cases, the taxable portion is less than 50%.[31]

To better understand the thresholds, if a taxpayer is filing Single or HOH and combined income* is

- Between $25,000 and $34,000 the taxpayer may have to pay income tax on up to 50% of Social Security benefits.
- More than $34,000, up to 85% of Social Security benefits may be taxable.

If a taxpayer filed jointly and combined income* is

- Between $32,000 and $44,000, the taxpayer has to pay income tax on up to 50% of Social Security benefits.
- More than $44,000, up to 85% of Social Security benefits may be taxable.

If a taxpayer is filing MFS, he will probably pay taxes on his Social Security benefits.

> *Formula: The T/P adjusted gross income
> + Non-taxable interest
> + ½ of Social Security benefits
> = "combined income"

If the taxpayer also received other income in addition to Social Security, such as income from a job, the benefits will not be taxed unless modified adjusted gross income (MAGI) is more than the base amount for the taxpayer's filing status. If a taxpayer has any income *in addition* to Social Security, he may be required to file a tax return *even if* none of the Social Security benefits are taxable. Social Security benefits are reported to the taxpayer on **Form SSA-1099**. Benefits (income) from Railroad Retirement are reported on **Form RRB-1099**.

Figuring the taxable portion of Social Security benefits is a little tricky. To find out the taxable portion of Social Security, first compare the BASE AMOUNT (shown below) for the taxpayer's filing status with the total of:

- One-half of the Social Security benefits, plus
- All other income, including tax-exempt interest.

---

[31] Social Security income is NOT THE SAME thing as SSI (Supplemental Security Income). SSI is a federal income supplement program for the poor and the disabled. SSI is not taxable.

When making this comparison, do not reduce other income by any exclusions for:
- Interest from qualified U.S. savings bonds,
- Employer-provided adoption benefits,
- Foreign earned income or foreign housing, or
- Income earned by bona fide residents of American Samoa or Puerto Rico.

BASE AMOUNTS: SOCIAL SECURITY

A taxpayer's BASE AMOUNT for figuring the taxability of Social Security is:

$25,000 for Single, Head of Household, or Qualifying Widow(er),

$32,000 for Married Filing Jointly, or

$25,000 for Married Filing Separately (and lived *apart* from his spouse all year)

$-0- if the taxpayer is MFS (if lived with spouse at any time during the tax year)

How to Figure the Taxability of Social Security

To figure out what percentages of a taxpayer's Social Security benefits are taxable, the taxpayer must first determine the sum of modified AGI (MAGI) and add one-half of the Social Security benefits. After doing this calculation on a worksheet, if the amount is less than the "base amount," then none of the Social Security is taxable.

Example: Bo and Marie are both over 65. They file jointly and they both received Social Security benefits during the year. At the end of the year, Bo received a **Form SSA-1099** showing net benefits of $7,500. Marie received a **Form SSA-1099** showing net benefits of $3,500. Bo also received wages of $20,000 and interest income of $500. Bo did not have any tax-exempt interest.

1. Total Social Security benefits: $11,000
2. Enter one-half of SS: $5,500
3. Enter taxable interest and wages: $20,500
4. Add ($5,500 + $20,500): $26,000

Bo and Marie's benefits are not taxable for 2011 because their income is not more than the base amount ($32,000) for Married Filing Jointly.

Taxable State Income Tax Refunds

State income tax refunds are reportable as taxable income in the year received only if the taxpayer itemized deductions in the prior year. The state should send **Form 1099-G**, *Certain Government Payments*, by January 31. The IRS also will receive a copy of the **Form 1099-G.**

Example: Wally claimed the standard deduction on last year's tax return and received a state tax refund of $600. The state tax refund is not taxable. Only taxpayers who itemize deductions and receive a state or local refund in the prior year are required to include the state tax refund in their taxable income.

Rents and Royalties

Income from rents and royalties must be included in gross income. Rental income is income from the use (or occupation) of property (such as income from a rental home). Income from royalties includes income from copyrights, trademarks, and franchises. Rental and royalty income is reported on **Schedule E**. Rental and royalty income will be covered at length in a later unit.

Non-taxable Income

Some types of income are non-taxable. You need to understand the most common types of non-taxable income for the Enrolled Agent exam. Some non-taxable income must be reported to the IRS, and some does not. Some common types of non-taxable income are covered below.

Veterans' Benefits

Veterans' benefits are non-taxable. Amounts paid by the Department of Veterans Affairs to a veteran or his family are non-taxable if they are for education, training, disability compensation, work therapy, dependent care assistance, or other benefits or pension payments given to the veteran because of disability.

Workers' Compensation

Workers' compensation is not taxable income if it is received because of an occupational injury. However, disability benefits paid by an employer (also called "sick pay") are taxable to the employee. Long-term disability income payments are included in gross income and are taxable to the employee.

Life Insurance Proceeds

Proceeds from life insurance are not taxable to the recipient. Consequently, life insurance premiums are not deductible by the payor, but an employer may choose to provide employees with life insurance as a fringe benefit and deduct the cost. However, a private individual, such as a sole proprietor purchasing life insurance for himself, may not deduct the premiums.

Sometimes, a taxpayer will choose to receive life insurance in installments, rather than a lump sum. In this case, part of the installment usually includes interest income. If a taxpayer receives life insurance proceeds in installments, he can exclude part of each installment from his income. To determine the excluded part, divide the amount held by the insurance company (generally the total lump sum payable at the death of the insured person) by the number of installments to be paid. Include anything over this excluded part as interest income.

> **Example:** Libby's brother died in 2011, and she is the beneficiary of his life insurance. The face amount of the policy is $75,000 and, as beneficiary, Libby chooses to receive 120 monthly installments of $1,000 each. The excluded part of each installment is $625 ($75,000 ÷ 120), or $7,500 for an entire year. The rest of each payment, $375 a month (or $4,500 for an entire year), is interest income to Libby.

Compensatory Damages and Court Settlements

Compensatory damages for personal physical injury or physical sickness are not taxable income, whether they are from a settlement or from an actual court award.

> **Example:** Felix was injured in a car accident in 2011. His legs were broken and he suffered other serious physical injuries. He received a settlement from the insurance company for his injuries totaling $950,000. This is non-taxable income, because it is payment for a physical injury.

Compensatory damages for "emotional distress" are usually taxable. Emotional distress itself is not a physical injury. If the emotional distress is due to unlawful discrimination or injury to reputation, the taxpayer must include the damages in taxable income, except for any damages received for medical care due to that emotional distress.

> **Example:** Kristina recently won a court award for emotional distress due to unlawful discrimination. Kristina was hospitalized for a nervous breakdown due to the emotional distress. She received damages of $100,000, including $20,000 to refund the cost of her medical care due to the nervous breakdown. In this case, $80,000 ($100,000 - $20,000) would be considered a taxable court award. The $20,000 of damages for her medical care would be non-taxable.

Punitive damages are taxable income. It does not matter if they relate to a physical injury or physical sickness. Court awards for lost wages are always taxable as ordinary income.

Non-taxable Types of Interest Income

There are numerous examples of interest income that are not taxable to the recipient.

I. Municipal Bonds

A taxpayer may exclude interest income on municipal or "muni" bonds, which are debt obligations by state and local governments. Taxpayers must still report the interest on their income tax returns, but it is not taxable. Although a muni bond is generally exempt from federal income tax, it is often still taxable at the state level.

II. Frozen Deposits

A taxpayer may EXCLUDE interest income on frozen deposits. A deposit is considered frozen if, at the end of the year, the taxpayer cannot withdraw any part of the deposit because:

- The financial institution is bankrupt or insolvent, or
- The state where the institution is located has placed limits on withdrawals because other financial institutions in the state are bankrupt or insolvent.

> **Example:** Creed earned $2,500 in interest at Belly-Up Bank in 2011. The bank became insolvent at the end of 2011 and all of Creed's money was frozen. He was unable to access any of his accounts until the following year. Creed does not have to recognize the income as taxable in 2011, because the interest qualified as a frozen deposit. Creed would recognize the income in 2012, when the funds finally became available for him to withdraw and use. Creed must still report the income on his 2011 tax return, but he may mark it as a "frozen deposit" and therefore not subject to income tax in the current tax year.

III. Mutual Funds Investing in Tax-Exempt Securities

Distributions from a fund investing in tax-exempt securities will be tax-exempt interest. Tax exempt interest must be reported on **Form 1040,** (line 8b).

IV. Education Savings Bond Interest Exclusion

Taxpayers may choose to purchase and then eventually redeem Series EE bonds on a tax-free basis to pay college expenses. The expenses must be for the taxpayer, the taxpayer's spouse, or the taxpayer's dependents.

For 2011, the amount of the interest exclusion is phased out for Married Filing Jointly taxpayers or Qualifying Widow(er) taxpayers whose modified AGI is between $106,650 and $136,650. If the modified AGI is $136,650 or more, no deduction is allowed.

> **Caution:** Married taxpayers who file separately do not qualify for the educational savings bond interest exclusion.

For Single and Head of Household filing statuses, the interest exclusion is phased out for taxpayers whose modified AGI is between $71,100 and $86,100. If the modified AGI is $86,100 or more, no deduction is allowed.

The exclusion is calculated and reported on IRS **Form 8815,** *Exclusion of Interest from Series EE and I U.S. Savings Bonds.* There are certain rules that must be followed in order for the educational exclusion to qualify:

- The bonds must be purchased by the owner. The bonds cannot be a gift.

- The money received on redemption must be used for tuition and fees. The taxpayer cannot use tax-exempt bond proceeds for tuition and also attempt to take educational credits (such as the Lifetime Learning Credit) for the same amount. No "double dipping" is allowed.
- Couples who file "Married Filing Separately" tax returns do not qualify for the educational savings bond exclusion.
- The total interest received may *only* be excluded if the combined amounts of the principal and the interest received *do not exceed* the taxpayer's qualified educational expenses.

Example: In February 2011, Daniel and Blythe, a married couple, cash a qualified Series EE savings bond they bought ten years ago. They receive proceeds of $8,124, representing principal of $5,000 and interest of $3,124. In 2011, they paid $4,000 of their daughter's college tuition. They are not claiming an education credit for that amount, and their daughter does not have any tax-free educational assistance (scholarships or grants). Daniel and Blythe can exclude $1,538 ($3,124 × ($4,000 ÷ $8,124)) of interest in 2011. They must pay tax on the remaining $1,586 ($3,124 − $1,538) interest, since not all the interest was used for qualified tuition costs.

Example: In 2011, Denise redeems her Series EE Bonds and receives a total of $4,000. Of that amount, $1,000 is interest income and the remainder is the return of principal ($3,000). Denise's qualified educational expenses (tuition and fees) are $5,800. Therefore, all of the interest earned on her Series EE Bonds qualifies for tax-exempt treatment.

If the taxpayer does not use the bonds for educational expenses, the interest income is taxable. When taxpayers cash in their savings bonds, they should receive a **Form 1099-INT** from the bank. Most taxpayers report the total interest when they cash the bonds. Some taxpayers also choose to report savings bond interest as it accrues. Either method is acceptable.

Foreign Earned Income Exclusion

Generally, the income of U.S. citizens is taxed even if the income is earned outside the United States. Foreign earned income is income received for services performed in a foreign country while the taxpayer's tax home is ALSO in a foreign country. The taxpayer must pass one of two tests in order to claim the foreign earned income exclusion.

- Test #1: "Bona Fide Residence Test," OR
- Test #2: The "Physical Presence" Test.

Bona Fide Residence Test: A U.S. citizen (or U.S. resident alien) who is a bona fide resident of a foreign country for an uninterrupted period that includes an entire tax year.

The Physical Presence Test: A U.S. citizen (or U.S. resident alien) who is physically present in a foreign country or countries for at least 330 full days during 12 consecutive months. A taxpayer may qualify under the physical presence test, and the income may span over a period of multiple tax years. If so, the taxpayer must prorate the foreign earned income exclusion based on the number of days spent in the foreign country.

For 2011, the maximum foreign earned income exclusion is $92,900. If the taxpayer is Married Filing Jointly and both individuals live and work abroad, both taxpayers can choose to claim the foreign earned income exclusion.

> **Example:** Brenda earned $80,000 while employed overseas, and she qualifies for the foreign earned income exclusion. Brenda also has $6,000 in work-related expenses. Brenda cannot deduct any of her expenses, because she is already excluding all of her income from taxation by taking the foreign earned income exclusion.

> **Example:** Leila was a bona fide resident of China for all of 2011. In 2011, Leila was paid $103,400 for her work in China. She can exclude $92,900 of the amount she was paid.

It does not matter whether the income is paid by a U.S. employer or a foreign employer.

The foreign earned income exclusion is figured using **Form 2555**, *Foreign Earned Income*, which must be attached to Form 1040. Once the choice is made to exclude foreign earned income, that choice remains in effect for the year the election is made and all later years, unless revoked.

Non-resident aliens do not qualify for the foreign earned income exclusion. A taxpayer must be either a U.S. citizen or a legal resident alien of the United States who lives and works abroad and who meets certain other qualifications to exclude a specific amount of his foreign earned income.

The exclusion **does not** apply to the wages and salaries of members of the Armed Forces and civilian employees of the U.S. government.

Foreign Tax Credit

Foreign tax credits allow U.S. taxpayers to avoid or reduce double taxation. The "foreign tax credit" is not the same as the foreign earned income exclusion. A taxpayer may claim either the foreign tax credit OR a deduction for foreign taxes paid each year. A taxpayer cannot take the foreign tax credit on income that has already been excluded from taxation by the foreign earned income exclusion.

Generally, the following four tests must be met for any foreign tax to qualify for the credit:

- The tax must be imposed on the taxpayer.
- The taxpayer must have paid or accrued the tax.
- The tax must be the legal and actual foreign tax liability.

- The tax must be an income tax.

A taxpayer can choose to alternate years, choosing to take a credit in one year and a deduction in the next year. The taxpayer can even change his credit to a deduction and vice versa by amending his tax return. To take the foreign tax credit, taxpayers complete **Form 1116**, *Foreign Tax Credit*.

> **Example:** Greer is a 3% shareholder of a German corporation. She received a $1,000 refund of the tax paid to Germany by the corporation on the earnings distributed to her as a dividend. The German government imposes a 15% withholding tax ($150) on the refund she received. Greer received a net check for $850. She includes $1,000 in her income, and the $150 of tax withheld is a qualified foreign tax and may be claimed as a credit.

The foreign tax credit cannot be more than the taxpayer's total U.S. tax liability multiplied by a fraction. The limit on this credit is figured by calculating the total tax liability multiplied by a fraction made up of total foreign income divided by total income from foreign and U.S. sources (see example next).

> **Example:** Harold's total tax liability is $1,000. In 2011, he made $20,000 from foreign-based investments, along with another $60,000 from U.S. sources. To figure the limit on the foreign tax credit, Harold must take his total foreign income ($20,000) and divide it by the total income from all sources ($20,000 + $60,000). This gives Harold a fraction of .25. Multiply this by his total tax liability ($1,000 x .25 = $250). This is the limit on his foreign tax credit.
>
> **(Foreign Source Taxable Income ÷ Worldwide Taxable Income) X (U.S. Income Tax before Credit = FTC Limitation.)**

Clergy: Special Rules

There are special rules regarding the taxation of clergy members. "Ministers" or "clergy" are individuals who are ordained, commissioned, or licensed by a religious body or church denomination. They are given the authority to conduct religious worship, perform religious functions, and administer ordinances or sacraments according to the prescribed tenets and practices of that church.

Clergy members must include offerings and fees received for marriages, baptisms, and funerals as part of their income. Generally a clergy member's salary is reported on IRS Form W-2. Additional payments for services are reported on the clergy member's Schedule C.

Minister's Housing Allowance

A minister's housing allowance (sometimes called a "parsonage" allowance or a rental allowance) is excludable from gross income for income tax purposes, but not for self-employment tax purposes. A minister who receives a housing allowance may exclude the allowance from gross income to the extent it is used to pay expenses in providing a home.

The exclusion for minister's housing is limited to:
- The lesser of the fair market rental value (including utilities, etc.), or
- The actual amount used to provide a home.

The housing allowance cannot exceed reasonable pay. The payments must be used for housing in the year they are received by the minister.

> **Example:** William is an ordained minister. He received $32,000 in salary in 2011. He also received an additional $4,000 for performing marriages and baptisms. His housing allowance was $500 per month, for a total of $6,000 per year. William must report the $32,000 as wages, $4,000 as self-employment income, and $6,000 as the housing allowance subject only to self-employment tax, not income tax. Report this "SE taxable income" on **Schedule SE.**

Both salary and housing allowances must be included in income for the purpose of determining self-employment tax.

> **Example:** Abby is a full-time ordained minister at Waterfront Presbyterian Church. The church allows her to use a cottage that has a rental value of $5,000. The church also pays Abby a salary of $12,000. Her income for self-employment tax purposes is $17,000 ($5,000 + $12,000 salary). Ministers must include the FMV of a home on Schedule SE.

> **Example:** Father Benicio is an ordained priest at the local Catholic Church. His annual salary is $26,000, and he also receives a $10,000 housing allowance. His housing costs for the year are $14,000. Therefore, Benicio's self-employment income is $36,000 ($26,000 salary + $10,000 housing allowance). But only his base salary ($26,000) is subject to income tax, because his actual housing expenses are more than his housing allowance.

Vow of Poverty

If a minister or other individual (nun, monk, etc.) is a member of a religious order who has taken a vow of poverty, the individual is exempt from paying SE tax on his earnings for qualified services. For income tax purposes, the earnings are tax-free, because the earnings are considered the income of the religious order, rather than of the individual.

Exemption from Social Security

A minister can request an exemption from self–employment tax for religious reasons. To request the exemption, ministers must file **Form 4361,** *Application for Exemption from Self-Employment Tax for Use by Ministers, Members of Religious Orders, and Christian Science Practitioners*, with the IRS.

Summary: Taxable vs. Non-taxable Income

TAXABLE INCOME	NON-TAXABLE INCOME
Wages, salaries, tips, bonuses, vacation pay, severance pay, commissions	Gifts and inheritances
Interest	Life insurance proceeds
Unemployment compensation	Child support
Dividends	Certain veterans' benefits
Strike benefits	Interest on muni bonds (state and local bonds)
Bank "gifts" for opening accounts	Employer-provided fringe benefits such as health insurance
Cancellation of debt (unless excludable)	Welfare payments, food stamps, other forms of public assistance
Alimony	Compensation or court awards for physical injury or illness
Gains from sales of property, stocks and bonds, stock options, etc.	Workers' compensation
Social Security benefits (above the base amount)	Combat pay
Most court awards or damages	Qualified scholarships, employer-provided educational assistance, and interest on U.S. Savings bonds used to pay college expenses
Barter income	Canceled debt from a primary residence, bankruptcy, or insolvency
Prizes, awards, gambling winnings	Foreign earned income (if qualifying for the exclusion)

Earned Income	Unearned Income	Can be variable
Salaries	Dividends	Business profits
Wages	Interest	Partnership income
Commissions	Capital gains	Royalties
Bonuses	Gambling winnings	Rents
Professional fees	Annuities	Scholarships
Vacation pay	Alimony	Fellowships
Tips	Social Security	Fringe benefits
Self-employment income	Pensions	Court/lawsuit proceeds

Unit 6: Questions

1. Hank received Social Security in 2011 totaling $11,724. Also in 2011, Hank sold all of his stock and moved into senior housing. He received $31,896 of taxable income from the sale of the stock. What is the maximum taxable amount of Hank's Social Security benefits?

A. $31,896.
B. $20,172.
C. $9,965.
D. Not enough information provided.

The answer is C. The maximum amount that can ever be taxable on the net Social Security benefits is 85% or $9,965. ###

2. Bruce and Ann are married and file jointly. They have three **Forms 1099-INT:**
- Epping National Bank, $62 (Bruce)
- Epping Credit Union, $178 (Ann)
- Breton Savings and Loan, $760 (Ann)

How much interest income should they report on **Schedule B (Form 1040)**?

A. None.
B. $760.
C. $240.
D. $1,000.

The answer is A. Schedule B is not used to report regular interest totaling $1,500 or less. Instead, these amounts can be reported directly on the taxpayer's **Form 1040.** ###

3. Which of the following types of income are exempt from federal tax?

A. Interest income.
B. Canceled debt.
C. Tips.
D. Inheritances.

The answer is D. Of the types of income listed here, only inheritances are exempt from federal taxes. ###

4. Ryan received a capital gain distribution in the amount of $75 and dividend income in the amount of $150, both from his mutual fund. Which of the following is correct?

A. Ryan may report both the capital gain distribution and the dividend directly on **Form 1040**.
B. Ryan must report the dividend on **Schedule B** and the capital gain distribution on **Schedule D**.
C. Ryan can report a capital gain distribution and the dividend on **Schedule B**.
D. Ryan can use **Schedule D** to report both amounts.

The answer is A. Ryan may report both of these amounts on his **Form 1040**. Dividend income of $1,500 or less may be reported on page 1 of **Form 1040 (or 1040A)**. He does not need to use **Schedule B** to report the dividend income. Ryan also meets the requirements for reporting the capital gain distribution directly on **Form 1040 (or Form 1040A)**, since the distribution is from a mutual fund. He is not required to use **Schedule D** to report the capital gain distribution.

5. Under what circumstances must a person report taxable income?
A. Always.
B. Always, unless the income is only from interest.
C. Always, unless the income is so small that reporting it is not required by law.
D. Always, unless the person is identified as a dependent on someone else's tax return.

The answer is C. All taxable income must be reported on a tax return, unless the amount is so small that the individual is not legally required to file a return. Filing thresholds depend on a taxpayer's marital status, age, and dependency status. ###

6. Which of the following types of income are taxable?

A. Credit union dividends.
B. Veterans' life insurance dividends.
C. Workers' compensation.
D. Child support.

The answer is A. Credit union dividends are considered interest income and are subject to federal income tax. ###

7. Toni owns a savings bond, which she purchased as an investment to help pay for her daughter's education. Toni redeems the bond in 2011 and immediately uses all the funds to pay for her daughter Tyler's college tuition. The bond's interest is reported on _____.

A. Toni's tax return and is 100% taxable.
B. Tyler's tax return and is 100% taxable.
C. Toni's tax return and is 100% exempt from taxes.
D. Nothing. It is not taxable and not required to be reported, so long as Toni uses all the funds to pay for qualified higher education costs.

The answer is C. As the buyer and owner of the bond, Toni reports the interest on her tax return, but excludes the interest from her income because she paid for qualified higher education expenses the same year.###

8. Joyce and Craig, a married couple, received $200 in interest from bonds issued by the State of Illinois. How should they report this on their **Form 1040?**

A. It must be reported as interest income, and it is 100% taxable.
B. It must be reported, but it is not taxable income.
C. They do not have to report it.
D. None of the above.

The answer is B. The interest is tax-exempt municipal bond interest (state and local bonds). Although it is not taxable, it must be reported on the taxpayer's return. ###

9. Leona received the following income: wages, interest, child support, alimony, inheritance, workers' compensation, and lottery winnings. Determine what amount of Leona's income is taxable.

Leona's Income:

SOURCE	Amounts
Wages	$13,000
Interest	$15
Child support	$6,000
Alimony	$2,000
Inheritance	$10,000
Workers' compensation	$1,000
Lottery winnings	$5,000

A. $13,015
B. $16,015
C. $20,015
D. $30,015

The answer is C. The wages, interest, alimony, and lottery winnings are taxable income and will appear on Leona's tax return ($13,000 + $15 + $2,000 + $5,000 = $20,015). Child support, inheritances, and workers' compensation are non-taxable income and will not appear on Leona's tax return. ###

10. Which of the following tip income is exempt from federal income tax?
A. Tips of less than $20 per month.
B. Non-cash tips.
C. Tips not reported to the employer.
D. All tips are taxable.

The answer is D. All tip income is subject to federal income tax, whether it is cash or non-cash. Individuals who receive less than $20 per month in tips while working one job do not have to report their tip income to their employer, but the income is still subject to federal income tax and must be reported on the taxpayer's **Form 1040.**###

11. Which of the following statements is TRUE?

A. Food servers do not need to report tips as taxable income.
B. Food servers are required to report tips on their tax return, even if the amounts have not been reported to the employer.
C. Tips received that total less than $20 a month are non-taxable.
D. Tips received that total less than $20 a month are subject to income tax, Social Security tax, and Medicare tax, just like regular wages.

The answer is B. All tips are taxable income and must be reported on the tax return, even if they have not been reported to the employer. Tips totaling less than $20 a month are not taxable for FICA tax (Social Security and Medicare tax) purposes. Tips under $20 a month do not need to be reported to an employer, but these amounts are still subject to regular income tax. ####

12. Tom has worked for Parkway Construction for three years. In November 2011, the owner of Parkway files for bankruptcy and leaves the country abruptly. Tom never received his **Form W-2**. What form may Tom use in order to file his 2011 tax return?

A: Form W-9.
B: Form 1099-MISC.
C: Form 4852.
D: Form W-3.

The answer is C. Tom may use IRS **Form 4852** in order to estimate the amounts on **Form W-2**, using his earning statement or some other similar document. Even if a taxpayer has not received a **Form W-2**, he must still file a tax return. The taxpayer may use a substitute W-2 form, **Form 4852**, to file with the IRS. ###

13. Salvador is a member of the armed forces and served in a combat zone from January 1 to September 2 of 2011. He returned to the United States and received his regular duty pay for the remainder of the year. How many months of income are taxable?

A. Zero. All the income is tax-free.
B. Three months are subject to tax.
C. Four months are subject to tax.
D. All twelve months are subject to income tax.

The answer is B. Since Salvador served for a few days in September, all the income in September is excluded as combat pay. If a taxpayer serves in a combat zone as an enlisted person for any part of a month, all of his pay received for military service that month is excluded from gross income. ###

14. Which form do banks use to report mutual fund distributions to a taxpayer?

A. Form 1099-DIV.
B. Schedule B.
C. Form 1099-Misc.
D. Form W-4.

The answer is A. Taxpayers who receive mutual fund distributions during the year will also receive a **Form 1099-DIV** identifying the type of distribution received. A mutual fund distribution may be an ordinary dividend, a qualified dividend, a capital gain distribution, an exempt-interest dividend, or a non-dividend distribution. ###

15. Which form is used by state taxing agencies to report state income tax refunds paid to a taxpayer?

A. Form 1099-MISC.
B. Form 1099-G.
C. Form 1098.
D. Form W-3.

The answer is B. State income tax refunds are reported to the taxpayer on Form 1099-G, *Certain Government Payments.* ###

16. Sven and Samantha file jointly in 2011. They received the following income for 2011. How much income should be reported on their 2011 joint tax return?
1. W-2 income for Samantha for wages of $40,000.
2. W-2 for Samantha for $2,000, the value of a trip she won to the Bahamas. She never went on the trip. But she is planning to take the trip in 2011.
3. Court settlement of $10,000 paid to Sven from a car accident for serious injuries he suffered.
4. $4,000 child support for Samantha's son from a previous marriage.

A. $40,000.
B. $42,000.
C. $46,000.
D. $52,000.

The answer is B. The wages earned and prize won by Samantha should be included on the joint return, and the accident settlement should be excluded from income. Samantha must recognize the prize, because even though she did not take the trip, she had constructive receipt of the winnings. Child support is not taxable. The answer is $42,000 ($40,000 wages + $2,000 prize). ###

17. A customer at a casino left a $10 poker chip as a tip for Steve, who is a hotel employee. Steve did not have any other tip income for the month. What is Steve's reporting requirement for this tip?

A. The poker chip is not legal tender, and is therefore not taxable.
B. Steve must report the tip income on his return at its fair market value, which would be $10.
C. Steve should report this tip income to his employer, and it will be taxed as wages on his Form W-2.
D. The tip is a gift, and therefore not taxable income.

The answer is B. Although this is not actual money, it is still taxable at its fair market value, which would be $10. The tip is not reportable to Steve's employer, since he earned less than $20 of tip income during the month. He should report the tip income on his return, subject to regular income tax. ###

18. Sandy received the following income in 2011:

1. Wages: $70,000.
2. Gambling winnings: $500 (Gambling losses, $1,000).
3. Dependent care benefits through her employer: $5,000.
4. Employer-provided parking pass: $220 per month.

Sandy had only $4,000 in qualified daycare expenses. How much gross income must she report on her tax return?

A. $70,000.
B. $70,500.
C. $71,500.
D. $73,300.

The answer is C. Dependent care assistance programs are not taxable, but only up to the amount of qualified expenses. Since Sandy received $5,000, but only had $4,000 in actual day care expenses, $1,000 is taxable to Sandy. The parking pass is an excluded benefit. Both the wages and gambling winnings must be included in the gross income total of $71,500 ($70,000 + $500 + $1,000). The gambling losses are not deductible from the net. Gambling losses are only allowable up to gambling winnings, and even then, only as an itemized deduction on **Schedule A.** ###

19. Ginny had the following income in 2011:

Social Security income: $14,000.
Interest income: $125.
Gambling winnings: $1,000.
Gambling losses: $2,000.
Settlement for a bodily injury: $20,000.
Child support payments: $13,000.
Food stamp benefits: $5,000.

How much income must Ginny report on her tax return?

A. $14,000.
B. $14,125.
C. $15,125.
D. $30,000.
E. $48,000.

The answer is C. The Social Security income, gambling income, and interest income must all be reported. The accident settlement and the child support are not taxable. Food stamps and welfare payments also are not taxable income. The gambling losses do not affect the reporting of the gambling income. Gambling losses are a deduction on Schedule A, should Ginny choose to itemize. If Ginny does not itemize, the gambling losses are not deductible. ###

20. Brandi, a flight attendant, received wages of $30,000 in 2011. The airline provided transportation on a standby basis, at no charge, from her home in Detroit to the airline's hub in Chicago. The fair market value of the commuting flights was $5,000. Also in 2011, Brandi received reimbursements under an accountable plan of $10,000 for overnight travel, but only spent $6,000. The excess was returned to Brandi's employer. Brandi became injured on the job in November of the current year and received workers' compensation of $4,000. What amount must Brandi include in gross income on her current year tax return?

A. $30,000.
B. $34,000.
C. $35,000.
D. $37,000.

The answer is A. Brandi only has to include her wages in her current year return. The free flights offered on standby to airline personnel are considered a non-taxable fringe benefit. Reim-Reimbursements under an accountable plan and amounts paid for workers' compensation are non-taxable. Since Brandi returned the unspent amounts to her employer, the travel reimbursements qualify under an accountable plan, and the amounts spent are not taxable to her. ###

21. Debby broke her leg in a car accident in 2011 and was unable to work for three months. She received an accident settlement of $13,000 from the car insurance company. During this time she also received $7,500 in sick pay from her employer. In addition, she received $5,000 from her personally purchased accident policy. How much of this income is taxable income to Debby?

A. $5,000.
B. $7,500.
C. $12,500.
D. $18,000.

The answer is B. Only Debby's sick pay is taxable as wages. Sick pay from an employer is taxable like wages (similar to vacation pay), and is therefore includable in Debby's gross income. If a taxpayer pays the full cost of an accident insurance plan, the benefits for personal injury or illness are not includable in income. If the employer pays the cost of an accident insurance plan, then the amounts are taxable to an employee. ###

22. Income was "constructively received" in 2011 in each of the following situations EXCEPT:

A. Wages were deposited in the taxpayer's bank account on December 26, 2011, but were not withdrawn by the taxpayer until January 3, 2012.
B. A taxpayer was informed his check for services rendered was available on December 15, 2011. The taxpayer did not pick up the check until January 30, 2012.
C. A taxpayer received a check by mail on December 31, 2011, but could not deposit the check until January 5, 2012.
D. A taxpayer's home was sold on December 28, 2011. The payment was not received by the taxpayer until January 2, 2012 when the escrow company completed the transaction and released the funds.

The answer is D. Constructive receipt does not require the taxpayer to have physical possession of the income. However, income is not considered constructively received if the taxpayer cannot access the funds because of restrictions. Since the taxpayer's control of the receipt of the funds in the escrow account was substantially limited until the transaction had closed, the taxpayer did not constructively receive the income until the closing of the transaction in the following year. ###

23. Luke and Barbie filed a joint return for 2011. Luke received $10,000 in Social Security benefits and Barbie received $16,000. No other income was received. What part of their Social Security benefits will be taxable for 2011?

A. $0.
B. $6,000.
C. $24,000.
D. $12,000.

The answer is A. If the only income received by the taxpayer is Social Security, the benefits generally are not taxable and the taxpayer probably does not have to file a return. If the taxpayer has additional income, he may have to file a return even if none of the Social Security benefits are taxable. ###

24. James is a self-employed attorney who performs legal services for a client, a small corporation. The corporation gives James 100 shares of its stock as payment for his services. The stock is valued at $2,000. Which of the following statements is true?

A. James does not have to include this transaction on his tax return.
B. James should report the income when he sells the stock.
C. The stock is taxable to James at its fair market value.
D. None of the above.

The answer is C. James must include the fair market value (FMV) of the shares in his gross income on Schedule C (Form 1040) in the year he receives them. The income would be considered payment for services he provided to his client, the corporation. ###

25. Rob owns a business that has a $10,000 profit in 2011. His wife, Cecilia, has a business loss of $12,000 for 2011. They both file **Schedule C** to report their self-employment income. Which of the following statements is true?

A. On their joint return, they will not have to pay self-employment tax because the losses from Cecilia's business offset Rob's income.
B. The spouses can file MFS and offset each other's self-employment tax.
C. Rob must pay self-employment tax on $10,000, regardless of his wife's losses.
D. If they choose to file separate returns, they may split the profits and losses equally between their two businesses.

The answer is C. Rob must pay self-employment tax on $10,000, regardless of how he and Cecilia choose to file. Taxpayers cannot combine a spouse's income or loss to determine their individual earnings subject to SE tax. However, if a taxpayer has more than one business, then he must combine the net profit or loss from each to determine the total earnings subject to SE tax. ###

26. Brent, a plastic surgeon, agreed to exchange services with a handyman. Brent removed a mole and the handyman fixed Brent's running toilet in his medical office. Mole removal is generally charged at $200, and the handyman generally charges $150 to fix a toilet. They agreed in advance that the fee would be $150. Neither exchanged actual cash. How much income must Brent recognize for this barter transaction?

A. $50.
B. $150.
C. $200.
D. $250.

The answer is B. Brent must include $150 in income. He may also deduct the cost of the repair ($150) if it qualifies as a business expense. If a taxpayer exchanges services with another person and both have agreed ahead of time on the value of those services, that value will be accepted as fair market value unless the value can be shown to be otherwise. ###

27. Ed received $32,000 in wages from his employer in 2011. He also won a prize from his employer because he helped develop a handbook for new employees. The prize was free lawn care service for a year, valued at $600. Ed also received $7,000 in child support and $2,000 in alimony from his ex-wife. Ed has full custody of his children. What is Ed's taxable income (before deductions and adjustments) for tax year 2011?

A. $32,000.
B. $32,600.
C. $34,600.
D. $39,600.

The answer is C. The wages and prize are both taxable income. Child support is not taxable to the receiver, nor deductible by the payor. The alimony is taxable to Ed and deductible by his ex-wife. The answer is figured as follows: ($32,000 + $600 + $2,000) = $34,600. ###

28. Scott opened a savings account at his local bank and deposited $800. The account earns $20 interest in 2011. Scott also received a $15 calculator as a gift for opening the account. How much interest income must Scott report on his IRS **Form 1040?**

A. $15.
B. $20.
C. $35.
D. $800.

The answer is C. If no other interest is credited to Scott during the year, the form 1099-INT he receives will show $35 interest for the year. Scott must report the fair market value of the calculator on his return as interest income. A gift for opening a bank account is taxed as interest income. ###

29. Jan owns and operates a store in the downtown shopping mall. She reports her income and expenses as a sole proprietor on Schedule C. Jan is having financial difficulties and cannot pay all of her debts. In 2011, one of the banks that she borrowed money from in order to start her business cancels her debt. Jan is not insolvent. She had a loan balance of $5,000 when the debt was canceled. Which of the following statements is true?

A. Jan does not have to report the forgiveness of the debt as income.
B. Jan must report the $5,000 debt cancellation on **Schedule A.**
C. Jan must report the $5,000 debt cancellation as business income on **Schedule C.**
D. Jan must report the $5,000 of canceled debt as a long-term gain on **Schedule D.**

The answer is C. Canceled debt that is related to business income must be included on a taxpayer's **Schedule C** as business income. Jan must report the canceled amount on **Schedule C** if the debt was incurred in a business. ###

30. Fran won $5,000 playing slot machines in Reno, Nevada. How will these winnings be reported to Fran?

A. Form 1099-G.
B. Form 1099-MISC.
C. Form W-2.
D. Form W-2G.

The answer is D. Form W-2G is used to report a taxpayer's income and withholding related to gambling. ###

31. During the current year, Andrew received interest income of $300 from municipal bonds and $200 in interest from a Certificate of Deposit (CD). Which of the following statements is TRUE?

A. Andrew is required to report the $500 in interest income on his income tax return, but none of the interest is taxable.
B. Andrew is NOT required to report any of the income on his tax return.
C. Andrew is required to report the total interest ($500) on his income tax return. The CD interest is taxable, but the muni bond interest is not.
D. Andrew is required to report only $200 of CD interest on his income tax return.

The answer is C. Under present federal income tax law, the interest income received from investing in municipal bonds is free from federal income taxes. However, the taxpayer is required to show any tax-exempt interest received on his tax return. This is an informational reporting requirement only. It does not change tax-exempt interest to taxable interest. The interest from the Certificate of Deposit ($200) is taxable and must be reported as interest income. ###

32. Kent invested in a mutual fund in 2011. The fund declared a dividend, and Kent earned $19. He did not get a **Form 1099-DIV** for the amount, and he did not withdraw the money from his mutual fund. Kent pulled the money out of his mutual fund on January 2, 2012. Which of the following statements is TRUE?

A. This dividend is not reportable in 2011 because Kent didn't receive the money yet.
B. This dividend is not reportable in 2011 because Kent didn't receive a **1099-DIV.**
C. This dividend must be reported in 2011.
D. This dividend is taxable and reportable in 2012.

The answer is C. Kent earned the money in 2011, and whether or not he received a 1099 for the income is irrelevant. Mutual fund dividends are taxable in the year declared regardless of whether the taxpayer withdraws the money or reinvests it. The money was constructively earned and available for withdrawal in 2011, so Kent must report the earnings in 2011. ###

33. Rashid owns shares in a Real Estate Investment Trust (REIT). The trust declares a dividend on October 25, 2011. However, the dividend is not actually paid to shareholders until January 3, 2012. How should Rashid report his earnings?

A. Rashid is not required to report this income, because income from a REIT is non-taxable.
B. Rashid must report this income in 2011.
C. Rashid must report this income in 2012.
D. Rashid is required to report this income as a capital gain from the sale of securities.

The answer is B. Rashid must report the dividend in 2011, the year it was declared. If a mutual fund or Real Estate Investment Trust (REIT) declares a dividend in October, November, or December but actually pays the dividend during January of the next calendar year, the shareholder is still considered to have received the dividend on December 31 of the prior tax year. ###

34. Willy's bank became insolvent in 2011. One hundred dollars in interest was credited to Willy's frozen bank account during the year. Willy withdrew $80, but could not withdraw any more as of the end of the year. Willy's **1099-INT** showed $100 in interest income. Which of the following is true?

A. Willy's tax return must reflect the full amount of the interest.
B. Willy must include the $20 in his income for the year he is able to withdraw it.
C. None of the interest is taxable on a frozen deposit.
D. There is no such thing as a "frozen deposit."

The answer is B. Willy must include $80 in his income for 2011 but may exclude $20. He must include the $20 in his income in the year he is able to withdraw it. A deposit is considered frozen if, at the end of the year, the taxpayer cannot withdraw the deposit because the financial institution is bankrupt or insolvent. ###

35. Lenore wanted to start investing. She deposited $4,000 of her own funds with a bank and also borrowed another $12,000 from the bank to make up the $16,000 minimum deposit required to buy a six-month Certificate of Deposit. The certificate earned $375 at maturity in 2011, but Lenore only received $175 in interest income, which represented the $375 she earned MINUS $200 in interest charged on the $12,000 loan. The bank gives Lenore a **Form 1099-INT** showing the $375 interest she earned. The bank also gives Lenore a statement showing that she paid $200 in interest. How should Lenore report all the interest amounts on her tax return?

A. Lenore can choose to report only $175 of income.
B. Lenore must report the $375 interest income. The $200 interest she paid to the bank is not deductible.
C. Lenore must include the $375 in her income. Lenore may deduct $200 on her Schedule A, subject to the net investment income limit.
D. Lenore does not have to report any income from this transaction.

The answer is C. Lenore must include the total amount of interest—$375—in her income. If she itemizes deductions on Schedule A (Form 1040), she can deduct $200 in interest expense, subject to the net investment income limit. To deduct investment expenses, the taxpayer must itemize. She may not "net" the investment income and expenses. ###

36. If a taxpayer's Social Security benefits are taxable, what is the maximum percent of taxable Social Security benefits?

A. 0%.
B. 50%.
C. 85%.
D. 100%.

The answer is C. Up to 85% of Social Security benefits may be taxable. No one pays federal income tax on more than 85% of his Social Security benefits. ###

37. Sheila and Ralph are married and both have life insurance. In December 2010, Ralph dies and Sheila, as the beneficiary, is awarded the life insurance. The face amount of the policy is $270,000. Instead of a lump sum, Sheila chooses to receive 180 monthly installments of $1,800 each over 15 years, starting January 1, 2011. How should Sheila treat these installments on her 2011 tax return?

A. All of the payments are excluded from income.
B. $18,000 is excluded from income per year, and $3,600 must be recognized as interest income.
C. $21,600 must be included in Sheila's income.
D. $18,000 will be excluded from income, and the remainder is taxed as a capital gain.

The answer is B. Life insurance proceeds are not taxable. However, the *interest* or investment gains earned on a life insurance installment contract are taxable. The face amount of the policy is $270,000. Therefore, the excluded part of each installment is $1,500 ($270,000 ÷ 180 months), or $18,000 for an entire year. The rest of each payment, $300 a month (or $3,600 for an entire year), is interest income to Sheila. ###

38. Randall is an ordained minister in the Evangelical Church of Chicago. Randall owns his own home and his monthly house payment is $900. His monthly utilities total $150. Fair rental value in his neighborhood is $1,000. Randall receives a housing allowance from his church in the amount of $950 per month. How much income must Randall include from his housing allowance amount?

A. $0.
B. $50 per month.
C. $150 per month.
D. $950 per month.

The answer is A. Ministers may exclude from gross income the rental value of a home or a rental allowance to the extent the allowance is used to provide a home, even if deductions are taken for home expenses paid with the allowance. A minister's housing allowance (sometimes called a "parsonage" allowance or a rental allowance) is excludable from gross income for income tax purposes, but not for self-employment tax purposes. ###

39. Alexander, age 64, is single and retired. He earned the following income in 2011. To determine if any of his Social Security is taxable, Alexander should compare how much of his income to the $25,000 base amount?

Part-time job	$8,000
Bank interest	$5,000
Social Security	$11,000
Taxable pension	$6,000
Total	$30,000

A. $30,000.
B. $11,000.
C. $24,500.
D. $25,000.

The answer is C. In order to figure out the taxable portion of Social Security, the taxpayer's modified adjusted gross income must be compared to the base amount.

Modified adjusted gross income EQUALS adjusted gross income PLUS tax-exempt interest. To figure the amount of income that should be compared to the $25,000 BASE AMOUNT:

Part-time job	$8,000
Interest	$5,000
1/2 of Social Security	$5,500
Taxable pension	$6,000
Total	$24,500

Alexander does not have to pay tax on his Social Security. His provisional income plus Social Security is less than the base amount ($25,000). However, he is still required to file a tax return, because his overall income exceeds the minimum filing requirement. ###

40. Supplemental wages and a holiday bonus are paid to Robert in 2011. Which items listed below are NOT considered taxable income to Robert?

A. Holiday bonus.
B. Overtime pay.
C. Vacation pay.
D. Travel reimbursements.

The answer is D. Travel reimbursements are considered part of an accountable plan and are not included in an employee's wages. ###

41. Joe is a priest at a Catholic church. He receives an annual salary of $18,000. Joe also receives a housing allowance of $2,000 to pay for utilities. Joe lives rent-free in a small studio owned by the church. The fair rental value of the studio is $300 per month. Only the $18,000 salary was reported on the W-2. How much of Joe's income is subject to income tax?

A. $0.
B. $18,000.
C. $20,000.
D. $21,600.

The answer is B. Only $18,000, Joe's wages, is subject to income tax. The other amounts for the housing allowance and use of the studio are not subject to income tax, but they are subject to self-employment tax. ###

42. Jacob's personal car is repossessed. His auto loan was a recourse loan. He later receives a Form 1099-C, showing $3,000 in cancellation of debt income. How must this transaction be reported by Jacob?

A. The repossession is treated as a sale. Jacob must report the cancellation of debt income and the gain or loss on the sale or repossession.
B. No reporting is required, because the loan was a recourse loan.
C. The amount must be reported as taxable interest income.
D. Not enough information to answer.

The answer is A. If a personal vehicle is repossessed, then the repossession is treated as a sale, and the gain or loss must be computed. If the taxpayer is personally liable for a loan (a recourse loan), then the canceled debt is taxable unless an exception applies. If a loan is "recourse," then the taxpayer must generally report two transactions: the cancellation of debt income and the gain or loss on the repossession.

43. Polly receives the following income and fringe benefits in 2011:

1. $30,000 in wages.
2. $2,000 Christmas bonus.
3. Parking pass at $90 per month.
4. Employer contributions to Polly's 401K plan in the amount of $900 for the year.
5. Free use of an indoor gym on the employer's premises, FMV valued at $500.

How much income must Polly report on her 2011 tax return?

A. $30,000.
B. $32,000.
C. $32,900.
D. $33,980.

The answer is B. Only the wages and the bonus are taxable. The parking pass is considered a non-taxable transportation benefit, and the employer contributions are not taxable until Polly withdraws the money from her retirement account. Polly does not have to report the use of the gym, because it is on the employer's premises and therefore not taxable. ###

44. Which of the following fringe benefits are taxable (or partially taxable) to the employee?

A. Health insurance covered 100% by the employer.
B. Employer-provided parking at $275 per month.
C. Group-term life insurance coverage of $50,000.
D. Employer contributions to an employee's 401K plan.

The answer is B. Employer-provided parking is an excludable benefit, but only up to $230 per month for qualified parking. Therefore, the amount above $230 ($275 - $230 = $45) becomes taxable to the employee. ###

45. Max owns a restaurant. He furnishes his employee, Caroline, a waitress, two meals during each workday. Max encourages (but does not require) Caroline to have her breakfast on the business premises before starting work so she can help him answer phones. She is required to have her lunch on the premises. How should Max treat this fringe benefit to Caroline?

A. Caroline's meals are not taxable.
B. Caroline's meals are ALL taxable.
C. Caroline's breakfast is not taxable, but her lunch is taxable.
D. Caroline's meals are taxed at a flat rate of 15%.

The answer is A. Meals furnished to Caroline are not taxable because they are for the convenience of the employer. Meals that employers furnish to a restaurant employee during, immediately before, or after the employee's working hours are considered furnished for the employer's convenience. For example, if a waitress works through the breakfast and lunch periods, employers can exclude from her wages the value of the breakfast and lunch they furnish in the restaurant for each day she works. Since Caroline is a waitress who works during the normal breakfast and lunch periods, Max can exclude from her wages the value of her breakfast and lunch. If Max were to allow Caroline to have meals without charge on her days off, those meals must be included in her wages. ###

46. Sheng spends two years working overseas in Australia as a computer programmer for a private company. He has qualified foreign earned income. He makes $120,000 in 2011. What is the maximum Sheng can exclude from his income?

A. $0.
B. $82,400.
C. $92,900.
D. $94,200.

The answer is C. For 2011, the maximum exclusion for the foreign earned income exclusion is $92,900. ###

47. Elaine is a cash-basis taxpayer and sells cosmetics on commission. She sells $200,000 in 2011, and her commission is 5% of sales. Elaine receives $10,000 in income from commissions, plus an advance of $1,000 in December 2011 for future commissions in 2012. She also receives $200 in expense reimbursements from her employer after turning in her receipts as part of an accountable plan. How much income should Elaine report on her 2011 tax return?

A. $0.
B. $11,000.
C. $11,200.
D. $10,200.

The answer is B. Elaine's commissions must be included in gross income, as well as advance payments in anticipation of future services, if the taxpayer is on a cash basis. The expense reimbursements from her employer would not be included in gross income. ###

48. Which IRS form is used to claim the foreign earned income exclusion?

A. Form 8228.
B. Form 2555.
C. Form 1040-NR.
D. Form 2848.

The answer is B. Form 2555 is used to claim the foreign earned income exclusion. The form must be attached to the taxpayer's **Form 1040.** ###

49. Antonio is employed as an accountant by the Giant Accounting Firm. When Antonio travels for his audit work, he submits his travel receipts for reimbursement by the Giant Accounting Firm, which has an accountable plan for its employees. Which of the following statements is TRUE?

A. Under an accountable plan, the reimbursed amounts are not taxable to Antonio.
B. Under an accountable plan, Antonio may still deduct his travel expenses on his tax return.
C. Under an accountable plan, Antonio's employer, Giant Accounting, may not deduct the travel expenses, even though Antonio was reimbursed in full.
D. Under an accountable plan, reimbursed expenses are taxable to the employee, and the employer may also deduct the expenses as they would any other current expense.

The answer is A. Under an accountable plan, employee reimbursements are not included in the employee's income. The employer can deduct the expenses as current expenses on their tax return. The employee is not required to be taxed on any amounts received under a qualified accountable plan. ###

50. Which form is used to calculate and report tax-free interest on educational savings bonds (Series EE Bonds)?

A. Form 1116.
B. Schedule B.
C. Form 1040.
D. Form 8815.

The answer is D. The exclusion for educational savings bonds is calculated and reported on IRS **Form 8815**, *Exclusion of Interest from Series EE and I U.S. Savings Bonds*. There are certain rules that must be followed in order for the educational exclusion to qualify. ###

51. Brad had a $15,000 loan from his local credit union. He lost his job and was unable to make the payments on this loan. The credit union determined that the legal fees to collect might be higher than the amount Brad owed, so it canceled the $5,000 remaining amount due on the loan. Brad did not file bankruptcy nor is he insolvent. How much must Brad include in his income as a result of this occurrence?

A. $0.
B. $5,000.
C. $10,000.
D. $15,000.

The answer is B. Since Brad's inability to pay his debt is not a result of bankruptcy nor insolvency, the amount of the canceled debt ($5,000) should be included in gross income. ###

52. Which of the following fringe benefits provided by the employer will result in taxable income to the employee?

A. $220 monthly parking permit.
B. Reimbursements paid by the employers for qualified business travel expenses.
C. Use of a company van for commuting.
D. Occasional coffee, doughnuts, and soft drinks.

The answer is C. Use of a company vehicle for commuting is not a qualified fringe benefit. Commuting expenses are not deductible. Use of a company van after normal working hours is a personal use and not a business use. This would result in taxable income to the employee. The parking permit, reimbursements for business travel, and the occasional coffee and doughnuts are considered non-cash fringe benefits that are not taxable. ###

53. Which of the following can be entered on Form 1040, line 8b (tax-exempt interest)?

A. Interest earned on a savings account in a bank.
B. Interest on insurance dividends.
C. Municipal bond interest.
D. All of the above are taxable.

The answer is C. Municipal or "muni" bond interest is not taxable at the federal level. Municipal bonds are debt obligations by state and local governments. Taxpayers must still report the interest on their federal income tax returns, but it is not taxable. ###

54. Gene bought his home in 2001. His basis in the home was $210,000. He injured himself and was unable to make the mortgage payments. The bank foreclosed in August 2011 and Gene moved out. At the time of the foreclosure, the FMV was $145,000 and the principal balance of the mortgage was $185,000. All of the debt was incurred to purchase the home, it was never used for business or as a rental, and Gene has not filed for bankruptcy. Gene has a **Form 1099-C.** Gene is personally liable for repayment of the debt (the debt is recourse debt). How should the foreclosure and loss be reported?

A. Report $25,000 in debt cancellation on **Form 982**
B. Report $40,000 debt cancellation on **Form 982**
C. Report $40,000 debt cancellation on **Form 982**, and the foreclosure on **Form 8949** and **Schedule D**
D. Report $40,000 debt cancellation on **Form 1040**, line 21 (other income).

The answer is C. The taxpayer must complete **Form 982**, **Form 8949**, and **Schedule D** should be completed. When a residence that is security for a mortgage is abandoned or foreclosed upon, it is treated as having been sold. This results in the foreclosure being reported on **Form 8949** and **Schedule D** as sale of home. ###

55. Brandi was released from her obligation to pay a large credit card debt. She owed $10,000 to her credit card company, which agreed to accept $2,500 as payment in full. Brandi was not insolvent and not in bankruptcy when the debt was cancelled. What amount would be reported on Brandi's Form 1040, line 21 (other income)?

A. $0
B. $10,000
C. $2,500
D. $7,500

The answer is D. Brandi would report $7,500 on line 21 of her Form 1040 as cancellation of debt income. ###

Unit 7: Rental and Royalty Income

> More Reading:
> Publication 527, *Residential Rental Property*
> Publication 550, *Investment Income and Expenses*
> Publication 946, *How to Depreciate Property*

Rental Income

Rental income is income from the use or occupation of property. Most people think of residential rental property when they think of rental income, but rental income can be earned from the rental of all types of property. Generally, rental and royalty activities are considered "passive activities" and subject to the passive activity rules. The income from rental real estate is subject to income tax, but not subject to self-employment tax, with an exception for bona fide real estate dealers/brokers.

Rental income and losses are reported on **Schedule E,** *Supplemental Income and Loss.* **Schedule E** is also used to report income from:

- Royalties
- Estates and trusts
- REMICs (Real Estate Mortgage Investment Conduits)[32]
- Pass-through income from a partnership and S Corporation

Property owners can deduct the expenses for managing, conserving, and maintaining their rental properties. Examples of common expenses include:

- Mortgage interest and property taxes
- Advertising
- Expenses incurred from the time a property is made available for rent to when it actually rented
- Maintenance, repairs, and utilities
- Insurance[33]

Major improvements that add to the value of a property or prolong its useful life are considered capital expenses and must be depreciated (covered in detail later in this chapter).[34]

Passive Activities: In General

Passive activity is any rental activity OR any business in which the taxpayer does not materially participate. A "passive activity" is an activity from which the taxpayer has the potential to profit, but in which the taxpayer does not materially

---

[32] Real Estate Mortgage Investment Conduits are a type of mortgage-based security.
[33] This list is not exhaustive.
[34] Discussion about whether an expense is an improvement or a repair is outlined in **Publication 946,** *How to Depreciate Property.*

participate. Rental income is generally considered passive income. "Non-passive" activities are businesses or activities in which the taxpayer works on a regular, continuous, and substantial basis.

Non-passive income includes wages and income from a sole proprietorship. It's important to understand the distinction, because ==losses from passive activities generally cannot offset "non-passive" income.== There are two types of passive activities:

- Rentals, including equipment and rental real estate, regardless of the level of participation. (A special exception exists for real estate brokers and dealers.)
- Businesses in which the taxpayer does not materially participate (such as a passive partnership interest).

The following entities are subject to the *passive activity loss* rules:
- Individuals
- Trusts and estates
- Personal Service Corporations
- Privately held corporations

The passive activity rules do not apply to S Corporations, grantor trusts, or partnerships. But the passive activity rules *do apply* to the owners of these pass-through entities.

If a taxpayer is a cash-basis taxpayer, as are most individual taxpayers, he must report rental income when it is "constructively received." Income is constructively received when it is available without restrictions to the taxpayer.

Income and losses from the following activities would generally be passive:
- Equipment leasing and equipment rental
- Rental real estate (with an exception for real estate professionals)
- A farm in which the taxpayer does not materially participate (rare)
- Limited partnership interests
- Partnerships, S Corporations, and Limited Liability Companies in which the taxpayer does not materially participate

Examples of Non-Passive Income

Non-passive income includes active income, such as wages, business income, and investment income. Income and losses from the following activities would generally be considered non-passive:
- Salaries, wages, and 1099-MISC income (independent contractors, sole proprietors, etc.)
- Guaranteed payments to partners
- Royalties derived from the ordinary course of business
- Businesses in which the taxpayer materially participates

- Partnerships, S Corporations, and Limited Liability Companies in which the taxpayer materially participates
- Trusts in which the fiduciary materially participates

> **Example:** Zach has a full-time job as a teacher making $32,000 a year. He also invests in a limited partnership and had $23,000 in passive income from his limited partnership. Zach's wages are ACTIVE income, and his investment income is PASSIVE INCOME (passive activity). Passive income is not subject to self-employment tax (Social Security and Medicare). The IRS sets strict limits on the amount of losses that can be claimed on passive activity.

The **"Passive Activity Rule"** states that passive activity losses may only be deducted against passive activity income and gains. The key regarding the passive activity loss rules is material participation. If the taxpayer does not "materially participate" in the activity, then the losses are disallowed against passive income.

If there is no passive income, then no passive losses can be deducted. Passive activity losses can only be carried forward; they cannot be carried back.

> **Example:** Kate, a single taxpayer, has $90,000 in wages, $15,000 income from a limited partnership, and an $18,000 passive loss from an investment in an LLC. Kate can use $15,000 of her $18,000 loss to offset her $15,000 passive income from the partnership. The unused passive losses ($3,000) must be carried over to the following year.

*Losses from Rental Real Estate: *Special $25,000 Rule**

Usually, taxpayers cannot deduct losses from passive activities from their active income. There is an exception in the IRC for losses relating to rental real estate activities. This is a special rule that is specific to rental real estate and does not apply to other types of passive rental activities.

If a taxpayer *actively participates* in a rental real estate activity, he can deduct up to $25,000 of losses against non-passive income. This special allowance for rental activity is *an exception* to the general rule disallowing losses in excess of income from passive activities.

> **Example:** Philip and Susanne have wages of $98,000 and a rental loss of $26,800 in 2011. They manage the rental property themselves. Because they meet both the active participation and the gross income tests, they are allowed to deduct $25,000 of the rental loss. The loss offsets their active income (wages). The remaining amount over the $25,000 limit ($1,800) that cannot be deducted is carried over to the next year.

The maximum amount of the "special allowance" is reduced if the taxpayer's modified adjusted gross income exceeds $100,000 ($50,000 if Married Filing Separately). The amount of the deduction is reduced by one dollar for every two dollars over $100,000. Once MAGI exceeds $150,000, the $25,000 allowance is reduced to zero.

So basically, if a married couple has $150,000 in wages, and they have $10,000 in rental losses in the current year, they cannot use the rental losses to offset their wage income. The rental losses are suspended and carried over to the next year.

Suspended passive losses can be carried forward indefinitely and used in subsequent years against passive activity income. Suspended losses are also released when a property is eventually sold or disposed of. Suspended passive losses are calculated on **Form 8582,** *Passive Activity Loss Limitations.* They are allowed in full upon the disposition of the activity (when the property is sold).

> **Example:** Hal and Sally file MFJ and have AGI of $140,000. They have accumulated $25,000 in expenses from their home rental that they actively manage. Because they actively manage the rental property, they qualify for the deduction of up to $25,000 in losses against non-passive income. Therefore, Hal and Sally's deduction is reduced by $20,000 (0.5 x ($140,000 - $100,000)). They will be able to deduct $5,000 ($25,000 - $20,000) against non-passive income. The additional $20,000 in expenses is carried forward to the following year.

If a taxpayer is married and filing a separate return, but lived apart from his spouse for the entire tax year, the taxpayer's special allowance for rental losses cannot exceed $12,500 (one-half of the $25,000 special limit).

If the taxpayer *lived with* his spouse at any time during the year and is filing MFS, the taxpayer cannot offset any active income with passive rental losses.

> **Example:** In March 2011, Campbell and Michelle legally separate and plan to divorce. They jointly own a residential rental. Campbell earned $40,000 in wages in 2011, and Michelle earned $33,000 in wages. Their jointly-owned rental generated a loss of $6,000 for the year. Michelle and Campbell both filed MFS and reported $3,000 ($6,000 ÷ 2) of rental loss on their returns. Although Campbell and Michelle meet the active participation rules and the gross income test, neither is allowed to deduct any of the rental losses because they did not live apart for the entire year, and they are filing MFS. So the loss is considered a "suspended passive activity loss" and must be carried over for use in a future year.

The Definition of "Active Participation"

To "actively participate" a taxpayer must own at least 10% of the rental property and make management decisions in a significant and bona fide way, such as approving new tenants and improvements, and establishing the lease and rental terms. Only individual persons can "actively participate" in rental real estate activities (not entities).

However, a decedent's estate is treated as "actively participating" for its tax years ending less than two years after the decedent's death, if the decedent would have satisfied the active participation requirement for the tax year in which the taxpayer died.

The concept of "active participation" is frequently litigated by the IRS.[35] The IRS expects taxpayers to be able to prove that they actively participated in the management of the rental. If the taxpayer is deemed to not have "actively participated," then rental losses are disallowed, and the taxpayer is not eligible for the special $25,000 loss allowance that is allowed to most residential rental activity.

Reporting Rental Income and Losses

If a property is strictly a rental property, the income and loss should be reported on IRS Form **Schedule E,** *Supplemental Income and Loss*. Schedule E is filed along with IRS **Form 1040.** Taxpayers use **Schedule E** to report income or loss from rental real estate, royalties, partnerships, S Corporations, estates, trusts, and residual interests in REMICs.

If a rental property is divided between personal use and rental use, the taxpayer must figure the income and losses differently (more on personal-use rental property later).

Treatment of Advance Rent

"Advance rent" is any amount received before the period that it covers. Include advance rent in income in the year it is received, regardless of the period covered.

Example: Earl signs a ten-year lease to rent his commercial office building. In 2011, the first year of the lease, Earl receives $5,000 for the first year's rent in a lump sum (in advance) and $5,000 as rent for the last year of the lease. It doesn't matter that the advance rent covers the last year of the rental agreement. Earl cannot postpone recognition of the payment. He must recognize the full $10,000 on his 2011 tax return.

If a tenant pays the taxpayer to cancel a lease, the amount received for the cancellation is rental income. The payment in income is included in the year received regardless of the taxpayer's accounting method or the period for which the rental income is covered.

Security Deposits

Security deposits are not considered taxable income, if the deposit is refundable to the tenant at the end of the lease. If the taxpayer (landlord) keeps the security deposit because the tenant does not live up to the terms of the lease or damages property, the retained deposit amount would be recognized in the year the deposit is retained. If the security deposit is to be used as a final payment of rent, it is advance rent, not a security deposit.

---

[35] Rules regarding active participation: Ref. IRC § 469(i), Reg. § 1.469-1T(e)(3).

Property or Services In Lieu Of Rent

Sometimes, tenants and landlords will barter services for rent. If a taxpayer (landlord) receives property or services instead of cash rents, the fair market value of the property or services must be recognized as rental income. Just like other barter exchanges, if the tenant and landlord agree in advance to a price, the agreed upon price is the fair market value unless there is evidence to the contrary.

> **Example:** Beth's tenant, Chris, is a professional chimneysweep. Chris offers to clean all Beth's chimneys in her apartment building instead of paying three months' rent. Beth accepts Chris's offer. Beth must recognize income for the amount Chris would have paid for three months' rent. Then Beth may include that same amount as a business expense for repairing the rental property. This is the correct procedure for recognizing rental income from an exchange of services.

If a tenant pays any expenses, those payments are rental income and the landlord (taxpayer) must recognize them as such. Consequently, the landlord can then deduct the expenses as deductible rental expenses.

> **Example:** Rosetta owns an apartment building. While she is out of town, the furnace in the apartment building stops working. Kerry, Rosetta's tenant, pays for the emergency repairs out-of-pocket. Kerry then deducts the furnace repair bill from his rent payment. Rosetta must recognize both the rent income and the amount Kerry paid for the repairs. Rosetta can then deduct the cost of the furnace repair as a rental expense.

Partial Rental Use

The concepts for "partial rental use" are heavily tested on the EA exam, so you must be clear about them. Different rules apply to a property that is partial rental use and partial personal use. The concept of "minimal rental use" is a situation where a taxpayer rents his actual home as a rental unit for a limited time.

The reason why the concept is so important is because if a property is deemed "personal use," then rental deductions are limited. If the taxpayer has a net profit from rental activity, he generally may deduct all of his rental expenses, including depreciation. However, if the taxpayer uses a rental for "personal use" and later has a net loss on the activity, then the deduction for rental expenses is limited, which means that the taxpayer cannot take a loss.

Taxpayers who use a property for personal and rental use must learn how to divide their expenses properly. If an expense is applied to both rental use and personal use, such as the heating bill for the entire house, the taxpayer must prorate the expense between the two. The taxpayer is allowed to use any reasonable method for dividing the expense, as long as it is consistent. It may be reasonable to divide the cost of some items (for example, the water bill) based on the number of people using the unit. The two most common methods for dividing an expense are:

- The number of rooms in the home, and
- The square footage of the home.

Another common situation is a "duplex" where the landlord (taxpayer) lives in one unit and rents out the other side. Certain expenses apply to the entire property, such as mortgage interest and real estate taxes, and must be split to determine rental and personal expenses.

Example #1: Pablo rents a granny cottage attached to his house. The granny cottage is 12 × 15 feet, or 180 square feet. Pablo's entire house, including the attachment, is 1,800 square feet. Pablo can deduct as a rental expense 10% of any expense that must be divided between rental use and personal use. Pablo's 2011 heating bill for the entire house was $600, and therefore $60 ($600 × .10) is considered a rental expense. The balance, $540, is a personal expense that Pablo cannot deduct.

Example #2: Gillian owns a duplex and lives in one half of it. She rents the other half. Both units are the same size. Last year, Gillian paid a total of $10,000 mortgage interest and $2,000 real estate taxes for the entire property. Gillian can deduct $5,000 mortgage interest and $1,000 real estate taxes on **Schedule E**. Then, Gillian can deduct the other $5,000 mortgage interest and $1,000 real estate taxes on **Schedule A** as an itemized personal expense.

Limit on Deductions for Personal-Use Property

Some property is rented out at times and used for personal use other times (such as a beach house or a summer home). In this case, expenses must be allocated based on the number of days the property is used for each purpose.

When a taxpayer uses a dwelling unit both as a home AND a rental unit, expenses must be divided between rental use and personal use, and the taxpayer may not deduct rental expenses that exceed the rental income for that dwelling unit.

On personal-use property, if rental expenses exceed rental income, the taxpayer cannot use the excess expenses to offset income from other sources. The excess deductions can be carried forward to the next year and treated as rental expenses for the same property. Any expenses carried forward to the next year will be subject to any limits that apply for that year.

Example: Jack owns a vacation condo on Miami Beach. He uses it as a personal residence four months out of the year and rents it out to tenants the rest of the year. Since Jack uses the condo more than 15 days for his own personal use, the condo is considered a personal-use dwelling. Jack's rental income is $5,000 in 2011. However, he had a bad tenant who damaged the property and was eventually evicted. Therefore, Jack's rental expenses were $7,000. Jack cannot deduct the full amount of rental expenses on his 2011 tax return, because the condo is still considered primarily a personal-use property for tax purposes. Jack may "carry over" the unused expenses and deduct them from future rental income.

Personal Use of a Home (Definition)

The rules for personal use are as follows: the taxpayer is considered to have used his unit "as a personal home" during the tax year if he uses the home for personal purposes greater than:
- Fourteen days, or
- 10% of the total days it is rented at a fair rental price.

How to Figure Days of Personal Use

A day of personal use is any day that the unit/home is used by any of the following persons:
- The taxpayer or any person who has ownership interest in the property.
- A member of the taxpayer's family (unless the family member pays a fair rental price and uses the property as a "main home.")[36]
- Anyone under an arrangement that allows for the use of some other dwelling unit (such as a housing swap).
- Anyone at less than a fair rental price.

Days Used for Repairs and Maintenance

Any day that the taxpayer or other owners spend working on repairs and maintaining the property is not counted as a day of personal use. The main purpose of the stay must be to complete the repairs or maintenance. Do not count such a day as a day of personal use even if family members use the property for recreational purposes on the same day.

> **Example:** Corey owns a cabin in the mountains that he normally rents out to tenants. He spends a week at the cabin with his family. Corey works on maintenance of the cabin each day during the week. Corey's family members, however, spend the rest of the time fishing and swimming. The main purpose of being at the cabin that week is to do maintenance work. Therefore, the use of the cabin during the week by Corey and his family will not be considered personal use by Corey.

> **Example:** Steve owns a rental condo in Hawaii. In March, Steve visits the unit to repaint, replace the carpet, and repair damage done by the former tenant. Steve has records to prove all of the purchases and repairs. He is at the condo performing repairs for three weeks and stays at the condo during that time. None of his time at the condo is considered "personal use" time.

Donated Rental Property

A taxpayer also "personally uses" a dwelling unit for personal purposes if:
- He donates the use of the unit to a charitable organization, and

---

[36] For this rental rule, "family" includes only brothers and sisters, half-brothers and half-sisters, spouses, and ancestors, meaning parents, grandparents, etc., and lineal descendants, meaning children, grandchildren, etc.

- The organization sells the use of the unit at a fundraising event, and the "purchaser" of the unit uses the unit.

Exception: Minimal Rental Use, or the "15 Day Rule"

If a taxpayer rents his main home for FEWER than 15 days (14 days or less), then he does not have to recognize any of the income as taxable. This is called the "15 Day Rule." If the taxpayer rents his home for *fewer than* 15 days during the year, he does not have to include any of the rent income. He also cannot deduct any rental expenses.

> **Example:** Janice owns a condo in a resort area. It is her main home. She rented her condo for 14 days during the summer and stayed with her mother during that time. Janice charged $100 per day, for a total of $1,400. She also had $320 in expenses during that time. Janice does not report any of the income or expenses, since the rental qualifies under the exception for minimal rental use.

> **Example:** April's main home is in Dallas, Texas. In 2011, April decided to rent her home during the Super Bowl. She rented her house for eight days, charging $150 a day. April stayed with her brother during that time. Since the rental period fell under the 15 day rule, the $800 that she earned is not taxable and not reported on her tax return.

An activity is also not considered a rental activity if any customer use of the property is seven days or less (this "seven-day" rule applies to all other types of property, not just residential rentals).

Rental Expenses and the "Placed in Service" Date

Rental property is "placed in service" when it is ready and available for rent. A taxpayer can begin to depreciate property and deduct expenses as soon as he places the property in service for the production of income.

If a taxpayer just holds property for rental purposes, he may still be able to deduct ordinary and necessary expenses (including depreciation) for managing, conserving, or maintaining the property while it is vacant.

However, a taxpayer cannot deduct any loss of rental income for the period the property is vacant. But if a taxpayer is actively trying to rent the property, he can deduct ordinary and necessary expenses for managing, conserving, or maintaining a rental property as soon as the property is *made available* for rent.

> **Example:** Rodrigo purchased a rental property in 2011. He made the property available for rent on March 1, 2011 by advertising the rental in the local newspaper. Rodrigo finally found a tenant on June 1, 2011. Even though the rental was unoccupied from March to June, Rodrigo may still deduct the mortgage interest and other expenses related to the property. Expenses incurred while a property is vacant but available for rent are generally deductible.

Expenses for a Rental Property That is Later Sold

If a taxpayer sells property originally held for rental purposes, he can deduct the ordinary and necessary expenses for managing, conserving, or maintaining the property until it is sold.

> **Example:** Gerry owns a rental property and wants to sell it. It is currently vacant, and Gerry still must pay the utility bills and landscaping costs. Gerry is also paying mortgage interest and property taxes. Gerry can deduct these expenses from his rental income.

Converting a Primary Residence to Rental Use

If a taxpayer changes a primary residence to rental use at any time other than the beginning of a tax year, he must divide yearly expenses, such as taxes and insurance, between rental use and personal use. A taxpayer can deduct as rental expenses only the portion that is for the part of the year the property was used or held for rental purposes. For depreciation purposes, the property is treated as being "placed in service" on the conversion date.

The taxpayer cannot deduct depreciation or insurance for the part of the year the property was held for personal use. However, the taxpayer can include the home mortgage interest, qualified mortgage insurance premiums, and real estate tax expenses for the part of the year the property was held for personal use as an itemized deduction on **Schedule A (Form 1040)**.

Figuring the Basis of a Converted Property

When a taxpayer converts a property from personal use to rental use (for example, a taxpayer rents his former main home), the tax practitioner must figure the basis for depreciation using the *lesser* of:

- Fair market value (this is the price at which the property would sell on the open market), OR
- The home's adjusted basis on the date of the conversion.

> **Example:** Five years ago, Lance purchased his home for $180,000. On the date of purchase, the assessed value of the land was $30,000. Lance lived in the home for a number of years and then converted the home to a rental property on April 1, 2011. Since land is not depreciated, Lance will include only the cost of the house when figuring the basis for depreciation. The basis of the house is $150,000 ($180,000 - $30,000). In 2011, the county assessor's office assigned the home an FMV of $185,000, of which $40,000 was for land and $145,000 for the house. The basis for depreciation on the house is the FMV on the date of change ($145,000), because it is less than Lance's adjusted basis ($150,000). Lance will use $145,000 as his basis for figuring depreciation on **Schedule E.**

Depreciation Rules for Rental Property

The IRS allows taxpayers to take a deduction each year for depreciation. Depreciation is an income tax deduction that allows a taxpayer to recover the cost of business-use property.[37] It is an annual allowance for the wear and tear, deterioration, and/or obsolescence of the property. Most types of tangible property (except land), such as buildings, machinery, vehicles, furniture, and equipment, are depreciable.

This is also called the "depreciation expense." Taxpayers must depreciate rental property; that is, they may deduct only a portion of the cost on their tax returns each year.

A taxpayer must claim the correct amount of depreciation each tax year. If a taxpayer does not claim all the depreciation he was entitled to deduct, he must still *reduce his basis* in the property by the full amount of depreciation that he could have deducted. This means that whether the taxpayer chooses to deduct the depreciation on his current return does not matter. For tax purposes, he will still be treated as if he had taken the allowable deduction, and the basis in the property will have to be reduced.

Three basic factors determine how much depreciation a taxpayer can deduct:

- Basis
- Recovery period for the property
- Depreciation method used

*NOTE: The Section 179 Deduction allows taxpayers to deduct the full cost of a business asset in the year it is purchased, rather than depreciate the asset over its useful life. A taxpayer cannot claim the Section 179 Deduction for property held to produce rental income. Buildings and other real property are also not eligible for Section 179.

Individuals report the income and loss for rental properties on **Schedule E**. The depreciation of rentals is reported on **Form 4562**, *Depreciation and Amortization*.

*NOTE! Raw Land is NEVER DEPRECIATED!

A taxpayer can never depreciate the cost of land because land does not wear out, become obsolete, or get used up. The costs of clearing, grading, planting, and landscaping are usually all part of the cost of land and cannot be depreciated.

Example: Diane owns an empty lot she purchased for $50,000, and she wishes to build an apartment complex. Diane pays an additional $15,000 to clear the property of trees and debris so she can begin construction. Diane's basis in the land is therefore $65,000 ($50,000 + $15,000). The cost of clearing the brush must be added to the basis of the land, and is not deductible or depreciable.

---

[37] Additional information about depreciation is in **Publication 946**, *How to Depreciate Property*.

Repairs vs. Improvements

A taxpayer can deduct the cost of repairs to rental property. A taxpayer cannot deduct the cost of "improvements." In order to pass the EA exam, you must understand the difference between a "repair" and an "improvement." A taxpayer recovers the cost of improvements by taking depreciation.

The taxpayer must separate the costs of repairs and improvements, and keep accurate records. The taxpayer will need to know the cost of improvements when the property is later sold, because improvements increase a property's basis.

A "repair" keeps a property in operating condition. It does not add to the value of a property or substantially prolong its life. Re-painting a property inside or out, fixing gutters or floors, fixing leaks, plastering, and replacing broken windows are examples of repairs.

Example: Keith owns a rental home. A neighborhood kid broke a window with a baseball last month, and Keith replaced the window with an upgraded model—an insulated double-pane window that helps control heating and cooling costs. Even though this window is a substantial upgrade from the previous one, it is still considered a repair, because the old window was broken and needed to be replaced. If Keith had decided to replace ALL the windows, the upgrade would have been considered an "improvement," and Keith would have been required to depreciate the cost.

An "improvement" adds to a property's useful life. For example, if a taxpayer makes an extensive remodeling or restoration of his property, the whole job may be considered an improvement.

If a taxpayer makes an "improvement" to a rental property, the cost of the improvement must be capitalized and depreciated. It cannot be deducted on the tax return as an expense. Remember, rental property purchases are not eligible for Section 179. The capitalized cost is usually depreciated as if the improvement were separate property from the dwelling unit.

Example: Keith's rental property also has a bad roof leak. Rather than repairing the roof for a third time, Keith replaces the entire roof at a cost of $7,000. This would be considered a substantial improvement and must be depreciated over time. Keith cannot expense the cost of the roof against current income.

Examples of Improvements

An *improvement* adds to the value of property, prolongs its useful life, or adapts it to new uses. Improvements include the following items:

- Putting a recreation room in an unfinished basement
- Paneling a den, putting in a fireplace, or other major construction
- Adding another bathroom or bedroom
- Putting decorative grillwork on a balcony

- Putting up a fence
- Installing new plumbing or wiring
- Putting in new cabinets
- Putting on a new roof
- Paving a driveway or adding a garage

> **Example:** Glenna owns a rental home. In 2011, she spent $7,000 replacing the carpet, $2,540 to pay the driveway, and $350 to repair a cracked window. Only the window repair ($350) can be expensed on her 2011 tax return. The cost of the new carpet and the new driveway must be capitalized and depreciated over time.

The depreciation periods for business and rental property vary from 3 years to 20 years. Land improvements must be depreciated over 15 or 20 years. Land improvements include items like fences, bridges, and shrubbery.

For property used in rental activities, a taxpayer must use the Modified Accelerated Cost Recovery System (MACRS). MACRS is the current method of accelerated asset depreciation required by the United States income tax code. Under MACRS, all assets are divided into classes that dictate the number of years over which an asset's cost will be recovered. Residential rentals are depreciated over 27.5 years.

Buildings are always depreciated using the straight-line method. Residential real estate is always recovered over 27.5 years, and commercial buildings are depreciated over 39 years. Residential real estate is any structure that at least 80% of the gross rental income of the building is derived from dwelling units (such as an apartment complex), or a common residential rental home.

All other real property is classified as "commercial non-residential property" and must be depreciated over 39 years. An example of commercial property is depreciated over 39 years is a factory building.

Only the building portion of the rental can be depreciated, so the value of the land must be separated from the value of the building. If a taxpayer is uncertain of the fair market value of the land and the buildings, he can calculate the basis using the assessed values for real estate tax purposes.

> **Example:** In 2011, Fidel buys a rental property for $200,000. The most recent real estate tax assessment on the property was based on an assessed value of $160,000, of which $136,000 was for the house and $24,000 was for the land. Fidel can allocate 85% ($136,000 ÷ $160,000) of the purchase price to the house and 15% ($24,000 ÷ $160,000) of the purchase price to the land. Therefore, his basis in the house is $170,000 (85% of $200,000) and his basis in the land is $30,000 (15% of $200,000). Fidel may use $170,000 as his basis for depreciation on the property.

> **Example:** A residential rental building with a cost basis of $137,500 would generate depreciation of $5,000 per year ($137,500 / 27.5 years).

IRS Recovery Periods for Depreciable Property Used in Rental Activities

Class of Property	Items Included
3-year property	Most computer software, tractor units, some manufacturing tools, and some livestock.
5-year property	Automobiles, computers and peripheral equipment, office machinery (faxes, copiers, calculators, etc.), appliances, stoves, refrigerators.
7-year property	Office furniture and fixtures, and any property that has not been designated as belonging to another class.
15-year property	Depreciable improvements to land such as shrubbery, fences, roads, and bridges.
20-year property	Farm buildings that are not agricultural or horticultural structures.
27.5-year property	Residential rental property (residential rental homes, condos, etc.)
39-year property	Non-residential real estate, such as factory buildings. (Remember that the value of land is not depreciated.)

Other Rental Property Expenses

There are many types of expenses that rental property owners may legitimately deduct. Examples of other expenses a taxpayer may deduct from rental income include advertising, cleaning, maintenance, utilities, fire and liability insurance, taxes, interest, commissions for the collection of rent, and ordinary and necessary travel and transportation. If a taxpayer buys a leasehold for rental purposes, he can deduct an equal part of the cost each year over the term of the lease.

Travel Expenses Related to Rental Property

A taxpayer can deduct the ordinary and necessary expenses of traveling away from home if the primary purpose of the trip was to collect rental income or to manage, conserve, or maintain his rental property.

Example: Walt owns a rental property 200 miles from his home. Part of the rental home was damaged by fire. Walt travels to the property to inspect the damage and hire someone to do the repairs. His travel expenses are deductible as ordinary and necessary costs.

Cannot Deduct Prepaid Insurance Premiums: If a taxpayer pays an insurance premium on rental property for more than one year in advance, each year he can deduct the part of the premium payment that applies to that year. He cannot deduct the total premium in the year paid.

Example: Connie owns a rental home. She gets a substantial discount from her insurance agent if she agrees to pay her hazard insurance two years in advance. Connie cannot deduct the full payment of the insurance in the year that she pays. She must prorate the insurance expense, even though she is a cash-basis taxpayer.

Cannot Deduct Local Benefit Taxes: Generally, a taxpayer cannot deduct charges for local benefits that increase the value of a property, such as charges for putting in streets, sidewalks, or water and sewer systems. These charges are non-depreciable capital expenditures. A taxpayer must add them to the basis of a property. He can deduct local benefit taxes if they are for maintaining, repairing, or paying interest charges for the benefits.

Exception for Real Estate Professionals

Real estate professionals are *exempt* from the passive activity rules if certain conditions are met. Rental activities in which real estate professionals materially participated during the year are not passive activities. A real estate professional may elect to treat his rental income as non-passive income. If the real estate professional elects this treatment, then the rental income is subject to self-employment tax. The taxpayer must file a Schedule C, rather than a Schedule E.

Real estate "dealers" are defined as those who are engaged in the business of selling real estate to customers with the purpose of making a profit from those sales. The benefit of being classified as a "real estate professional" is that the taxpayer is treated like a Schedule C business and there is no limit on the amount of losses the taxpayer can claim on the activity. A taxpayer will qualify as a real estate professional for the tax year if he meets BOTH of the following requirements:

- More than half of the services performed during the tax year are performed in real estate or real property businesses in which the taxpayer materially participates.
- The taxpayer performs more than 750 hours of services during the tax year in real property trades or businesses in which he materially participates.

Rental income received from the use of or occupancy of hotels, boarding houses, or apartment houses is included in self-employment income *if* the real estate professional provided services to the occupants.

Services are considered "provided to the occupants" if they are for the convenience of the occupants and not normally provided with the rental of rooms or space for occupancy only. Daily maid service, for example, is a service provided for the convenience of occupants, while heat and light, cleaning of stairways, and the collection of trash are not.

Royalty Income

Royalties from copyrights, patents, and oil, gas, and mineral properties are taxable as ordinary income. Royalty income is generally considered passive income and subject to the passive activity rules.

"Royalties" are payments that are received for the use of property. The most common types of royalties are for the use of copyrights, trademarks, and patents.

Royalties are also paid by companies that extract minerals and other substances from the earth, such as oil or gas. Mineral property includes oil and gas wells, mines, and other natural deposits, such as geothermal deposits.

Many different types of royalties exist. Royalties can be paid to a taxpayer for the use of his name or image. Royalty income and expenses are reported on **Schedule E,** *Supplemental Income and Loss*. Many special rules apply to the ownership and taxation of mineral property, and most of these complex concepts will not show up on the EA exam. But exam-takers should still have a basic understanding of royalties and how they should be reported.

*Exception: There are special rules for taxpayers who are self-employed writers, artists, photographers, or inventors. In this case, the royalties are generated by a *self-created* copyright, trademark, or patent. Therefore, the royalties would be reported as business income on **Schedule C** and be subject to self-employment tax.

Royalties from copyrights on literary, musical, or artistic works, and similar property, or from patents on inventions, are amounts paid for the right to use the property over a specified period of time. Royalties generally are based on the number of units sold, such as the number of books, tickets to a performance, or machines sold.

Example: In 2011, Don's brother died. Don inherited a copyright from his brother, who was an author. It was the copyright to an instruction manual for woodworking. Don then leased the copyrighted material to schools and colleges for their use in the classroom. Since this was not a self-created copyright, the income is considered passive income. Don would report the income from this copyright on **Schedule E.**

Unit 7: Questions

1. Thomas, who is single, owns a rental apartment building property. This is the only rental property that he owns. He "actively participates" in this rental activity as he collects the rents and performs ordinary and necessary repairs. In 2011, Thomas had an overall loss of $29,000 on this rental activity and had no other passive income. His total income from wages is $60,000. How much of the rental loss may Thomas deduct on his 2011 return?

A. $0.
B. $6,000.
C. $25,000.
D. $29,000.

The answer is C. Thomas may deduct $25,000 in rental losses. The remaining amount, $4,000 ($29,000 - $25,000), must be carried over to the following year. ####

2. In 2011, Jane is single and has $40,000 in wages, $2,000 of passive income from a limited partnership, and $3,500 of passive losses from a rental real estate activity in which she actively participated. Which of the following statements is TRUE?

A. $2,000 of Jane's $3,500 loss offsets her passive income. Jane may deduct the remaining $1,500 loss from her $40,000 wages.
B. Jane may not deduct the passive losses from her $40,000 in wages.
C. Jane may deduct any other losses.
D. Jane must carry over her losses to the subsequent tax year.

The answer is A. Jane may deduct the remaining $1,500 loss from her $40,000 wages. A taxpayer may deduct up to $25,000 per year of losses for rental real estate activities. This special allowance is an exception to the general rule disallowing losses in excess of income from passive activities. ###

3. Which of the following costs incurred on rental property should be classified as a capital improvement and must be depreciated, rather than expensed?

A. Replacing an entire deck.
B. Repairing a broken toilet.
C. Refinishing the existing wood floors.
D. Replacing a broken window pane.

The answer is A. The replacement of the deck would be considered a depreciable improvement. The other choices are repairs and may be deducted as current expenses. ###

4. Mike, a single taxpayer, had the following income and loss during the tax year:

Salary $52,300.
Dividends $300.
Bank interest $1,400.
Rental losses ($4,000).

The rental loss came from a rental property that Mike owned. He advertised and rented the house to the current tenant himself. He also collected the rents and did the repairs or hired someone to do them. Which of the following statements is true?

A. Mike can claim the entire rental loss against his active income.
B. Mike cannot claim the rental loss because his income exceeds $50,000.
C. Mike cannot claim the rental loss because he is not a real estate professional.
D. Mike can claim $1,700 in rental losses and the remaining amount ($2,300) will be carried over to the following year.

The answer is A. Even though the rental loss is a loss from a passive activity, Mike can use the entire $4,000 loss to offset his other income because he actively participated. If a taxpayer *actively participates* in a rental real estate activity, he can deduct up to $25,000 of losses against non-passive income. This special allowance for rental activity is *an exception* to the general rule disallowing losses in excess of income from passive activities. ###

5. Gene signs a three-year lease to rent his business property. In December 2011, he receives $12,000 for the first year's rent and $12,000 as rent for the last year of the lease. He also receives $1,500 in 2011 as a refundable security deposit. How much of this income must Gene include in his 2011 tax return?

A. $1,500.
B. $12,000.
C. $24,000.
D. $25,500.

The answer is C. Gene must include $24,000 in his income in the first year. He must recognize all the advance rent as income immediately. The security deposit does not have to be recognized as income as it is refundable to the tenant. ###

6. Rosemary's home is used exclusively as her residence all year except for 13 days. During this time, Rosemary rents out her home to alumni while the local college has its homecoming celebration. She made $3,000 in rental income and had $500 in rental expenses. Which of the following statements is TRUE?

A. All of the rental income may be excluded.
B. Rosemary may exclude only $2,500 of the rental income.
C. Rosemary may deduct her rental expenses when she reports her rental income on **Schedule E**.
D. Rosemary must recognize $3,000 in rental income.

The answer is A. All the rental income may be excluded. This is called the "15 Day Rule." This home is primarily personal use, and the rental period is "disregarded," which means the IRS does not consider it a rental. The rental income is not taxable, and any of the rental expenses (such as utilities or maintenance costs) are considered non-deductible personal expenses. ###

7. Eric incurred the following expenditures in connection with his rental property. Which of them should be capitalized and depreciated?

A. New roof.
B. New cabinets.
C. Paving of driveway.
D. All of the above.

The answer is D. All of the property listed must be capitalized and depreciated. A taxpayer can deduct only the cost of repairs to his rental property. He cannot "deduct" the cost of improvements, but can recover the cost of improvements by taking depreciation over the life of the asset. ###

8. Terry purchased a heating, ventilating, and air conditioning (HVAC) unit for her rental property on December 15, 2011. It was delivered on December 28, 2011, and was installed and ready for use on January 2, 2012. When should the HVAC unit be considered "placed in service" for depreciation purposes?

A. December 15, 2011.
B. December 28, 2011.
C. January 1, 2011.
D. January 2, 2012.

The answer is D. The placed-in-service date is the day on which an asset becomes available for use. In most cases, the placed-in-service date and the purchase date are the same, but that is not necessarily the case. Depreciation begins on the placed-in-service date. Since Terry did not actually have the HVAC unit in use until January 2, 2012, she must wait until 2012 to begin depreciating the unit. ###

9. Passive rental income and losses are reported on which IRS form?

A. Schedule E.
B. Schedule A.
C. Schedule C.
D. Schedule D.

The answer is A. Rental income and loss is reported on Schedule E, which is then attached to the taxpayer's Form 1040. Rental income is any payment received for the use or occupation of property, and is generally passive income. An exception exists for real estate professionals, who may report rental income on **Schedule C.** ###

10. Brian has a house in Arizona that is rented out for eight months each year. How many days can he use the house without losing income tax deductions?

A. As many days as he wants.
B. 14 days.
C. Zero days.
D. 24 days.

The answer is D. Brian can personally use his rental home the longer of 14 days OR 10% of the time the rental was in use. The rental home was used for 240 days (30 x 8). Brian can use his rental home for 24 days (240 x 10%) with no impact in deducting expenses from his rental property.###

11. In January 2011, Kimberly purchased a commercial office building and used office furnishings. The used office furnishings consisted of chairs, desks, and file cabinets. Nine hundred thousand dollars of the purchase price was allocated to the office building and $50,000 of the purchase price was allocated to the used office furnishings. According to the guidelines for MACRS depreciation, what recovery period must she use for the purchased items?

A. 27.5 years for the entire purchase (building and furnishings).
B. 39 years for the building and 5 years for the used office furnishings.
C. 15 years for the building and 5 years for the used office furnishings.
D. 39 years for the building and 7 years for the used office furnishings.

The answer is D. Commercial real estate is depreciated as 39-year property. The recovery period under MACRS for furniture is seven years. ###

12. Nick decides to convert his residence into rental property. Nick moved out of his home in May and started renting it out on June 1. He had $12,000 in mortgage interest on the home. How should Nick report his mortgage interest expense?

A. Nick can report $7,000 on Schedule E as interest expense and $5,000 on Schedule A as mortgage interest.
B. Nick should report the entire $12,000 on Schedule A.
C. Nick should report the entire $12,000 on Schedule E.
D. Nick can report $8,000 on Schedule E as interest expense and $4,000 on Schedule A as mortgage interest.

The answer is A. Nick must allocate his expenses between personal use and rental use. He can deduct as rental expenses seven-twelfths (7/12) of his yearly expenses, such as taxes and insurance. Starting with June, he can deduct as rental expenses the amounts he paid for items generally billed monthly, such as utilities. When figuring depreciation, he should treat the property as placed in service on June 1. ###

13. In 2011 Jacqueline has modified adjusted gross income of $120,000. She owns a rental house that has losses of $22,000 for the year. How much of the rental loss may she deduct on her tax return?

A. $0.
B. $11,000.
C. $15,000.
D. $22,000.

The answer is C. Jacqueline may only deduct $15,000 of the loss. The rental loss allowance is phased out when a taxpayer's MAGI is over $100,000. For every two dollars of income over $100,000, the rental loss allowance is reduced one dollar. The answer is figured as follows:
Jacqueline's income-MAGI threshold: ($120,000 - $100,000 = $20,000)
$20,000 X 50% = $10,000
$25,000 (normal rental allowance) - $10,000 = $15,000
$15,000 is the maximum in rental losses that Jacqueline can claim as a deduction. The remaining unused losses ($7,000) must be carried over to the following year. ###

14. Jake is a full-time freelance writer. He earns $23,000 in royalty income from one of his copyrighted books in 2011. He also has $4,000 in travel expenses related to the promotion of the book. How should this income be reported?

A. Jake must report $23,000 in taxable income on Schedule C.
B. Jake must report $23,000 in taxable income on Schedule E.
C. Jake must report $19,000 in taxable income on Schedule E.
D. Jake must report $19,000 in taxable income on Schedule C.

The answer is D. As a full-time writer, his royalty income is not considered passive income and therefore is subject to self-employment tax. Jake must report $19,000 in taxable income on Schedule C ($23,000-$4,000 in expenses). ###

15. Aaron converted his basement level into a separate apartment with a bedroom, a bathroom, and a small kitchen. Aaron rented the basement apartment at a fair rental price to college students during the regular school year. He rented to them on a 9-month lease (273 days). He figured that 10% of the total days rented at a fair rental price is 27 days (273 days X 10%). In June Aaron's brothers stayed with him and lived in the basement apartment rent-free for 30 days. Which is the TRUE statement?

A. Aaron may deduct all of his expenses for the converted basement apartment, as it is 100% rental use.
B. Aaron may not deduct any of his rental losses because the converted basement apartment is considered personal use.
C. Aaron must recognize imputed rental income from his brothers' use of the property, even if he did not actually receive it.
D. Aaron must divide his expenses from personal use and rental use, but he is still allowed to deduct losses from the property.

The answer is B. Since Aaron's family members use the basement apartment for free, this usage counts as personal use for Aaron. Therefore, the basement apartment is no longer considered a 100% rental unit. Aaron's personal use (the 30 days his family used it for free) exceeds the greater of 14 days or 10% of the total days it was rented (27 days). When a taxpayer uses a dwelling unit both as a home AND a rental unit, expenses must be divided between rental use and personal use, and the taxpayer may not deduct rental expenses that exceed the rental income for that dwelling unit. Aaron's losses, if he has any, are not deductible. ###

16. In general, income from a residential rental property is subject to what kind of tax?

A. Income tax.
B. Income tax, Social Security tax, and Medicare tax.
C. Income tax and Social Security tax (but not Medicare tax.)
D. Income tax and Medicare tax (but not Social Security tax).

The answer is A. In general, income from rental real estate is subject to income tax, but not subject to self-employment tax, with a rare exception for bona fide real estate dealers/brokers. ###

Unit 8: Adjustments to Gross Income

> **More Reading:**
> **Publication 590**, *Individual Retirement Arrangements*
> **Publication 521**, *Moving Expenses*
> **Publication 970**, *Tax Benefits for Education*

In this chapter, we will cover "adjustments to income." An "adjustment" is not the same thing as a "tax deduction." That is because an adjustment is the best type of deduction—it happens "above-the-line."

The "line" is the taxpayer's adjusted gross income (AGI). Adjustments are taken before arriving at final AGI and appear as direct subtractions from gross income.

Adjustments are subtracted from gross income to arrive at adjusted gross income. This is a difficult concept to understand, but you can visualize it much better if you look at the front of IRS Form 1040.

Common Adjustments to Gross Income

There are many types of adjustments to gross income. Some of them are obscure, and some of them are very common. We will cover the most common ones in this unit. These are also the most common adjustments tested on the IRS Enrolled Agent exam:

1. Educator Expense deduction (Line 23 of Form 1040)
2. Certain business expenses of reservists, performing artists, and fee-basis government officials (Line 24)
3. Health Savings Account deduction from **Form 8889** (Line 25)
4. Moving expenses from **Form 3903** (Line 26)
5. Self-employment tax deduction (Line 27)
6. Deductible contributions to retirement plans (self-employed, SEP, SIMPLE, and Qualified Plans, Line 28)
7. Self-employed health insurance deduction (Line 29)
8. Penalty for early withdrawal of savings (Line 30)
9. Alimony paid (Line 31)
10. Deductible IRA contributions (Line 32)
11. Student Loan Interest deduction (Line 33)
12. Tuition and Fees deduction (Line 34)
13. Domestic Production Activities deduction (Line 35)[38]
14. Other adjustments (Line 36)
    - Archer MSA
    - Jury duty pay remitted to an employer
    - Repayment of unemployment benefits
    - Other adjustments

---

[38] The Domestic Production Activities Deduction (Line 35) applies almost exclusively to large businesses and is covered extensively in Part 2 (Businesses) of the EA exam coursework.

Line 23: Educator Expense Deduction

Teachers are allowed to deduct up to $250 of unreimbursed expenses that they pay for books, supplies, computer equipment (including related software and services), other equipment, and supplementary materials used in the classroom. This is sometimes mistakenly called the "Teacher Credit." In reality, it is not a credit; rather, it is an adjustment to income.

Teachers can deduct these expenses even if they do not itemize deductions. Previously, educator expenses were deductible only as a miscellaneous itemized deduction (subject to the 2% of adjusted gross income limit).

For courses in health and physical education, expenses are deductible only if they are related to athletics. Non-athletic supplies for physical education and expenses related to health courses do not qualify. Materials used for home schooling also cannot be deducted. Only certain teachers qualify. An eligible educator must work at least 900 hours a school year in a school that provides elementary or secondary education (K-12). College instructors do not qualify. The term "educator" includes:

- Teacher or instructor
- Counselor
- Principal
- Teacher's aide

> Example: Devina is a third grade teacher who works full-time in a year-round school. She had 1,600 hours of employment during the tax year. She spent $262 on supplies for her students. Of that amount, $212 was for educational software. The other $50 was for supplies for a unit she teaches on health. Only the $212 is a qualified expense that she can deduct.

On a joint tax return, if both taxpayers are teachers, they both may take the credit, up to a maximum of $500. Any expenses that exceed the adjustment to income may still be deducted as "unreimbursed employee expenses" on **Schedule A,** subject to the 2% AGI limit (more on unreimbursed employee expenses later).

Line 24: Certain Business Expenses of Reservists, Performing Artists, and Fee-Basis Government Officials

Certain employees are allowed to take their work-related expenses as an adjustment to income, rather than a deduction on Schedule A. The expenses are calculated first on **Form 2106**, *Unreimbursed Employee Business Expenses*, and then carried over to page 1 of **Form 1040**. The following individuals qualify for this special adjustment to income:

- **Reservist:** Members of the reserve component of the Armed Forces of the United States, National Guard, or the Reserve Corps of the Public Health Service. The adjustment is allowed for work-related expenses incurred while traveling more than 100 miles away from the taxpayer's home. The expense is limited to the regular federal per diem rate.

- **Qualified Performing Artist:** To qualify, the taxpayer must have:
  - Worked in the performing arts as an employee for at least two employers during the tax year,
  - Received at least $200 in wages (or more) per employer,
  - Had qualified business expenses attributable to the performing arts of more than 10% of gross income from the performing arts, and
  - Had adjusted gross income of $16,000 *or less* before deducting expenses as a performing artist.
- **Fee-Based Government Official:** An official who is a government official and is compensated on a fee basis.

In the case of these special occupations, the workers' business expenses are deductible whether or not the taxpayer itemizes deductions.

Line 25: HSA: Health Savings Accounts

An HSA is a Health Savings Account, and the IRS allows a deduction for the contributions made to this type of account. An HSA allows taxpayers to save and pay for health care expenses on a tax-preferred basis. The taxpayer can then take withdrawals from the HSA based on the amount of his qualifying medical expenses.

Unlike Flexible Spending Accounts, HSA funds carry over from year to year.

Beginning in 2011, HSA funds cannot be used for over-the-counter medicines unless specifically prescribed by a doctor.

An HSA must be set up exclusively for paying medical expenses for the taxpayer, his spouse, and his dependents. To qualify, the taxpayer:

- Must NOT be enrolled in Medicare
- May NOT be claimed as a dependent on anyone else's tax return

In 2011, Health Savings Accounts allow a taxpayer to avoid federal income tax on up to $3,050 for singles or $6,150 for joint filers. HSA owners who are 55 and over may save an extra $1,000, which means $4,050 for an individual and $7,150 for a family.

A 6% penalty applies to excess contributions to an HSA.

2011 Health Savings Account Contribution Limits (HSA)

Taxpayer	Minimum Deductible	Maximum Out-of-Pocket	Contribution Limit	55 and Over
Single	$1,200	$5,950	$3,050	+$1,000
Family	$2,400	$11,900	$6,150	+$1,000

HSA contributions are 100% tax deductible from gross income. The amounts deposited in an HSA become an "above the line" deduction on **Form 1040**. A taxpayer does not have to itemize in order to take this deduction.

If an employer makes a Health Savings Account contribution on behalf of an employee, it is excluded from the employee's income and not subject to income tax or payroll tax.

In order to qualify as an HSA, a High Deductible Health Plan (HDHP) must be used in conjunction with the HSA. A *"High Deductible Health Plan"* has an annual deductible of at least $1,200 for self-only coverage or $2,400 for family coverage and annual out-of-pocket expenses of up to $5,950 for self-only coverage or $11,900 for family coverage.

Withdrawals for non-medical expenses from an HSA are allowed, but non-medical distributions are subject to a 20% penalty tax,[39] except in the following instances:
- When a taxpayer turns age 65 or older
- When a taxpayer becomes disabled
- When a taxpayer dies

The deduction for an HSA is reported on **Form 8889**, *Health Savings Accounts*. Taxpayers will receive Form 5498-SA from the HSA trustee showing the amount of their contributions for the year.

HSA accounts are usually set up with a bank, an insurance company, or by an employer. For an employee's HSA, the employee AND the employer may contribute to the employee's HSA in the same year. Contributions made by the employer are pretax and not subject to employment taxes (Social Security and Medicare). Similarly, any contributions made by a self-employed individual are deductible from AGI.

Contributions to an HSA must be made in cash. Contributions of stock or property are not allowed. To claim the HSA deduction for a particular year, the HSA contributions must be made on or before that year's tax filing date. For example, 2011 HSA contributions must be made on or before the filing deadline, which is April 17, 2012.

Line 26: Moving Expenses

If a taxpayer moves due to a change in job or business location, he may deduct moving expenses. The move must be work-related in order to qualify for this deduction.

A taxpayer who starts a first job or returns to full-time work after a long absence can also qualify for the deduction. Moving expenses incurred within one year from the date the taxpayer first reported to work at the new location can generally be deducted. Although the move must be work-related, there is no requirement that the job be in the same field or similar employment.

If a taxpayer does not move within one year of the date he begins the new job, the moving expenses are not deductible unless he can prove that circumstances exist-

---

[39] This penalty was increased from 10% to 20% for the 2011 tax year.

ed that prevented the move within that time. Simply failing to sell one's former home, for example, would not be an adequate excuse.

Moving expenses are figured on **Form 3903**, *Moving Expenses*. The amount is then transferred to **Form 1040** as an adjustment to income. To qualify for the moving expense deduction, the taxpayer must satisfy these tests:

- The move must be related to work or business, and
- The taxpayer must meet the **"Distance Test"** and the **"Time Test."**

The Time Test

The *Time Test* is different for employees than for people who are self-employed. For employees, moving costs are deductible only if the taxpayer works full-time at the new work location for at least 39 weeks (in the first 12 months). For joint filers, only one spouse has to qualify for the Time Test in order to deduct moving expenses.

Self-employed taxpayers must work full-time 39 weeks in the first 12 months at the new location, and then at least 78 weeks within the first 24 months (two years) at the new location. For this test, any combination of full-time work as an employee or as a self-employed person qualifies.

If the taxpayer fails to meet the Time Test, the taxpayer must report the moving expenses as "other income" on a later tax year, or amend the tax return on which the moving expenses was claimed.

Example: Randy quit his job and moved from Texas to California to begin a full-time job as a mechanic for Motorcycle Customs, Inc. Randy worked at the motorcycle shop 40 hours each week. Shortly after his move, Randy also began operating a part-time motorcycle repair business from his home garage for several hours each afternoon and on weekends. Because Randy's principal place of business is Motorcycle Customs, he can satisfy the time test by meeting the 39-week test. However, if Randy is unable to satisfy the requirements of the 39-week test during the 12-month period, he can satisfy the 78-week test because he also works as a self-employed person.

Exceptions to the Time Test

There are exceptions to the Time Test. These are examples where the Time Test does not need to be met, and the moving expenses will be deductible regardless. These exceptions are frequently tested on the EA exam, especially the exception for armed services personnel.

A taxpayer does NOT have to meet the time test if any of the following applies:
- The taxpayer is in the armed forces and moved because of a permanent change of station.
- The taxpayer's main job location was outside the United States and he moved back to the United States because he retired from his position.

- A taxpayer is the surviving widow(er) of a person whose main job location at the time of death was outside the United States.
- The taxpayer's job at the new location ends because of death or disability.
- The taxpayer is transferred or laid off for a reason other than willful misconduct.

Example: Darrell moves to Georgia from New York because he is transferred by his employer. He correctly deducts his moving expenses. Darrell expects to continue his full-time employment in Georgia for many years and does not expect it to be a temporary move. A few months later, Darrell's employer is forced into bankruptcy and closes the entire Georgia division. Darrell is laid off. He does not have to satisfy the time test.

Example: Shelby moves from Michigan to Ohio for a new job as a building manager. Six months after she starts the job, Shelby dies. On Shelby's final tax return, her executor will be able to deduct Shelby's moving expenses, because her job ended at the new location because of death.

The Distance Test

The "Distance Test" says that the new job must be at least 50 miles farther from the taxpayer's old home than the old job location was from the taxpayer's old home. If the taxpayer had no previous workplace, the new job must be at least 50 miles from the old home (see the diagram for clarification).

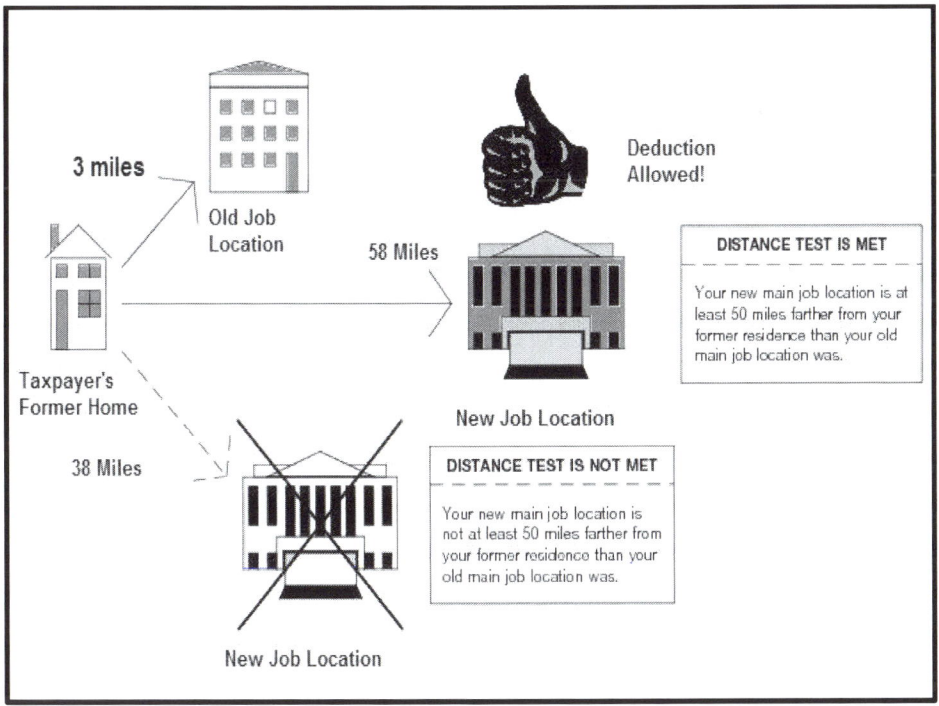

This means that if a taxpayer starts a job for the first time, the place of work must be at least 50 miles from his former home to meet the Distance Test.

> **Example:** Abe took a job as a plumber in another city. His old job was three miles from his former home. Therefore, in order to deduct his moving expenses, his new job location must be at least 53 miles from that former home. The distance test considers only the location of the former home, NOT the location of the former job.

Members of the armed forces moving because of a permanent change of station are NOT required to meet the Distance Test OR the Time Test.

> **Example:** Matt is enlisted in the Air Force, and has been transferred to another base 32 miles from his former home. Matt may still deduct his moving expenses without meeting the Distance Test or the Time Test, since he is a member of the armed forces.

Qualifying Moving Expenses

Only certain expenses qualify for the moving expense deduction. Deductible moving expenses are:

- The cost of moving household goods, pets, and family members.
- Storage costs (only while in transit and up to 30 days after the day of the move).
- Travel expenses (including lodging but NOT meals) for one trip per person. However, family members are not required to travel together. The taxpayer may choose to deduct actual costs or mileage.
- Any costs of connecting or disconnecting utilities required because a taxpayer is moving his household goods, appliances, or personal effects.
- The cost of shipping a car, pet, or belongings to a new home.

Actual car expenses such as gas and oil are tax deductible if accurate records are kept, or a taxpayer can use the standard mileage rate instead. Parking fees and tolls are also tax deductible, but general car repairs, maintenance, insurance, or depreciation of a taxpayer's car are not tax deductible.

> **Example:** In February 2011, Ethan and Jackie moved from Minnesota to Washington, D.C. where Ethan was starting a new job. He drove the family car to Washington, D.C., a trip of 1,100 miles. His actual expenses were $181.50 for gas, plus $40 for tolls and $150 for lodging, for a total of $371.50. One week later, Jackie flew from Minnesota to Washington, D.C. Her only expense was a $400 plane ticket. The couple's moving expense deduction is $771.50 (Ethan's $371.50 + Jackie's $400).

For the purpose of this rule, a taxpayer's home means a taxpayer's main residence. It can be a house, apartment, condominium, houseboat, house trailer, or similar dwelling. It does not include other homes owned by the taxpayer, such as vacation homes.

Non-deductible Moving Expenses

Only certain moving expenses are deductible. Moving expenses that cannot be deducted for income tax purposes include:

- Pre-move "house hunting" expenses.
- Temporary living expenses.
- Meals while traveling.
- Expenses of buying or selling a home, home improvements to help sell a home, or loss on a home sale.
- Real estate taxes.
- Car tags, driver's license renewal fees.
- Storage charges (except those paid in-transit and for foreign moves).

Extended Example: Non-deductible Expenses

Brandon and Peggy Smith are married and have two children. They owned a home in Detroit where Brandon worked. On February 8, 2011, Brandon's employer told him that he would be transferred to San Diego as of April 10, 2011. Peggy flew to San Diego on March 1 to look for a new home. She put a down payment of $25,000 on a house being built and returned to Detroit on March 4, 2011. The Smiths sold their Detroit home for $1,500 less than they paid for it. They contracted to have their personal belongings moved to San Diego on April 3, 2011. The family drove to San Diego where they found that their new home was not finished. They stayed in a nearby motel until the house was ready on May 1. On April 10, 2011, Brandon went to work at his new job in San Diego.

They had $43,282 in total expenses:
Pre-move house hunting expenses of $524
Down payment on the San Diego home of $25,000
Real estate commission of $3,500 paid on the sale of the Detroit home
Loss of $1,500 on the sale of the Detroit home
Meal expenses of $320 for the drive to San Diego
Motel expenses of $3,730 while waiting for their home to be finished
Moving truck expense of $8,000
Gas and hotel expenses of $708 while driving to San Diego

Out of all the expenses that Brandon and Peggy incurred, only the cost of the moving truck and the actual trip to San Diego (the gas and hotel expense) can be deducted ($8,000 + $708 = $8,708). The rest of the expenses totaling $34,574 ($43,282 − $8,708) cannot be deducted. Meals are not deductible as moving expenses. Losses on the sale of a primary residence are not deductible.

Employer-Reimbursed Moving Expenses

Sometimes employers will reimburse a taxpayer for his moving expenses. If so, reimbursed moving expenses are excluded from taxable income and unreimbursed moving expenses are tax deductions in computing AGI rather than as an itemized tax deduction.

However, if an employer reimburses an employee for "non-deductible" expenses (such as the expense incurred from breaking a lease), this reimbursement is taxable as wages. It must be treated as paid under a non-accountable plan and be included as income on the employee's **Form W-2**.

Expenses of buying or selling a home or breaking a lease (including closing costs, mortgage fees, and points) are never deductible as moving expenses.

Example: Xavier is an engineer who has been offered a job at GenCorp Engineering. Xavier only agrees to accept the offer if GenCorp pays all his moving expenses. The cost of his professional movers was $4,600, which GenCorp agrees to pay. This amount is deductible by GenCorp as a business expense and not taxable to Xavier, since it is a legitimate moving expense and allowable by the IRS. However, in order to entice Xavier to move out of state, GenCorp also reimburses Xavier for a $7,500 loss on the sale of his home. Because this is a reimbursement of a non-deductible expense, it is treated as taxable to the employee and must be included in Xavier's **Form W-2.** Xavier has $7,500 added to his wages, which is taxable to the employee as regular compensation. The $7,500 is also deductible to GenCorp, but it is categorized as a wage expense and subject to payroll tax.

Seasonal Work and Temporary Absences: Exceptions

For the purpose of the moving expense deduction, if a taxpayer's trade or business is seasonal, the off-season weeks when no work is available may still be counted as weeks during which he worked full time. In order to qualify, the off-season must be less than six months and the taxpayer must work full-time before *and* after the off-season.

Temporary absences from work are allowed. A taxpayer is still considered to be employed on a full-time basis during any week he is temporarily absent from work because of illness, strikes, natural disasters, or similar causes. There are some exceptions to the time test in case of death, disability, and involuntary separation, among other things.

Example: Marcus moves from Colorado to Jackson Hole, Wyoming to take a job as a manager of a ski resort. He works full-time during the ski season, and he is off for five months during the summer. Marcus may still count this time as full-time work, since his regular employment is expected to be seasonal.

> **Example:** Marlene moves to Florida from Missouri to take a job with a new employer. After working 25 weeks, her union votes to go on strike. She is off work for five weeks until the issue is resolved. Those five weeks count as a temporary absence and still may be counted as full-time work for the purpose of satisfying the time test. Marlene still qualifies for the moving expenses deduction, because the time she spent on strike is considered a "temporary absence" for the purposes of this test.

Line 27: One-Half of Self-Employment Tax

Self-employed taxpayers can subtract half of their self-employment tax from their income. This is equal to the amount of Social Security tax and Medicare tax that an employer normally pays for an employee, which is excluded from an employee's income. Self-employment tax is calculated on **Schedule SE**, *Self-Employment Tax.* .

SE tax must be paid if either of the following applies:
- The taxpayer had income as a church employee of $108.28 or more, or
- The taxpayer had self-employment income of $400 or more.

Adjusted Gross Income	23	RESERVED (see page 29)	23	
	24	Certain business expenses of reservists, performing artists, and fee-basis government officials. Attach Form 2106 or 2106-EZ	24	
	25	Health savings account deduction. Attach Form 8889	25	
	26	Moving expenses. Attach Form 3903	26	
	27	One-half of self-employment tax. Attach Schedule SE	27	
	28	Self-employed SEP, SIMPLE, and qualified plans	28	
	29	Self-employed health insurance deduction (see page 30)	29	
	30	Penalty on early withdrawal of savings	30	

Extensions to the *2010 Tax Relief Act* reduced the self-employment tax by 2% for self-employment income earned in tax year 2011.

The self-employment tax rate in 2011 is 13.3% (10.4% for Social Security and 2.9% for Medicare).

This deduction only affects *income tax.* It does not affect either net earnings from self-employment or SE tax. This deduction is reported as an adjustment to income and is claimed **on Form 1040**. It is available whether or not the taxpayer itemizes deductions.

Line 28: Deductible Contributions to Retirement Plans

On the EA exam, you will be expected to understand the concept of retirement plans from the perspective of the individual (such as an employee) and also from the perspective of the employer (a business). Sometimes these concepts intersect, and you must understand them from both sides. The concept of self-employed retirement plans is one of those instances, because a self-employed person is an individual, but also a business owner. And as a business owner, he may set up a retirement plan not only for himself but also for his employees.

Self-employed taxpayers are allowed to set up a qualified retirement plans for themselves and their employees, and they have many choices of retirement plans. These plans are available for sole proprietorships (taxpayers who report income on **Schedule C** or **Schedule F**), as well as other business types.[40]

Self-employed individuals are allowed to take a deduction for contributions to certain types of self-employed retirement plans. Line 28 of **Form 1040** is used to report contributions to the following types of plans:

- Self-employed SEP (Simplified Employee Pension)
- Self-employed SIMPLE (Savings Incentive Match Plan for Employees)
- Self-employed qualified plans

Generally under these plans, contributions that are set aside for retirement may be currently deductible by the taxpayer, but are not taxable until later. Therefore, the contribution grows tax-free until the monies are distributed.

A taxpayer must have self-employment income in order to contribute to his own plan. However, a self-employed person with employees may still contribute to his employee's retirement plans, even if his business shows a loss for the year.

Traditional IRA contributions are reported on Line 32 and will be covered at length in a later unit.

Line 29: Self-Employed Health Insurance Deduction

A self-employed taxpayer may also deduct 100% of his health insurance premiums as an adjustment to income. Premiums paid by the taxpayer for his spouse and dependents are also deductible as an adjustment to income. For the first time, health insurance premiums paid for coverage of an adult child under age 27 at the end of the year also qualify for this deduction, even if the child is NOT the taxpayer's dependent.

In addition, long-term care insurance is considered "health insurance" for the purpose of this deduction. The policy can be in the name of the business or in the name of the business owner.

*Note: In 2011, the health insurance deduction no longer reduces self-employment tax. This means that self-employed individuals cannot use the self-employed health insurance deduction to reduce their Social Security self-employment tax liability as they did in 2010.

As in the past, eligible taxpayers claim this deduction on **Form 1040**, Line 29.

---

[40] Also see **Publication 560**, *Retirement Plans for Small Business* (SEP, SIMPLE, and Qualified Plans).

In order to take the deduction, the taxpayer cannot be eligible to participate in an employer-sponsored health plan (neither spouse can be eligible to participate in an employer-sponsored health plan). This is true even if the taxpayer declines the employer-sponsored coverage.

Details, including a worksheet, are in the instructions to **Form 1040.**

A self-employed taxpayer must have a net profit for the year in order to take this deduction. So, if the taxpayer is showing a loss on his **Schedule C,** he may not take this deduction.

Line 30: Penalty for Early Withdrawal

If a taxpayer withdraws money from a Certificate of Deposit (CD) prior to the certificate maturing, he usually incurs a penalty for early withdrawal. This penalty is charged by the bank and withheld directly from a taxpayer's proceeds from the certificate.

Taxpayers can take an adjustment to income for early withdrawal penalties. Early withdrawal penalties are reported on a taxpayer's **Form 1099-INT,** *Interest Income*, or **Form 1099-OID**, *Original Issue Discount*. These forms will list the interest income, as well as the penalty amount.

The reason why this adjustment is tested often on the EA exam is because of a special rule that allows taxpayers to claim a penalty for early withdrawal, even if the penalty exceeds their interest income for the year.

This is very different from the normal rule that governs regular investment expenses. A penalty for early withdrawal is treated as an adjustment to income, rather than a deduction on **Schedule A**.

> **Example:** Earlier in 2011, Gloria invested in a Certificate of Deposit. However, in November, she had an unexpected medical expense and had to withdraw all the money early. Gloria made an early withdrawal of $15,000 from a one-year, deferred-interest CD in the current tax year. She had to pay a penalty of three months' interest, which totaled $150. Gloria can claim the penalty ($150) as an adjustment to income.

***Note:** The penalty for early withdrawal of an IRA (retirement plan) is NOT tax-deductible.

Line 31: Alimony PAID as an Adjustment to Income

Earlier in the book, we covered alimony as taxable income. Alimony is also a deductible expense by the individual who PAYS the alimony. By definition, alimony is a payment to a former spouse under a divorce or separation instrument.

The payments do not have to be made directly to the ex-spouse. For example, payments made on behalf of the ex-spouse for expenses such as medical bills, housing costs, and other expenses can also qualify as alimony.

Example: Victoria divorced two years ago. Her divorce settlement agreement states that she must pay her ex-husband $16,000 a year. She is also required, per the divorce agreement, to pay his ongoing medical expenses. In 2011, the medical expenses were $9,500. She can deduct the full amount ($25,500) because it is all required by her divorce agreement.

Alimony does NOT include child support. Child support is never deductible. Child support payments are not deductible by the payer and are not taxable to the recipient. Alimony will be disallowed and reclassified as child support if the divorce decree states that the "alimony" will discontinue based on a contingency relating to the child.

Example: Neil pays child support and alimony to his ex-wife. They have one child together. The divorce decree states that he must pay $400 per month in child support and $500 per month in alimony. However, Neil's divorce agreement states that all payments will discontinue if the child gets married. This means that for tax purposes, ALL the payments must be treated as child support.

Requirements for Payments to Qualify as Alimony

Non-cash property settlements, whether in a lump sum or installments, are not considered alimony. Voluntary payments (i.e., payments not required by a divorce decree or separation instrument) do not qualify as alimony. To qualify as alimony, all of these requirements must be met:

- The payments must be in cash or cash equivalents (checks or money orders).
- Payments must be required by the divorce decree.
- Spouses may not live in the same household (if only legally separated).
- The payment may not be child support.
- The payor's liability for the alimony payments must stop upon the death of the recipient spouse.
- The parties may not file jointly.

A taxpayer does not have to itemize deductions in order to deduct alimony payments. Taxpayers may claim the deduction for "alimony paid" on Page 1 of **Form 1040**. They cannot use **Form 1040A** or **Form 1040EZ**.

The PAYOR must provide the Social Security Number of the ex-spouse *receiving* the alimony payments.

Payments after Death and Voluntary Payments are NOT Alimony

If any alimony payments must continue after the ex-spouse's death, those payments are not considered alimony for tax purposes, even if they are made before death. These payments would normally be reclassified as child support, and therefore are not taxable to the recipient and non-deductible to the payor. Voluntary payments *outside* the divorce agreement do not count as alimony.

> **Example:** Anthony has been divorced for three years. Under his divorce instrument, he paid his ex-wife $12,600 in 2011. As a favor, he also made $2,400 in payments to cover part of her vehicle lease so she could keep steady employment. Anthony can take the $12,600 as an adjustment to income. He cannot count the lease payments because they were not required by the divorce agreement.

The person paying alimony can subtract it as an adjustment to income; the person RECEIVING alimony claims it as taxable income. If a taxpayer's decree of divorce or separate maintenance provides for alimony and child support, and the payor pays *less* than the total amount required, the payments apply first to child support. Any remaining amount is considered alimony.

> **Example:** Jeff must pay alimony and child support to his ex-wife, Liz. His monthly payment for alimony is $200, and his monthly payment for child support is $800. Jeff falls behind on his payments and is only able to pay $500 per month in 2011. Since he is behind on his payments, none of his payments qualify as alimony. All of his payments must be allocated to child support first. The amount is calculated as follows: $200 x 12 = $2,400 (alimony due), $800 x 12 = $9,600 (child support due). Jeff can only pay $500 x 12 = $6,000; therefore he is short by $6,000 ($2,400 + $9,600 = $12,000 − $6,000). Since the $6,000 he can pay falls short of the required child support payment by itself, all of his $6,000 will be reclassified as child support. Therefore, Jeff can deduct NONE of his payments as alimony. Also, Jeff's ex-wife does not have to claim any of the payments as alimony income. Child support is not taxable and not deductible by either party.

Line 32: Deduction for Traditional IRA Contributions

An IRA (Individual Retirement Arrangement) is a personal savings plan that offers tax advantages for setting aside money for retirement. A taxpayer generally sets up an IRA with a financial organization, such as a bank, a mutual fund, or a life insurance company. Generally, amounts in an IRA, including earnings and gains, are not taxed until they are distributed.

The complex rules regarding contributions, withdrawals, and rollovers to IRAs will be covered extensively in a later unit. Here, we will only discuss the adjustment to income that is allowed on Page 1 of **Form 1040**. Some contributions to IRAs may be deducted from income.

Only **traditional IRAs** qualify for tax-deductible contributions. Amounts that do NOT qualify for a deduction include:

- Roth IRA contributions
- Contributions made in the calendar year 2011, which apply to the previous tax year
- Rollovers

- Non-deductible contributions due to the taxpayer's active participation in an employer-sponsored plan

To contribute to a traditional IRA, the taxpayer must:
- Be *under* the age of 70½ at the end of the tax year.
- Have taxable compensation, such as wages income from self-employment. Taxable alimony and non-taxable combat pay are treated as "compensation" for IRA purposes (but not child support!)

For the purpose of a contribution to a traditional IRA, "compensation" does NOT include passive income such as:
- Pension income
- Rental income
- Interest and dividend income

Contributions can be made to a traditional IRA at any time during the year or by the *due date* for filing the return, NOT including extensions. Because April 15, 2012 falls on a Sunday and Emancipation Day, a legal holiday in the District of Columbia, falls on Monday, April 16, 2012, the due date for making contributions for 2011 to an IRA is April 17, 2012.

Example: Daniel wants to make a contribution to his traditional IRA for 2011, but he is unsure how much he should contribute. He sees his accountant on April 1, 2012, and Daniel decides that he wants to contribute the maximum amount. Daniel files his tax return on April 1 and takes the deduction for his contribution. Daniel now has until April 17, 2012 to make a tax deductible contribution to his traditional IRA for the 2011 tax year.

For 2011, the most a taxpayer can contribute to his traditional IRA generally is the *smaller* of the following amounts:
- 5,000 ($6,000 if age 50 or older), or
- The amount of taxable compensation.

Example: Wes is 52 and self-employed. Normally, he would be able to contribute $6,000 to a traditional IRA. However, in 2011, he has $3,700 in self-employment income, and $23,000 in dividend income. Since only his self-employment income counts as "compensation" for the purposes of an IRA contribution, the maximum he can contribute for the 2011 tax year is $3,700.

Line 33: Student Loan Interest Deduction

Generally, personal interest (other than mortgage interest) is not deductible on a tax return. However, there is a special deduction for interest paid on a student loan (also known as an education loan) used for higher education.

Only student loan interest paid to an accredited college or university is eligible for this deduction. A "qualified student loan" is used solely to pay qualified education expenses for the taxpayer (or the taxpayer's spouse and/or dependents).

The maximum deduction for student loan interest in 2011 is $2,500. Modified adjusted gross income (MAGI) must be less than $75,000 ($150,000 if filing a joint return).

> **Example:** Veronica and her husband file jointly. Their MAGI is $162,000. She completed her doctoral degree in 2011 and paid $3,400 in student loan interest in 2011. Due to their high MAGI, they may not deduct their student loan interest as an adjustment to income.

Loans from "related persons" do not qualify for this deduction. A taxpayer cannot deduct interest on an educational loan from a related person. Related persons include:

- A spouse, brothers and sisters, half-brothers, and half-sisters
- Direct ancestors (parents, grandparents, etc.)
- Lineal descendants (children, grandchildren, etc.)

Loans from an employer plan also do not qualify for the deduction.

In order for the student loan interest to qualify, the student must be enrolled at least half-time in a higher education program leading to a degree, certificate, or other recognized educational credential. A student who is taking classes "just for fun" does not qualify.

> **Example:** Natalie is going to her local community college and attends part-time to take a typing course. She is not attempting to earn a degree. Therefore, Natalie cannot take the Student Loan Interest Deduction.

> **Example:** Peter attends a local technical college where he is enrolled full-time in a certificate program for automotive repair. Peter may take the Student Loan Interest Deduction.

For purposes of the Student Loan Interest Deduction, these expenses are the total costs of attending an eligible educational institution, including graduate school. They include amounts paid for the following items:

- Tuition and fees
- Room and board
- Books, supplies, and equipment
- Other necessary school-related expenses, such as transportation

The cost of room and board qualifies *only* to the extent that it is not more than the greater of:

- The allowance for room and board, as determined by the eligible educational institution, that was included in the cost of attendance (for federal financial aid purposes) for a particular academic period and living arrangement of the student, or

- The actual amount charged if the student is residing in housing owned or operated by the eligible educational institution.

Before calculating "qualified expenses" on a tax return, the following tax-free income amounts must be subtracted:
1. Employer-provided educational assistance benefits
2. Tax-free withdrawals from a Coverdell Education Savings Account
3. U.S. savings bond interest already excluded from income
4. Tax-free scholarships and fellowships
5. Veterans' educational assistance benefits
6. Any other non-taxable payments (EXCEPT gifts, bequests, or inheritances) received for educational expenses

Example: In 2011, Katelyn's educational expenses are $7,200. She also receives a gift of $1,000 from her aunt and $1,000 in veterans' educational assistance. Therefore, in 2011 Katelyn's qualified higher education expenses for the purpose of the Student Loan Interest Deduction are $6,200. This is because veterans' assistance benefits must be subtracted from the taxpayer's educational expenses. The gift from her aunt does not have to be subtracted.

Qualified Student Loan Interest: Requirements

In addition to simple interest on the loan, certain loan origination fees, capitalized interest, interest on revolving lines of credit, and interest on refinanced student loans can be deducted as "qualified student loan interest."

"Qualifying interest" includes both required and voluntary interest payments.

Example: The payments on Curtis's student loan were scheduled to begin in June 2010, six months after he graduated from Mississippi State. He began making payments as required. In September 2011, Curtis enrolled in graduate school. He was granted deferment of his loan payments while in graduate school. Wanting to pay down his student loan as much as possible, Curtis made loan payments in October and November 2011. Even though these were voluntary (not required) payments, he can deduct the interest paid as qualifying student loan interest.

In order to qualify for this deduction, the loan must be a bona fide student loan. Simply paying tuition on a credit card does not make the credit card interest "qualified student loan interest."

A taxpayer cannot deduct student loan interest paid on a loan that the taxpayer is not legally obligated to pay.

> **Example:** Josh took out a student loan years ago to help defray his college expenses. During 2011, Josh paid $600 interest on his qualified student loan. The loan is in his name, and only Josh is legally obligated to make the payments. No one claimed Josh as a dependent in 2011. Assuming all other requirements are met, Josh can deduct the $600 of interest he paid as an adjustment to income.

Generally, the taxpayer can claim the Student Loan Interest Deduction if all FOUR of these requirements are met:
- The taxpayer's filing status cannot be "Married Filing Separately."
- No other taxpayer is claiming the student on another tax return.
- The taxpayer is legally obligated to pay the interest on the loan.
- The taxpayer must actually PAY interest on the loan (not just accrue it).

*Exceptions: For purposes of the Student Loan Interest Deduction, the following are exceptions to the general rules for dependents:
- An individual can be a dependent even if he is the dependent of another taxpayer.
- An individual can be a dependent even if the individual files a joint return with a spouse.
- An individual can be a dependent even if the individual had gross income for the year that was equal to or more than the exemption amount for the year ($3,700 for 2011).

Student Loan Interest Deduction Thresholds

The Student Loan Interest Deduction for 2011 is the *smaller* of:
- $2,500, or
- The interest actually paid in 2011.

A taxpayer can deduct a maximum of $2,500 per tax year, no matter *how many* qualifying students there are.

The Student Loan Interest Deduction is "per return" not "per student." So, for example, if a taxpayer has three children in college and pays over $2,000 in student loan interest for each of them, the maximum deduction is still only $2,500.

If a taxpayer pays over $600 of interest on a qualified student loan during the year, the taxpayer will receive **Form 1098-E**, *Student Loan Interest Statement*, from the lender.

Student Loan Interest Deduction: A Summary

?s	Description
benefit	$2,500 per tax return, per year
Loan qualifications	The student loan:
	o Must have been taken out solely to pay qualified education expenses, and
	o Cannot be from a related person OR made under a qualified employer plan.
Student qualifications	The student must be:
	o The taxpayer, a spouse, or a dependent, and
	o Enrolled at least half-time in a degree program.
Time limit	The taxpayer can deduct interest paid during the remaining period of the student loan.
Phase-out range	In 2011, the deduction is phased out at $75,000 of MAGI ($150,000 if filing jointly). MFS filers do not qualify.

Line 34: Tuition and Fees Deduction

The *Tuition and Fees Deduction* is another education-related adjustment. A taxpayer may deduct qualified tuition and related expenses as an adjustment to income. The deduction is allowed for qualified higher education expenses paid for academic periods beginning in 2011 and the **first three months** of 2012.

In 2012, the maximum deduction is either $2,000 or $4,000, depending on MAGI. The deduction is calculated as follows:

- $4,000 if MAGI is $65,000 or less ($130,000 if MFJ)
- $2,000 if MAGI is $80,000 or less ($160,000 if MFJ)

The deduction is eliminated completely once a taxpayer's MAGI exceeds $80,000 ($160,000 if filing jointly).

A "qualified student" is:
- The taxpayer
- The taxpayer's spouse (if filing jointly)
- The taxpayer's dependent

Qualifying Educational Expenses: Tuition and Fees Deduction

The expenses that qualify for the Tuition and Fees Deduction are very different than the expenses that qualify for the Student Loan Interest Deduction, so do not be confused by the differences.

Generally, for the Tuition and Fees Deduction, "qualified education" expenses are amounts paid at an eligible college or vocational institution. It does not matter whether the expenses were paid in cash, by check, by credit card, or with student loans. Qualified education expenses do **NOT** include amounts paid for:

- Room and board, medical expenses (including student health fees), transportation, or other personal expenses
- Course-related books, supplies, equipment, and non-academic activities, UNLESS they are required as a condition of enrollment
- Any course or other education involving sports, games, or hobbies, or any non-credit course

A taxpayer cannot claim the Tuition and Fees Deduction based on expenses that have already been paid with a tax-free scholarship, fellowship, grant, or education savings account funds such as a Coverdell Education Savings Account, tax-free savings bond interest, or employer-provided education assistance.

Tuition Received as a Gift (Special Rule)

Another individual may make a payment directly to an eligible educational institution to pay for a student's education expenses. In this case, the student is treated as receiving the payment as a gift from the other person and, in turn, paying the institution. In order for the taxpayer to claim the deduction for tuition received as a gift, the taxpayer may not be claimed on anyone else's tax return. If someone else can claim an exemption for the student, no one will be allowed a deduction for the tuition payment. In this case, there is also a special exemption in the law; the giver does not have to file a gift tax return.

Specifically, any tuition payments made by a grandparent (or anyone else) directly to a college to cover a student's tuition expenses are exempt from federal gift tax. The money will not qualify for a gift tax exemption if it is first given to the student, with instructions to pay the college.

How to Report Refunded Tuition After Claiming the Deduction

Sometimes, a student will have his tuition refunded. If, after a tax return, a student receives a refund of amounts that were previously used to figure the Tuition and Fees Deduction, the taxpayer must report the refund as income in the following year. The refunded amount is added to income by entering it on the "Other Income" line of **Form 1040** in the following year—the year the refund of tuition is received. The taxpayer's current year tax return does not need to be amended.

> **Example:** Keith has one daughter named Robin. Keith paid $8,000 in tuition and fees for Robin's college education in December 2011, and Robin began college in January 2012. Keith filed his 2011 tax return on March 1, 2012 and properly claimed a Tuition and Fees Deduction of $4,000. After Keith filed his return, Robin dropped three classes and Keith received a refund of $5,600. Keith must refigure his Tuition and Fees Deduction using $2,400 of qualified expenses instead of $8,000 ($8,000 - $5,600). He must include the difference of $1,600 ($4,000 - $2,400) on his 2012 **Form 1040** (the following year).

*Study Tip: On the EA exam, be prepared to understand the difference between the Tuition and Fees Deduction and the Student Loan Interest Deduction; qualifying expenses, AGI limits, and deduction amounts are all different. A common "trick question" will be to verify a type of qualifying expense. Remember that in the case of the Student Loan Interest Deduction, qualifying expenses include housing. For the Tuition and Fees Deduction, housing expenses are not considered a "qualified expense."

A taxpayer cannot take the Tuition and Fees Deduction if his filing status is "Married Filing Separately." Non-resident aliens do not qualify for this deduction.

A taxpayer cannot claim the Tuition and Fees Deduction AND an education credit for the *same student*. A taxpayer who is eligible to claim the American Opportunity Credit or Lifetime Learning Credit[41] is allowed to figure his return both ways and choose the deduction that results in the lowest tax.

The Tuition and Fees Deduction isn't affected by the phase-out rule for itemized deductions, and a taxpayer does not have to itemize in order to take this deduction. This deduction is claimed on IRS **Form 8917**.

Line 35: Domestic Production Activities Deduction

The Domestic Production Activities Deduction (DPAD) is a tax deduction that is given to businesses that have employees and also do manufacturing and other qualifying activities in the United States. The aim of this deduction is to stimulate domestic production.

This deduction is covered extensively in Part 2 of the exam, because it applies mainly to businesses. However, it is possible for a sole proprietor to qualify for this deduction, so long as the taxpayer has employees and pays wages to those employees.

Individuals and businesses use **Form 8903** to figure their allowable DPAD from certain trade or business activities.

Line 36 Other Adjustments

Line 36 of **Form 1040** is reserved for more obscure deductions. There is a dotted line on the form that allows the taxpayer to indicate what type of adjustment is being taken, and most software programs will fill this in automatically. Here are some of the miscellaneous adjustments that are entered on line 36:

1. **Archer MSA:** An Archer MSA[42] is a tax-exempt account that is set up with a U.S. financial institution (such as a bank or an insurance company) in which a

---

[41] These education credits are discussed later in the chapter on tax credits.
[42] Although Archer MSAs still exist, they were superseded by HSAs, which were created in 2003 and are more widely available.

taxpayer can save money exclusively for future medical expenses. It is similar to a Health Savings Account.

2. **Jury duty pay remitted to an employer:** Jury duty pay is reported as taxable income on **Form 1040**. However, some employees continue to receive their regular wages when they serve on jury duty even though they are not at work, and their jury pay is turned over to their employers. The amount is reported as a write-in adjustment.

3. **Repayment of unemployment benefits:** A taxpayer who repaid unemployment benefits may take the repaid amounts as an adjustment to income in the year the amount is repaid.[43]

---

[43] Sometimes, a person will be forced to repay unemployment benefits back to the state. This happens most often when an individual continues to draw unemployment after he has started working again.

Unit 8: Questions

1. Jermaine and Anna have a MAGI of $45,000. They are married and file a joint return. Two years ago, they took out a loan so their daughter, Miranda, could earn her degree. Miranda is their dependent. In 2011, they paid $3,000 in student loan interest. How much student loan interest can Jermaine and Anna deduct on their tax return?

A. $0.
B. $1,000.
C. $2,500.
D. $3,000.

The answer is C. The maximum deduction for student loan interest is $2,500. The deduction is limited to the lesser of $2,500 or the amount of interest actually paid. ###

2. Contributions to a traditional IRA can be made:

A. Any time during the year or by the due date of the return, NOT including extensions.
B. Any time during the year or by the due date of the return, including extensions.
C. By December 31 (the end of the tax year).
D. Any time during the year, but only while the taxpayer is gainfully employed.

The answer is A. IRA contributions for tax year 2011 must be made by April 17, 2012. A taxpayer cannot make a contribution to an IRA after the due date of his tax return, even if he files for an extension. ###

3. Which of the following statements is FALSE?

A. A school counselor may qualify for the Educator Expense Deduction.
B. A part-time teacher may qualify for the Educator Expense Deduction.
C. A school principal may qualify for the Educator Expense Deduction.
D. A college instructor qualifies for the Educator Expense Deduction.

The answer is D. College instructors do not qualify. An "eligible educator" must work 900 hours a year in a school that provides elementary or secondary education (K-12). Part-time teachers qualify, so long as they meet the yearly requirement for hours worked. The term "educator" includes teachers, instructors, counselors, principals, and aides. ###

4. What is the maximum Educator's Expense Deduction for two teachers who are married and file jointly?

A. $100.
B. $250.
C. $500.
D. $750.

The answer is C. On a jointly filed tax return, if both taxpayers are teachers, they both may take the credit, up to a maximum of $500 ($250 each). ###

5. Which of the following statements is TRUE?

A. Credit card interest can be deductible as student loan interest if qualifying educational expenses are paid.
B. On a Married Filing Jointly return, a taxpayer may deduct student loan interest paid on behalf of his spouse.
C. The maximum deduction for student loan interest is $5,000 per student.
D. Taxpayers may deduct student loan interest even if they are not liable for the loan.

The answer is B. On a MFJ return, a taxpayer may deduct student loan interest paid on behalf of his spouse or dependents. This deduction is a maximum of $2,500 in 2011. Credit card interest does not qualify, and taxpayers must be liable for the loan in order to deduct the interest expense. ###

6. Drew borrowed $15,000 from his sister to pay for college. He signed a notarized loan statement and is paying regular payments of $500 per month at 10% interest. In 2011, he paid $3,200 in student loan interest. Which of the following is TRUE?

A. Drew can deduct all the interest as qualified student loan interest.
B. Drew can deduct $2,500 of the interest as qualified student loan interest.
C. Drew cannot deduct the interest.
D. Drew can deduct $6,000 ($500 X 12 months).

The answer is C. Interest paid to a related person is not "qualified interest" for the purposes of the Student Loan Interest Deduction. Related persons include a spouse, brothers and sisters, half-brothers and half-sisters, ancestors (parents, grandparents, etc.), and lineal descendants (children, grandchildren, etc.). ###

7. Years ago, Sammy took out a student loan for $90,000 to help pay the tuition at Ivy League University. He graduated and began making payments on his student loan in 2011. Sammy made twelve payments in 2011, and he paid $1,600 in required interest on the loan. He also paid an additional $1,000 in principal payment voluntarily, attempting to get the debt paid off faster. How much is Sammy's Student Loan Interest Deduction?

A. $1,600.
B. $2,500.
C. $2,600.
D. $90,000

The answer is A. Only the interest is deductible. A payment toward the principal on the loan is not a deductible expense. Student loan interest is interest a taxpayer paid during the year on a qualified student loan. It includes both required and voluntary interest payments. ###

8. Which of the following expenses does NOT qualify for the Student Loan Interest Deduction?

A. Tuition.
B. Required books.
C. Required equipment.
D. Tuition for a non-degree candidate.

The answer is D. The student must be enrolled at least half-time in a program leading to a degree, certificate, or other recognized educational credential in order to qualify for the Student Loan Interest Deduction. Tuition for a non-degree candidate or someone who is taking classes just for fun or for general improvement does not qualify. ###

9. On which form is student loan interest reported to the taxpayer?

A. Form 1098.
B. Form 1099-Misc.
C. Form 1099-R.
D. Form 1098-E.

The answer is D. Taxpayers who pay student loan interest will receive **Form 1098-E**, *Student Loan Interest Statement,* from their lender. A lender (or bank) that receives interest payments of $600 or more in one year must send out this statement, reporting the interest to the taxpayer. A copy of this form is also sent to the IRS. ###

10. In the case of the Tuition and Fees Deduction, qualified education expenses do NOT include amounts paid for:

A. Insurance.
B. Medical expenses (including student health fees).
C. Room and board.
D. All of the above.

The answer is D. None of the above expenses qualifies for the Tuition and Fees Deduction. This is true even if the amount must be paid to the institution as a condition of enrollment or attendance. Student activity fees, course-related books, supplies, and equipment may be deductible only if they are required by the institution as a condition of enrollment. ###

11. Which form is used by the taxpayer to figure and report the Tuition and Fees Deduction?

A. Form 8917.
B. Form 8883.
C. Form 1099-INT.
D. Form 1098-T.

The answer is A. The deduction is calculated on **Form 8917**, *Tuition and Fees Deduction*. The amount is then transferred over to page 1 of **Form 1040**. ###

12. Ty is a sophomore at Iowa State University's degree program in Anthropology. This year, he paid $3,000 in tuition and $10,000 to live in optional on-campus housing. In addition to tuition, he is required to pay a fee to the university for the rental of the equipment he will use in this program. The fee to rent the equipment is $300 per year. How much of these expenses qualify for the Tuition and Fees Deduction?

A. $3,000.
B. $3,300.
C. $13,000.
D. $13,300.

The answer is B. The rental fee and the tuition costs qualify for the Tuition and Fees Deduction, and Tyler may deduct the cost on his tax return. Because the equipment rental fee must be paid to the university and is a requirement for enrollment and attendance, it is a qualified expense. Student activity fees and expenses for course-related books, supplies, and equipment can be included in qualified educational expenses if the fees and expenses paid to the institution are required. The housing is not a qualified educational expense. ###

13. Addie paid $2,000 tuition and fees in December 2011, and she began college in January 2012. Addie filed her 2011 tax return on February 1, 2012, and correctly claimed a Tuition and Fees Deduction of $2,000. But after Addie filed her return, she became ill and dropped two courses. She received a refund of tuition in the amount of $1,100 in April 2012. How must Addie report the refund of fees?

A. Addie may use the refund to pay qualified tuition in 2012 and not report the refund.
B. Addie may report the refund on her next year's tax return as "Other Income."
C. Addie is not required to report the refund.
D. Addie is required to amend her 2011 return and remove the deduction for tuition and fees.

The answer is B. Addie may include the difference of $1,100 on the "Other Income" line of her **Form 1040** in the following year. Her 2011 return does not have to be amended. ###

14. On which form must taxpayers report deductible moving expenses?

A. Form 3903.
B. Form 1041.
C. Form 8821.
D. Schedule A.

The answer is A. Taxpayers must report deductible moving expenses on IRS **Form 3903**, *Moving Expenses*. The form must be attached to the taxpayer's Form 1040. ###

15. Alimony does NOT include:
A. Non-cash property settlements.
B. Payments to a third-party on behalf of an ex-spouse.
C. Medical expenses paid on behalf of an ex-spouse.
D. Cash alimony payments.

The answer is A. Non-cash property settlements do not qualify as alimony. Alimony does not include child support, non-cash property settlements, payments to keep up the payor's property, or use of the payor's property. Payments made to a third party or medical expenses paid on behalf of a former spouse may qualify as alimony. ###

16. In 2011, Patricia was offered a new job in a different state. She had the following moving expenses:

$1,200 for transporting her household goods.
$550 in lodging for travel between her old home and her new home.
$250 in meals during the trip.
$250 to break the lease on her old home. Patricia moved to start a new job and met the Distance and Time tests. What are the total moving expenses that can be deducted on her tax return?

A. $2,150.
B. $1,900.
C. $1,750.
D. $2,000.

The answer is C. The answer is figured as follows:

Cost of moving goods:	$1,200
Lodging	$550
Deductible expenses	**$1,750**

A taxpayer cannot deduct any moving expenses for meals. The cost of breaking a lease to move to a new location is also not a deductible expense. ###

17. Dave and Bea file jointly. In March 2011, they move from Arizona to Connecticut, where Dave is starting a new job. Dave drives the car to Hartford. His expenses are $400 for gas, $40 for tolls, $150 for lodging, and $70 for meals. One week later, Bea drives to Hartford. Her expenses are $500 for gas, $40 for tolls, $35 for parking, $100 for lodging, and $25 for meals. A week later, they pay $600 to ship their pet, a miniature horse, to Connecticut. How much is their deduction for moving expenses?

A. $590.
B. $1,265.
C. $1,300.
D. $1,865.

The answer is D. The cost of meals is not deductible. The costs of travel, transportation, and lodging are all deductible. The costs of moving personal items and pets are deductible. The answer is figured as follows:
Dave's expenses $400 + $40 + $150 = $590
Bea's expenses $500+ $40 +$35 + $100 = $675
Cost of shipping horse = $600
Total deductible expenses: $590 + $675 + $600 = $1,865
If a married couple files jointly, *either* spouse can qualify for the full-time work test. Family members are not required to travel together. ###

18. Chase is moving for a new job. He has the following expenses:

$500 cost of moving truck rental.
$300 cost of moving family and pets.
$200 cost for a storage unit while moving.
$400 cost of breaking his existing apartment lease.
$500 pre-move house-hunting.

Assuming that Chase passes all the required tests, what is his Moving Expense Deduction?

A. $500.
B. $800.
C. $1,000.
D. $1,900.

The answer is C. The cost of breaking a lease is not a deductible moving expense. House-hunting before a move is also not deductible. The cost of a storage unit while moving (and up to thirty days before and after) is deductible. Therefore, Chase may deduct the following: ($500 + $300 + $200 = $1,000). ###

19. Lynn was offered a position in another city. Her new employer reimburses her for the $9,500 loss on the sale of her home because of the move. How should this reimbursement be treated?

A. The employer can reimburse Lynn and make the payment non-taxable through an accountable plan, if properly documented.
B. Because this is a reimbursement of a non-deductible expense, it is treated as wages and must be included as pay on Lynn's **Form W-2.**
C. The reimbursement is tax-exempt because it is a qualified moving expense.
D. The expense is non-taxable so long as Lynn's employer makes the payment directly to her mortgage lender.

The answer is B. Because this is a reimbursement of a non-deductible expense, it is treated as paid under a non-accountable plan and must be included as pay on Lynn's **Form W-2.** Expenses of buying or selling a home (including closing costs, mortgage fees, and points) are never deductible as moving expenses. If an employer offers to pay these expenses as a condition of employment, then the amounts are treated like taxable compensation (wages) and must be reported and treated as such.###

20. Ian and Pam are divorced. Pam has an auto accident and dies. Under their divorce decree, Ian must continue to pay his former spouse's estate $30,000 annually. The divorce decree states that upon Pam's death, the continued payments will be put into trust for their daughter, who is 12 years old. What is true about the $30,000 annual payment?

A. For tax purposes, it is alimony.
B. For tax purposes, it is child support.
C. For tax purposes, it is a gift.
D. Once Pam dies, the payments are taxable to the daughter.

The answer is B. The trust is to be used for the child's benefit and must continue after Pam's death. Therefore, the $30,000 annual payment is not alimony and is instead classified as child support for tax purposes. Any payment that is specifically designated as child support or treated as specifically designated as child support under a divorce agreement is not alimony. ###

21. Under his divorce decree, Rick must pay the medical expenses of his former spouse, Linda. In January 2011, Rick sends a check totaling $4,000 directly to General Medical Hospital in order to pay for Linda's emergency surgery. Which of the following statements is TRUE?

A. This payment qualifies as alimony, and Linda must include the $4,000 as income on her return.
B. This payment does not qualify as alimony, but Rick can claim a deduction for the medical expenses on his return.
C. Linda must include the $4,000 as income on her return, but Rick cannot deduct the expense as alimony because it was paid to a third party.
D. None of the above.

The answer is A. The payment may be treated as alimony for tax purposes, because the medical payments are a condition of the divorce agreement. Payments to a third party on behalf of an ex-spouse under the terms of a divorce instrument can be alimony, if they qualify. These include payments for a spouse's medical expenses, housing costs (rent and utilities), taxes, and tuition. The payments are treated as received by the ex-spouse and included as income. ###

22. George paid $14,000 in alimony to his wife during the year. Which of the following is TRUE?

A. George can only deduct alimony if he itemizes on his tax return.
B. The deduction for alimony is entered on Schedule A as an itemized deduction.
C. George can deduct alimony paid, even if he does not itemize.
D. George can deduct alimony paid on Form 1040EZ.

The answer is C. George can deduct alimony paid, even if he does not itemize. He must file **Form 1040** and enter the amount of alimony paid as an adjustment to income. An adjustment for alimony cannot be claimed on **Form 1040EZ** or **Form 1040A**. ###

23. Under the terms of a divorce decree, Blake transfers appreciated property to his ex-wife, Ming. The property has a fair market value of $75,000 and an adjusted basis of $50,000 to Blake. This transaction creates taxable alimony of _____ to Ming.

A. $0.
B. $25,000.
C. $75,000.
D. $50,000.

The answer is A. Transfers of property in the fulfillment of a divorce decree are not taxable events. Property settlements due to a divorce decree are NOT alimony; they are simply a division of assets and are treated as such. ###

24. If a taxpayer's decree of divorce provides for alimony and child support, and the payor pays LESS than the total amount required, the payments apply first to _____.

A. Alimony.
B. Child support.
C. Separate maintenance.
D. Tax delinquencies.

The answer is B. If a taxpayer's decree of divorce or separate maintenance provides for alimony and child support, and the payor pays LESS than the total amount required, the payments apply first to child support. Any remaining amount is considered alimony. ###

25. Which form is used to report HSA contributions to the IRS?

A. Form 8889.
B. Form 5498.
C. Schedule A.
D. Form 2848.

The answer is A. HSA contributions are reported to the IRS on **Form 8889**, *Health Savings Accounts.* Taxpayers will receive **Form 5498-SA** from the HSA trustee showing the amount of their contributions for the year. ###

26. Kyle has an HSA, and he becomes permanently disabled in 2011. Which of the following statements is true?

A. Kyle may withdraw money from his HSA for non-medical expenses, but the withdrawals will be subject to income tax and also an additional penalty.
B. Kyle may withdraw money from his HSA for non-medical expenses. The withdrawals will be subject to income tax, but will not be subject to penalty.
C. Kyle may not take non-medical distributions from his account.
D. Kyle must be at least 65 to take non-medical distributions from an HSA.

The answer is B. Kyle is disabled, so his withdrawals are not subject to penalty. Withdrawals for non-medical expenses from an HSA are allowed, but non-medical distributions are subject to an additional penalty tax, except when the taxpayer turns 65, becomes disabled, or dies. ###

27. Seth makes an excess contribution to his HSA, by accidentally contributing over the maximum allowable amount. What is the penalty on excess contributions if Seth does not correct the problem?

A. No penalty.
B. 6% penalty.
C. 10% penalty.
D. 20% penalty.

The answer is B. The 6% penalty applies to excess contributions. Excess contributions made by an employer must be included in an employee's gross income. Excess contributions to an HSA are not deductible. ###

28. In 2011, Caylie had an HSA account set up with her employer. At the end of the year, she had $3,000 in the account. Then she quit her job and withdrew all the funds from her HSA. She did not use the $3,000 for qualifying medical expenses. What is the consequence of this action?

A. Nothing; taxpayers are allowed to withdraw from their HSA accounts at any time.
B. Non-medical withdrawals from an HSA are prohibited and will result in a forfeiture of the funds.
C. Withdrawals from an HSA for non-eligible expenses are subject to a 20% penalty.
D. Withdrawals from an HSA for non-eligible expenses are subject to a 6% penalty.

The answer is C. Withdrawals from an HSA for non-eligible expenses are allowed, but the withdrawal will be subject to a 20% penalty, in addition to regular income tax.###

29. During 2011, Deborah was self-employed. She had self-employment tax of $4,896. Which of the following statements is true?

A. Deborah may deduct 100% of the self-employment tax she paid on Schedule C.
B. Deborah may deduct 50% of the self-employment tax she paid on Schedule C.
C. Deborah may deduct 50% of the self-employment tax she paid as an adjustment to income on **Form 1040**.
D. Deborah may not deduct self-employment tax.

The answer is C. Deborah may deduct 50% of the self-employment tax she paid as an adjustment to income on page 1 of her **Form 1040**. A taxpayer can deduct one-half (not 100%) of self-employment tax paid as an adjustment on **Form 1040**. ###

30. Joe lost his job last year and withdrew money from a number of accounts. He paid the following penalties:

$100 penalty for early withdrawal from a Certificate of Deposit (CD).
$200 penalty from early withdrawal from a traditional IRA.
$50 late penalty for not paying his rent on time.
How much of these listed amounts can Joe deduct as an adjustment to income on his **Form 1040?**

A. $0.
B. $100.
C. $200.
D. $250.

The answer is B. Early withdrawal penalties are tax-deductible if made from a time deposit account, such as a Certificate of Deposit. Taxpayers deduct any penalties on **Form 1040** as an adjustment to income. ###

31. Jasmine is a part-time art teacher at an elementary school. She spends $185 on qualified expenses for her art students and $75 on materials for a health course that she also teaches. She has 440 hours of documented employment as an educator during the tax year. How much can she deduct as a qualified educator expense (as an adjustment to income)?

A. $0.
B. $185.
C. $250.
D. $260.

The answer is A. Because she has only 440 hours of documented employment as an educator during the tax year, she cannot deduct her educator expenses as an adjustment to income. The educator must have at least 900 hours of qualified employment during the school year in order to take this deduction as an adjustment to income. ###

31. Chuck and Diana are married and file jointly. Chuck is self-employed and his profit was $50,000 in 2011. They pay $500 per month for health insurance coverage. Diana was a homemaker until March 1, 2011, when she got a job working for a local construction company. Diana was eligible to participate in an employer health plan, but she and Chuck didn't want to switch doctors, so she declined the coverage. Which of the following statements is TRUE?

A. No deduction is allowed in 2011 for self-employed health insurance.
B. Chuck and Diana may only deduct $1,000 in self-employed health insurance, which is for January and February, the two months they were not eligible to participate in an employer plan.
C. Chuck and Diana may deduct 100% of their insurance premiums because they declined the employer coverage.
D. Chuck and Diana may deduct 50% of their health insurance premiums on Chuck's **Schedule C.**

The answer is B. Chuck and Diana may only deduct $1,000 in self-employed health insurance for the two months that they were ineligible to participate in an employer plan. No deduction is allowed for self-employed health insurance for any month that the taxpayer has the option to participate in an employer-sponsored plan. This is true even if the taxpayer declines the coverage. Self-employed taxpayers may deduct 100% of health insurance premiums as an adjustment to income but only if they are unable to participate in an employer health plan. ###

Unit 9: Individual Retirement Arrangements

> **More Reading:**
> **Publication 590,** *Individual Retirement Arrangements (IRAs)*
> **Publication 575,** *Pension and Annuity Income*

There are several types of IRA accounts, but in this unit, we will only discuss traditional IRAs and Roth IRAs.[44] These are the two most common types of retirement accounts and the ones most heavily tested on Part 1 of the EA exam. Each IRA has different eligibility requirements.

Traditional IRA: A traditional IRA is the most common type of retirement savings plan. In most cases, taxpayers can deduct their traditional IRA contributions as an adjustment to income. Generally, amounts in a traditional IRA, including earnings and gains, are not taxed until distributed. If a taxpayer's income is too high, then the taxpayer's contributions to his traditional IRA might not be deductible.

Roth IRA: A Roth IRA is a retirement account that features non-deductible contributions and tax-free growth. In other words, a taxpayer funds his Roth IRA with after-tax income, and the income then grows tax-free. When a taxpayer withdraws money from a Roth, the withdrawal will not be subject to income tax. Not everyone can participate in a Roth IRA. There are strict income limits, and higher wage earners may be prohibited from participating in a Roth IRA account because of their income threshold.

*NOTE: Only contributions to a traditional IRA are deductible as an adjustment to gross income. Roth IRA contributions are NOT deductible. Although contributions to a Roth IRA cannot be deducted, the taxpayer may still be eligible for the Retirement Savings Contribution Credit (the Saver's Credit).

Example: In 2011, Fred contributes $2,200 to a traditional IRA and $1,000 to a Roth IRA. The most Fred will be able to deduct as an adjustment to income is the $2,200 contribution to his traditional IRA. Roth IRA contributions are never deductible.

Traditional IRA Rules

There are many rules regarding traditional IRAs, and you must understand them for the EA exam. First, remember that not everyone can contribute to a traditional IRA. In addition, not everyone who contributes to a traditional IRA is allowed to deduct the contribution.

In order to make contributions to a traditional IRA:
1. The taxpayer must be *under* age 70½ at the end of the year.

---
[44] For more detailed information on all types of IRAs, refer to the Individual Retirement Arrangements (IRAs) chapter in **Publication 17** and **Publication 590,** *Individual Retirement Arrangements*.

2. The taxpayer must have qualifying compensation, such as wages, self-employed income, and alimony income. Investment income does not count.
3. If a taxpayer's income is too high, then he will not be allowed to deduct his IRA contribution (if covered by an employer plan).

> ***Note:** The contribution rules are very strict. Only certain types of compensation qualify as contributions to an IRA. For purposes of making an IRA contribution, taxable alimony and non-taxable combat pay count as qualifying income. This rule allows taxpayers to build retirement savings in IRAs even if they rely on alimony income for support. The rule applies only to taxable alimony income and does not include child support payments.

Contributions can be made to a traditional IRA at any time on or before the due date of the return (not including extensions).

IRAs cannot be owned jointly. However, a married couple who files jointly may choose to contribute to each of their IRA accounts, even if only one taxpayer has qualifying compensation. This means that one taxpayer may choose to make an IRA contribution on *behalf* of his or her spouse, even if only one spouse had compensation during the year. Each spouse must have a separate IRA account.

> **Example:** Joaquin, 48, and Meg, 52, are married and file jointly. Joaquin works as a paramedic and makes $46,000 per year. Meg is a homemaker and has no income. Even though Meg has no taxable compensation, Joaquin may still contribute to her IRA account. Their combined maximum contribution for 2011 is $11,000. Joaquin may deposit $5,000, and Meg may deposit $6,000 because she is over 50 years of age.

For the 2011 tax year, a person may make an IRA contribution all the way up until April 17, 2012. This makes an IRA contribution a rare opportunity for after-tax planning, because it can occur after the tax year has already ended. A taxpayer can even file his return claiming a traditional IRA contribution *before* the contribution is actually made. However, if a contribution is reported on the taxpayer's 2011 return but is not made by the deadline, the taxpayer must file an amended return.

The contribution must be made no later than the **due date of the tax return** (NOT including extensions).

> **Example:** Paul files his 2011 tax return on March 5, 2012. He claims a $4,000 IRA contribution on his tax return. Paul may wait as late as April 17, 2012 (the due date of the return) to finally make the IRA contribution for tax year 2011.

In order to contribute to an IRA, the taxpayer must have "non-passive" income, such as wages, salaries, commissions, tips, bonuses, or self-employment income. Taxable alimony and non-taxable combat pay are also treated as "non-passive" compensation for this purpose.

Example: Stan is an Army medic serving in a combat zone for all of 2011. Although none of his pay is taxable, it is still qualifying compensation for the purposes of an IRA contribution. Stan may contribute the maximum to his traditional IRA. Since none of his income is taxable anyway, Stan would not take an adjustment to income on his tax return for his contribution.

A taxpayer must have taxable income in order to contribute to an IRA, so a self-employed person who shows an overall LOSS for the year would not be able to contribute. However, if a taxpayer has wages *in addition* to self-employment income, do not subtract the *loss* from self-employment from the taxpayer's wages when figuring total compensation.

Example: Marcy is 45 and works part-time as an employee for a local library. She earns $10,000 in wages during 2011. She also works part of the year as a self-employed photographer. In 2011, her photography business has a loss of $5,400. Even though the taxpayer's *net income* for 2011 is only $4,600 ($10,000 wages – $5,400 loss from self-employment), her qualifying income for the purposes of an IRA contribution is still $10,000 (the amount of her wages). This means that Marcy can make a full IRA contribution of $5,000 in 2011.

"Compensation" for the purposes of contributing to an IRA does NOT include passive income such as:

- Rental income
- Interest income
- Dividend and portfolio income
- Pension or annuity income
- Deferred compensation
- Income from a limited partnership
- Prize winnings or gambling income
- Any other income that is excluded from income, such as foreign earned income and housing costs (other than non-taxable combat pay)

Taxpayers cannot make IRA contributions that are greater than their qualifying compensation for the year. This means that if a taxpayer only has passive income for the year, he cannot contribute to an IRA at all.

Example: Larry is 54 and wants to contribute to his traditional IRA. He has $10,000 in passive rental income from residential rental properties (he is not a real estate professional). He also received $8,000 in interest income and has $3,000 in wages from a part-time job. The rental and interest income is passive income and not considered "compensation" for IRA purposes, so cannot be used to fund his retirement account. Therefore, the maximum Larry can contribute to his traditional IRA is $3,000, the amount of his wage income.

2011 Traditional and Roth IRA Contribution Limits

Under 50 years of age:
- 2011 Contribution Limit: $5,000 per taxpayer
- Filing Jointly: $10,000

50 years and over:
- 2011 Contribution Limit: $6,000 per taxpayer
- Filing Jointly (Both 50 or older): $12,000

A taxpayer may choose to split his retirement plan contributions between a traditional IRA and a Roth IRA; however, the maximum contribution limits still apply. Although a person may have IRAs with several different financial institutions, for the purpose of the contribution limits, tax law treats all of a taxpayer's IRAs as a single IRA.

Example: Alan is 32. He has a traditional IRA at his regular bank and a Roth IRA through his stockbroker. Alan can contribute to both of his retirement accounts this year, but the combined contributions for 2011 cannot exceed $5,000. Alan decides to contribute $3,000 to his Roth IRA and $2,000 to his traditional IRA.

Example: Naomi, 25, had only $3,000 in interest income in 2011. Naomi marries Carl during the year. In 2011, Carl has taxable wages of $34,000. He plans to contribute $5,000 to his traditional IRA. If he and Naomi file a joint return, each can contribute $5,000 to a traditional IRA. This is because Naomi, who has no "qualifying" compensation, can include Carl's compensation, reduced by the amount of his IRA contribution ($34,000 − $5,000 = $29,000) to her own compensation ($0) to figure her maximum contribution to a traditional IRA. Since they are filing a joint return, she can substitute Carl's qualifying compensation in order to contribute to her own traditional IRA. They both may contribute the maximum in 2011 ($5,000 each).

However, even if they file a joint return, married taxpayers' combined IRA contributions cannot exceed their combined compensation, and neither spouse can contribute more than $5,000 (or $6,000 for 50 and older) to his or her own IRA.

Example: Elliott and June are both age 49 and married. Elliott has $23,000 in pension income for the year. June has $13,000 in pension income and $7,000 in wages. Only June's wages count as "qualifying compensation" for the purposes of an IRA. June may contribute the maximum to her IRA ($5,000). If they file jointly, then Elliott can contribute $2,000 (the remaining amount of June's qualifying compensation, $7,000 − $5,000 = $2,000).

Once again, a married couple cannot set up a "joint" IRA account. Each individual must have his or her own IRA, but married spouses may choose to make contributions to a spouse's IRA, up to the legal limit, if they file jointly. If taxpayers choose to file separately, then they must consider only their own qualifying compensation for IRA purposes.

> **Example:** Greg is 35, works full-time, and made $65,000 in 2011. His wife, Laverne, is 34, has a part-time job, and made $3,600 in 2011. They choose to file separately (MFS). Since they file MFS and Laverne only has $3,600 in compensation, Laverne is limited to a $3,600 IRA contribution. Greg may contribute a full $5,000 to his own IRA account.

A taxpayer cannot claim the adjustment for an IRA contribution on **Form 1040EZ;** the taxpayer must use either **Form 1040A** or **Form 1040**.

Rules for Deductibility of a Traditional IRA

A *contribution* to a traditional IRA and *the deductibility* of the contribution are two different things. Not everyone is allowed to deduct his IRA contributions. The deduction for contributions made to a traditional IRA depends on whether the taxpayer is covered by an employer retirement plan. The deduction is also affected by income and by filing status.

A taxpayer is permitted to have a traditional IRA whether or not he is covered by an employer retirement plan. However, if the taxpayer is covered by an employer retirement plan, he may be entitled to only a partial deduction or no deduction at all.

Even if a taxpayer exceeds the income limits for making a tax-deductible contribution to a traditional IRA, he may always make an after-tax contribution to a traditional IRA. This means that, even though the contribution may not be deductible, a taxpayer may still choose to contribute to his retirement on an after-tax basis. In either case, earnings will grow on a tax-deferred basis.

If a taxpayer makes **non-deductible** contributions to a traditional IRA, he must attach **Form 8606,** *Non-deductible IRAs.* **Form 8606** reflects a taxpayer's cumulative non-deductible contributions, which is his tax basis in the IRA. If a taxpayer does not report non-deductible contributions properly, then all future withdrawals from the IRA will be taxed unless the taxpayer can prove, with satisfactory evidence, that non-deductible contributions were made.

Traditional IRA Phase-Outs

Phase-Out Ranges for Deductibility

A taxpayer can take a deduction for IRA contributions of:
- $5,000 ($6,000 if he is age 50 or older), or
- 100% of qualifying compensation (whichever is smaller).

If the taxpayer (or spouse) is not covered by an employer plan, then the traditional IRA contribution is deductible. However, the contribution will be phased-out (reduced) if either the taxpayer or his spouse (or both) are covered by a retirement plan at work. The rules get more complicated at this point.

Out Ranges When Covered by an Employer Plan

a taxpayer is covered by an employer retirement plan, then the tax-deductible bution to a traditional IRA is phased out at the following income limits:

Phase-outs for Those Covered by an Employer Plan	
Filing Status	Income Range
MFJ or QW	$90,000 - $110,000
MFS (living with spouse)	$0 - $10,000
Single, HOH, or MFS (living apart)	$56,000 - $66,000

Taxpayer's Spouse Covered By An Employer's Retirement Plan:	
Filing Status	Income Range
MFJ (spouse covered)	$169,000 - $179,000
MFS (spouse covered)	$0 - $10,000
Single, QW, HOH, or MFS (spouse not covered)	No limit

If the taxpayer's income for the year is *under* the phase-out limits, the IRA contribution is fully tax-deductible. If the income falls *within* the phase-out range, the IRA contribution is partially deductible. If the income falls *above* the phase-out range, none of the IRA contribution is deductible.

Example: Tamara is single and earned $95,000 in 2011. She is covered by a retirement plan at work, but she still wants to contribute to a traditional IRA. She is phased out for the deduction because her income exceeds the threshold for single filers. If she contributes to an IRA in 2011, she must file **Form 8606** to report her non-deductible contribution.

Married taxpayers who are filing separately (MFS) have a much lower phase-out range than any other filing status. However, if a taxpayer files a separate return and **did not live** with his or her spouse at any time during the year, the taxpayer is not treated as married for the purpose of these limits, and the applicable dollar limit is that of a single taxpayer.

Example: Don is separated from his wife, although they are not divorced. They have lived in separate residences for the past three years. In 2011, Don earned $40,000 and files MFS. He is allowed to deduct his full IRA contribution. This is because he did not live with his spouse at any time during the year, and therefore he is not subject to the normal IRA phase-out limits that apply to MFS filers.

Required Minimum Distributions

A person cannot keep funds in a traditional IRA indefinitely. Eventually they must be distributed. Traditional IRAs are subject to Required Minimum Distributions (RMDs). When a retirement plan account owner reaches 70½ years of age, he is required to take a minimum distribution from the IRA every year. The amount is based on IRS tables.[45]

IRA owners are responsible for taking the correct amount of RMDs on time every year from their accounts. Taxpayers face stiff penalties for failure to take RMDs. Failure to take an RMD can result in a penalty tax equal to 50% of the amount the taxpayer *should* have withdrawn, but did not. If the taxpayer fails to make a required minimum distribution, then he must file IRS **Form 5329**, *Additional Taxes on Qualified Plans*, to report the excise tax that applies on the failure to take a required RMD.

RMDs must be taken starting with the year the taxpayer reaches age 70½. The latest the taxpayer may take an RMD is by April 1 following the year he turns 70½. The required minimum distribution for any year after the year a taxpayer turns 70½ must be made by December 31.

Taxpayers must figure their required minimum distribution for each year by dividing the IRA account balance at the end of the *preceding year* by the applicable distribution period on the IRS tables.[46]

Example: Dinah was born on October 1, 1940. She reaches age 70½ in 2011. Her required RMD beginning date is April 1, 2012. As of December 31, 2011, her IRA account balance was $26,500. Using IRS tables, the applicable distribution period for someone her age (71) is 26.5 years. Her required minimum distribution for 2011 is $1,000 ($26,500 ÷ 26.5). That amount must be distributed to her by April 1, 2012, in order to avoid the 50% excise tax.

Example: Ron is 73. He must take his first Required Minimum Distribution by December 31, 2011.

When the owner of an IRA owner dies before RMDs have begun, different RMD rules apply to the beneficiary of the IRA. Generally, the entire amount must be distributed to the beneficiary either:

- Within five years of the owner's death, or
- Over the life of the beneficiary, starting no later than one year following the owner's death.

However, if the beneficiary of a traditional IRA is a spouse, then he or she is granted special treatment. Surviving spouses may "roll over" their deceased spouse's IRA into their own. Only spouses are allowed this beneficial treatment. Spousal rollovers are covered more extensively later.

---

[45] An RMD is calculated for each account by dividing the balance of the IRA account by a life expectancy factor that the IRS publishes in tables in **Publication 590**, *Individual Retirement Arrangements (IRAs)*.

[46] Once again, these tables are printed in IRS **Publication 590**. For the EA exam, you will not need to memorize the tables, but you may be asked to figure a problem regarding RMDs. If that is the case, the IRS will provide the distribution period and you will be asked to figure the RMD.

Withdrawal Penalties on Early Distributions from an IRA

A taxpayer may choose to withdraw funds anytime from a traditional IRA account. However, early withdrawals from a traditional IRA before age 59½ will generally be subject to a 10% penalty, in addition to income tax on the distributed amount.

To discourage the use of retirement funds for purposes other than retirement, the IRS imposes a 10% additional "penalty" tax on certain early distributions from a traditional IRA.

There are some exceptions to the general rule for early distributions, however. An individual will not have to pay the additional 10% penalty in the following situations:

- When the taxpayer has unreimbursed medical expenses that exceed 7.5% of adjusted gross income
- When the distributions do not exceed the cost of the taxpayer's medical insurance
- Distributions that are due to permanent disability or death
- Distributions that are not more than qualified higher education expenses
- Distributions that are used to buy, build, or rebuild a first home (up to $10,000 of distributions)
- Distributions that are used to pay the IRS due to a levy
- Distributions that are made to a qualified reservist (an individual called up to active duty)

Even though these distributions will not be subject to the penalty, they WILL be subject to income tax.

Distributions that are properly rolled over into another retirement plan are not subject to either income tax or the 10% additional penalty. Taxpayers must complete a rollover within 60 days after the day they receive the distribution.

Example: Lauren is 43 years old and she takes a $5,000 distribution from her traditional IRA account. Lauren does not meet any of the exceptions to the 10% additional tax, so the $5,000 is an early distribution. Lauren must include the $5,000 in her gross income and pay income tax on it. Lauren must also pay an additional 10% penalty tax on the early distribution. The penalty is $500 (10% × $5,000).

Qualified Charitable Distribution (QCD)

A taxpayer may choose to may a "qualified charitable contribution" from his IRA without tax consequences. This election may be made from a Roth or a Traditional IRA. This special tax-free treatment of distributions for charitable purposes has been extended through December 31, 2011, with the following special rule:

For QCDs made during January 2011, taxpayers can elect to have the distribution deemed to have been made on December 31, 2010. If this election is made, the

QCD counts toward the 2010 exclusion limit of $100,000, as well as the 2010 m required distribution.

To qualify as a QCD, the IRA trustee must make the distribution directly to the qualified charity (the taxpayer CANNOT request a distribution and then donate the money later). Any distributions, including any RMDs, which the IRA owner actually receives cannot qualify as QCDs. Likewise, any tax withholdings on behalf of the owner from an IRA distribution cannot qualify as QCDs.

Roth IRA Rules

Many taxpayers prefer the Roth IRA, because it allows for tax-free growth. However, unlike a traditional IRA, a Roth IRA has income limits. That means high income earners are prohibited from contributing to a Roth. In contrast, there are no income limits to who can participate in a traditional IRA. In 2011, the following income limit rules apply to Roth IRAs:

2011 Roth IRA Participation Limits

Filing Status	Full Contribution	Phase-Out Range	No Roth IRA Allowed
Single, HOH filers[47]	Less than $107,000	$107,000 - $122,000	$122,000 or more
MFJ and QW filers	Less than $169,000	$169,000 - $179,000	$179,000 or more
MFS (lived with spouse)	N/A	$0 - $10,000	$10,000 or more

Anyone who earns income above the Roth threshold amount is not allowed to participate, contribute, or roll over into a Roth IRA.

Here are the major differences between a Roth IRA and a traditional IRA:

- Contributions to a Roth IRA are not deductible by the taxpayer, so participation in an employer plan is irrelevant.
- There are no required minimum distributions from a Roth IRA. A distribution is not required until a Roth IRA owner dies.
- Contributions to a Roth IRA can be made by persons who are over the age of 70½.
- Roth IRAs have income limits, but traditional IRAs do not.
- Roth IRA owners have a five-year initial holding period to qualify for tax-free distributions.

---

[47] This phase-out range also applies to MFS taxpayers who did not live with their spouses at all during the year.

IRA Rollovers in General

Generally, a "rollover" is a tax-free transfer from one retirement plan to *another* retirement plan. The contribution to the second retirement plan is called a "rollover contribution." *Most* rollovers are non-taxable events. However, sometimes taxpayers will choose to roll a traditional IRA into a Roth IRA (explained previously). In this case, the conversion will result in taxation of any untaxed amounts in the traditional IRA.

A taxpayer can always choose to receive a distribution from an IRA. The most common property in an IRA is stock or other securities, although some IRAs invest in other commodities such as bullion and real estate.

If a taxpayer sells the distributed property (such as stocks distributed from an IRA) and rolls over *all the proceeds* into another traditional IRA, no gain or loss is recognized. The sale proceeds (including any increase in value) are treated as part of the distribution and are not included in the taxpayer's gross income.

Example: On September 4, 2011, Mike begins a new job. He decides to transfer his retirement account to his new employer's plan. Mike receives a total distribution from his employer's retirement plan of $50,000 in cash and $50,000 in stock. On October 4, he rolls over the entire amount totaling $100,000 into another IRA account.

Any taxable distribution paid from an employer-sponsored retirement plan is subject to a mandatory withholding of 20%, even if the taxpayer intends to roll it over later. If the taxpayer does roll it over and wants to defer tax on the entire taxable portion, he will be forced to add funds from other sources equal to the amount withheld. In order to avoid this, a taxpayer should always request a direct transfer—where the employer transfers the distribution directly to another eligible retirement plan. Under this option, the 20% mandatory withholding does not apply. It is called a "direct rollover" when a taxpayer has a check for his rollover funds made payable directly to his new retirement account.

Rollover Time Limit: 60 Days to Complete

If a taxpayer receives an IRA distribution and wishes to make a rollover, he must complete the transaction by the 60th day after the day he receives the distribution from a traditional IRA account (or an employer's plan). The IRS may waive the 60-day requirement when the failure to do so would be inequitable, such as in the event of a casualty, disaster, or other event beyond the taxpayer's reasonable control.

The IRS allows only one rollover per IRA account in a 12-month period. However, a trustee-to-trustee transfer (or "direct transfer") can be done more than once a year. A "trustee to trustee" transfer is when an IRA's current custodian (such as a bank) directly transfers the funds to a new custodian. The transfer is done between the two companies and the money never touches the taxpayer's hands.

In 2011, Congress has permitted rollovers to be made directly from an IRA to a qualified public charity. This enables an IRA owner who is age 70½ or older to make a direct transfer to charity. The transfer may be up to $100,000 in one year and qualifies as an RMD. An inherited IRA cannot be rolled over, unless the beneficiary is the taxpayer's spouse.

Rollover after the Death of an IRA Owner

After the death of an IRA owner, a surviving spouse can elect to treat the IRA as being his or her own. Surviving spouses may "roll over" their deceased spouse's IRA into their own. ONLY spouses are allowed this beneficial treatment.

An IRA may not be rolled over into the account of any other family member or beneficiary after death. However, any amounts remaining in an IRA upon a taxpayer's death can be paid to beneficiaries without penalty (although the amounts will still be subject to tax).

After an IRA owner dies, the beneficiary can generally take distributions over his remaining life expectancy. The beneficiary's "life expectancy" is calculated by using the age of the beneficiary in the year following the year of the IRA owner's death. The IRS has tables for making these calculations.

Example: Allison, 42, and Lorenzo, 53, are married. Allison dies in 2011, and at the time of her death she has $50,000 in her traditional IRA account. Lorenzo chooses to roll over the entire $50,000 into his own IRA account, thereby avoiding taxation on the income until he retires and starts taking distributions.

Rollovers From a Traditional IRA to a Roth IRA

In 2010 and 2011, Congress eliminated the AGI and filing status requirements for *converting* a traditional IRA to a Roth IRA. Before 2010, high income taxpayers could not participate, contribute, or roll over funds to a Roth IRA. Although there are still income limits to who can *participate* in a Roth IRA, the new rules allow anyone to *convert* an existing traditional IRA to a Roth IRA. Congress has made a *conversion* to a Roth IRA possible, even for high wage earners.

In the case of a high-wage earner that is phased out for regular participation in a Roth IRA, this means that a taxpayer must first have a traditional IRA, and then rollover (convert) the funds to a Roth. This is an important concept to understand, because in 2011, any taxpayer is allowed to convert a traditional IRA to a Roth IRA *regardless* of income thresholds. Taxpayers who decide to convert to Roth IRAs must declare the conversion amounts on their individual returns.

Remember, the Roth conversion is treated as a rollover, not as participation in a Roth. If a taxpayer desires to convert his traditional IRA to a Roth IRA, he is required to pay federal income taxes on any pretax contributions, **as well as any growth** in the investment's value. Once the funds are converted to a Roth, all of the investment grows tax free, and funds can be withdrawn on a tax-free basis.

> **Example:** Becky converted her traditional IRA to a Roth IRA in 2011. The traditional IRA had a balance of $100,000. She reports the conversion and must pay the tax on the conversion. She is in the 28% federal tax bracket, so Becky is required to pay $28,000 in taxes on the conversion.

Any Roth conversions in subsequent years are included in income during the tax year in which the conversion is made. A Roth conversion is reported on **Form 8606, Non-deductible IRAs**. Rules for Roth conversions:

- Taxpayers who decide to convert to a Roth must pay taxes on the amount they convert.
- Penalties apply if the taxpayer withdraws from the Roth within five years of the conversion.
- Taxpayers can choose to do a partial conversion.

In the case of an inherited IRA, only an IRA inherited from a spouse may be converted to a Roth. As a general rule, a taxpayer is allowed to treat an inherited IRA from his deceased spouse as his own IRA, which also includes the choice to do a Roth conversion. This rule only applies to spouses. Non-spousal inheritors (for example, a child who inherits an IRA from a deceased parent) are not allowed to roll over or convert a traditional IRA to a Roth.

Excise Tax on Excess Contributions

If a taxpayer *accidentally* contributes more to his IRA than he is legally entitled to, the excess contribution is subject to a 6% excise tax. The IRS will allow a taxpayer to *correct* an excess contribution if certain rules are followed. If he makes an excess contribution that exceeds his yearly maximum or his qualifying compensation, the excess contributions (and all related earnings) must be withdrawn from the IRA before the due date.

The excess contributions must be withdrawn by the due date of the tax return, *including* extensions. If a taxpayer corrects the excess contribution in time, the 6% penalty will apply only to the interest earned on the excess contribution. Contributions made in the year a taxpayer reaches 70½ are also considered excess contributions.

Each year that the excess amounts remain in the traditional IRA the taxpayer must pay a 6% tax. However, this tax can never exceed more than 6% of the combined value of all the taxpayer's IRAs at the end of the tax year. In order to correct an "improper contribution" to an IRA, the taxpayer must withdraw the contribution and any earnings on that amount. Relief from the 6% excise penalty is available only if the following are true:

- The taxpayer must withdraw the full amount of the excess contribution on or before the due date (including extensions) for filing the tax return for the year of the contribution.
- The withdrawal must include any income earned that is attributable to the excess contribution.

Taxpayers must include the earnings on the excess contribution as taxable income, and that income is reported on the return for the year in which the withdrawal was made.

> **Example:** Betsy is 66, self-employed, and also owns rental properties. Betsy contributes the maximum amount of $6,000 to her traditional IRA in December 2011. She is very busy and her records are poor, so she files for an extension to prepare her tax return. When Betsy finally gives her records to her accountant, he discovers that her taxable income from self-employment is only $3,000. Her passive rental income is $18,000. Only the self-employment income counts as "compensation" for the purposes of contributing to a traditional IRA, so Betsy has inadvertently made an excess contribution of $3,000. She must withdraw the excess contribution (and any interest earned on the excess contribution) by the due date of her return or face an excise tax of 6% on the $3,000.

Differences Between a Traditional IRA and a Roth IRA

Issue	Traditional IRA	Roth IRA
Age limit	A person over 70½ cannot contribute.	No age limit.
2011 Contribution limits	$5,000, or $6,000 if age 50 or older by the end of 2011.	$5,000, or $6,000 if age 50 or older by the end of 2011.
Are contributions deductible?	Usually, yes. Deductibility depends on AGI, filing status, and whether the person is covered by a retirement plan at work.	No. You can never deduct contributions to a Roth IRA. Participation in an employer plan is irrelevant, since contributions are not deductible
Filing requirements	No filing requirement unless non-deductible contributions are made.	No filing requirement.
Mandatory distributions	A person must begin receiving required minimum distributions by April 1 of the year following the year he or she reaches age 70½.	No. There are no required distributions unless the IRA owner dies.
How distributions are taxed	Distributions from a traditional IRA are taxed as ordinary income.	Distributions from a Roth IRA are not taxed.
Income limits	No income limits.	Income limits exist, but in 2011 anyone can convert a traditional IRA to a Roth IRA. Taxes apply on the conversion.

Unit 9: Questions

1. Lucas, an unmarried college student working part-time, earns $3,500 in 2011. He also receives $500 in interest income and $4,000 from his parents to help pay tuition. What is his maximum IRA contribution in 2011?

A. $0.
B. $3,500.
C. $5,000.
D. $6,000.

The answer is B. His IRA contribution for 2011 is limited to $3,500, the total amount of his wages. The other income (the interest income and the gifted money from his parents) are not qualifying compensation for IRA purposes. ###

2. Vic, age 36 and single, is in the Marines. Vic has the following income in 2011 totaling $35,100:

$30,500 of non-taxable combat pay.
$2,100 of regular wages.
$4,600 of interest income.
What is the maximum amount of money that Vic can contribute to a traditional IRA?

A. $2,100.
B. $4,600.
C. $5,000.
D. $6,000.

The answer is C. Vic may contribute $5,000, the maximum contribution allowed for his age. That is because a taxpayer may elect to treat non-taxable combat pay as taxable compensation for IRA purposes. The interest income would not be considered "compensation" for IRA purposes. ###

3. Rafael, 40, earns $26,000 in 2011. Although he is allowed to contribute up to $5,000 for 2011, he only has enough cash to contribute $2,000. On May 15, 2012, Rafael expects to get a big bonus, and he wishes to make a "catch-up" contribution for 2011. Rafael filed a timely extension for his tax return. Which of the following statements is TRUE?

A. Rafael can contribute an additional $3,000 in May 2012 for his 2011 tax year so long as he files his tax return by the extended due date.
B. Rafael cannot contribute an additional $3,000 after April 17, 2012.
C. Rafael can contribute an additional $3,000 in May 2012 for his 2011 tax year only if he files his return by April 17, 2012.
D. Rafael cannot make a 2011 contribution to his IRA after December 31, 2011.

The answer is B. Rafael cannot contribute an additional $3,000 after April 17, 2012, regardless of whether he files an extension. If contributions to a traditional IRA for the year were less than the limit, a taxpayer cannot contribute more after the original due date of the tax return to make up the difference. ###

4. Celeste, who is 50 and single, worked recently for a telephone company in France and earned $48,500 for which she claimed the foreign earned income exclusion. In addition to that she earned $3,200 as an employee of an answering service while she was in the U.S. She also received alimony of $400 for the year. What is her maximum amount of allowable contribution to a traditional IRA for year 2011?

A. $3,200.
B. $3,600.
C. $5,000.
D. $6,000.

The answer is B. Foreign earned income and any other income that is excluded from tax is also excluded for IRA purposes (with the exception of non-taxable combat pay). Alimony and wages earned in the U.S. are both earned income for IRA purposes. Therefore, only the $400 alimony and the $3,200 earned in the U.S. would be considered "compensation" for the purposes of an IRA contribution. ###

5. Kristin, 42, is a full-time graduate student with $1,200 in wages. She marries Omar, 50, during the year. Omar has taxable compensation of $46,000 in 2011. What is the maximum they can contribute to their traditional IRA accounts in 2011 if they file jointly?

A. $1,200.
B. $6,200.
C. $10,000.
D. $11,000.

The answer is D. They can contribute $11,000 ($5,000 for Kristin and $6,000 for Omar). If they file jointly, Kristin can contribute $5,000 to a traditional IRA, and Omar can contribute $6,000 (because he is 50—the increased contribution starts at 50 years of age). Even though Kristin only has $1,200 in compensation, she can add Omar's compensation to her own compensation to figure her maximum contribution to a traditional IRA. ###

6. Jody is single, 51, and has the following compensation in 2011:

$1,600 in annuity income.
$3,000 in wages.
$2,300 in alimony.
$3,000 in interest income.
$6,000 in rental income.

What is the maximum amount that she can contribute to her traditional IRA in 2011?
A. $3,000.
B. $5,000.
C. $5,300.
D. $6,000.

The answer is C. Only Jody's wage income of $3,000 and the $2,300 in alimony qualify as "compensation" for the purposes of an IRA. The annuity income and the interest income do not qualify. ###

7. Derek, age 62, is retired with $11,000 in interest income. He has no other taxable income in 2011. Derek marries Virginia, age 46, on March 15, 2011. Virginia has taxable compensation of $50,000 for the year. She plans to contribute $5,000 to a traditional IRA. How much can Derek contribute to an IRA?

A. $0.
B. $4,000.
C. $5,000.
D. $6,000.

The answer is D. Since Derek is over 50, he can choose to contribute $6,000 to an IRA. Even though Derek only has interest income, his wife has wage income. If spouses file a joint return, each can contribute to a traditional IRA, even if only one spouse has qualifying compensation. ###

8. An "excess contribution" to an IRA is subject to a tax. Which of the following is TRUE?

A. The taxpayer will not have to pay the 6% tax if he withdraws the excess contribution and any income earned on the excess contribution before the due date of the tax return for the year it is due, including extensions.
B. The 6% tax is due on both the excess contributions and any income earned on the excess contribution, even if the taxpayer withdraws the excess from the account.
C. A taxpayer will not have to pay the 6% tax if he withdraws the excess contribution and any income earned on the excess contribution before the due date of the tax return for the year it is due, NOT including extensions.
D. A taxpayer will not have to pay the 6% on interest earned on the excess contributions so long as the taxpayer is disa-disabled.

The answer is A. The taxpayer will not have to pay the 6% tax if the excess contribution is withdrawn by the due date of his return, *including extensions*. The taxpayer must also withdraw interest or other income earned on the excess contribution. He must complete the withdrawal by the due date of the tax return, including extensions, in order to avoid the 6% excise tax. ###

9. Elizabeth and Landon are 62 years old, married, and lived together all year. They both work and each has a traditional IRA. In 2011, Landon earned $4,000 in wages and $11,000 in annuity income. Elizabeth earned $52,000. They prefer to file separately. If they file separate returns, what is the maximum that Landon can contribute to his IRA?

A. $1,000.
B. $4,000.
C. $5,000.
D. $6,000.

The answer is B. If Married Filing Separately, Landon can contribute no more than his $4,000 in wages, which is his only qualifying compensation for IRA purposes. ###

10. Colton, 49, and Molly, 52, are married and file jointly. They both work and each has a traditional IRA. In 2011, Molly earned $2,000 and Colton earned $50,000. If they file jointly, what is the maximum Molly can contribute to her IRA?

A. $2,000.
B. $5,000.
C. $6,000.
D. $12,000.

The answer is C. They can both agree to contribute up to $6,000 to Molly's IRA account. Colton can contribute $5,000 to his own IRA because he is under 50 years old. ###

11. Preston and Ruby are 50 years old and married. They both work and each has a traditional IRA. In 2011, Preston earned $5,000 and Ruby earned $32,000. If they file jointly, what is the maximum they can contribute to all their IRAs?

A. $5,000.
B. $6,000.
C. $10,000.
D. $12,000.

The answer is D. If Married Filing Jointly, they can contribute up to $12,000 to all their IRAs. This is because they are over 50. The maximum contribution for taxpayers who are 50 and above is $6,000 per person. ###

12. Frank, 72, and Sue, 61, are married and file jointly. In 2011, Frank earned $30,000 and Sue earned $7,500. If Frank and Sue file jointly, how much can they contribute to their traditional IRAs?

A. $5,000.
B. $6,000.
C. $11,000.
D. $12,000.

The answer is B. Only Sue can contribute to an IRA. Frank **cannot** contribute because he is over 70½ years old. Sue can contribute up to $6,000 to her IRA because she is over 50. ###

13. Which IRS form is used to report *non-deductible* retirement plan contributions?

A. Form 8606.
B. Form 1040.
C. Form 8886.
D. Form 8889.

The answer is A. To designate IRA contributions as non-deductible, a taxpayer must file Form 8606. ###

14. Miguel is 47. In 2011, he contributed $1,000 to a Roth IRA. He also wants to contribute to a traditional IRA account. What is the maximum he can contribute to a traditional IRA in 2011?

A. $0.
B. $3,000.
C. $4,000.
D. $5,000.

The answer is C. The answer is $4,000; the 2011 maximum for contributions to all types of IRAs is $5,000 for taxpayers under 50. Taxpayers are allowed to have different types of IRA accounts, but they must still follow the maximum contribution thresholds. ###

15. Annette, age 40, and Gill, age 48, are married and file jointly. Annette is covered by a retirement plan at work, but Gill is not. Annette contributed $2,000 to her traditional IRA and $3,000 to a traditional IRA for Gill. Annette has a modified AGI of $90,000; Gill has a modified AGI of $98,000. What is their allowable traditional IRA deduction?

A. $5,000.
B. $3,000.
C. $2,000.
D. Zero.

The answer is D. Annette and Gill's allowable traditional IRA deduction is zero because their modified AGI is over the phase-out limit of $179,000. They are still allowed to make a non-deductible IRA contribution. Non-deductible IRA contributions are reported on **Form 8606**. ###

16. Shari wants to roll over her retirement account to another bank. She received a distribution in 2011. How long does Shari have to complete the rollover in order to avoid income tax on the distribution?

A. 30 days.
B. 60 days.
C. Until the end of the year.
D. Until the due date of the return.

The answer is B. Shari has 60 days to complete the rollover. If she does not complete the rollover within 60 days, the distribution is treated as a taxable event and is subject to income tax. ###

17. Janelle plans to make a contribution to her traditional IRA. She files her 2011 tax return on March 1, 2012, claiming a deduction for her IRA contribution. However, she forgets to make the contribution in time and misses the deadline. What must Janelle do?

A. Janelle must file an amended return.
B. Janelle may claim the contribution as income in the following year.
C. Janelle must file an extension.
D. Janelle must pay an early withdrawal penalty.

The answer is A. If a contribution is reported on the 2011 return but is not made by the deadline, the taxpayer must file an amended return. IRA contributions must be made by the due date for filing the return, NOT including extensions. ###

18. David is 57 and he contributed $2,000 to his Roth IRA. What is the maximum he can contribute to a traditional IRA?

A. $0.
B. $3,000.
C. $4,000.
D. $5,000.

The answer is C. The answer is $4,000; the 2011 maximum for contributions to all types of IRAs is $6,000 for taxpayers who are 50 or older. Since David is 57, he is allowed to contribute a maximum of $6,000 combined. ###

19. Which of the following is considered an excess contribution to an IRA?

A. A traditional IRA contribution made in the year a taxpayer reaches 70½.
B. A rollover to a Roth IRA.
C. A contribution made by a taxpayer who only has alimony income.
D. A Roth contribution made by a taxpayer who is 75.

The answer is A. Contributions to a traditional IRA made in the year a taxpayer reaches 70½ (and any later years) are considered excess contributions. In general, an excess contribution and any earnings on it are subject to an additional 6% tax if the taxpayer does not withdraw the contribution by the due date of the tax return, including extensions.###

Unit 10: The Standard Deduction and Itemized Deductions

> **More Reading:**
> Publication 502, *Medical and Dental Expenses*
> Publication 529, *Miscellaneous Deductions*
> Publication 600, *State and Local General Sales Taxes*
> Publication 936, *Home Mortgage Interest Deduction*
> Publication 547, *Casualties, Disasters, and Thefts*
> Publication 526, *Charitable Contributions*
> Publication 561, *Determining the Value of Donated Property*
> Publication 587, *Business Use of Your Home*

The Standard Deduction in General

Taxpayers may choose to take the "standard deduction" or "itemize" their deductions on their tax return. If a taxpayer chooses to itemize, then he must file a **Schedule A** along with his **Form 1040**. When taxpayers make the choice, they should use the type of deduction that results in the lower tax.

The standard deduction eliminates the need for taxpayers to itemize actual deductions, such as medical expenses, charitable contributions, and taxes. It is available to U.S. citizens and resident aliens who are individuals, married persons, and heads of household. The standard deduction is adjusted every year for inflation. In some cases, the standard deduction can consist of two parts: the *basic* standard deduction and an *additional* standard deduction amount for age, blindness, or both.

The additional amount for blindness will be allowed if the taxpayer is blind on the last day of the tax year, even if he did not qualify as "blind" the rest of the year. A taxpayer must obtain a statement from an eye doctor that states:

- The taxpayer cannot see better than 20/200 even while corrected with eyeglasses, or
- The taxpayer's field of vision is not more than 20 degrees (the taxpayer has disabled peripheral vision).

The additional amount for age will be allowed if the taxpayer is at least age 65 at the end of the tax year.

Some taxpayers are not allowed to use the standard deduction. The following taxpayers are not eligible:

- Non-resident aliens and dual-status aliens.
- Individuals who file returns for periods of less than 12 months.
- A married couple who file separate returns (MFS) and one spouse itemizes deductions. The other spouse must also itemize deductions, even if the other spouse has no expenses to itemize.

11 Standard Deduction Amounts

The standard deduction is a dollar amount that reduces the amount of income at is taxed. The standard deduction amount is based on the taxpayer's filing status.

Standard Deduction Amounts	
Filing Status	2011
Single or MFS	$5,800
Married Filing Jointly	$11,600
Head of Household	$8,500
Qualifying Widow(er)	$11,600

An *increased* standard deduction is available to taxpayers who are:

- 65 or older and/or
- Blind or partially blind

*Note: Don't be confused by this concept. The "additional" standard deduction is NOT a credit or an itemized deduction. It is simply an increase over the regular standard deduction amount that Congress has decided to give to taxpayers who are over 65 and/or blind.

The increased standard deduction amount in these cases is $1,150 per taxpayer for married filers and $1,450 for Single and Head of Household.

Example: Joel, 46, and Christine, 33, are filing a joint return for 2011. Neither is blind. They decide not to itemize their deductions. Their standard deduction in 2011 is $11,600.

Example: Darius, 66, and Lisa, 59, are filing a joint return for 2011. Darius is over 65 and Lisa is blind. They do not itemize deductions. Because they are Married Filing Jointly, their base standard deduction is $11,600. Because Darius is over age 65, he can claim an additional standard deduction of $1,150. Because Lisa is blind, she can also claim an additional $1,150. Therefore, their total standard deduction is $13,900 ($11,600 + $1,150 +$1,150).

The standard deduction for a deceased taxpayer is the same as if the taxpayer had lived the entire year, with one exception: if the taxpayer died *before* his 65th birthday, the higher standard deduction for being 65 does not apply.

Example: Richard is single and died on November 1, 2011. He would have been 65 if he had reached his birthday on December 12, 2011. He does not qualify for a higher standard deduction for being 65, because he died before his 65th birthday. His standard deduction would be $5,800 on his final tax return, which should be filed by his executor.

Standard Deduction for Dependents (who File a Return)

A dependent is also allowed a standard deduction. If a dependent is claimed on another person's return, his standard deduction amount is the GREATER of:
- $950, or
- The dependent's *earned* income (such as wages) plus $300 (but not more than the regular standard deduction amount. For a single person, this is $5,800 in 2011).

> **Example:** Georgia is single, 22, and a full-time student. Georgia works a part-time job on campus. Her parents supported her, so they claimed her as a dependent on their 2011 tax return. Georgia will also file a return, and she will take the standard deduction. In 2011, Georgia has interest income of $120, taxes withheld from her wages totaling $35, and total wages of $780 from her part-time job. Her standard deduction is $1,080 ($780 wages + $300).

However, the standard deduction may be higher if the dependent is 65 or older or blind.

> **Example:** Amy is 19, single, and legally blind. She is claimed on her parents' 2011 return. Amy has interest income of $1,300 and wages from a part-time job of $2,900. She has no itemized deductions. Her base amount for the standard deduction is $3,200 ($2,900 + $300, which equals her wages plus $300). Because Amy is also blind, she is allowed an *additional* standard deduction amount of $1,450. So her standard deduction is figured as follows: ($2,900 + $300 + $1,450) = $4,650.

Itemized Deductions

Itemized deductions allow taxpayers to reduce their taxable income based on specific personal expenses. Itemized deductions are taken *instead* of the standard deduction. If the total itemized deductions are greater than the standard deduction, they will result in a lower taxable income and lower tax.

In general, taxpayers benefit from itemizing deductions if they have mortgage interest, large unreimbursed medical expenses, or other large expenses such as charitable contributions. Generally, the taxpayer may choose whether to take itemized deductions or the standard deduction, and may take whichever deduction gives him the highest benefit. However, the following taxpayers are *forced* to itemize:

- Married Filing Separately when one spouse itemizes: the other spouse is also forced to itemize.
- A non-resident or dual-status alien during the year (who is not married to a U.S. citizen or resident).
- A taxpayer with a short year return.

If any of the above situations applies, the taxpayer must itemize personal deductions. He cannot choose the standard deduction.

> **Example:** Shannon files as Married Filing Separately. Her husband, Grant, will itemize his deductions. Shannon cannot use the standard deduction; she is also forced to itemize her deductions. A married taxpayer, filing separately, whose spouse itemizes deductions is not allowed to claim the standard deduction; if one spouse itemizes, the other must itemize (even if the amount is "0").

Itemized deductions are claimed on **Schedule A**. Itemized deductions include amounts paid for:

- Qualified medical and dental expenses
- Certain taxes (property tax and state income tax are the most common)
- Mortgage interest
- Gifts to charity
- Casualty and theft losses
- Certain miscellaneous deductions

Medical and Dental Expenses (Subject to the 7.5% Limit)

Medical and dental expenses are deductible only if taxpayers itemize their deductions. Further, taxpayers can deduct only the amount of unreimbursed medical expenses that exceeds 7.5% of their adjusted gross income (AGI). Qualified medical expenses include expenses paid for:

- The taxpayer
- The taxpayer's spouse
- Dependents (the individual must have been a dependent at the time the medical services were provided or at the time the expenses were paid)

> ***Exception:** If a child of divorced or separated parents is claimed as a dependent on *either* parent's return, each parent may deduct the medical expenses he or she individually paid for the child. There is also an exception for medical expenses paid on behalf of former spouses pursuant to a divorce decree. A taxpayer may also deduct medical expenses that were paid on behalf of an adopted child, even before the adoption is final. The child must qualify as a dependent and must be a member of the taxpayer's household during the year the medical expenses were paid.

> **Example:** Colby and Carmen are divorced. Their son, Raymond, lives with Carmen, who claims him as a dependent. Carmen deducts Raymond's annual medical and dental bills. However, in April, Raymond fell on the playground and fractured his leg and arm. The out-of-pocket expenses were $5,500. Raymond's father, Colby, paid for the emergency room visit and the expenses related to the injury. Therefore, Colby may deduct the emergency bill he paid, even though he does not claim his son as a dependent on his return. Colby can claim the expenses based on the exception for divorced/separated parents.

A taxpayer can deduct medical expenses paid for a dependent parent. All the standard rules for a dependency exemption apply, so a dependent parent would not have to live with the taxpayer in order to qualify.

> **Example:** Julie pays all the medical expenses for her mother, Rose, who is her dependent. Rose does not live with Julie. The medical expenses are still deductible on Julie's tax return as an itemized deduction if the 7.5% limit is reached.

Taxpayers may deduct unreimbursed medical and dental expenses and long-term care insurance premiums. Even vehicle mileage may be deducted if the transportation was for medical reasons, such as trips to and from medical appointments.

The 2011 standard mileage rate allowed for out-of-pocket expenses when used for medical reasons is:

- 19 cents per mile before 7/1/2011
- 23.5 cents per mile after 6/30/2011

The taxpayer can also deduct parking fees and tolls, the cost of a ferry or taxi, or other types of transportation, so long as it is for medical reasons.

In this section, the term *"7.5% limit"* is used to refer to 7.5% of adjusted gross income. A taxpayer must subtract 7.5% (.075) of his AGI from gross medical and dental expenses to figure the medical expense deduction.

> **Example:** Tracy's AGI is $40,000. She had actual medical expenses totaling $2,500. Tracy cannot deduct any of her medical expenses because they are not more than 7.5% of her AGI (7.5% of which is $3,000).

> **Example:** Olivia's AGI is $100,000. In 2011, she paid for a knee operation. She had $10,000 of out-of-pocket medical expenses related to the surgery. In this case, $2,500 would be allowed as an itemized deduction, the amount in excess of the $7,500 base ($100,000 X .075 = $7,500).

Qualifying Medical Expenses

Qualifying medical expenses include the costs of diagnosis, cure, mitigation, treatment, or prevention of disease, and the costs for medical (not cosmetic) treatments. They include the costs of:

- Medically necessary equipment, supplies, and diagnostic devices
- Dental and vision care expenses, such as prescription eyeglasses and contact lenses
- Transportation costs to obtain medical care
- Qualified long-term care insurance

Deductible medical expenses may include but are not limited to:

- Fees paid to doctors, dentists, surgeons, chiropractors, psychiatrists, psychologists, and nontraditional medical practitioners

- In-patient hospital care or nursing home services, *including* the cost of meals and lodging charged by the hospital or nursing home
- Payments for acupuncture treatments
- Lactation supplies (new for 2011)
- Treatment at a center for alcohol or drug addiction, for participation in a smoking-cessation program, and for prescription drugs to alleviate nicotine withdrawal
- A weight-loss program prescribed by a physician (but NOT payments for diet food items or the payment of health club dues)
- Payments for insulin and payments for drugs that require a prescription
- Payments for admission and transportation to a medical conference relating to a chronic disease (but NOT the costs for meals and lodging while attending the conference)

Some examples of deductible medical expenses include the cost of false teeth, laser eye surgery, hearing aids, crutches, wheelchairs, and guide dogs for the blind or deaf.

In some cases, even veterinary care can be deducted as a medical expense. The IRS allows taxpayers to include the cost of service animals in medical expenses. An animal trained to assist persons with other physical disabilities may also be deducted. Guide dogs or other service animals to be used by a visually-impaired, disabled, or hearing-impaired person are considered "medical devices" for the purpose of this rule. Specifically, amounts paid for the care of these specially-trained animals are deductible as medical expenses.

Medical Insurance and Long-Term Care Premiums

Qualifying medical expenses include medical insurance premiums that the taxpayer has paid with after-tax dollars. A taxpayer may only include the medical expenses paid during the year, regardless of when the services were provided. If a taxpayer pays medical expenses by check, the day a taxpayer mails the check is generally accepted as the date of payment. If a medical expense is paid by credit card, the date the credit card is charged is accepted as the date of payment.

Along with regular medical insurance, a taxpayer may also deduct the costs of qualified long-term care insurance as a medical expense. For 2011, the maximum deductible amount of qualified long-term care premiums has increased. Qualified long-term care premiums, up to the amounts shown below, can be included as medical expenses on **Form 1040, Schedule A:**

- $340 - age 40 or under
- $640 - age 41 to 50
- $1,270 - age 51 to 60
- $3,390 - age 61 to 70

- $4,240 - age 71 and over

These limits are per person.

If a taxpayer (or a dependent) is in a nursing home, and the primary reason for being there is medically related, the entire cost, including meals and lodging, is a medical expense.

Medical expenses must be primarily to alleviate or prevent a physical or mental defect or illness. Medical expenses do NOT include expenses that are merely "beneficial" to general health, such as vitamins, spa treatments, gym memberships, or vacations. In addition, over-the-counter medications cannot be deducted as medical expenses on **Schedule A**.

Medically Related Legal Fees

A taxpayer can deduct legal fees that are necessary to authorize treatment for a mental illness. However, legal fees for the management of a guardianship estate, or legal fees for conducting the affairs of a person being treated are not deductible as medical expenses.

Medical Expenses of Deceased Taxpayers

An election can be made to deduct medical expenses paid by a deceased taxpayer. This is legal for one year *after* the date of the taxpayer's death. The expenses may be treated as if paid when the medical services were provided (even if the medical expenses are not actually paid until after the taxpayer's death). In some cases the taxpayer's **Form 1040** must be amended. **Form 1040X** is the correct form to submit an amended tax return. The medical expenses of a deceased taxpayer are still subject to a 7.5% floor.

Example: Anne had heart surgery in November 2011 and incurred $20,000 in medical bills. Anne died on January 2, 2012. The 2011 medical bills were still unpaid at the time of her death. The executor of Anne's estate may elect to deduct her medical expenses in 2011, even though the medical expenses are paid at a later date.

Cosmetic Surgery

Cosmetic surgery is only deductible if it is used to correct a defect or disease. Cosmetic procedures simply for the enhancement of someone's physical appearance are not deductible medical expenses.

Example: Adrienne undergoes surgery to remove a breast as part of treatment for cancer. She pays a surgeon to reconstruct her breast. The surgery to reconstruct the breast corrects a deformity directly related to the disease. The cost of the surgery is includable in her medical expenses.

Example: Miles is two years old and was born with a congenital deformity. His parents pay for cosmetic surgery to correct the deformity. The surgery is deductible as a medical expense because it corrects a defect.

Medically Related Meals, Lodging, and Transportation

A taxpayer can deduct the cost of meals and lodging at a hospital or similar institution if the principal reason for being there is to receive medical care. The taxpayer can deduct the cost of lodging if all of the following requirements are met:

- The lodging is primarily for medical care.
- The medical care must be provided by a doctor, hospital, or a medical care facility.
- There is no significant element of personal pleasure or recreation.

The IRS imposes a $50 limit, per person, per night, for lodging for medically-related issues. There is no deduction for meals.

Capital Improvements for Medical Reasons

Capital improvements such as home improvements are usually not deductible by the taxpayer. However, a home improvement may qualify as a deductible expense if its main purpose is to provide a medical benefit to the taxpayer or to dependent family members.

The deduction for capital improvements is limited to the excess of the actual cost of the improvements over the increase in the fair market value of the home. Home improvements that qualify as deductible medical expenses include:

- Wheelchair ramps
- Lowering of kitchen cabinets
- Railings and support bars
- Elevators

Tenants may deduct the entire cost of disability-related improvements, since they are not the owners of the property.

Example: Jay has a heart condition. He cannot easily climb stairs or get into a bathtub. On his doctor's advice, he installs a special sit-in bathtub and a stair lift on the first floor of his rented house. The landlord did not pay any of the cost of buying and installing the special equipment and did not lower the rent. Jay can deduct the entire amount as a medical expense.

Medical Expenses: A Summary

1. In order to claim medical expenses, the taxpayer must itemize on **Schedule A.**
2. The deduction is limited. A taxpayer can only claim medical expenses that exceed 7.5 percent of adjusted gross income for the year.
3. In order to claim expenses, they must have been paid during the year, *regardless* of when the services were provided.
4. Taxpayers cannot deduct any reimbursed expenses. Therefore, total medical expenses for the year must be reduced by any insurance reimbursement.

5. A taxpayer may include qualified medical expenses paid for themselves, a spouse, and any dependents. Special rules apply to divorced or separated parents.

6. Taxpayers can deduct medical expenses paid for the diagnosis, cure, mitigation, treatment or prevention of disease, or treatment affecting any structure or function of the body. Taxpayers can also include premiums for medical, dental and some long-term care insurance. For drugs, taxpayers can only deduct prescription medication and insulin.

7. Taxpayers may deduct transportation costs related to medical care. Taxpayers can deduct the actual costs for a taxi, bus, train, plane, or ambulance as well as tolls and parking fees. If a taxpayer uses his own car for medical transportation, he can deduct actual out-of-pocket expenses such as for gas and oil, or he may opt to deduct the standard mileage rate for medical expenses.

8. Distributions from Health Savings Accounts and withdrawals from Flexible Spending Arrangements are generally tax free if used to pay qualified medical expenses.

9. These expenses are NOT deductible as medical expenses: funeral or burial expenses, non-prescription medicines, toiletries, cosmetics, any program for the general improvement of health, maternity clothes, and most cosmetic surgery (unless it is to correct a defect).

Deductible Taxes in General

Taxpayers can deduct certain taxes if they itemize their deductions. To be deductible, the tax must have been imposed on the taxpayer and paid by the taxpayer during the tax year. Taxes that are deductible include:

- State, local, and foreign income taxes
- Real estate taxes
- Personal property taxes (such as DMV fees)
- State and local sales taxes

State and local taxes

In 2011, Congress extended the provision allowing taxpayers to deduct sales taxes in lieu of state income taxes. The taxpayer may choose whatever method gives them the larger deduction. Taxpayers can choose one of the following taxes, but NOT both:

- **Income taxes:** This includes withheld taxes, estimated tax payments, or other tax payments such as a prior year refund of a state or local income tax that taxpayers applied to their estimated state or local income taxes.
- **Sales taxes:** Taxpayers may deduct state and local sales taxes paid.

Personal property taxes (DMV fees)

Personal property taxes are deductible if they are:

- Charged on personal property

- Based on the value of the property, and
- Charged on a yearly basis, even if collected more or less than once a year.

The most common type of personal property tax is a DMV fee. In order to be deductible, the tax must be based on the value of a property, such as a boat or car.

> **Example:** Genevieve makes the following tax payments: state income tax, $2,000; real estate taxes, $900; homeowners' association fee, $250. Genevieve's total tax deduction is $2,900 ($2,000 + $900 = $2,900). The $250 homeowners' association fee is not deductible.

Foreign income taxes

Under the foreign earned income exclusion or the foreign housing exclusion, these taxes can be deducted on income that is not exempt from U.S. tax. Generally, income taxes paid to a foreign country can be deducted as:

- An itemized deduction on **Schedule A**, OR
- A credit against U.S. income tax.

A taxpayer can choose between claiming the Foreign Tax Credit or claiming any foreign tax paid on **Schedule A** as an itemized deduction. The taxpayer may use whichever method results in the lowest tax.

Real Estate Taxes

State, local, or foreign real estate taxes that are based on the assessed value of the taxpayer's real property (such as a house or land) are deductible. Real estate taxes are reported to the taxpayer on Form 1098, *Mortgage Interest Statement*. A taxpayer may deduct real estate taxes on any real estate property he owns. Real estate taxes paid on foreign property are also deductible.

If a portion of a taxpayer's monthly mortgage payment goes into an escrow account, the taxpayer can only deduct the amount *actually paid* out of the escrow account during the year to the taxing authority. Some real estate taxes are not deductible, including taxes for local benefits, itemized charges for services, and homeowners' association fees.

If a property is sold, the real estate taxes must be "prorated" between the buyer and the seller according to the number of days that each owned the property. It doesn't matter who actually paid the real estate taxes. If, for example, the buyer paid all the taxes including delinquent taxes on a property, the amounts paid while the buyer was not the LEGAL owner must be added to the property's basis, rather than deducted on the taxpayer's current year return.

> **Example:** Mandy bought her home on September 1. The property tax was already overdue on the property when Mandy decided to purchase it. The real estate taxes on the home were $1,275 for the year and were paid by Mandy as a condition of the sale. Since Mandy did not own the home during the time the property tax was due, then the amount paid must be added to the basis of the residence. Mandy cannot deduct the $1,275 on her **Schedule A** as an itemized deduction.

Mortgage Interest and Other Deductible Interest

Certain types of interest are deductible as itemized deductions. The types of interest a taxpayer can deduct as an itemized deduction on **Form 1040, Schedule A** are:

- Investment interest
- Home mortgage interest (including certain points and mortgage insurance premiums)
- Mortgage interest on a second home or vacation home, with a maximum of two homes

Qualifying Home Mortgage Interest

Home mortgage interest is interest paid on a loan secured by a taxpayer's home. The loan may be a mortgage, a second mortgage, a home equity loan, or a line of credit. A taxpayer is allowed to deduct the interest on a primary residence and one second home. In order to qualify, the "home" can be a house, condominium, mobile home, house trailer, or houseboat. So long as a residence has sleeping, cooking, and toilet facilities, it may qualify for this deduction.

A second home can include any other residence a taxpayer owns and treats as a second home. A taxpayer does not have to actually use the home during the year in order to get a deduction of the mortgage interest paid on a second home. Home mortgage interest and points are reported to a taxpayer on **Form 1098**, *Mortgage Interest Statement*, by the financial institution to which the taxpayer made the payments.

Home mortgage interest is only deductible if the mortgage is secured debt. The taxpayer must be legally liable for the debt in order to deduct the mortgage interest.

An empty lot (bare land) does not qualify for the Mortgage Interest Deduction. In order for interest to be deductible as home mortgage interest, the loan must be secured by an actual home. If the taxpayer is planning to build a house, the taxpayer can start deducting mortgage interest once construction begins.

*Note: Although a taxpayer may deduct real estate taxes on *more than* two properties, a taxpayer may NOT deduct mortgage interest on more than two homes.

A taxpayer may deduct late charges on the loan as mortgage interest.

Qualified Mortgage Insurance Premiums (PMI)

Taxpayers can deduct Private Mortgage Insurance (PMI) premiums paid during the tax year on **Schedule A**. The following qualifications are required in order to deduct PMI:

- The borrower bought or refinanced the home
- The AGI is $100,000 or less ($50,000 if Married Filing Separately): full deduction
- The AGI is more than $100,000 ($50,000 if Married Filing Separately): reduced deduction
- The AGI is more than $109,000 ($54,500 if Married Filing Separately): no deduction

Payments made during 2011 for qualified mortgage insurance can be treated as home mortgage interest.

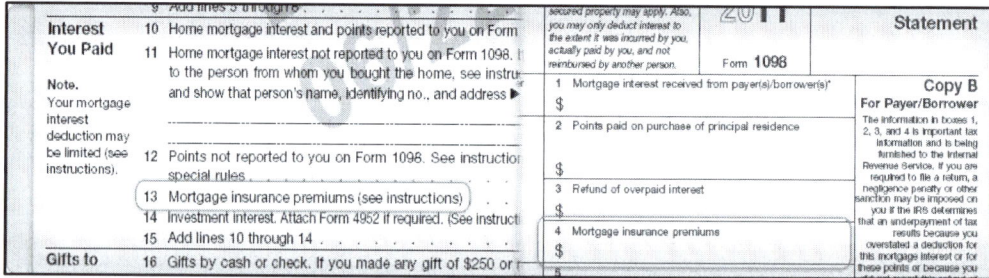

Home Mortgage Points

Points are the charges paid by a borrower to secure a loan. They are actually prepaid interest that a buyer pays at closing in order to secure a lower interest rate. They are also called:

- Loan origination fees (including VA and FHA fees)
- Maximum loan charges
- Premium charges
- Loan discount points
- Prepaid interest

Only points paid as a form of interest can be deducted. Points paid to refinance a mortgage are generally not deductible in full the year the taxpayer paid them, unless the points are paid in connection with the improvement of a main home. Some loan fees do not qualify as "points." Points paid for specific services, such as home appraisal fees, document preparation fees, VA funding fees, or notary fees are not interest and are not deductible.

In order to deduct points in the year paid, the taxpayer must meet these requirements:

- The mortgage must be secured by the taxpayer's main home, and the mortgage must have been used to buy or build the home.
- The points must be an established practice in the area where the loan is funded, and the amount paid not an excess or unusual amount for the area.
- The total points paid must not be more than the total unborrowed funds.
- The points must be computed as a percentage of the loan principal, and the points must be listed on the settlement statement.

Although this seems like a long list of restrictions, most homebuyers still qualify to take the deduction for points on the purchase of their primary residence. The deduction for points is reported on **Schedule A.**

Interest Paid on Home Equity Debt

The interest paid on a home equity line of credit is deductible by the taxpayer if certain rules are met. There is a limit on the amount of debt that can be treated as home equity debt. Home equity debt is not deductible if it exceeds the property's fair market value.

Example: Carla bought her home for cash ten years ago. The fair market value of her home is $80,000. Carla did not have a mortgage on her home until last year, when she took out a $45,000 loan, secured by her home, to pay for her daughter's college tuition and her father's medical bills. This loan is home equity debt. Since the $45,000 loan is secured by her home (and the loan amount is less than $100,000 in equity debt), the mortgage interest on the equity line is deductible.

The interest on home equity indebtedness is deductible by the taxpayer no matter how the proceeds are used.

Example: Jeremy and Ashley obtained two home equity loans totaling $90,000. They used the loans to pay off gambling debts, overdue credit payments, and some nondeductible medical expenses. Jeremy and Ashley can deduct the interest on their home equity loans because the total does not exceed $100,000.

Example: Chad bought his home five years ago. Its FMV now is $110,000, and the current balance on Chad's original mortgage is $95,000. Shaky Bank offers Chad a home mortgage loan of 125% of the FMV of the home. To consolidate some of his other debts, Chad agrees to take out a $42,500 home mortgage loan [(125% × $110,000) − $95,000] with Shaky Bank. Chad's home equity line exceeds the fair market value of the home. Therefore, his Mortgage Interest Deduction relating to his equity line is limited. For tax purposes, Chad's qualified home equity debt is limited to $15,000. This is the amount that the FMV of $110,000 exceeds the amount of home acquisition debt of $95,000.

Limits on the Mortgage Interest Deduction

If all of the taxpayer's mortgages fit into one or more of the following three categories, he can deduct the interest:

- Any mortgage the taxpayer obtained on or before 1987 (grandfathered debt.)
- Any mortgage obtained after 1987 to buy or improve a home (called home acquisition debt), but only if the mortgage debt totaled $1 million or less ($500,000 if MFS).
- A home equity mortgage, even if used for expenses other than to improve the home (called home equity debt), but only if the home equity line is $100,000 or less. The limit is $50,000 if MFS.

Example: Shirley borrowed $800,000 against her primary residence and $500,000 against her secondary residence. Both loans were used solely to acquire the residences. The loan amounts add up to $1.3 million. Since the total loan amount exceeds the $1 million limit for home acquisition debt, Shirley's Mortgage Interest Deduction is limited.

Deductible Investment Interest

If a taxpayer borrows money to buy property held for investment, the interest paid is investment interest. The deduction for investment interest expense is limited to the amount of net investment income. A taxpayer cannot deduct interest incurred to produce tax-exempt income (such as the purchase of municipal bonds). Investment interest expense is calculated on IRS **Form 4952**, *Investment Interest Expense Deduction*.

Example: Andy borrows money from a bank in order to buy $3,000 worth of short-term bonds. The bonds mature during the year and Andy makes $400 in investment interest income. He also has $210 in investment interest expense, which he paid on the loan originally taken out to buy the bonds. Andy must report the full amount of $400 as investment interest income. The $210 in investment interest expense is a deduction on **Schedule A.**

A taxpayer can "carry over" to the next tax year the amount of investment interest that he could not deduct because of the passive activity rules. The interest carried over is treated as investment interest paid or accrued in that next year.

Example: Jackson borrows money from a bank in order to buy $10,000 worth of U.S. gold coins. During the year, the coins lose value and he has no investment income. Jackson has $326 in investment interest expense, which he paid on the loan originally taken out to buy the coins. He had no other investment income. Jackson may not take a deduction for the investment interest expense, because he has no investment income to offset it. Jackson must "carry over" to the next tax year the amount of investment interest that he could not deduct because of this limit.

Investment income is any income that is produced by property that is held for investment. A taxpayer must first determine net investment income by subtracting his investment expenses (other than interest expense) from the investment income.

Non-deductible Interest and Investment Expenses

The following expenses cannot be deducted:
- Interest on personal car loans
- Other personal loans
- Annual fees for credit cards
- Credit card investigation fees
- Loan fees for services needed to get a loan
- Interest on a debt the taxpayer is not legally obligated to pay
- Finance charges for non-business credit card purchases
- Personal interest (to be discussed later)
- Service charges
- Interest to purchase or carry tax-exempt securities
- Late payment charges paid to a public utility
- Stockholders' meetings or investment-related seminars
- Interest expenses from single-premium life insurance, endowment, and annuity contracts
- Interest incurred from borrowing on insurance
- Expenses incurred to produce tax-exempt income (this includes expenses incurred for both tax-exempt and taxable income that cannot be properly allocated)
- Short-sale expenses

A taxpayer cannot deduct fines and penalties paid to any government entity for violations of the law, regardless of their nature.

> **Example:** José and Petronila file a joint return. During the year, they paid:
> $2,180 of home mortgage interest reported to them on **Form 1098**
> $400 in credit card interest
> $1,500 paid to a lender for an appraisal fee
> $2,000 in interest on a car loan
> José and Petronila may report only their home mortgage interest ($2,180) as deductible interest. None of the other charges are deductible.

Charitable Contributions in General

Charities need funds to operate their tax-exempt programs. Most of the time, these contributions come from taxpayers. A "charitable contribution" is a donation to a qualified organization. Taxpayers must itemize deductions to be able to deduct a

charitable contribution. Taxpayers can deduct contributions to qualifying organizations that:
- Operate exclusively for religious, charitable, educational, scientific, or literary purposes, or
- Work to prevent cruelty to children or animals, or
- Foster national or international amateur sports competition.

Other qualifying organizations include:
- War veterans' organizations, and
- Certain non-profit cemetery companies or corporations.

Qualified donations also include donations for public purposes to the federal government of the United States, to any state, or to an Indian tribal government (example: a donation to the state capital's yearly toy drive).

To be deductible, contributions must be made to a qualifying organization, not to an individual. Taxpayers *must keep records* to prove the amounts of cash and non-cash contributions they make during the year. Taxpayers can only deduct a contribution in the year it is actually made.

Non-Qualifying Organizations

Not all non-profit organizations that accept donations qualify as "charities." Even if an organization is a non-profit, that doesn't automatically mean that contributions to the organization are deductible by donors.

There are some organizations that still qualify as non-profit groups for tax purposes, but they do not qualify as charitable organizations for the purposes of deductible contributions. The following are examples of donations that do not qualify:
- Gifts to civic leagues, social and sports clubs, labor unions, and Chambers of Commerce
- Gifts to groups run for personal profit
- Gifts to political groups, candidates, or political organizations
- Gifts to homeowners' associations
- Direct donations to needy individuals
- The cost of raffle, bingo, or lottery tickets, even if the raffle is part of a qualified organization's fundraiser
- Dues paid to country clubs or similar groups

Even though these groups may have non-profit status, they do not qualify for a deductible contribution for the taxpayer. An exemption from tax does not automatically grant an entity to accept donations that are deductible to the grantor.

Example: Renee ran a 10K race organized by the Chamber of Commerce, with the Chamber to donate proceeds to a cancer charity. She paid the race organizers a $30 entry fee and received a "free" T-shirt and pancake breakfast after the race. Renee did not make a contribution directly to the qualifying organization (the cancer charity). She paid the Chamber of Commerce, which is not a qualifying charitable organization. Therefore, none of her entry fee is tax deductible as a charitable expense. If the race had been organized by the qualifying organization itself, part of her entry fee may have been deductible.

Charitable Contributions: Substantiation Requirements

There are very strict recordkeeping requirements for charitable contributions. Taxpayers must keep records to prove the amounts of cash and non-cash contributions they make during the year. In the following section, we will cover the recordkeeping and substantiation requirements for cash contributions. There are a few major categories of contributions, and the substantiation requirements are different for each. These are:

- Cash contributions of $250 or less
- Cash contributions of $250 or more
- Non-cash contributions less than $500
- Non-cash contributions more than $500
- Special rule for donated vehicles
- Volunteering expenses

CASH Donations of $250 or Less

Cash contributions include those paid by cash, check, debit card, credit card, or payroll deduction. For a contribution by cash or check, the taxpayer must maintain a record of the contribution. It must be either a bank record or a written receipt from the organization. If the value of the individual donation is *less than* $250, the taxpayer must keep at least a canceled check or credit card slip, a receipt, or some other reliable written record or evidence.

A taxpayer cannot deduct a cash contribution, regardless of the amount, unless he keeps ONE of the following:

- A bank record that shows the name of the qualified organization, the date of the contribution, and the amount of the contribution. Bank records may include:
    - A canceled check,
    - A bank or credit union statement, or
    - A credit card statement.

- A receipt (or a letter or other written communication) from the qualified organization showing the name of the organization, the date of the contribution, and the amount of the contribution.

> **Example:** Gary donates $10 per week to the Humane Society. He always pays by check, and he keeps the canceled check as a record of his contribution. This is a valid method of recordkeeping for small donations under $250.

CASH Donations OVER $250

For cash donations OVER $250 dollars, the taxpayer can claim a deduction ONLY if he has a receipt or written acknowledgement from the organization. A canceled check is not sufficient. The receipt (or acknowledgment) must meet certain tests. It must include:

- The amount of cash the taxpayer contributed
- The date of the contribution
- Whether the qualified organization gave any goods or services as a result of the contribution (other than certain token items and membership benefits)
- A description and good faith estimate of the value of any goods or services provided in return by the organization (if applicable)

The taxpayer must obtain the receipt on or before:

- The date the taxpayer files his tax return for the year he makes the contribution, or
- The due date, including extensions, for filing the return.

If a charitable gift is made via an automatic payroll deduction, the taxpayer does NOT need an acknowledgement letter unless any single deduction exceeds $250. In that case, the taxpayer may save a copy of his pay stub.

Non-cash Contributions: Substantiation Rules

In order to claim a deduction for non-cash donations, the donated items must be in good condition. The taxpayer must get a receipt from the receiving organization and keep a list of the items donated. In most cases, the taxpayer will be able to claim a deduction for the fair market value of the contribution (generally what someone would be willing to pay at a garage sale or thrift store).

No deduction is allowed for items that are in poor or unusable condition, meaning the charity must be able to use the items. Deductible items include:

- Fair market value of used clothing and furniture in good condition.
- Unreimbursed expenses that relate DIRECTLY to the services the taxpayer provided for the organization. Only out-of-pocket expenses that are directly related to the donated services can be deducted. The value of time or services donated cannot be deducted.

- Part of a contribution above the fair market value for items received such as merchandise and tickets to charity balls or sporting events.
- Transportation expenses, including bus fare, parking fees, tolls, and either the cost of gas and oil or a standard mileage deduction of 14 cents per mile in 2011.

Example: Virgil is an attorney who donates his time to his local church for their legal needs. In 2011, he spent 10 hours drafting documents for his church, which is a qualified organization. He also has $200 in out-of-pocket expenses because he purchased a new printer and office supplies for the church. The printer and office supplies were delivered directly to the church rectory for its use. Virgil can take a charitable deduction for $200, the amount he spent on behalf of his church. He cannot take a deduction for the "value" of his time.

Non-cash Contributions: Donations Less Than $500

For each single contribution of at least $250 but not exceeding $500, the taxpayer must have all the documentation described for non-cash contributions less than $250. In addition, the organization's written acknowledgement must state whether the taxpayer received any goods or services in return and a description and good faith estimate of any such items.

Non-cash Contributions: Donations of More Than $500

If a taxpayer's total deduction for all non-cash contributions for the year is over $500, he must also file **Form 8283**, *Non-cash Charitable Contributions*. If any single donation is valued at over $5,000, the taxpayer must also get an appraisal.

*Special "$500 Rule" for Donated Vehicles, Boats, and Airplanes

Special rules apply to any donation of a vehicle. This rule also applies to the donation of a boat or airplane. If the taxpayer donates a vehicle to a charity and the taxpayer claims a deduction of more than $500, the taxpayer can only deduct the smaller of:
- The gross proceeds from the sale of the vehicle, or
- The vehicle's fair market value on the date of the contribution.

Example: Kevin donates his used motorcycle to his church fundraiser. The FMV ("Blue Book" value) of the motorcycle is $2,500. The church sells the motorcycle 60 days later; the organization sends Kevin a **Form 1098-C** showing the proceeds from the sale of the donated item. The church was only able to sell the motorcycle for $1,700. Therefore, Kevin may only deduct $1,700 on his **Schedule A, Form 1040** (the smaller of the FMV or the gross proceeds from the sale). He must attach a copy of **Form 1098-C**, *Contributions of Motor Vehicles, Boats, and Airplanes*, to his tax return.

Form 1098-C shows the gross proceeds from the sale of the vehicle. If the taxpayer does not attach **Form 1098-C,** he cannot deduct a contribution over $500 for a donated vehicle. Unless documented with **Form 1098-C** (or comparable documentation), the maximum value that can be taken for a vehicle donation is $500. Vehicles that are not in working condition may have zero donation value.

*Exceptions to the "$500 Rule" for Donated Vehicles

There are two exceptions to the strict rules regarding vehicle donations. This is called "Significant Intervening Use" and allows the donor to take a special exception for the value of the vehicle. It applies when the charity uses the vehicle for its own use, or otherwise sets the vehicle aside for specific purposes for a needy individual.

- **Exception 1:** The vehicle is used by the organization. If the charity takes the vehicle for its own use, the taxpayer can deduct the vehicle's FMV.
- **Exception 2:** The vehicle is given (or sold) to a needy individual. If the charity gives or sells the vehicle directly to a needy person, the taxpayer generally can deduct the vehicle's FMV at the time of the contribution.

Example: Bonnie donates a used van to a charity that delivers meals to needy individuals. The charity does not sell her van. Instead, the charity uses her donated van every day to deliver meals. Since this qualifies as "Significant Intervening Use," Bonnie may take a deduction for the FMV of the van at the time of the donation. The charity must have provided a written receipt and a statement to substantiate the "Significant Intervening Use."

Deductible Volunteering Expenses

A taxpayer may claim a charitable contribution deduction for out-of-pocket expenses incurred while away from home performing services for a charitable organization only if there is no significant element of personal pleasure in the travel. However, a deduction will not be denied simply because the taxpayer enjoys providing services to a charitable organization.

The taxpayer is still allowed to take a charitable contribution deduction for the expenses if he is on-duty in a genuine and substantial sense throughout the trip.

Expenses that are incurred on behalf of the charitable organization are deductible as out-of-pocket expenses. Taxpayers may not deduct the "value of their time" when they volunteer for an organization. However, travel expenses such as transportation, meals, and lodging are deductible. Travel expenses can be deducted in actual expenses, or the taxpayer may use the standard mileage rate for charitable miles, which is 14 cents per mile in 2011.

Example: Charles volunteered for the Boy Scouts in 2011. He was the den leader and regularly paid out-of-pocket expenses for travel, gas, and parking while performing duties and picking up supplies on behalf of the Scouts. Charles was not paid for his work. Charles may deduct his out-of-pocket costs related to the volunteer work, but he may not take a deduction for the value of his time.

Example: Francine regularly volunteers at her local animal shelter. She uses her own car to travel back and forth to the shelter. She is not reimbursed for mileage. Francine also fosters kittens on behalf of the shelter. She pays for food and other supplies out-of-pocket while she's fostering the kittens. Once the kittens are old enough for adoption, she returns them to the animal shelter so that they may be adopted by the public. Francine may deduct her mileage and her out-of-pocket costs as a charitable contribution.

Deductible Contributions and the "50% Limit"

There are limits to the amounts that can be claimed as a deductible donation. A taxpayer may not take a deduction for charitable contributions that exceed 50% of adjusted gross income. In other words, if a taxpayer had $20,000 in gross income in 2011, the maximum he could deduct as a charitable contribution in 2011 would be $10,000 (50% of AGI). Any amounts that are disallowed by this limit may be carried forward to a future year (explained later).

There is a reduced limit of 30% or 20% that applies to certain organizations. This means that for certain non-profit organizations, a taxpayer's contribution cannot exceed 20% of his AGI.

Examples of 50% limit organizations include churches, hospitals, most schools, state or federal government units, and animal welfare organizations. Also included are corporations, trusts, or foundations organized solely for charitable, religious, educational, scientific, or literary purposes, or to prevent cruelty to children or animals, or to foster certain national or international amateur sports competition.

Organizations Subject to the 30% Limit

Certain organizations only qualify for the "30% limit." This means that the deductible amount of the contribution cannot exceed 30% of the taxpayer's AGI. A 30% limit applies to the following organizations:

- Veterans' organizations
- Fraternal societies (such as Freemasons or Kiwanis)
- Non-profit cemeteries

In addition, the 30% limit applies in the following cases:

- Gifts for the actual use of any organization (such as the donation of a table that the organization uses for itself)
- Any gift of appreciated property (such as stocks)

Appreciated property, also called "capital gain property," may be given to an organization that is normally a "50%" organization, such as a church. However, capital gain property is always subject to the 30% limit (or 20% limit); regardless of the organization type that actually receives the donation.

This means that the donation of capital gain property will always be subject to limitations.

> **Example:** Howard's adjusted gross income is $50,000. During the year, he gave appreciated stocks with an FMV of $15,000 to his synagogue, which is a 50% limit organization. Howard also gave $10,000 cash to a veteran's organization. The $15,000 gift of capital gain property is subject to the special 30% limit, even though it was given to a religious organization. The $10,000 gift is subject to the other 30% limit. However, both gifts are fully deductible by Howard because neither is more than the 30% limit that applies ($15,000 in each case), and together they are not more than the 50% limit of Howard's AGI ($50,000 x 50% = $25,000).

Charitable gifts of appreciated property held long-term are subject to a lower deductibility ceiling—30% of AGI—with a five-year carryover of any excess deduction (example: a gift of appreciated stock).

Appreciated Property and the 20% Limit

The 20% limit applies to all gifts of capital gain property (appreciated property) to qualified organizations that are NOT 50% organizations.

> **Example:** Henry's adjusted gross income is $23,000. During the year, he gave appreciated stocks with an FMV of $10,000 to his fraternal society, Kiwanis, which is a 30% limit organization. Henry makes no other donations during the year. The $10,000 donation of capital gain property (the stocks) is subject to the special 20% limit because it is capital gain property that was donated to a 30% limit organization. The donation is not fully deductible by Henry, because it exceeds 20% of his AGI ($23,000 x 20% = $4,600). Therefore, the maximum deduction for charitable contributions that Henry can take is limited to $4,600. He must carry over the remaining $5,400 to a future tax year.

Any contributions made by the taxpayer and carried over to future years retain their original character. For example, contributions made to a 30% organization are always subject to the 30% limit of AGI.

Non-Qualified Types of Donations

There are some expenses that do not qualify as charitable deductions, even if the amounts are given to a qualified charity or organization. Amounts that may not be deducted include:

- The cost of raffle, bingo, or lottery tickets (even if the amounts go to a qualified charity)

- Tuition costs
- The value of a person's time or service
- Blood donated to a blood bank or to the American Red Cross
- Car depreciation, insurance, general repairs, or maintenance
- Direct contributions to an individual
- Sickness or burial expenses for members of a fraternal society
- Part of a contribution that benefits the taxpayer, such as the fair market value of a meal eaten at a charity dinner

Example: Bill goes to a local church fundraiser. His church is a qualified organization. During the fundraiser, the church deacon holds a bingo game, with all the proceeds going to the church. Bill spends $200 on bingo cards, but does not win anything. Even though the $200 went to the church, the cost of the bingo game is not considered a charitable gift and is therefore not deductible.

Charitable Contribution Carryovers

A carryover is simply an amount that a taxpayer is unable to deduct in the current year. Charitable contributions are subject to a five-year carryover period. The taxpayer can deduct the unused contribution for the next five years until it is used up, but not beyond that time.

A carryover of a "qualified conservation contribution" can be carried forward for 15 years. A qualified conservation contribution is the donation of a qualified real property interest (e.g., an easement) to an organization that uses it exclusively for conservation purposes.

Example: Taylor owns 200 acres of wetlands. She decides to donate the property to the Wildlife Conservation Society, a 501(c)(3) organization. The property is then used for wildlife conservation and research only. This is a "qualified conservation contribution" eligible for a 15-year carryover.

Non-Business Casualty and Theft Losses in General

In this section, we will cover deductible non-business casualty losses, which are reported on **Schedule A.** Casualty losses related to a business (including self-employed businesses that are reported on **Schedule C** and **Schedule F**) are treated differently and are covered extensively in Part 2, Businesses.

The rules regarding non-business casualty losses are very complex. A "casualty loss" is an unexpected loss. A casualty loss does not include normal wear and tear or progressive deterioration from age or insect damage. The loss must be caused by a sudden, unexpected, or unusual event (e.g., car accident, fire, earthquake, flood, vandalism, or theft).

Lost or mislaid property is NOT considered a casualty loss.

Sometimes, a casualty loss will create a gain for the taxpayer. For example, this happens when the insurance reimbursement is more than the taxpayer's basis in the property.

If the taxpayer has a gain, he may have to pay tax on it. In most cases, however, the gain can be deferred until the property is later sold.

A taxpayer must have proof of the casualty or theft in order to deduct it. The taxpayer must also prove that the loss was actually caused by the event. Specifically, the taxpayer must be able to prove:

- The type of casualty loss (car accident, fire, storm, etc.) and the date of occurrence
- That the taxpayer was the legal owner of the property, or at least legally liable for the damage (such as leased property where the lessee is responsible for damage)
- Whether insurance reimbursement exists

Example: Gregory rents a car from Good Rentals, Inc. He declines renter's insurance and signs a contract stating he will be responsible for any damage. The rental car is stolen and now Gregory is responsible for paying back Good Rentals. Gregory's car insurance does not have rental car coverage, so he is liable for the full amount. Gregory may deduct the loss as a casualty loss, subject to the applicable rules.

Personal casualty losses are calculated on IRS **Form 4684**, and the amount is then transferred to Schedule A as an itemized deduction.

Non-deductible Losses Include:

- Damage done by pets
- Slow insect damage to trees, clothing, or household items (termite or moth damage is included)
- Any fire willfully set by the taxpayer (arson)
- Lost property
- Progressive deterioration
- Losses in real estate value from market fluctuations
- Accidental breakage of china, dishes, or other items during regular use

Non-Business Casualty Loss Limits ($100 & 10% Rule)

Each personal casualty or theft loss is limited to the excess of the loss over $100. In addition, a 10%-of-AGI limit applies to the net loss. The "$100 Rule" and "10% Rule" only apply to non-business casualty losses. Losses on business property are not subject to these rules. Personal casualty losses are also subject to the "Single Event Rule."

Generally, events closely related in origin are considered a "single event." It is a "single casualty" when the damage is from two or more closely related causes, such as wind and flood damage caused by the same storm. A single casualty may also damage two or more pieces of property, such as a hailstorm that damages both a taxpayer's home and his car parked in the driveway.

> **Example:** A fire damaged Dick's house in January, causing $3,000 in damage. In September, storm damaged his house again, causing $5,000 in damage. Dick must reduce each loss by $100.

1. The $100 Rule

After a taxpayer has figured the casualty loss on personal-use property, he must reduce that loss by $100. This reduction applies to each total casualty or theft loss. It does not matter how many pieces of property are involved in an event; the taxpayer only has to reduce the losses for each EVENT by $100.

> ***Note:** If a taxpayer has *more than one* casualty loss during the year, he must reduce each loss by $100 separately. Then the taxpayer must reduce the total of ALL losses by 10% of adjusted gross income.

2. The 10% Rule

Personal casualty losses are further reduced by AGI. The taxpayer must reduce the total of all casualty losses on personal-use property by 10%. This rule does not apply to a net disaster loss within a federally declared disaster area.

Reporting a Casualty Loss or Gain

Taxpayers use **Form 4684**, *Casualties and Thefts*, to report a gain or loss from a personal casualty. **Form 4684** must be attached to the taxpayer's return. The taxpayer may claim a deductible loss on personal-use property only if he itemizes deductions.

Sometimes, taxpayers will have a gain from casualty losses because the insurance reimbursement will exceed their basis. However, if a taxpayer has a gain on damaged property, he can postpone reporting the gain if the insurance reimbursement is spent to restore the property.

To determine a taxpayer's deduction for casualty losses:
1. Calculate the *lesser* of the FMV or adjusted basis of the item prior to the loss.
2. Subtract any payments/reimbursements from insurance.
3. Subtract $100 for each event (2011 limit).
4. Subtract 10% of the taxpayer's AGI.

> **Example:** Many years ago, Al bought a vacation cottage for $18,000. A storm destroyed the cottage in 2011. The FMV of the cottage in 2011 was $250,000. Al received $146,000 from his insurance company. He had a gain of $128,000 ($146,000 – $18,000 basis). Al spent the full $146,000 to rebuild his cottage. Since he used the insurance proceeds to rebuild his cottage, he can postpone reporting or recognizing the gain until the cottage is sold.

Although casualty losses are treated differently depending on whether the loss occurred to business property or personal property, all casualty losses are still reported on **Form 4684.**

Decrease in FMV from a Casualty Loss

A decrease in the value of property because it is near an area that suffered a casualty cannot be taken into consideration. Casualty losses are deductible only for actual damage caused to a property.

> **Example:** In 2011, Nicole purchased a condo for $200,000. Two months after the purchase, a hurricane destroyed five other properties on her block. A resulting appraisal showed that all of the properties within a five-mile radius had declined in fair market value by 15% because people were afraid to purchase homes in "hurricane territory." The reduction in the home's fair market value is not a deductible casualty loss.

Insurance Reimbursements

Taxpayers can deduct qualified casualty losses to their homes, household items, and vehicles. A taxpayer may not deduct casualty and theft losses that are covered by insurance unless he files a claim for reimbursement. The taxpayer must reduce his casualty loss by the amount of the insurance reimbursement. If the taxpayer decides not to file an insurance claim but has a deductible, he may still claim the amount of the insurance deductible, since that amount would not have been covered by the policy anyway.

> **Example:** Sonny has a $750 deductible on his car insurance. He has a car accident in 2011, incurring $6,000 of damage. The insurance company pays Sonny for the damage minus the $750 deductible. The amount of Sonny's casualty loss is based solely on his deductible. Sonny's actual casualty loss is only $650 ($750 – $100).

> **Example:** Caitlyn has homeowners' insurance on her home. In 2011, she has a small fire and incurs $8,000 in damage. She does not want her insurance premium to go up, so she declines to file a claim and pays for the damage out-of-pocket. Her insurance policy carries a $1,500 deductible. Caitlyn cannot deduct the loss because she declined to file an insurance claim. However, she is allowed to deduct $1,500, the amount of the deductible, because her insurance would not have covered that amount in any case.

Rules for Determining Fair Market Value and Adjusted Basis

A casualty loss is limited to the LESSER of the FMV of the property, or the property's adjusted basis right before the loss. The cost of replacement property is not part of a casualty or theft loss. Usually, a property's basis is its cost. For property that is acquired by inheritance or by gift, basis is figured differently (to be covered in a later unit).

Example: Don purchased an antique vase at a garage sale for $600. Later, he discovered that the vase was actually a rare collectible and its fair market value was $20,000. The vase was stolen two months later during a robbery. Don's casualty loss is limited to the $600 he paid for it, which is his basis in the property. Don cannot claim a casualty loss deduction for $20,000 (the value of the item).

Example: Raquel bought a new leather sofa four years ago for $3,000. In April, a fire destroyed the sofa. Raquel estimates that it would now cost $5,000 to replace it. However, if she had sold the sofa before the fire, she probably would have received only $900 for it because the sofa was already four years old. Raquel's casualty loss is $900 (still subject to the $100 and 10% rules), the FMV of the sofa before the fire. Her loss is not $3,000 (her basis) and it is not $5,000 (the replacement cost).

Theft Losses in General

A theft loss may be deducted in the year that the theft is discovered. It doesn't matter when the theft actually occurred. Qualifying theft losses include:

- Ponzi investment schemes
- Burglaries
- Embezzlement by an employee
- Identity theft
- Mail fraud
- Blackmail, kidnapping for ransom

Some theft losses are not deductible. If the taxpayer has theft losses from his own illegal activity, the losses are not deductible.

Decline in value of stock: A taxpayer may not deduct the decline in value of stock as a casualty loss, even if it is related to accounting fraud. There is an exception for Ponzi scheme losses. However, the taxpayer may deduct these losses as capital losses, and the regular rules for capital losses apply.

The cost of insurance: The cost of insurance or other protection is not deductible as a casualty loss. This rule applies to non-business assets only.

Example: Jordan pays for renter's insurance to cover the furniture and appliances in his home from theft or other disaster losses. Jordan may not deduct the cost of the renter's insurance as a casualty loss.

Example: Sydney is self-employed and owns a clothing boutique. She pays for hazard insurance on the boutique. Sydney may deduct the cost of the insurance on her shop as a regular business expense.

Recovered property: If a taxpayer takes a deduction for stolen property and the property is later recovered by the police, he must report the recovery as income in the year the property is recovered. However, he must only report the amounts that actually reduced tax in an earlier year.

Business Casualty Losses

A business-related casualty loss is treated much differently than a personal casualty loss. Business casualty losses may be tested on either Part 1 and Part 2 of the exam. This is because a business loss may affect a self-employed taxpayer, as well as an investor who owns rental units. Self-employed taxpayers and rental income are both tested on Part 1 of the EA exam.

If income-producing property (such as rental property) is subject to a casualty loss, the amount of the taxpayer's loss is the adjusted basis in the property minus any salvage value and minus any insurance or other reimbursement received.

The loss is figured as follows:

The taxpayer's adjusted basis in the property
MINUS
Any salvage value
MINUS
Any insurance reimbursement

Example: Mario is a self-employed florist who owns his own shop. Mario has a utility van that he uses to make floral deliveries. While he was making a delivery, the van was involved in an accident. Mario had purchased the van for $70,000. The accumulated depreciation on the van prior to the accident was $35,000. Mario's insurance company reimbursed him $20,000. His casualty loss is determined as follows:

Acquisition cost	$70,000
Less accumulated depreciation	($35,000)
Initial loss from accident	$35,000
Minus insurance reimbursement	($20,000)
Amount of casualty loss	**$15,000**

Business casualty losses are also reported on **Form 4684**, *Casualties and Thefts*. Section A of the form is used for personal-use property, and Section B is used for business (or other income-producing) property.

For self-employed taxpayers who file a **Schedule C**, business-related casualty losses are reported on Part V of **Schedule C**. The taxpayer must also attach a completed **Form 4684** to the return.

Business casualty losses are covered more extensively in Book 2, Businesses for Part 2 of the EA exam.

Miscellaneous Itemized Deductible Expenses

Miscellaneous deductible expenses include all other categories of expenses that do not fall into the major categories of medical, taxes, interest, or charitable contribu-

tions. These "miscellaneous" expenses are further divided into two very important categories:
- Miscellaneous expenses subject to the 2% of AGI limit, and
- Miscellaneous expenses deductible in full (NOT subject to the 2% AGI limit).

Miscellaneous Expenses Subject to the 2% Limit

A taxpayer may deduct certain expenses as miscellaneous itemized deductions on **Schedule A (Form 1040).** The taxpayer may ONLY claim the amount that exceeds 2% of his AGI. There are many common types of miscellaneous expenses that are subject to the 2% limit. Some examples are:

- Unreimbursed job-related expenses
- Credit or debit card fees incurred when paying income tax charged by the card processor
- Union dues and fees
- Professional society dues
- Uniforms for work
- Small tools and supplies used for business
- Professional books, magazines, and journals
- Employment-related educational expenses
- Job-hunting expenses
- Investment counseling fees
- Investment expenses
- Safe deposit box rental for investment documents
- Tax counsel and assistance
- Fees paid to an IRA custodian[48]

Investment expenses are allowed as a deduction if the expenses are directly connected with the production of investment income. Investment expenses are included as a miscellaneous itemized deduction on **Schedule A (Form 1040),** and are allowable deductions only *after* applying the 2% limit.

> **Example:** Craig's AGI is $45,000. Craig has $1,100 in miscellaneous deductible work-related expenses. He must first figure out the 2% limit before he can start deducting these expenses (2% X $45,000 = $900). He can therefore only deduct $200 of those expenses ($1,100 - $900 = $200). He adds this amount to his **Schedule A** as an itemized deduction.

Unreimbursed Employee Business Expenses

An employee may deduct certain work-related expenses as itemized deductions. These expenses are first reported on **Form 2106**, *Employee Business Expenses*, and the amount is transferred to **Schedule A.** The taxpayer can deduct only unreimbursed employee expenses that are:

---

[48] This list is not exhaustive.

- Paid or incurred during the tax year,
- For carrying on the business of being an employee, and
- Ordinary and necessary.

An expense does not have to be required to be deductible. However, it must be a common expense that would be accepted in the taxpayer's trade or profession. Employee business expenses are deductible if they are for the convenience of an employer or required as a condition of employment. A taxpayer may deduct the following items as unreimbursed employee expenses:

- Business liability insurance premiums
- Damages paid to a former employer for breach of an employment contract
- Depreciation on an asset the employer requires for work
- Dues to professional societies
- A home office used regularly and exclusively in a taxpayer's work
- Expenses of looking for a new job in the taxpayer's present occupation
- Legal fees related directly to a job
- Licenses and regulatory fees
- Malpractice insurance
- Occupational taxes and research expenses of a college professor
- Rural mail carriers' vehicle expenses
- Subscriptions to professional journals
- Tools and supplies used for work
- Travel, transportation, meals, and lodging related to the taxpayer's work
- Union dues
- Work clothes and uniforms (if required and not suitable for everyday use)
- Work-related education
- Employee meals and entertainment
- Tax counseling, preparation, and assistance

An employee may deduct unreimbursed business-related meals and entertainment expenses he has for entertaining a client, customer, or another employee. The limit on deductible meals and entertainment is 50% (the same for self-employed taxpayers and businesses). The taxpayer must apply the "50% limit" *before* applying the "2% of adjusted gross income" limit. The taxpayer can deduct meals and entertainment expenses only if they meet the following tests:

- The main purpose of the meal or entertainment was the active conduct of business,
- The taxpayer conducted business during the entertainment period, and
- The taxpayer had more than a general expectation of some other specific business benefit at a future time.

Non-deductible Employee Meals or Entertainment

There are cases where an employee cannot deduct certain types of entertainment, even if it is substantially business-related. The taxpayer cannot deduct dues (including initiation fees) for membership in any country club or social club.

This is an IRS rule that applies specifically to country clubs. The purpose of a club (not its name) will determine whether or not a taxpayer can deduct the dues. Generally, the taxpayer cannot deduct any expense for the use of an "entertainment facility." Examples include a yacht, hunting lodge, fishing camp, swimming pool, tennis court, bowling alley, car, airplane, apartment, hotel suite, or home in a vacation resort.

Example: Alejandro is an employee of Yarrow Plastics, Inc. He regularly entertains at Rich Guy's Country Club, where he takes clients golfing and closes many business contracts. Alejandro's membership dues to Rich Guy's Country Club do not qualify as a deductible business expense, even if he uses the club substantially for business use.

Entertainment Facilities and Employee Business Expenses

A taxpayer can deduct out-of-pocket expenses, such as for food and beverages, catering, gas, and fishing bait that the taxpayer provided during entertainment at a facility. The taxpayer may also deduct the cost of transportation to a meal or an event. These are not considered expenses for the use of an entertainment facility.

Example: Stanley rents a summer cottage on the river that he occasionally uses for entertaining clients. He cannot deduct the cost of renting this facility. He can, however, deduct the out-of-pocket costs of entertaining a client, which include meals and beverages during the actual entertainment or business meeting.

Deducting a Work-Related Home Office

An employee can deduct expenses for the business use of his home if certain rules are followed and tests are met. The home office must be used by the employee for the *convenience of the employer* in order to be deductible.

The space does not need to be marked off by a permanent partition, but the space needs to be exclusively and regularly used for business. The area used for business can be a room or other separately identifiable space, such as a shed or garage. If an area is not exclusively or regularly used in the employee's profession, the taxpayer cannot claim a deduction for the business use space.

If an employee is not required to work from home, he will not meet the convenience-of-the-employer test and cannot claim a deduction for the business use of the home.

> **Example:** Kathleen is employed as a teacher. The school provides her with an office where she can work on her lesson plans, grade papers and tests, and meet with parents and students. The school does not require her to work at home. Kathleen prefers to use her home office and does not use the one provided by the school. She uses this home office exclusively and regularly for the administrative duties of her teaching job. Since the school provides Kathleen with an office and does not require her to work at home, she does not meet the "convenience-of-employer" test and cannot claim a deduction for her home office.

> **Example:** Glenn is a tool salesman working for Tremendous Tools Co. He is on the road most of the time, and his home is the only fixed location for selling tools. Glenn regularly uses the right half of his basement for storage of inventory and product samples. The expenses for the space are deductible as an "employee-related" home office expense.

There is a special rule for "multiple offices." If a taxpayer has a home office and also uses an office at his regular workplace, the home office may still qualify for a deduction. If the employee meets with patients, clients, or customers in his home in the normal course of business even though he also carries on business at another location, the employee can deduct expenses for that part of the home. The following tests must be met if there are multiple offices:

- The space must be used exclusively and regularly for business
- The taxpayer must physically meet with patients, clients, or customers on the premises (not just over the phone)

The use of the home office must be substantial and integral to the conduct of business.

Calculating the Home Office Percentage

Generally, the home office deduction depends on the percentage of the home that is used for business. A taxpayer can use any reasonable method to compute business percentage, but the most common methods are to:

- Divide the area of the home used for business by the total area of the home, or
- Divide the number of rooms used for business by the total number of rooms in the home if all rooms in the home are about the same size.

Taxpayers may not deduct expenses for any portion of the year during which there was no business use of the home.

Example: Lillian is a self-employed bookkeeper, and she has a qualified home office. The entire square footage of her home is 1,200 square feet. Her home office is 240 square feet, so therefore, her home office percentage is 20% (240 ÷ 1,200) of the total area of her home. Her business percentage is 20%.

Deductible Employee Travel Expenses

An employee may not deduct commuting expenses, which are the expenses incurred when going from a taxpayer's home to his main workplace. However, there are numerous instances where an employee may deduct mileage or other travel expenses relating to his employment. Deductible employee travel expenses include:

- Getting from one work location to another in the course of business
- Visiting clients or customers
- Going to a business meeting away from the regular workplace
- Traveling from a first job to a second job in the same day
- Getting from a taxpayer's home to a temporary workplace

Any amounts reimbursed by the employer would not be deductible by the employee. A taxpayer can deduct travel expenses related to a temporary work assignment. Travel expenses paid in connection with an indefinite work assignment are NOT deductible. Examples of deductible travel expenses include:

- The cost of getting to a business destination (air, rail, bus, car, etc.)
- Meals and lodging while away from home
- Taxi fares
- Baggage charges

"Tax Home" For the Purpose of Employee Travel Expenses

To determine the deductibility of employee travel, the employee must determine his "tax home." Generally, a taxpayer's tax home is his regular place of business, regardless of where the taxpayer maintains his residence. A taxpayer may deduct work-related expenses of traveling away from home for his profession or job.

Example: Alec is a railroad conductor. He leaves his home terminal on a regularly scheduled round-trip run between two cities and returns home 16 hours later. During the run, Alec has six hours off at his turnaround point. Alec stops, eats a meal, and rents a hotel room to get necessary sleep before starting the return trip. Alec is considered to be away from his tax home. His travel expenses are deductible.

Multiple Business Locations and the Effect on Tax Home

If a taxpayer has multiple business locations, his "tax home" is the main place of business. If the taxpayer does NOT have a regular or main place of business because of the nature of the taxpayer's work, then his tax home may be the place where he actually lives.

> **Example:** Crystal is a guitarist in a rock band. She travels with her band to multiple playing locations and venues, and also works as a freelance musician. Because of the nature of her business, Crystal has no "regular" place of business. She maintains a primary residence in Los Angeles. Crystal's tax home is in Los Angeles.

If a taxpayer does not have a regular place of business or post of duty and there is no place where he regularly lives, the taxpayer is considered a transient (an itinerant) and his tax home is wherever he works. As a transient, the taxpayer cannot claim a travel expense deduction because he is never considered to be traveling away from home.

Conventions: Special Rules

A taxpayer may deduct the cost of travel and attendance to conventions. In order for the travel cost to be deductible, the convention must be in the U.S. or in the "North American area" (including Canada and Mexico). For cruises, there is a $2,000 cap on deductions. A deduction is not allowed for conventions focused exclusively on investments or financial planning.

Job Search Expenses

A taxpayer may deduct job search expenses, if the expenses relate to the same profession. Expenses incurred can be deducted, even if the taxpayer does not find a new job. However, a taxpayer may not deduct the costs of searching for a job in a brand new occupation.

If the job search qualifies, the taxpayer can deduct costs for using an employment agency or career counselor, and for traveling to interviews. The taxpayer may also deduct the cost of printing, preparing, and mailing resumes.

The following expenses are not deductible:

- Job search expenses for a new occupation
- Living expenses incurred during a period of unemployment between the ending of the last job and a new period of employment
- A taxpayer looking for a new job the first time

Job-Related Education

The cost of courses designed to maintain or improve the skills needed for a present job (or required by an employer or the law) is deductible as an employee business expense. The taxpayer may also choose to take an education credit. These educational expenses are deductible, even if the education later leads to a degree. The education must meet at least one of the following tests:

- The education maintains or improves skills that are required for the taxpayer's current line of work
- The education is required by law or by the taxpayer's employer as a condition of his employment

If a taxpayer has a regular job and then enrolls in work-related education courses on a temporary basis, he can also deduct the round-trip costs of transportation between his home and school. This is true regardless of the location of the school, the distance traveled, or whether the taxpayer attends school on non-work days.

In some cases, a taxpayer may choose to take either an education credit (as an adjustment to income) or take a miscellaneous itemized deduction, depending on the circumstances. In this case, the taxpayer may choose to take whichever method gives him a lower tax.

Deductible Uniforms

The cost of uniforms and other special work clothes required by an employer can be deducted as work-related expenses. The uniforms must NOT be suitable for everyday use. The taxpayer may also deduct the cost of upkeep, including laundry and dry cleaning bills.

Examples of employees who may deduct their uniforms include delivery workers, firefighters, health care workers, law enforcement officers, letter carriers, professional athletes, and transportation workers (air, rail, bus, etc.) Musicians and entertainers can deduct the cost of theatrical clothing and accessories that are not suitable for everyday wear. An employee can deduct the cost of protective clothing, such as safety shoes or boots, safety glasses, hard hats, and work gloves.

Full-time active-duty military personnel cannot deduct the cost of their uniforms. However, they may be able to deduct the cost of insignia, shoulder boards, and related items.

Non-deductible Expenses

A taxpayer cannot deduct the following expenses:
- Commuting expenses
- Political contributions
- The cost of entertaining friends
- Lost or misplaced cash or property
- An attorney's fee to prepare a will (considered a personal legal expense, so it is not deductible)
- Brokers' commissions that are paid on an IRA or other investment property
- Burial or funeral expenses, including the cost of a cemetery lot
- Campaign expenses, lobbying expenses, illegal bribes or kickbacks
- Check-writing fees
- Athletic or country club dues and health spa expenses
- Fees and licenses, such as car licenses, marriage licenses, and dog tags
- Fines and penalties, such as parking tickets
- Investment-related seminars
- Life insurance premiums
- Losses from the sale of a primary residence, furniture, personal car, etc.

- Personal disability insurance premiums
- Legal expenses related to personal, living, or family expenses (divorce fees, etc.)
- Professional accreditation fees
- Residential telephone lines
- Expenses of attending stockholders' meetings
- Expenses of earning or collecting tax-exempt income

Miscellaneous Deductions (NOT Subject to the 2% Limit)

There are also some expenses that are NOT subject to the 2% limit. A taxpayer can fully deduct the expenses that fall under this category on **Schedule A,** without regard to any percentage of income limits.

The expenses that are NOT subject to the "2% Rule" are:

1. Gambling losses to the extent of gambling winnings. (Taxpayers must have kept a written record of their losses.) The full amount of a taxpayer's gambling winnings is reported on line 21 of his **Form 1040**. Gambling losses are deducted on **Schedule A,** up to the total amount of gambling winnings.

2. Work-related expenses for individuals with a disability that enable them to work, such as attendant care services at their workplace.

Example: Erin has a visual disability. She requires a large screen magnifier at work in order to see well enough so she can perform her work. Erin purchased her screen magnifier for $550. She may deduct the cost of the screen magnifier as an itemized deduction NOT subject to the 2% floor.

3. Amortizable premium on taxable bonds: If the amount a taxpayer pays for a bond is greater than its stated principal amount, the excess is called a "bond premium." If this occurs, the excess is treated as a miscellaneous itemized deduction that is not subject to the 2% limit.

4. Casualty or theft losses from *income-producing* property: A taxpayer can deduct a casualty or theft loss as a miscellaneous itemized deduction not subject to the 2% limit if the damaged or stolen property was income-producing property (property held for investment, such as stocks, notes, bonds, gold, silver, vacant lots, and works of art).

5. A taxpayer can deduct the federal estate tax attributable to income "in respect of a decedent" that the taxpayer includes in gross income. Income "in respect of a decedent" is income that a deceased taxpayer would have received had the death not occurred and which was not properly includable in the decedent's final income tax return.

*Note: Gambling losses in excess of winnings are not deductible. The full amount of winnings must be reported as income and the losses (up to the amount of winnings) can be claimed as an itemized deduction.

Summary: Itemized Deductions

Medical and Dental Expenses

Deductible medical and dental expenses are reported and calculated on **Schedule A**. Qualified medical and dental expenses are expenses the taxpayer paid during the tax year for himself, his spouse, and his dependents.

Taxes

Deductible taxes are reported on **Schedule A**. Taxpayers can deduct the following:
1. State and local income taxes
2. State, local, or foreign real estate taxes
3. State and local personal property tax payments

Deductible Interest

Deductible interest is reported on **Schedule A**. The taxpayer should receive **Form 1098**, *Mortgage Interest Statement*, which shows the deductible amount of interest he paid during the tax year. Only taxpayers who are legally liable for the debt can deduct the interest. Taxpayers can treat amounts paid in 2011 for qualified mortgage insurance as home mortgage interest.

Only points paid as a form of interest can be deducted on **Schedule A**. This interest, even if it qualifies for home mortgage interest, must generally be spread over the life of the mortgage. However, if the loan is used to buy or build a taxpayer's main home, the taxpayer may be able to deduct the entire amount in the year paid.

Points paid to refinance a mortgage are generally not deductible in full the year the taxpayer paid them, unless the points were paid in connection with the improvement of a main home and certain conditions were met.

Charitable Deductions

Qualified charitable contributions are reported on **Schedule A**. The contributions to qualifying organizations that taxpayers can deduct include cash donations, dues paid to qualified organizations, fair market value of used goods, and unreimbursed volunteer and travel expenses that relate directly to the services the taxpayer provided for the qualifying organization. Any donation over $250 requires a receipt from the organization. Any non-cash donation over $500 must be reported using IRS **Form 8283**, *Non-cash Charitable Contributions*. If any single non-cash donation is valued over $5,000, the taxpayer must also get an appraisal.

Unit 10: Questions

1. All of the following may be claimed as miscellaneous itemized deductions EXCEPT _____.

A. Unreimbursed commuting expenses to and from work.
B. Professional society or union dues.
C. Expenses of looking for a new job.
D. Work-related expenses for individuals with a disability.

The answer is A. The expenses of commuting to and from work are not deductible expenses. ###

2. Eli purchased a used car for $10,000 in 2011. He forgot to purchase auto insurance, and three months later, he totaled his car in an auto accident. He was able to sell the car to a salvage yard for $500. Eli's AGI for 2011 was $35,000. What is Eli's deductible loss?

A. $0.
B. $3,500.
C. $5,900.
D. $8,910.

The answer is C. This is a non-business casualty loss, so Eli must first reduce his loss by $100 and then 2% of his AGI. The answer is calculated as follows:

Basis:	$10,000
Insurance	$0
Salvage value	(500)
Statutory reduction	(100)
10% of AGI	(3,900)
Deductible Loss	$5,900

Eli's deductible casualty loss on **Schedule A** is $5,900. ###

3. Which of the following taxes can taxpayers deduct on **Schedule A**?

A. Federal income tax.
B. Real estate tax.
C. Tax on alcohol and tobacco.
D. Foreign sales taxes.

The answer is B. Only the real estate taxes are deductible. Taxpayers can deduct real estate tax on **Schedule A** as an itemized deduction. ###

4. Angie and Chuck file a joint return and claim their two children as dependents. They have an adjusted gross income of $95,400. Last year the family accumulated $6,620 in unreimbursed medical and dental expenses that included the following:

Prescription eyeglasses for Angie ($320)
Prescription contacts for Chuck ($1,000)
Chuck's stop smoking-cessation program ($5,300)

The total of Chuck and Angie's deductible medical expenses is _____.

A. $6,620.
B. $6,300.
C. $5,620.
D. $0.

The answer is D. Angie and Chuck cannot deduct any of their medical expenses. Only the portion of total medical expenses that exceeds 7.5% of the taxpayer's AGI is deductible. The total of Angie and Chuck's medical expenses, $6,620, is less than $95,400 x 7.5%=$7,155. ###

5. All of the following are deductible medical expenses EXCEPT _____.

A. Transportation for medical care.
B. Transportation to a medical conference related to the chronic disease of a dependent.
C. Smoking-cessation programs.
D. Non-prescription nicotine gum and patches.

The answer is D. Taxpayers may deduct transportation related to medical care. The cost of smoking programs and prescription drugs are also deductible. However, non-prescription and over-the-counter medicines are not deductible as medical expenses. ###

6. Which of the following is a deductible medical expense?

A. Non-prescription ointment for treating poison oak.
B. Premiums for life insurance.
C. Prescription hearing aids.
D. Cost of childcare while a parent is in the hospital.

The answer is C. Only the cost of the hearing aids is a deductible medical expense. Life insurance premiums, childcare, and non-prescribed medicines are not deductible. ###

7. Max and Wendy are both 30 years old and file jointly for 2011. They decide not to itemize their deductions. Max is legally blind. What is their standard deduction amount in 2011?

A. $8,500.
B. $11,600.
C. $12,750.
D. $13,050.

The answer is C. The answer is figured as follows: ($11,600 + $1,150) on their Form 1040. Max is blind, so he and Wendy are allowed an additional $1,150 as a standard deduction amount. Their standard deduction is $12,750. ###

8. Which of the following taxpayers must either itemize deductions or claim zero as their deduction?

A. Mindy, who files a joint return with her husband.
B. Leslie, who claims two dependents and files **Form 1040.**
C. Pearl, whose itemized deductions are more than the standard deduction.
D. Gabe, whose wife files a separate return and itemizes her deductions.

The answer is D. Married taxpayers who file separately and whose spouses itemize deductions must either claim "0" as their deduction or itemize their deductions. ###

9. All of the following factors determine the amount of a taxpayer's standard deduction EXCEPT _____.

A. The taxpayer's filing status.
B. The taxpayer's gross income.
C. Whether the taxpayer is 65 or older, or blind.
D. Whether the taxpayer can be claimed as a dependent.

The answer is B. The standard deduction amount depends on the taxpayer's filing and dependent status, and whether the taxpayer is blind or at least 65 years old. It is not based on the taxpayer's income. ###

10. Sara and James are both 25, and they have been married for two years. What is their standard deduction in 2011?

A. $11,600.
B. $8,500.
C. $5,800.
D. $3,750.

The answer is A. Sara and James meet the requirements for the standard deduction for most people. Their standard deduction is $11,600 in 2011. ###

11. Brenda is 22, single, and recently graduated from college. She has no dependents. She provides all of her own support. What is her standard deduction in 2011?

A. $950.
B. $3,700.
C. $5,800.
D. $8,600.

The answer is C. Brenda is Single, with no dependents. Her standard deduction is $5,800. ###

12. Which of the following taxpayers is *required* to itemize deductions?

A. Sophie, who has one dependent child.
B. Andrea, who wants to deduct the alimony she paid to her ex-husband.
C. Gabrielle, whose itemized deductions are more than the standard deduction.
D. Samir, who is a non-resident alien.

The answer is D. A non-resident or dual-status alien during the year (who is not married to a U.S. citizen or resident) must itemize personal deductions. He cannot choose the standard deduction. The other taxpayers listed are not required to itemize their deductions. ###

13. All of the following are deductible medical expenses EXCEPT _____.

A. Elective cosmetic surgery.
B. Transportation to a medical conference related to the chronic disease of a dependent.
C. Legal abortion.
D. Prescription birth control pills.

The answer is A. Elective cosmetic surgery is not a deductible medical expense. All the other expenses listed are acceptable as deductible medical expenses. ###

14. All of the following home improvements may be itemized and deducted as medical expenses EXCEPT:

A. The cost of installing porch lifts and other forms of lifts.
B. The cost of lowering cabinets to accommodate a disability.
C. The cost of making doorways wider to accommodate a wheelchair.
D. The cost of an elevator costing $4,000 that adds $5,000 to the FMV of the home.

The answer is D. The deduction for capital improvements is limited to the excess of the actual cost of the improvements over the increase in the fair market value of the home. Since the elevator adds value to the home, it cannot be deducted as a medical expense. ###

15. Which of the following items is NOT a deductible medical expense?

A. Dental implants to replace broken or missing teeth.
B. Over-the-counter aspirin.
C. Guide dog expenses for a blind person.
D. Prescription contact lenses.

The answer is B. The cost of medical items such as false teeth, prescription eyeglasses or contact lenses, laser eye surgery, hearing aids, crutches, wheelchairs, and guide dogs for the blind or deaf are all deductible medical expenses. Over-the-counter medicines are not deductible. ###

16. Justin had the following medical expenses in 2011:

- $450 for contact lenses
- $800 for eyeglasses
- $9,000 for a broken leg, of which $8,000 was paid for by his insurance
- $200 for prescription drugs
- $1,900 for a doctor-prescribed back brace
- $200 for childcare while in the hospital

What is his medical expense deduction BEFORE the imposition of the 7.5% income limit?

A. $1,900.
B. $4,350.
C. $4,550.
D. $12,350.

The answer is B. His medical expense deduction before limitations is $4,350. The babysitting is not deductible, even though it was incurred while he was obtaining medical care. The amounts reimbursed by insurance are not deductible as medical expenses. ###

17. Jesse is in the process of adopting a child. In 2011, the child lived with Jesse and he provided all of the child's support. However, the adoption is not final. Which of the following statements is TRUE?

A. Jesse can include medical expenses that he paid before the adoption becomes final, if the child qualified as his dependent when the medical services were provided or paid.
B. Jesse cannot claim the medical expenses because the adoption is not final.
C. Jesse must save his receipts and, once the adoption becomes final, he may amend his tax return.
D. A taxpayer may only claim medical expenses for a biological child or a stepchild.

The answer is A. Jesse can include medical expenses that he paid before the adoption becomes final, so long as the child qualified as a dependent when the medical services were provided or paid. ###

18. All of the following expenses do not qualify as deductible medical expenses, EXCEPT:

A. Non-corrective cosmetic surgery.
B. Maternity clothes.
C. Final burial expenses.
D. Braces to correct teeth.

The answer is D. A taxpayer may deduct the cost of dental expenses, including orthodontia. None of the other expenses are deductible as medical expenses. ###

19. Which of the following is a deductible medical expense?

A. Acupuncture for back pain.
B. Karate lessons for an overweight person.
C. Marriage counseling.
D. Teeth whitening.

The answer is A. In this instance, only acupuncture qualifies as an IRS-allowed medical expense. Medical care expenses must be primarily to alleviate or prevent a physical or mental defect or illness. They do not include expenses that are merely beneficial to general health, such as vitamins, gym classes, or vacations. ###

20. Dora's AGI is $40,000. She paid medical expenses of $3,500. Taking into account the AGI limit, how much can Dora deduct on her **Schedule A**?

A. $0.
B. $500.
C. $2,313.
D. $2,500.

The answer is B. Dora can deduct only $500 of her medical expenses because that is the amount that exceeds 7.5% of her AGI. Dora's AGI is $40,000, 7.5% of which is $3,000. ###

21. Which of the following taxes can taxpayers deduct on **Schedule A?**

A. Local sales taxes.
B. Fines for speeding.
C. Social Security taxes.
D. Homeowner's association fees.

The answer is A. In 2011, taxpayers have the option of claiming state and local sales taxes as an itemized deduction instead of claiming state and local income taxes (a taxpayer cannot claim both). Taxpayers may deduct sales taxes on **Schedule A**. The other expenses listed are not deductible as taxes on **Schedule A**. ###

22. Which of the following expenses are deductible on **Schedule A**?

A. Stamp taxes.
B. Parking ticket obtained while getting emergency medical care.
C. Drivers' license fees.
D. Personal property taxes paid on a speedboat.

The answer is D. Only the property taxes paid on the boat are deductible. These are also called "DMV fees." Parking tickets and fines are never deductible. Drivers' license fees and stamp taxes are not deductible. ###

23. Ryan is having money troubles and agrees to sell his home to Janie. Janie agrees to pay all the delinquent real estate taxes on the residence, totaling $2,000. How must Janie treat the property tax payment of $2,000?

A. Janie may deduct the taxes as an itemized deduction on her **Schedule A.**
B. Janie may not deduct the taxes. She must add the taxes paid to her basis in the property.
C. The taxes may be prorated and deducted over the life of her loan.
D. Janie may deduct the taxes paid as an adjustment to income.

The answer is B. Janie can only deduct the property taxes that are legally imposed on her. Janie cannot deduct property taxes because she was not the legal owner of the property when the taxes were imposed. Property taxes paid during a purchase may be added to the buyer's basis if the taxes are for the time period that the property was owned by the seller. ###

24. Which of the following taxes is NOT deductible on Schedule A?

A. Property tax on a vacation home.
B. Special assessments to improve the sidewalks.
C. DMV fees based on the vehicle's value.
D. Property taxes paid on a home in Mexico.

The answer is B. The assessment to improve sidewalks is not deductible. Many states, cities, and counties also impose local benefit taxes for improvements to property, such as assessments for streets, sidewalks, and sewer lines. These taxes cannot be deducted, but they can be added to the property's basis. ###

25. For a tax to be deductible, all of the following must be true EXCEPT _____.

A. The tax must be imposed during the tax year.
B. The taxpayer must be legally liable for the tax.
C. The tax must be paid during the tax year.
D. The tax must be paid by the taxpayer.

The answer is A. Taxpayers can deduct tax imposed during a *prior* year, so long as the taxes were paid during the current tax year. ###

26. Christopher and Angie file a joint return. During the year, they paid:

- $5,000 in home mortgage interest that was reported to them on **Form 1098**
- $600 in credit card interest
- $4,000 interest on an auto loan
- $3,000 loan interest on an empty lot that was purchased for building a home

How much can Christopher and Angie report as deductible interest?

A. $0.
B. $5,000.
C. $8,000.
D. $8,600.

The answer is B. Only their home mortgage interest ($5,000) is deductible as interest on **Schedule A.** The other types of interest are all personal interest that is not deductible. Interest paid on a plot of land is not deductible as mortgage interest, even if the taxpayer later decides to build on the property. ###

27. Nathaniel owns a home, and he also has a vacation home in the mountains that he maintains. The vacation home sat empty all year. Which of the following statements is true?

A. Only the mortgage interest and property tax on his main home is deductible.
B. Both the mortgage interest and property tax on his main home and the second residence are deductible.
C. The mortgage interest on both homes is deductible, but the property tax on the vacation property is not.
D. The mortgage interest and property tax on his main home is deductible, and the property tax on the second home is deductible. Any mortgage interest on the second home is not deductible.

The answer is B. Both the mortgage interest and property tax on his main home and the second residence are deductible. The mortgage interest on a second home is deductible, even though the taxpayer did not use the home during the year. ###

28. For the Mortgage Interest Deduction, which of the following choices would qualify as a home?

A. An empty lot where the taxpayer plans to build his main home.
B. A sailboat with a camp stove and no bathroom.
C. A vacation cabin without running water.
D. An RV with a small kitchen, bathroom, and sleeping area.

The answer is D. A qualified home includes a house, condominium, cooperative, mobile home, house trailer, boat, or similar property that has sleeping, cooking, and toilet facilities.###

29. Harvey refinanced his home and paid closing costs in 2011. He used the proceeds from the refinance to put on a new roof and also to pay off one of his credit cards. He paid the following fees:

- $400 Loan origination fee (points)
- $500 Home appraisal fee
- $45 Document prep fee
- $60 Loan closing fee
- $70 Title insurance

How much of the fees Harvey paid to the bank for the loan is fully deductible in 2011?

A. $0.
B. $400.
C. $900.
D. $945.
E. $1,005.

The answer is A. Harvey may not fully deduct any of the expenses listed. He cannot "fully deduct" the points because the home loan is a refinance, not a purchase. Deductible fees are limited to home mortgage interest and certain real estate taxes. Points that represent interest on a refinancing are generally amortized over the life of the loan. Fees that are not associated with the acquisition of a loan (other than fees representing interest for tax purposes) generally only affect the basis of the home. Fees related to the acquisition of a loan, such as a credit report fee, are not deductible. ###

30. Ingrid is single with the following income and expenses:
- Wages $70,000
- Interest income $3,000
- Mortgage interest paid $24,000
- Investment interest expense $5,000
- Personal credit card interest $3,400
- Car loan interest $1,200
- Late fees on her mortgage $50

What is Ingrid's total allowable deduction for interest expense on her **Schedule A?**
A. $24,000.
B. $27,000.
C. $27,050.
D. $32,400.

The answer is C. The answer is: $24,000 + $3,000 + $50 = $27,050. The deduction for investment interest expense is limited to investment income. Late fees paid on a qualifying mortgage are deductible as interest. The remaining amount of interest expense must be carried over to the next tax year and may be used to offset income in future tax years. The credit card interest is not deductible. ###

31. Alexander and Melinda are married and file jointly. They have the following interest expenses in the current tax year. How much deductible interest do they have after limitations?

- $10,000 in mortgage interest on a main home
- $2,000 in mortgage interest on a second home
- $4,600 in interest on a car loan
- $600 in credit card interest
- $3,000 in margin interest expense
- $2,400 in investment income

A. $10,000.
B. $12,000.
C. $14,400.
D. $15,000.

The answer is C. The answer is figured as follows: $10,000 + $2,000 + $2,400 = $14,400. The mortgage interest on both homes is deductible. The interest on the auto loan and credit cards is not deductible. The margin interest expense is deductible, but limited to the amount of investment income, which is $2,400. Investment interest is deductible by individuals only to the extent of investment income. The remaining investment interest expense may be carried over to a future tax year. ###

32. All of the following are deductible charitable contributions that Larissa made to a qualifying battered women's shelter EXCEPT _____.

A. Fair market value of the used kitchen appliances, in good condition, she donated to the shelter.
B. $35 of the $50 admission Larissa paid for a shelter fundraising dinner. (The fair market value was $15.)
C. Fair market value of the hours Larissa spent staffing the shelter.
D. Larissa's transportation costs for driving to and from her shift at the shelter.

The answer is C. Larissa cannot deduct the value of her volunteer hours. The value of a person's time and service is never deductible. ###

33. Which taxpayer is required to fill out **Form 8283** and attach it to his or her return?

A. Lenny, who made a single cash contribution of $650 to a qualified organization.
B. Hunter, whose deductible cash contributions totaled $550.
C. Marilyn, whose non-cash contributions totaled $250.
D. Debra, whose non-cash contributions totaled $600.

The answer is D. Debra would be required to fill out **Form 8283**, *Non-Cash Charitable Contributions*, and attach it to her return. That is because any non-cash donation over $500 must be described on **Form 8283**. ###

34. Julia made the following contributions last year:

- $600 to St. Martin's Church (The church gave her a receipt)
- $32 to the SPCA
- $40 to a family whose house burned
- $50 for lottery tickets at a fundraiser
- $100 for playing bingo at her church
- Furniture with a fair market value of $200 to Goodwill

The amount that Julia can claim as deductible cash contributions is $_____.

A. $672.
B. $632.
C. $72.
D. $32.

The answer is B. Julia's donations to her church and to the SPCA are her only deductible cash contributions. Lottery tickets and bingo (or any type of gambling) is not a charitable contribution, even if the proceeds go to a qualifying organization. The donation of furniture to Goodwill is not a cash contribution, and therefore would not be included in the calculation. Non-cash contributions are reported separately from cash contributions. ###

35. Amelia donates $430 in cash to her church. What is required on the receipt to substantiate the donation correctly for IRS recordkeeping requirements?

A. The reason for the contribution.
B. Amelia's home address.
C. The amount of the donation.
D. Amelia's method of payment.

The answer is C. A taxpayer can claim a deduction for a contribution of $250 or more only if he has a receipt from the qualified organization. The receipt (acknowledgment) must include:
- The amount of cash contributed
- Whether the qualified organization gave the taxpayer any goods or services in return
- A description and good faith estimate of the value of any goods or services provided in return by the organization (if applicable)

A receipt for the donation must also show the amount, the date, and the name of the organization that was paid. ###

36. Lindy donates her used car to a qualified charity. She bought it three years ago for $15,000. A used car guide shows the FMV for this type of car is $5,000. Lindy's friend, Buck, offered her $4,500 for the car a week ago. Lindy gets a Form 1098-C from the organization showing the car was sold for $1,900. How much is Lindy's charitable deduction?

A. $15,000.
B. $5,000.
C. $4,500.
D. $1,900.

The answer is D. Lindy can only deduct $1,900 for her donation. She must attach **Form 1098-C** and **Form 8283** to her return. This is because she is only allowed to take the lesser of the car's FMV or the amount for which the charity was able to sell the car. Since the car only sold for $1,900, that is the amount of the donation. ###

37. Joshua's adjusted gross income is $20,000. Determine which expenses he would include in the total for his miscellaneous itemized deductions.

Expense Description:
- Income tax preparation fee $100
- Safe deposit box rental (to store bonds) $75
- Life insurance premiums $600
- Credit card convenience fee for income tax payment $70
- Loss on sale of a personal vehicle $1,800
- Investment journals and newsletters $250
- Investment expenses $200
- Attorney fees for preparation of a will $1,000

What is the total of Joshua's qualified miscellaneous itemized expenses (before the application of any income limits)?

A. $2,895.
B. $2,295.
C. $1,095.
D. $695.

The answer is D. The deductible expenses are the income tax preparation fee ($100); the safe deposit box rental ($75); and the investment expenses, journals, newsletters, and advisory fees ($520). Therefore, his total deduction before application of the 2% floor is $695.

38. Oscar donated a nice leather coat to a thrift store operated by his church. He paid $450 for the coat three years ago. Similar coats in the thrift store sell for $50. What is Oscar's charitable deduction?

A. $0.
B. $50.
C. $400.
D. $450.

The answer is B. Oscar's donation is limited to $50. Generally, the FMV of used clothing and household goods is far less than their original cost. For used clothing, a taxpayer should claim as the value the price that buyers of used items actually pay in used clothing stores, such as consignment or thrift shops. ###

39. Kendra made $1,500 in non-cash (property) contributions to a qualified charity. What form must she file and attach to her tax return in addition to **Schedule A**?

A. Form 8283.
B. Form 2815.
C. Form 1098-C.
D. Form 1065.

The answer is A. If a taxpayer's total deduction for all non-cash contributions for the year is over $500, he must file **Form 8283**, *Non-cash Charitable Contributions*. Taxpayers report their charitable contributions on **Schedule A (Form 1040)**. If any single gift or group of similar gifts is valued over $5,000, the taxpayer must also get an appraisal of the item or items from a qualified appraiser. ###

40. Laney pays $105 for a ticket to a church dinner. All the proceeds go to the church. The ticket to the dinner has an FMV of $20, the cost of the dinner. At the dinner, Laney buys $35 worth of raffle tickets, which the church is selling as a fundraiser. She doesn't win any raffle prizes. What is Laney's deductible charitable contribution to her church?

A. $85.
B. $120.
C. $140.
D. $195.

The answer is A. To figure the amount of Laney's charitable contribution, she must subtract the value of the benefit received ($20) from the total payment ($105). Therefore, Laney can deduct $85 as a charitable contribution to the church. The cost of raffle tickets or other wagering activity is never deductible as a charitable contribution. ###

41. Deductions to the following organizations are subject to the 50% limitation on deductible contributions:

A. Churches.
B. Hospitals.
C. Fraternal societies such as the Kiwanis and the Lions Club.
D. Both A and B.

The answer is D. The 50% limit applies to the total of all charitable contributions made during the year. This means that the deduction for charitable contributions cannot exceed 50% of a taxpayer's AGI. A 30% limit applies to veterans' organizations, fraternal societies, non-profit cemeteries, and certain private non-operating foundations. ###

42. Vera and Jack are married and file jointly. They contributed $15,000 in cash from their savings to their synagogue during 2011. They also donated $3,000 to a private foundation that is a non-profit cemetery organization. A 30% limit applies to the cemetery organization. Their adjusted gross income for 2011 was $30,000. Vera and Jack's deductible contribution for 2011 and any carryover to next year is:

A. $18,000 with zero carryover to next year.
B. $15,000 with $2,100 carryover to next year.
C. $7,500 with $2,100 carryover to next year.
D. $15,000 with $3,000 carryover to next year.

The answer is D. Vera and Jack cannot deduct more than $15,000, which is 50% of their income of $30,000. The remaining amount must be carried forward to a future tax year. ###

43. During a fundraising auction at his local church, Lyle pays $600 for a week's stay at a beachfront hotel, where he stays during a vacation in August. He intends to make the payment as a contribution, and all the proceeds go to help the church. The FMV of the stay is $590. What is Lyle's charitable contribution?

A. $0.
B. $10.
C. $590.
D. $600.

The answer is B. Lyle can only deduct $10, because he received the benefit of staying at the property. Only the excess contribution over the FMV of the item qualifies as a charitable contribution. ###

44. Maya is a church leader and she supervises the group on a prayer trip. She is responsible for overseeing the setup of the trip and really enjoys the activities. She also oversees the breaking down of the campsite and helps transport the group home. Which of the following statements is TRUE?

A. Maya may not deduct her travel expenses because she enjoyed the trip. Therefore, it is a vacation and is not deductible.
B. Maya may deduct her out-of-pocket expenses.
C. Maya may deduct only the travel expense to and from the campsite.
D. None of the above.

The answer is B. A taxpayer may claim a charitable contribution deduction for out-of-pocket expenses incurred while away from home performing services for a charitable organization only if there is no significant element of personal pleasure in the travel. However, a deduction will not be denied simply because the taxpayer enjoys providing services to a charitable organization. The taxpayer is still allowed to take a charitable contribution deduction for the expenses if he is on-duty in a genuine and substantial sense throughout the trip. Since Maya had substantial supervisory and leadership duties throughout the trip, her out-of-pocket expenses are deductible. ###

45. Nancy donates $300 in cash to her local food bank. What type of documentation is required for her donation?

A. No documentation.
B. A canceled check.
C. A self-prepared statement.
D. A receipt for the donation showing the amount, date, and who was paid.

The answer is D. A taxpayer can claim a deduction for a contribution of $250 or more only if he has an acknowledgment or receipt of the contribution from the charity. The receipt must reflect the amount, date, and the name of the organization that was paid. ###

46. Julio spent the entire day attending his church organization's regional meeting as a chosen representative. He spent $50 on travel to the meeting and $25 on materials for the meeting. In the evening, Julio went to the movies with two other meeting attendees. He spent $50 on movie tickets. The charity did not reimburse Julio for any of his costs. How much can Julio deduct as a charitable expense?

A. $25.
B. $50.
C. $75.
D. $150.

The answer is C. Julio's charitable contribution is $75 ($50 + 25 = $75). He can claim his travel and meeting expenses as charitable contributions, because they are directly related to his charitable activities. However, he cannot claim the cost of the evening at the movies. Those costs are personal entertainment costs. ###

47. Ted pays a babysitter $100 to watch his children while he does volunteer work at the Red Cross. He also has $50 in transportation expenses, of which $10 was reimbursed by the organization. What is Ted's deductible expense?

A. $0.
B. $40.
C. $50.
D. $150.

The answer is B. Only Ted's transportation costs are deductible ($50 - $10 reimbursement =$40). A taxpayer cannot deduct payments for child care expenses as a charitable contribution, even if they are necessary so he can do the volunteer work. ###

48. In March 2011, Sonia volunteers for 15 hours in the office of a local homeless shelter. The full-time receptionist is paid $10 an hour to do the same work Sonia does. Sonia makes $15 per hour as a cashier at her regular job. She also has $16 in out-of-pocket expenses for bus fare to the shelter. How much can Sonia deduct on her taxes as a charitable contribution?

A. $16.
B. $150.
C. $225.
D. $241.

The answer is A. A taxpayer cannot deduct the "value" of his time or services as a charitable deduction. However, a volunteer may deduct out-of-pocket expenses and the costs of gas and oil or transportation costs for getting to and from the place where he volunteers. Sonia cannot use the standard mileage rate because she did not use her own car for transportation. ###

49. Oliver pays $70 to see a special showing of a movie at a church fundraising event. The regular price of a movie ticket is $8. Pre-printed on the ticket it says "Contribution: $100." How much is Oliver's charitable deduction?

A. $8.
B. $62.
C. $70.
D. $100.

The answer is B. If the regular price for the movie is $8, the taxpayer contribution is $62 ($70 payment-$8 regular price). If a taxpayer pays MORE than the FMV to a qualified organization for merchandise, goods, or services, the amount paid that is more than the value of the item can be a charitable contribution. No matter what the ticket says, the taxpayer may never deduct more than his actual contribution. ###

50. All of the following are non-profit organizations. However, not all of them qualify as deductible contributions. Sam donated to each non-profit listed. What is his total qualified deduction for 2011?

Amount	Organization
$100	Catholic Church
$120	County animal shelter
$75	Salvation Army
$25	Red Cross
$50	Political contribution
$300	Chamber of Commerce
$670	Total Contributions

A. $320.
B. $370.
C. $220.
D. $670.

The answer is A. The contributions to the political organization and the Chamber of Commerce are not deductible on **Schedule A.** The deduction is figured as follows:
($100 + $120 + $75 + $25 = $320). ###

51. Ali participated in a fundraising raffle event for his local mosque. All the money collected by the mosque, a qualified organization, went to feed the homeless. Ali purchased $300 in bingo cards and won movie tickets valued at $60. What is Ali's charitable deduction?

A. $0.
B. $60.
C. $240.
D. $300.

The answer is A. Ali may not deduct any amount as a contribution. Deducting the cost of raffle, bingo, or lottery tickets is specifically prohibited by IRS Publication 17, even if the money goes to a qualified charity. The cost of raffle, bingo, or lottery tickets is never deductible as a charitable contribution. ###

52. Martin contributes to many organizations. In 2011, he contributes $5,000 in cash to his church and $4,000 to his local Chamber of Commerce. He also contributes land with a fair market value of $16,000 to his church. Martin has a basis of $5,000 in the land. His taxable income for the year is $45,000. What is the maximum amount he can deduct for charitable contributions?

A. $9,000.
B. $18,500.
C. $22,500.
D. $25,000.

The answer is B. The contribution to the Chamber of Commerce is not a deductible contribution. The $5,000 contribution in cash is fully deductible, but gifts of appreciated property (the land) are subject to a maximum deduction of 30% of the taxpayer's contribution base. However, charitable gifts of appreciated property held long-term are subject to a lower deductibility ceiling: 30% of AGI, with a five-year carryover of any excess deduction. So, Martin figures his charitable contribution as follows:

($45,000 x 30%) = $13,500
($5,000 + $13,500) = $18,500
Carryover = $2,500
($16,000 - $13,500 = $2,500)###

53. Patrice's antique Persian rug was damaged by a new kitten before it was housebroken. Patrice estimates the loss at $4,500. Her AGI for the year is $50,000. How much of the casualty loss may she deduct?

A. $0.
B. $4,500.
C. $3,000.
C. $2,900.

The answer is A. A casualty loss is not deductible if the damage is caused by a family pet. Because the damage was not unexpected and unusual, the loss is not deductible as a casualty loss. ###

54. Brady's garage caught fire in 2011. The garage is not attached to his primary residence. Brady estimates the property damage at $6,000. He declines to file an insurance claim because he fixes the damage himself. Brady pays $3,000 for the cost of the materials. He estimates the value of his labor to be approximately $2,800. His insurance company has a $1,000 deductible for any casualty loss claim filed. What is Brady's deductible casualty loss before any deductions or income limitations?

A. $0.
B. $1,000.
C. $3,000.
D. $6,000.

The answer is B. If a taxpayer's property is covered by insurance, he cannot deduct a loss unless he files an insurance claim for reimbursement. However, if the taxpayer declines to file an insurance claim, the IRS limits eligible casualty losses to the amount that is not normally covered by insurance, such as the amount of the insurance deductible. ###

55. Isaac's home was damaged by a tornado. He had $90,000 worth of damage, but $80,000 was reimbursed by his insurance company. Isaac's employer had a disaster relief fund for its employees. Isaac received $4,000 from the fund and spent the entire amount on repairs to his home. What is Isaac's deductible casualty loss before applying the deduction limits?

A. $0.
B. $4,000.
C. $6,000.
D. $10,000.

The answer is C. Isaac's casualty loss before applying the deduction limits is $6,000. Isaac must reduce his unreimbursed loss ($90,000 - $80,000 = $10,000) by the $4,000 he received from his employer. Isaac's casualty loss before applying the deduction limits is $6,000 ($10,000 - $4,000). ###

56. All of the following may be claimed as miscellaneous itemized deductions EXCEPT _____.

A. Funeral expenses.
B. Union dues.
C. Laundry costs for uniforms.
D. Investment expenses.

The answer is A. Funeral expenses are not deductible as a miscellaneous itemized deduction. All of the other expenses listed are deductible as itemized deductions on **Schedule A**. ###

57. All of the following miscellaneous itemized deductions are subject to the 2% of AGI limit EXCEPT _____.

A. Tax preparation fees.
B. Union dues.
C. Investment expenses.
D. Gambling losses to the extent of gambling winnings.

The answer is D. Gambling losses to the extent of gambling winnings are not subject to the 2% AGI limit. ###

58. Kim uses her home office while she works as a translator for an online translating company. Kim meets the requirements for deducting expenses for the business use of her home. Her home office is 480 square feet and her home is 2,400 square feet. What is Kim's "business use" percentage in order to figure her allowable deduction?

A. 5%.
B. 10%.
C. 15%.
D. 20%.

The answer is D. Kim uses 20% of her home for business. Her office is 20% (480 ÷ 2,400) of the total area of her home. Therefore, her business percentage is 20%. ###

59. Simon's AGI is $75,000. Therefore, the first _____ of miscellaneous employee work-related expenses are not deductible.

A. $1,000.
B. $1,500.
C. $5,625.
D. Some other amount.

The answer is B. Simon's employee work-related expenses are subject to the 2% limit of adjusted gross income. Therefore, Simon must figure his deduction on Schedule A by first subtracting 2% of his AGI (75,000 x 2% = $1,500) from the total amount of these expenses. ###

60. Marissa works as a bookkeeper for A+ Bookkeeping. She was hired as a bookkeeper three years ago, but this year her employer changed his educational requirements. Now all the bookkeepers are required to take three additional courses in order to keep their current positions. Marissa incurred the following expenses when she took these courses:

- $100 Required supplies
- $550 Tuition
- $120 Required books
- $50 Credit card interest from paying tuition
- $65 Bus passes to and from school
- $885 Total educational expenses

What is Marissa's deductible work-related educational expense on her **Schedule A** before the 2% limitation?

A. $550.
B. $670.
C. $835.
D. $885.

The answer is C. Marissa may deduct all the costs as work-related educational expenses, with the exception of the credit card interest, which is a personal expense and not deductible. ###

61. Which of the following expenses does NOT qualify as a deductible transportation expense?

A. Getting from one client to another in the course of a taxpayer's business or profession.
B. Commuting expenses.
C. Traveling overseas to sign a business contract with a foreign supplier.
D. Going to a business meeting out-of-state.

The answer is B. A taxpayer can include in business expenses amounts paid for transportation primarily for and essential to business or trade. A taxpayer cannot deduct personal commuting expenses, no matter how far his home is from his regular place of work. ###

62. Which of the following will qualify for a deduction on **Schedule A** as an employee business expense?

A. The employer reimburses expenses under a tuition reimbursement (nontaxable) program.
B. Taking classes that maintain or improve skills needed in the taxpayer's present work.
C. Taking classes that are required by a taxpayer's employer or the law to keep his present salary, status, or job. The required education must serve a bona fide business purpose to the taxpayer's employer.
D. Both B and C.

The answer is D. Both B and C are correct. A taxpayer can deduct the costs of qualifying work-related education as business expenses. Choice "A" is incorrect because any amounts that are reimbursed by an employer cannot be deducted by the taxpayer. ###

63. What form is used to figure a taxpayer's unreimbursed employee business expenses?

A. Form 1040-EZ.
B. Form 2106.
C. Form 8821.
D. Form W-2.

The answer is B. The taxpayer must figure the gross expenses on **Form 2106**, *Employee Business Expenses*, and attach it to his **Form 1040**. ###

64. During the year, Leon paid $350 to have his tax return prepared. He also paid union dues of $450 and paid an attorney $3,000 to draft his will. What is Leon's miscellaneous itemized deduction on his Schedule A before the 2% limitation?

A. $350.
B. $450.
C. $800.
D. $3,800.

The answer is C. The attorney fees for drafting the will are not deductible. The tax preparation fees and union dues are deductible and subject to a 2% of AGI floor. ###

65. Connor is deaf. He purchased a special device to use at work so he can identify when his phone rings. He paid for the device out-of-pocket, and his employer did not reimburse him. How should Connor report this on his tax return?

A. Connor may deduct the purchase as an itemized deduction, NOT subject to the 2% floor.
B. Connor may deduct the purchase as an itemized deduction, subject to the 2% floor.
C. Connor may not deduct the purchase because he is not totally disabled.
D. Connor may not deduct the purchase because he is not self-employed.

The answer is A. Connor may deduct the expenses for the special device as an impairment-related work expense. The deduction is not limited. If a taxpayer has a physical or mental disability that limits employment, he can choose to deduct the expense as a miscellaneous itemized deduction, NOT subject to the 2%-of-income floor.###

66. Brooke had a number of unreimbursed medical expenses during the year. Which of the following is not a deductible medical expense?

A. Long-term care premiums.
B. Acupuncture treatments.
C. Transportation costs to a doctor's office.
D. Non-prescription medication.

The answer is D. Non-prescription medication is not deductible as a medical expense. ###

67. Abby has the following income and losses in 2011:

1. $45,000 in wages.
2. $10,000 in gambling winnings.
3. $13,000 in gambling losses.
4. $1,500 in attorney fees for a divorce.

How should these transactions be treated on her tax return?

A. Report $55,000 in taxable income and $10,000 in miscellaneous itemized deductions on Schedule A, NOT subject to the 2% floor.
B. Report $53,000 in taxable income and $13,000 in miscellaneous itemized deductions, subject to the 2% floor.
C. Report $55,000 in taxable income and $13,000 in miscellaneous itemized deductions on Schedule A, subject to the 2% floor.
D. Report $45,000 in taxable income and $14,500 in miscellaneous itemized deductions on Schedule A, NOT subject to the 2% floor.

The answer is A. The full amount of income must be reported on **Form 1040** ($45,000 + $10,000 = $55,000). The gambling losses are deductible only up to the amount of gambling winnings; a taxpayer must report the full amount of gambling winnings on **Form 1040**. The taxpayer then may deduct gambling losses on **Schedule A (Form 1040)**. Gambling losses are not subject to the 2% of income limitation, but taxpayers cannot report more gambling losses than they do gambling winnings. ###

68. Louis has a car insurance policy with a $900 deductible. He has a car accident in 2011 and has $2,600 worth of damage. Louis doesn't want his insurance to go up, so he chooses not to file an insurance claim. Instead, Louis decides to do the work himself. He pays $1,200 for replacement parts to repair the damage. What is his casualty loss, before applying the $100 and 10% of income limit?

A. $0.
B. $900.
C. $1,200.
D. $2,600.

The answer is B. If Louis had filed a claim with his insurance company, his insurance would not have covered the first $900 of an auto collision, so the $900 is deductible as a casualty loss (still subject to the $100 and 10% rules). A taxpayer may not deduct casualty and theft losses that are covered by insurance unless he files a claim for reimbursement. If the taxpayer decides not to file an insurance claim but has a deductible, he may still claim the amount of the insurance deductible, since that amount would not have been covered by the policy anyway.
###

Unit 11: Tax Credits

> **More Reading:**
> Publication 972, *Child Tax Credit*
> Publication 503, *Child and Dependent Care Expenses*
> Publication 596, *Earned Income Credit*
> Publication 970, *Tax Benefits for Education*
> Publication 524, *Credit for the Elderly or Disabled*
> Publication 514, *Foreign Tax Credit for Individuals*

A tax credit directly reduces tax liability. A tax credit is usually more valuable than a tax deduction of the same dollar amount. It is important to understand this distinction for the EA exam. A tax deduction will reduce income that is subject to tax, but a tax credit will actually reduce tax *liability*—the amount the taxpayer is required to pay the IRS.

In some cases (such as the Earned Income Tax Credit), a tax credit is refundable. This can create a tax refund—even if the taxpayer does not owe any tax! There are two types of tax credits:

- **Refundable credits**
- **Non-refundable credits**

Non-refundable Tax Credits

A non-refundable credit is a dollar-for-dollar reduction of the tax liability. A non-refundable credit can reduce a taxpayer's tax liability down to zero, but not beyond that. Most tax credits are "non-refundable" credits. Non-refundable tax credits include the following:

1. Child and Dependent Care Credit
2. Credit for the Elderly and Disabled
3. Child Tax Credit
4. Mortgage Interest Credit
5. Lifetime Learning Credit
6. Retirement Savings Contribution Credit (the Saver's Credit)
7. Non-business Energy Property Credit
8. Residential Energy Efficient Property Credit

Refundable Tax Credits

A refundable tax credit can produce a tax refund even if the taxpayer does not owe any tax. Refundable tax credits that can reduce tax liability below zero include the following:

1. Credit for Excess Social Security Tax or Railroad Retirement Tax Withheld
2. Additional Child Tax Credit
3. Earned Income Credit (*heavily tested on the EA exam)
4. Adoption Credit (refundable in 2011)

5. First-Time Homebuyer Credit (in 2011, this credit is only available to service members on qualified extended duty)
6. Health Coverage Tax Credit
7. American Opportunity Credit

Other Credits (Covered Later)
1. Health Coverage Tax Credit (refundable)
2. Foreign Tax Credit
3. Credit for Prior Year Alternative Minimum Tax (AMT)
4. Alternative Fuel Vehicle Refueling Property Credit
5. Electric Vehicle Credit

Child and Dependent Care Credit

The Child and Dependent Care Credit is a non-refundable credit that allows taxpayers to reduce their tax liability by a percentage of their dependent care expenses. The credit may be claimed by taxpayers who work and pay for daycare (or adult care services) for someone who is their dependent or spouse. The Child and Dependent Care Credit is calculated using **Form 2441.**

The credit can range from 20% to 35% of a taxpayer's qualifying expenses. The percentage is based on the taxpayer's income. Since this credit is non-refundable, it cannot exceed the amount of income tax on the return; that is, it can reduce an individual's tax to $0, but it cannot result in a refund. The credit for child and dependent care is available without regard to the taxpayer's income (it is not phased out at higher income levels).

Because the Child and Dependent Care Credit is a non-refundable credit, only taxpayers with taxable income can claim the credit. In order to qualify, the childcare expenses must be incurred in order for the taxpayer to work. The taxpayer may be employed in full-time or part-time work. The expenses may also be incurred while a taxpayer is searching for a job.

Some taxpayers receive dependent care benefits from their employers, which may also be called "Flexible Spending Accounts" or "reimbursement accounts." Taxpayers usually can exclude these benefits from their income. Employer-provided dependent care benefits are reported on the employee's **Form W-2**.

All taxpayers who receive employer-provided dependent care benefits are required to complete **Form 2441,** *Child and Dependent Care Expenses*, to determine if they can exclude these benefits from their taxable income.

A taxpayer must pass five eligibility tests in order to qualify for this credit:
1. **Qualifying person test**
2. **Earned income test**
3. **Work-related expense test**
4. **Joint return test**
5. **Provider identification test**

Qualifying Person Test

To meet the *qualifying person test*, the taxpayer's expenses must be for the care of a qualifying individual. In most cases, this is the taxpayer's minor child. However, expenses paid for the care of other dependents (such as a dependent parent who requires in-home care) are also allowable.

For the purposes of this credit, a "qualifying person" is:
- A dependent child under the age of 13
- A spouse who is unable to care for himself or herself (a disabled spouse)
- Any other dependents who are unable to care for themselves

Only a custodial parent can take the Child and Dependent Care Credit. If the child is not being claimed as a dependent by the taxpayer because the non-custodial parent is taking the exemption under the special rules for children of divorced and separated parents, only the custodial parent may treat the child as a qualifying person for this credit.

Example: Samuel paid someone to care for his wife, Janet, so he could work. Janet is permanently disabled and requires an in-home care aide. Samuel also paid to have someone prepare meals for his 12-year-old daughter, Jill. Both Janet and Jill are "qualifying persons" for the credit.

The Earned Income Test

The next test is the "earned income test." The taxpayer (AND spouse if married) must have earned income during the year in order to qualify for this credit. Usually, this means that the taxpayer must have worked for an employer, or else he must be self-employed. If a taxpayer has only passive income during the year (such as rental income or interest income), then he will not qualify for the credit.

A taxpayer may claim daycare expenses while he is seeking employment. However, the taxpayer must still have earned income for the year in order to take this credit. For couples filing MFJ, this means both spouses must work. This credit is not available to taxpayers who file separately.
Example:

A spouse is exempted if he is a full-time student or is disabled (explained below). Childcare expenses that are incurred so that the taxpayer may volunteer for a charity or other tax-exempt organization do NOT qualify for the credit. Earned income includes:

- Wages, salaries, tips
- Other taxable employee compensation
- Earnings from self-employment, including self-employment income earned by a general partner in a partnership
- Strike benefits
- Disability pay reported as wages

The taxpayer's spouse is treated as having earned income for any month he is:
- A full-time student, or
- Disabled

In either case, for the purposes of the credit, the spouse's income is considered to be $250 for each month. If, in the same month, the taxpayer and spouse are either full-time students or unable to care for themselves, only one of them can be treated as having earned income in that month (up to $500 or $250 for each).

Example: Jessica and Quincy are married. Quincy worked full-time all year and earned $40,000 in 2011. Jessica attended school full-time from January 1 to June 30. She was unemployed during the summer months and did not attend school the rest of the year. Jessica should be treated as having earned income for the months she attended school full-time, which were January through June of the tax year.

Example: Patsy is a stay-at-home mom. Her husband works and had earned income for the tax year. They have a young son. Patsy volunteers 12 hours a week at a local autism information hotline. She and her husband pay a caregiver to stay with their son during the hours she does her volunteer work. They do not qualify for the Dependent Care Credit because the caregiver expense is not work-related; that is, Patsy is not using it in order to work or to look for work. Also, to qualify for the credit, Patsy and her husband must BOTH have earned income for the tax year. Since Patsy does not have a job (and is not disabled or a full-time student), then the expenses would not qualify.

Work-Related Expense Test

Qualifying expenses must be "work related," meaning that the childcare must be incurred while a taxpayer is working or searching for work. Daycare expenses incurred during a short, temporary absence from work, such as for vacation or a minor illness, may still qualify as childcare expenses. An absence of two weeks or less is considered a short, temporary absence.

Example: Ernie and Grace have full-time jobs. They pay $45 to a babysitter once a week so they can go out to eat on a date. Since this is not a work-related expense, it is not qualifying childcare for the purposes of the Child Care Credit.

Example: Darcy works only three days a week. While she works, her six-year-old child attends a daycare center. Darcy pays the center $150 for three days a week or $250 for five days a week. Sometimes Darcy pays the $250 so she can run errands or do other tasks. However, the extra charge for daycare during the time Darcy is not working is not a qualifying expense. Darcy's deductible expenses are limited to $150 a week, which is the amount of work-related daycare expense.

The following expenses qualify as work-related:
- Cost of care outside the home for dependents under 13; for example, preschool or home daycare, before or after-school care for a child in grade school.
- Cost of assistive care for any other qualifying person; for example, dependent care for a disabled adult.
- Household expenses that are at least partly for the well-being and protection of a qualifying person; for example, the services of a housekeeper or cook.

Preschool expenses are deductible for children below the first grade. Private school tuition for kindergarten (or a higher grade) is not a qualifying expense, but after-school care at a private school may still qualify as a deductible expense.

Example: Roger's 10-year-old child attends a private school. In addition to paying for tuition, Roger pays an extra fee for the before-school and after-school program so Roger can go to work. Roger can count the cost of the before and after-school program when figuring the credit, but not the cost of tuition.

Example: Emily is single and her elderly mother, Lorraine, is her dependent. Lorraine is completely disabled and must be in an adult daycare so she does not injure herself. Emily pays $8,000 per year for Lorraine to be in the daycare. Emily may take the Dependent Care Credit, because Lorraine is disabled and incapable of self-care.

Examples of childcare expenses that do not qualify include:
- Education, such as expenses for a child to attend kindergarten or a higher grade
- The cost of sending a child to an overnight camp
- The cost of transportation not provided by a care provider
- A forfeited deposit to a daycare center (a forfeited deposit is not actually a daycare cost, and therefore is not deductible)

Example: Ellie is divorced and has custody of her 12-year-old daughter, Terri. Terri takes care of herself after school. In the summer, Ellie spends $2,000 to send Terri to an overnight camp for two weeks. The cost of sending a child to an overnight camp is not considered a work-related expense. Ellie does not have any qualifying expenses for the purpose of this credit.

Care expenses do not include amounts paid for food, clothing, education, or entertainment. Small amounts paid for these items, however, can be included if they are incidental and cannot be separated from the cost of care.

> **Example:** Krista takes her three-year-old child to a nursery school that provides lunch and educational activities as part of its preschool childcare service. The meals are included in the overall cost of care, and they're not itemized on her bill. Krista can count the total cost when she figures the credit.

Payments for childcare made to an individual will not qualify for the credit if the payment is made to a family member who is either:

- The taxpayer's own child under age 19
- Any other dependent listed on the taxpayer's tax return

There is a limit on the amount of work-related expenses taxpayers can include in figuring the Child and Dependent Care Credit. The limit is:

- $3,000 for expenses paid for one qualifying person, or
- $6,000 for two or more qualifying persons

No matter how many dependents a taxpayer has, the credit cannot be more than $6,000 in a single tax year.

Taxpayers may combine costs for multiple dependents. For example, if a taxpayer pays daycare for three qualifying children, the $6,000 limit does not need to be divided equally among them.

> **Example:** Lee has three children. His qualifying daycare expenses for his first child are $2,200. Lee's qualifying expenses for his second child are $2,800, and the expenses for his last child are $900. He is allowed to use the total amount, $6,000, when figuring his credit.

> **Example:** Diego and Valeria both work and have three children. They have $2,000 in daycare expenses for their son, Miguel; $3,000 for their son, Cesar; and $4,000 for their daughter, Cecilia. Although their total childcare expenses are $9,000, they may only use the first $6,000 as their basis for the Child Care Credit.

> **Example:** Lori is a single mother with a dependent child. Her son, Noah, is five years old. Lori takes Noah to daycare five days per week so she can work. Lori makes $46,000 in wages and spends $5,200 per year on daycare for Noah. The maximum that Lori can claim as a dependent care credit is $3,000, even though her actual expenses exceed that amount.

Joint Return Test

The joint return test specifies that married couples who wish to take the credit for child and dependent care must file jointly. However, a married taxpayer can be "considered unmarried" for tax purposes if they qualify for Head of Household filing status.[49] Taxpayers who file separately (MFS) are not eligible for the Child and Dependent Care Credit.

In the case of divorced or separated taxpayers, only the custodial parent is allowed to take the Child and Dependent Care Credit.

Provider Identification Test

The "provider identification test" requires that taxpayers provide the name, address, and Taxpayer Identification Number (TIN) of the person or organization who provided the care for the child or dependent. If the daycare provider is an individual, the Social Security Number should be provided. If the care provider is a business or an organization, then the Employer Identification Number (EIN) must be provided. If the provider is a tax-exempt organization (church, school, etc.), it is not necessary to provide identification – a taxpayer may enter "TAX-EXEMPT."

If a daycare provider refuses to supply the taxpayer with identification information such as a Social Security Number, the taxpayer may still claim the credit. She must report whatever information she has about the provider (such as the name and address) and attach a statement to **Form 2441** explaining the provider's refusal to supply the information. Returns that do not include the provider information cannot be filed electronically.

Education Credits in General

Education credits are for postsecondary education expenses (college). Education credits reduce the amount of tax due. The amount of the credit is based on qualified education expenses the taxpayer paid during the tax year. There are two education credits:

- The American Opportunity Credit[50] and
- The Lifetime Learning Credit

IRS **Form 8863,** *Education Credits (American Opportunity and Lifetime Learning Credits),* is used to claim both of the education credits.

*Note: The American Opportunity Credit allows 40% of the credit to be refundable. The Lifetime Learning Credit is not a refundable credit.

There are general rules that apply to these credits, as well as specific rules for each credit. For example, taxpayers can take education credits for themselves, their spouse, and their dependents who attended an eligible educational institution during the tax year. Eligible educational institutions include colleges, universities, vocational schools,

---

[49] In this case, the taxpayer will still be eligible for the Dependent Care Credit if he files as Head of Household. The taxpayer who claims the Dependent Care Credit must be the custodial parent.

[50] The American Opportunity Credit modified the Hope Credit beginning in 2009. The American Opportunity Credit (which is partially refundable) was extended for tax year 2011.

or community colleges. Taxpayers can claim payments that were prepaid for the academic period that begins in the first three months of the next calendar year.

> **Example:** Tom paid $1,500 in December 2011 for college tuition for the spring semester that begins in January 2012. He can use the $1,500 paid in December 2011 to compute his credit for 2011. Tom can deduct the education credit on his 2011 return, even though he won't start college until 2012. Taxpayers who prepay qualified expenses for an academic period that begins in the first three months of the following year can use the prepaid amount in figuring the credit.

All of the following conditions will DISQUALIFY a taxpayer from claiming education credits:

- If the taxpayer can be claimed as a dependent on someone else's tax return
- If the taxpayer files as Married Filing Separately
- If the taxpayer's adjusted gross income (AGI) is above the limit for the taxpayer's filing status
- If the taxpayer (or spouse) was a non-resident alien for any part of the tax year[51]

To claim the credit for a dependent's education expenses, the taxpayer must claim the dependent on his return. The taxpayer doesn't necessarily have to pay for all of the dependent's qualified education expenses in order to qualify for the credit.

In some circumstances, eligible students can claim education credits for themselves even if their parents actually paid the qualified tuition and related expenses. This would be the same tax treatment as if the parent had given the student a gift.

If a taxpayer does not claim an exemption for a dependent who is an eligible student, the student may claim the American Opportunity or Lifetime Learning Credit on his own return, if the situation applies.[52]

> **Example:** Cathy has a 19-year-old son named Trent, who is a full-time college student and her dependent. Trent's grandmother paid his tuition directly to the college. For purposes of claiming an education credit, Cathy is treated as receiving the money as a gift and paying for the qualified tuition and related expenses. Since Cathy claims Trent as a dependent, she may still claim an education credit. Alternatively, if Trent claims himself on his own return (and his mother does not), he might be able to claim the expenses as if he paid them himself.

If a taxpayer has education expenses for more than one student, he can take the American Opportunity Credit and the Lifetime Learning Credit on a "per student"

---

[51] In a case when one spouse is a U.S. citizen or a resident alien and the other spouse is a non-resident alien, the taxpayers may ELECT to treat the non-resident spouse as a U.S. resident. If the taxpayers make this choice, both spouses are treated as residents for income tax purposes and for withholding purposes.

[52] This concept is covered in more detail in **Publication 970**, with various examples.

basis. This means that a taxpayer may claim the American Opportunity Credit for one student and the Lifetime Learning Credit for another student on the same tax return.

> **Example:** Reed pays college expenses for himself and for his dependent daughter, who is 18. Reed goes to graduate school, and he qualifies for the Lifetime Learning Credit. His daughter is an undergraduate, and she qualifies for the American Opportunity Credit. He can choose to take both credits on his tax return because he has two eligible students (his daughter and himself).

Qualified Education Expenses

In the case of these two educational credits, "qualified education expenses" are:

- Tuition
- Required related expenses (enrollment expenses)

For the American Opportunity Credit, the definition for "qualified education expenses" is different from the Lifetime Learning Credit. For tax year 2011, "qualified tuition and related expenses" are expanded to include expenditures for course materials for the American Opportunity Credit. These materials are eligible even if the college does NOT require them to attend the school.

> **Example:** Toby had receipts for books and supplies during his first year at college. He spent $1,291 for required books, lab supplies, and rock-hunting equipment he needed for his introductory chemistry and geology courses. He purchases some of the equipment from the university bookstore, and some of it online. He has receipts for all the purchases. These are qualified expenses for the American Opportunity Credit.

Tuition expenses are reported to the taxpayer on **Form 1098-T**, *Tuition Statement*, issued by the school. Taxpayers must identify the expenses that qualify for education credits.

Non-qualifying Expenses

For the purpose of education credits, qualified tuition and related expenses do not include expenses such as:

- Insurance
- Medical expenses (including insurance and student health fees)
- Room and board
- Transportation or personal, living, or family expenses

Any course of instruction or other education involving sports, games, or hobbies is not a qualifying expense *unless* the course is part of the student's degree program.

Example: Elias is a college sophomore who is studying to be a dentist. This year, in addition to tuition, he pays a fee to the university for the rental of the dental equipment he will use in the program. Elias's equipment rental fee is a qualified education expense.

Excluded Amounts

Taxpayers who pay qualified higher education expenses with tax-free funds cannot claim a credit for those amounts. Qualified expenses must be reduced by the amount of any tax-free educational assistance taxpayers receive. The taxpayer must reduce his qualified educational expenses by any of these tax-free educational benefits:

- Pell grants
- Employer-provided educational assistance
- Veterans' educational assistance
- Tax-free portions of scholarships and fellowships
- Any other non-taxable payments received as educational assistance (other than gifts or inheritances)
- Refunds of the year's qualified expenses paid on behalf of a student (e.g., if the student dropped a class and received a refund of tuition)

Example: Faith received **Form 1098-T** from the college she attends. It shows her tuition was $9,500 and that she received a $1,500 tax-free scholarship. She had no other scholarships or non-taxable payments. Her maximum qualifying expenses for the education credit would be $8,000 ($9,500 - $1,500).

Example: In 2011, Jacqueline paid $3,000 for tuition and $5,000 for room and board at her university. She was also awarded a $2,000 scholarship and a $4,000 student loan. The scholarship is a qualified scholarship that is excludable from Jacqueline's income—in other words, it is tax-free. For purposes of the education credit, she must first subtract the tax-free scholarship from her tuition (her only qualified expense). A student loan is not considered tax-free educational assistance because it must be paid back—it isn't income, it's a loan. To calculate her education credit, Jacqueline only had $1,000 in qualified expenses ($3,000 tuition - $2,000 scholarship).

The American Opportunity Credit

The American Opportunity Credit allows taxpayers to claim a credit of up to $2,500 based on qualified tuition and related expenses paid for each eligible student. The credit covers:

- 100% of the first $2,000 and
- 25% of the second $2,000 of eligible expenses

This credit applies *per student*, up to the amount of tax.

> **Example:** Floyd is a single father who has two dependent daughters, Vanessa and Jasmine. Vanessa is a freshman in college. Floyd paid $4,500 in qualified education expenses for Vanessa in 2011. Jasmine is a senior in college. Floyd paid $5,300 in qualified expenses for Jasmine. Floyd can claim a $5,000 American Opportunity Tax Credit on his return. This is because Floyd is allowed to claim the full credit ($2,500) for each one of his daughters. The credit is calculated as 100% of the first $2,000 in expenses, and 25% of the second $2,000 of eligible expenses.

In 2011, 40% of the American Opportunity Credit is a refundable credit, which means the taxpayer can receive up to $1,000 even if no taxes are owed. The American Opportunity Credit is available for the first four years of college per eligible student (generally, freshman through senior years). Graduate school programs do not qualify. Under current law, the American Opportunity Tax Credit is for amounts paid through 2012.

To be eligible for the American Opportunity Credit, the student must meet these basic requirements during the 2011 time period:

- Be enrolled in a program that leads to a degree, certificate, or other recognized educational credential
- Be enrolled at least half time for at least one academic period
- Be enrolled as a student in the first four years of college only
- Have no felony conviction for possessing or distributing a controlled substance

The credit phases out for married couples filing joint returns with income between $160,000 to $180,000 and for Single filers with income between $80,000 to $90,000. Couples with income above $180,000 and Single filers with income above $90,000 do not qualify for the credit.

If the student doesn't meet all of the conditions for the American Opportunity Credit, the taxpayer may still be able to take the Lifetime Learning Credit.

Lifetime Learning Credit

The Lifetime Learning Credit is not based on a student's workload. It is allowed for one or more courses, even if the student is not a degree candidate. Unlike the American Opportunity Credit, a taxpayer may claim the Lifetime Learning Credit for courses at any postsecondary school, regardless of the number of years he has attended in the past. This credit can be claimed an unlimited number of years, regardless of the number of courses taken, student workload, and educational goals. It is eligible for students who are merely acquiring or improving their existing job skills.

The Lifetime Learning Credit can be up to $2,000 per tax return (not per student!), depending on the amount of eligible expenses and the amount of tax liability. The credit is 20% of the first $10,000 of eligible expenses paid for all students, up to the amount of tax on the return. The Lifetime Learning Credit is not refundable. Books and other course materials are only eligible expenses if they are required by the college as a condition of enrollment or attendance.

The taxpayer can take the Lifetime Learning Credit even if the student is not enrolled at least half-time. The student does not have to be in a degree program, and a felony drug conviction does not disqualify the student.

Example: Colleen spent three months in prison for a felony cocaine conviction. She now attends Creek Community College, an eligible education institution. She paid $4,400 for the course of study, which included tuition, equipment, and books required for the course. The school requires that students pay for the books and equipment when registering for the course. The entire $4,400 is an eligible educational expense under the Lifetime Learning Credit. Colleen does not qualify for the American Opportunity Credit because she has a drug conviction.

Example: Zoe, a designer, enrolls in an advanced photography course at a local community college. Although the course is not part of a degree program, she enrolls in it to improve her job skills. The course fee she pays is considered qualified tuition for the purpose of claiming the Lifetime Learning Credit.

Example: Lai works full-time and takes one course a month at night school. Some of the courses are not for credit, but she is taking them to advance her career. The education expenses qualify for the Lifetime Learning Credit, but not the American Opportunity Credit.

For 2011, the phase-out for the Lifetime Learning Credit for Single filers is between $51,000 and $61,000. For joint filers, the phase-out is $102,000 to $122,000 or more (no credit is allowed). All education tax credits are claimed on **Form 8863**.

Education Credits: Summary

1. The American Opportunity Credit

- The credit can be up to $2,500 per eligible student.
- It is only available for the first four years of postsecondary education, and the student must be pursuing an undergraduate degree (or other qualifying credential).
- Forty percent of the credit is refundable, which means that a taxpayer may be able to receive up to $1,000 (even if there is no tax liability).
- The student must be enrolled at least half time for at least one academic period.
- Qualified expenses include tuition and fees, coursed-related books and supplies, and equipment.
- The full credit is available to taxpayers whose modified adjusted gross income is less than $80,000 (or $160,000 for MFJ).
- Taxpayers with felony drug convictions are ineligible for this credit.

2. Lifetime Learning Credit

- The credit is a maximum of $2,000 per return (regardless of how many eligible students there are).
- There is no limit on the number of years for this credit. It is available for all years of postsecondary education and for courses to acquire or improve job skills. The student does not need to be pursuing a degree.
- The credit is not refundable and can reduce tax to zero, but not below that.
- Qualified expenses include tuition and fees, course-related books and supplies, and equipment.
- The full credit is generally available to eligible taxpayers whose modified adjusted gross income is less than $60,000 (or $120,000 for MFJ).
- Felony drug convictions are permitted.

If the taxpayer doesn't qualify for either of these education credits, he may still qualify for the Tuition and Fees Deduction (as an adjustment to income, covered earlier), which can reduce the amount of taxable income by up to $4,000. However, a taxpayer cannot claim the Tuition and Fees Deduction in the same year that he claims the American Opportunity Tax Credit or the Lifetime Learning Credit. A taxpayer must choose to take *either* the tax credit or the deduction, and should consider which is more beneficial.

Credit for the Elderly or the Disabled

The Credit for the Elderly or the Disabled is calculated on **Schedule R** and reported on **Form 1040** or **Form 1040A**. The credit applies only to:

- Taxpayers 65 or older
- Taxpayers under 65 who retired on permanent disability, receiving taxable disability income, and have not reached the mandatory retirement age[53]

It is a non-refundable tax credit that has such strict income limitations that tax practitioners rarely see anyone who qualifies for it. The EA exam does not test this credit very often, but you should know that it exists and the basic qualifications for the credit.

A taxpayer with a permanent disability is defined as "unable to engage in substantial, gainful activity," (in other words, the taxpayer is unable to work). Working in a sheltered workshop setting,[54] however, is not considered substantial, gainful activity, and will not disqualify the taxpayer from claiming the credit.

---

[53] Mandatory retirement age is the age set by a taxpayer's employer at which the taxpayer would have been required to retire had the taxpayer not become disabled.

[54] A "sheltered workshop" is a workplace that provides an environment where physically or mentally challenged persons can acquire job skills and vocational experience.

> **Example:** Jeannie, 49, is on disability from her job as a construction worker. She now works as a full-time babysitter at minimum wage. Although Jeannie's disability forced her to retire from her previous job, she now works full-time. She cannot take the credit because she is engaged in a substantial, gainful activity.

Generally, disability income comes from an employer's disability insurance or pension plan. The disability payments replace wages.

> **Example:** Rolando is 54 and single with no dependents. He had to stop working last year because of his disability. He started receiving his disability benefits last August. His adjusted gross income was $15,430. His non-taxable Social Security benefits were $4,430. Ronaldo's AGI ($15,430) is under the limit of $17,500, and his income from non-taxable Social Security or pension benefits ($4,430) is within the limit of $5,000 for the credit. Therefore, Rolando qualifies for the credit.

> **Example:** Cornelius is 67 years old and single. He received $12,000 in non-taxable Social Security benefits in the tax year. His AGI is $9,000. Even though Cornelius is a qualified individual, he is not eligible to claim the credit since his non-taxable Social Security benefits exceed $5,000.

In actual practice, few taxpayers qualify for this credit because the income calculation includes the taxpayer's non-taxable Social Security and veterans' benefits, or other excludable pension, annuity, or disability benefits. Most taxpayers' Social Security benefits alone exceed the limit.

Income Limits for the Credit for the Elderly or the Disabled

In addition to being a qualified individual, the taxpayer's total income must be within the following limits:

Taxpayers CANNOT take the credit IF filing status is:	AND AGI is equal to or exceeds:	OR non-taxable Social Security is equal to or more than:
S, HOH, or QW	$17,500	$5,000
MFJ (both spouses qualify)	$25,000	$7,500
MFJ (only one spouse qualifies)	$20,000	$5,000
MFS (did not live with spouse at any time during the year)	$12,500	$3,750

Child Tax Credit and Additional Child Tax Credit

The Child Tax Credit is unique because it has two components: a non-refundable credit and a refundable credit. Taxpayers who cannot benefit from the *non-refundable* credit may be able to qualify for the *refundable* "Additional Child Tax Credit."

- **Child Tax Credit:** This is a *non-refundable* credit that allows taxpayers to claim a tax credit of up to $1,000 per qualifying child, which reduces their tax liability. Taxpayers whose tax liability is zero cannot take the Child Tax Credit because there is no tax to reduce. However, a taxpayer may be able to take the Additional Child Tax Credit, which is refundable, even if his tax liability is zero.

- **Additional Child Tax Credit:** This is a refundable credit that may result in a refund even if the taxpayer doesn't owe any tax. The Additional Child Tax Credit is claimed on **Form 8812**, *Additional Child Tax Credit*. Taxpayers who claim the Additional Child Tax Credit must claim the Child Tax Credit as well, even if they do not qualify for the full amount.

Both credits are very similar, but they are considered separate credits. The Child Tax Credit is claimed directly on **Form 1040**. It cannot be claimed on **Form 1040EZ**.

The maximum amount taxpayers may claim for the non-refundable Child Tax Credit is $1,000 for each qualifying child. The amount actually claimed on **Form 1040** depends on the taxpayer's tax liability, modified adjusted gross income (MAGI), and filing status.

The credit is limited if modified adjusted gross income is above a certain amount. The amount at which this phase-out begins varies by filing status. In 2011, the amount of the credit is reduced if the taxpayer's MAGI is above the threshold amounts shown below based on the following filing statuses:

- Married Filing Jointly - $110,000
- Single, Head of Household, or Qualifying Widow(er) - $75,000
- Married Filing Separately - $55,000

The credit is phased out incrementally as the taxpayer's income increases. The credit is reduced by $50 for each $1,000 of modified adjusted gross income that exceeds the threshold amounts listed above.

In addition, the Child Tax Credit is limited by the amount of income tax and any Alternative Minimum Tax owed.

Example: Cordell and Roxana file jointly and have two children who qualify for the Child Tax Credit. Their MAGI is $86,000 and their tax liability is $954. Even though their AGI is less than the threshold limit of $110,000, they can only claim $954, reducing their tax to zero. Because Cordell and Roxana cannot claim the maximum Child Tax Credit of $1,000, they may still be eligible for the Additional Child Tax Credit.

Example: Clint files as Head of Household and has three children who qualify for purposes of the Child Tax Credit. Clint's MAGI is $54,000 and his tax liability is $4,680. Clint is eligible to take the full credit of $1,000 per child ($3,000) because his MAGI is less than $75,000 and his tax liability is greater than $3,000.

Definition of a "Qualifying Child" for the Child Tax Credit

To be eligible to claim the Child Tax Credit, the taxpayer must have at least one qualifying child. To qualify, the child must:

- Be claimed as the taxpayer's dependent.

- Meet the relationship test: must be the son, daughter, adopted child, stepchild, foster child, brother, sister, stepbrother, stepsister, or a descendant of any of them (for example, a grandchild, niece, or nephew).
- Meet the age criteria: *under* the age of 17 at the end of the year.
- Not have provided over half of his or her own support.
- Have lived with the taxpayer for more than six months of the tax year (there are special rules for divorced, separated, or unmarried parents)[55].
- Be a U.S. citizen, U.S. national, or resident of the U.S. (being a resident of Canada or Mexico does not qualify). Foreign-born adopted children will still qualify if they lived with the taxpayer *all year*, even if the adoption is not yet final.
- The taxpayer cannot file a **Form 2555** (relating to foreign earned income).

Example: Ed's son, Jeff, turned 17 on December 30, 2011. He is a citizen of the United States and has a valid SSN. According to the Child Tax Credit rules, he is not a qualifying child because he was not under the age of 17 at the end of 2011.

Example: Laura's adopted son, Nash, is 12. He is a citizen of the United States and lived with Laura for the entire tax year. Laura provided all of her son's support. Nash is a qualifying child for the Child Tax Credit because he was under the age of 17 at the end of the tax year; he meets the relationship requirement; he lived with Laura for at least six months of the year; and Laura provided his complete support.

*Note: Do not confuse the **Child Tax Credit** with the **Child and Dependent Care Credit**!

Additional Child Tax Credit

The Additional Child Tax Credit is for certain individuals who do not qualify for the full amount of the non-refundable Child Tax Credit. The Additional Child Tax Credit is *refundable*, so it can produce a refund, even if the taxpayer does not owe any tax.

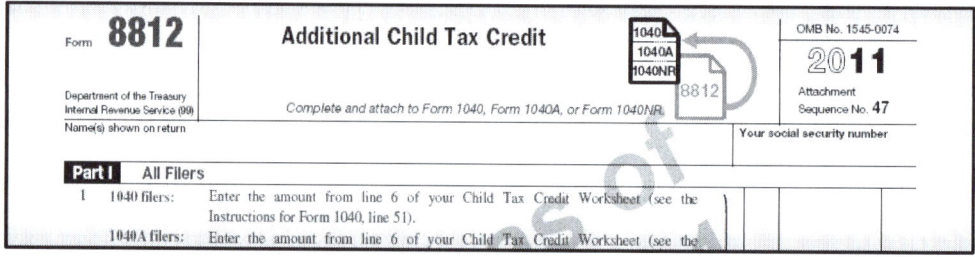

---

[55] There are special rules for children of divorced or separated parents, as well as children of parents who never married. In most cases the custodial parent will claim the dependency exemption for a qualifying child. The non-custodial parent, however, may be entitled to claim the dependency exemption for a child and thus the Child Tax Credit and Additional Child Tax Credit. A custodial parent's release of the dependency exemption will also release the Child Tax Credit and the Additional Child Tax Credit, if either applies, to the non-custodial parent. Non-custodial parents must attach **Form 8332** to their return each year the exemption is claimed.

Like the Child Tax Credit, the Additional Child Tax Credit allows eligible taxpayers to claim up to $1,000 for each qualifying child after subtracting the allowable amount of Child Tax Credit. For taxpayers with earned income over $3,000, the credit is based on the lesser of:

- 15% of the taxpayer's taxable earned income that is more than $3,000, or
- The amount of unused Child Tax Credit (caused when tax liability is less than the allowed credit),

Example: May and Dmitri have two qualifying children, a MAGI of $66,000, and a tax liability of $850. Because their tax liability is less than the full amount of the Child Tax Credit, they may be able to take the Additional Child Tax Credit of up to $1,150 ($2,000 - $850). Since the Additional Child Tax Credit is refundable, it will produce a refund of $1,150, even when a taxpayer doesn't owe any tax.

*Note: Non-taxable combat pay counts as earned income for calculating the Additional Child Tax Credit.

The Child Tax Credit: Key Points

Taxpayers can reduce their federal income tax by up to $1,000 for each qualifying child. To qualify, a child must have been under age 17 (age 16 or younger) at the end of 2011.

To claim a child for purposes of the Child Tax Credit, the child must be a son, daughter, stepchild, foster child, brother, sister, stepbrother, stepsister, or a descendant of any of these individuals. (This includes a grandchild, niece, or nephew).

The child must not have provided more than half of his or her own support.

The taxpayer must claim the child as a dependent on his federal tax return.

The qualifying child cannot file a joint return for the year (or files it only as a claim for refund).

The child must be a U.S. citizen, U.S. national, or U.S. resident alien.

The child must have lived with the taxpayer for more than half of 2011.[56]

---

[56] There are some exceptions to the residence test (such as for hospitalization, school, or other temporary absences). These exceptions are listed in IRS **Publication 972**, *Child Tax Credit*.

The Adoption Credit (Refundable in 2011)

In 2011, a maximum credit of up to $13,360 can be taken for qualified expenses paid to adopt a child. In 2011, this credit is fully refundable. For a special needs child, the credit is allowed even if the taxpayer *does not have* any adoption expenses.

In order to take the credit, **Form 8839**, *Qualified Adoption Expenses*, must be attached to the taxpayer's **Form 1040**. There is a new documentation requirement in 2011, and the taxpayer is required to submit the final adoption paperwork along with the date that the adoption was finalized. The forms cannot be e-filed, and a tax return claiming the Adoption Credit must be mailed along with the required paperwork.

The Adoption Credit phases out ratably between $185,210 and $225,210. A taxpayer cannot claim the Adoption Credit if his AGI is over $225,210. The phase-out ranges are the same for all taxpayers. There is not a separate phase-out for single or MFS filers.

"Qualified" adoption expenses are directly related to the adoption of a child. These include:
- Adoption fees
- Court costs
- Attorney fees
- Travel expenses related to the adoption
- Re-adoption expenses to adopt a foreign child

Qualified adoption expenses DO NOT include:
- Illegal adoption expenses
- A surrogate parenting arrangement
- The adoption of a spouse's child
- Any amounts that were reimbursed by an employer or any other organization

An "eligible child" for the purposes of the credit is:
- Under 18 years old, or
- Disabled (of any age)

Until the adoption becomes final, the taxpayer may take the credit in the year *after* expenses were paid. Once the adoption becomes final, a taxpayer can take the credit in the year the expenses were paid.

Foreign Adoptions: Special Rules

If the adoption is for a foreign child, then the taxpayer may only take the credit in the year the adoption becomes final. The Adoption Credit cannot be taken for a child who is not a United States citizen or legal U.S. resident (green card holder is okay) until the adoption becomes final. Any expenses paid in the year after the foreign adoption is finalized can be taken in the year they were paid.

> **Example:** Jude and Jada adopt a baby from China. They have $3,000 in adoption expenses in 2010 and $7,000 in adoption expenses in 2011. The adoption becomes final in November 2011. They may take the Adoption Credit in 2011 for the combined expenses from 2010 and 2011 ($10,000 in total adoption expenses).

The Adoption Credit is not available for any expenses that were already reimbursed by an employer.

Special Needs Children: Special Rules

In the case of an adoption of a "special needs" child, the taxpayer may claim the full Adoption Credit regardless of actual expenses paid or incurred. A child has special needs if:

- o   The child otherwise meets the definition of an eligible child,
- o   The child is a United States citizen or resident,
- o   A state determines that the child cannot or should not be returned to his or her parent's home, and
- o   A state determines that the child probably will not be adopted unless assistance is provided.

The credit and exclusion for qualifying adoption expenses are each subject to a dollar limit and an income limit.

Employer-Provided Adoption Assistance

Amounts reimbursed by an employer as part of a qualified benefit arrangement may be excludable from gross income. If a taxpayer has enough qualifying expenses and can take both the Adoption Credit and an exclusion, the $13,360 dollar amount applies separately to each.

Earned Income Tax Credit

(*Tested very frequently. Make sure you understand the details of the EITC!)

The Earned Income Tax Credit (EITC or EIC) is the most frequently tested credit on the EA exam. It is tested on both Part 1 and Part 3 (as part of due diligence requirements). The EITC is a fully refundable federal income tax credit for low-income individuals.

The EITC is increased for taxpayers who have a qualifying child. This means that the EITC may give the taxpayer a refund, even if he doesn't owe any tax. The EITC is claimed on **Schedule EIC**, *Earned Income Credit*. This must be attached to the taxpayer's **Form 1040**. The EITC may not be claimed on **Form 1040-EZ**.

Rules for Qualifying for the Earned Income Credit

There are very strict rules and income guidelines for the EITC. A taxpayer must have *earned* income in order to qualify for the EITC. Investment income does not qualify. In fact, investment income **must not exceed** $3,150 in 2011, or it will disqualify the taxpayer from claiming the EITC altogether.

To claim the EITC, the taxpayer must meet ALL of the following tests:

- Must have a valid Social Security Number (an ITIN or ATIN is not valid for the EITC). Any qualifying child must also have a valid SSN.
- Must have earned income from wages or self-employment (non-taxable combat pay qualifies.) Passive income (such as interest and dividends) does not qualify.
- Filing status cannot be MFS.
- Must be a U.S. citizen or legal resident all year (or a non-resident alien married to a U.S. citizen or resident alien filing MFJ).
- Cannot be a dependent of another taxpayer.

Individual Taxpayer Identification Numbers (ITINs) and Adoption Taxpayer Identification Numbers (ATINs) cannot be used when claiming the EITC. If a couple files a joint return, BOTH spouses (and all qualifying children) must have valid Social Security Numbers to qualify for the EITC. However, if a valid number is obtained later and the taxpayer meets all the qualifications, an amended return may be filed claiming the EITC.

Qualifying Income for the EITC

Only earned income (such as wages) qualifies for the EITC. Income that is excluded from tax is generally not considered earned income for the EITC. However, non-taxable combat pay qualifies as earned income for this credit. Qualifying "earned income" also includes:

- Tips
- Union strike benefits
- Net earnings from self-employment

Also, earned income includes "taxable long-term disability benefits received prior to minimum retirement age." These are disability pensions received by disabled taxpayers who are younger than the minimum retirement age at which taxpayers who are not disabled can first receive a pension or annuity from their company.

"Earned income" does NOT include Social Security benefits, workfare payments, alimony, or child support. Investment income does not qualify as "earned income" for EITC. Investment income includes taxable interest and dividends, tax-exempt interest, capital gain net income, and income from residential rental property.

*__Note:__ Inmate wages do NOT qualify as "earned income" when figuring the Earned Income Credit. This includes amounts for work performed while in a prison work release program or in a halfway house.

Taxpayers Without a Qualifying Child

Low-income taxpayers without children may still qualify for the EITC in certai es, but the rules are stricter and the amount of the credit is less.

Any taxpayer with a qualifying child may claim the EITC without any age limitations, but a taxpayer *without* a child can only claim the EITC if ALL of the following tests are met:

- Must be at least age 25 but under 65 at the end of the year (if married, either spouse can meet the age test)
- Must live in the United States for more than half the year[57]
- Must not qualify as a dependent of another person
- Cannot file Form 2555 (related to foreign earned income exclusions[58])

2011 EITC Thresholds and Limitations

In 2011, the EITC increased for taxpayers who had a third qualifying child. The rules also changed for how to determine a "qualifying child" for the EITC. Adjusted gross income (AGI) thresholds are as follows:

EITC 2011 Tax Year

Earned income and AGI must be less than:

- $43,998 ($49,078 for MFJ) if taxpayer has three or more qualifying children
- $40,964 ($46,044 for MFJ) if taxpayer has two qualifying children
- $36,052 ($41,132 for MFJ) if taxpayer has one qualifying child
- $13,660 ($18,740 for MFJ) if taxpayer does not have a qualifying child

Example: Graham is single and his AGI is $39,000. He has one qualifying child. Graham cannot claim the EITC because his AGI exceeds the income threshold for single filers.

The "Qualifying Child" Tests for the EITC

The definition of a "qualifying child" for the purposes of the EITC is different than the definition of a qualifying child for dependency. In order to qualify for the EITC, the taxpayer's qualifying child must meet the following four tests:

1. **Relationship Test**
2. **Age Test**
3. **Residency Test**
4. **Joint Return Test**

---

[57] Residence in U.S. possessions, such as Guam or Puerto Rico, does not qualify.
[58] Taxpayers who do NOT exclude their foreign income from their gross income (by filing Form 2555 or Form 2555-EZ) may still be eligible for the EITC.

Relationship Test for EITC

There is a strict "relationship test" for the EITC. The child must be related to the taxpayer in the following ways:

- Son, daughter, stepchild, eligible foster child, adopted child, or a descendant of any of them (for example, a grandchild), or
- Brother, sister, half-brother, half-sister, stepbrother, stepsister, or a descendant of any of them (for example, a niece or nephew).

An adopted child is always treated as a taxpayer's own child. An "eligible foster child" must be placed in the taxpayer's home by an authorized placement agency or by court order.

In the case of a foreign adoption, special rules apply. To claim the EITC, the taxpayer must have a valid SSN. Any qualifying child listed on **Schedule EIC** *also* must have a valid SSN. An ATIN number is not sufficient for the purposes of the EITC. However, the taxpayer can elect to amend the tax return once an SSN is granted and the adoption is final.

> **Example:** Rusty is 31 and takes care of his younger sister, Tiffany, who is 16. He has taken care of her since their parents died five years ago. Tiffany is Rusty's qualifying child for the purposes of the EITC.

Age Test for EITC

In order to qualify for the EITC, the child must meet the "age test." The child must be:

- Age 18 or younger, OR
- A full-time student, age 23 or younger, OR
- Any age, if permanently disabled.

In addition, the qualifying child must be younger than the taxpayer claiming him (unless the child or person is permanently disabled).

> **Example:** Garth is 45 and supports his older brother, Jeremiah, who is 56. Jeremiah lives with Garth and is profoundly retarded and permanently disabled. In this case, Jeremiah meets the criteria to be Garth's "qualifying child" for the purposes of the EITC.

Residency Test and Joint Return Test

The qualifying child (dependent) may not file a joint return with a spouse, except to claim a refund.

> **Example:** Margaret's 18-year-old son and his 18-year-old wife had $800 of interest income and no other income. Neither is required to file a tax return. Taxes were taken out of their interest income due to backup withholding, so they file a joint return only to get a refund of the withheld taxes. The exception to the Joint Return Test applies, so Margaret's son may still be her qualifying child if all the other tests are met.

The child must have lived with the taxpayer in the United States for more than half of 2011 (this does not apply to newborn infants or temporary absences). U.S. military personnel stationed outside the United States are considered to meet the residency test for purposes of the EITC.

A child who was born or died in 2011 meets the residency test for the entire year if the child lived with the taxpayer the entire time he or she was alive in 2011.

> **Example:** Tawanda gave birth to a baby boy in March 2011. The infant died one month later. The child would still be a qualifying child for the purposes of the EITC because he meets the other tests for age and relationship.

First-Time Homebuyer Credit

Most people do not qualify to take the First Time Homebuyer Credit in 2011. Only certain members of the uniformed services and Foreign Service can claim the credit for homes purchased in 2011.

Under a special provision, members of the uniformed services must have entered into a binding contract by April 30, 2011 and closed on the purchase by June 30, 2011 to get a refundable tax credit of up to $8,000. This credit only applies to individuals who served on qualified official extended duty outside of the United States for at least 90 days after Dec. 31, 2008 and before May 1, 2010.

The credit amount is the smaller of:
- $8,000 ($4,000 if Married Filing Separately), or
- 10% of the purchase price of the home.

In order to qualify as a "first-time homebuyer," the taxpayer must not have purchased a primary residence in the previous three years before the purchase of the home. The credit is fully refundable, meaning the credit will be paid out to eligible taxpayers even if they owe no tax.

If the taxpayer is married, both must be "first-time homebuyers" in order to take the credit. However, if two unmarried people purchase a home together and they later marry, the qualifying rules apply at the date of purchase.

If Taxpayer A (a first-time homebuyer) buys a house and then later that year marries Taxpayer B (not a first-time homebuyer), the credit is still allowed to Taxpayer A. Taxpayer A may take the maximum credit.

The First-Time Homebuyer Credit is claimed on IRS **Form 5405,** *First-Time Homebuyer Credit.*

Retirement Savings Contributions Credit (the Saver's Credit)

The Retirement Savings Contributions Credit[59] is a non-refundable credit eligible taxpayers may claim if they made a qualifying contribution to a retirement plan. If

---

[59] The Retirement Savings Contribution Credit is also called the Saver's Credit. The reason we use both names in this text is because in the most recent edition of **Publication 17**, the credit is

the contribution is tax deferred, the taxpayer receives the benefit of the tax deferral and a tax credit; for example, a taxpayer may be able to claim this credit AND a deduction for an IRA contribution. This is considered a double benefit and is rarely allowed.

Eligibility for this credit is affected by adjusted gross income, filing status, age, whether the taxpayer can be claimed as a dependent, or is a full-time student. For 2011, taxpayers may be able to claim the Retirement Savings Contribution Credit if their modified AGI is not more than:

- $56,500 for Married Filing Jointly
- $42,375 for Head of Household
- $28,250 for Single, Married Filing Separately, or Qualifying Widow(er)

To be eligible for the credit, the taxpayer must have made voluntary contributions to a qualified retirement plan. Plans that qualify are:

- Traditional IRAs and Roth IRAs
- Salary reduction contributions (elective deferrals, including amounts designated as after-tax Roth contributions) to a:
    - 401(k) plan (including a SIMPLE 401(k) and federal Thrift Savings Plan).
    - 403(b) annuity.
    - Governmental 457 plan.
    - SIMPLE IRA plan.
    - Salary reduction SEP.
    - 501(c)(18)(D) plan.
    - Voluntary after-tax employee contributions to a tax-qualified retirement plan or Section 403(b) annuity plan (***Note:** Contributions made as a condition of employment are not considered to be voluntary.)

To be eligible for the credit the taxpayer must be at least 18 years of age and cannot have been a full-time student during the year. Anyone claiming this credit cannot be claimed as a dependent on another person's return.

The Retirement Savings Contributions Credit is *in addition* to other tax benefits for retirement contributions. For example, most workers may deduct their contributions to a traditional IRA. This credit may be taken in addition to the adjustment for a traditional IRA contribution.

---

called the "Retirement Savings Contribution Credit," but in recent IRS newswires (IRS Tax Tip 2012-36) the name of the credit is also referred to as "the Saver's Credit." So it is possible that on the EA exam, you will see the credit referred to by either name. Do not be confused by this; it is the same credit.

> **Example:** Truman is 24 and earned $32,000 during the year. He is single and contributed $3,000 to his 401(k) plan at work. Truman is not eligible for the credit because his income exceeds the threshold limit of $28,250.

Factors that Reduce the Eligible Credit

Even if taxpayers qualify for the credit, their eligible contributions will be reduced by certain distributions (withdrawals) received during the "testing period." The testing period includes:

- The tax year,
- The two preceding tax years, and
- The period between the end of the tax year and the due date of the return, including extensions.

The types of distributions that reduce the eligible contributions include any distribution that is:

- Included in the taxpayer's gross income from a qualified retirement plan or from an eligible deferred compensation plan.
- From a Roth IRA (does not include a qualified rollover contribution).

> **Example:** Luther and Monica are married and filed joint returns for 2009 and 2010, and plan to do so for 2011. Luther made a withdrawal from his qualified plan in 2009 and a distribution from his deferred compensation plan in 2010. Monica received taxable distributions from her Roth IRA in 2010. Both Luther and Monica made qualifying contributions to their traditional IRAs in 2011 and otherwise qualify for the Retirement Savings Credit. They must reduce the amount of their qualifying contributions in 2011 by the total of the distributions they received in 2009 and 2010. This calculation is completed on **Form 8880**. If *either* spouse has a distribution during the testing period, *both* spouses must reduce their eligible contribution by that amount.

The credit is 10% to 50% of eligible contributions up to $1,000 ($2,000 for MFJ). The credit amount can be as low as 10% or as high as 50% of a maximum annual contribution of $2,000 per person, depending on filing status and AGI.

The credit is figured on **Form 8880**, *Credit for Qualified Retirement Savings Contributions*.

Residential Energy Credits

Taxpayers who purchase certain qualified energy-efficient improvements for their main home may be allowed a non-refundable tax credit. There are two types of residential energy credits:

- Non-Business Energy Property Credit
- Residential Energy-Efficient Property Credit

These credits may *sound* similar, but the qualifying property and threshold amounts are different for each. These credits are calculated and claimed on IRS **Form 5695,** *Residential Energy Credits.*

Because these are credits and not deductions, they reduce the amount of tax owed dollar for dollar. Neither credit is refundable, so it may reduce tax down to zero, but not beyond that. Any unused amounts cannot be carried over to future years. Eligible taxpayers can claim these credits regardless of whether they itemize deductions on **Schedule A.**

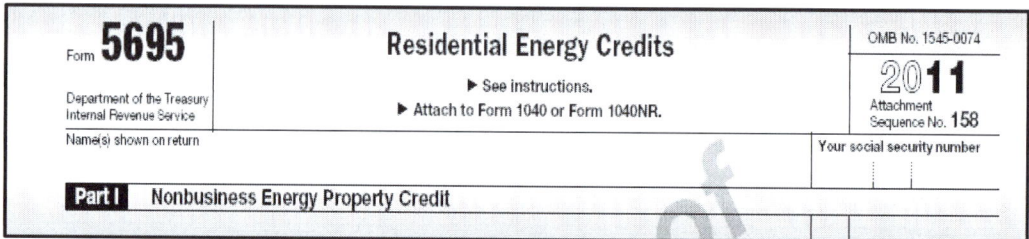

Non-Business Energy Property Credit

The Non-Business Energy Property Credit is available for certain qualifying energy efficiency improvements or residential energy property costs. In 2011, the credit is more limited than in past years. Qualifying improvements must have been placed into service before January 1, 2012. The residence must be located in the United States in order to qualify.

Congress extended the Non-Business Energy Property Credit through 2011,[60] with the following limitations:

- A total combined credit limit of $500 for all tax years after 2005 (see **Form 5695,** Part I).
- A combined credit limit of $200 for windows, for the total amount of all tax years after 2005.
- A maximum credit for residential energy property costs of:
    - $50 for any advanced main air circulating fan;
    - $150 for any qualified natural gas, propane, or oil furnace, or hot water boiler; and
    - $300 for any item of energy-efficient building property.

The energy-efficiency standards for qualified natural gas, propane, or oil furnaces, or hot water boilers have increased. The qualifying items are:

- Biomass stoves
- Heating, ventilating, air-conditioning (HVAC)
- Insulation

---

[60] This tax credit expired on December 31, 2011.

- Roofs (metal and asphalt)
- Water heaters (non-solar)
- Windows and doors

This credit is only available for existing homes that are the taxpayer's principal residence—new construction, vacation homes, and rentals do NOT qualify. The 2011 credit rate is 10% of the cost of qualified energy efficiency improvements. Energy efficiency "improvements" include:

- Adding insulation
- Energy-efficient exterior windows
- Certain roofs (metal and asphalt)

The cost of installing the improvements listed above does not count toward the credit.

This credit can also be claimed for the cost of residential energy property. Residential energy property includes certain high-efficiency heating and air conditioning systems, water heaters, and stoves that burn biomass fuel. In the case of these larger items, the credit includes the labor costs for installation.

There are no income limits, so any taxpayer can claim the credit, regardless of his income.

This credit has a look-back provision, and is limited to $500 for all non-business energy property for 2011. This is further limited to the combined credit amount for all tax years after 2005. So, for example, if the total credits taken in prior years since 2005 is more than $500, the credit may not be claimed in 2011.

The Non-Business Energy Property Credit is a non-refundable credit that reduces a taxpayer's tax liability. If the taxpayer has no tax liability, then he cannot use the credit and it is not carried over to the next year.

Example: Travis purchases a qualifying biomass stove for his main home in 2011. However, in 2010, Travis had already claimed the Non-Business Energy Property Credit for the installation of qualifying insulation. Travis had correctly claimed a $1,000 credit in 2010; therefore, he cannot claim the same credit in 2011, because of the look-back provision in 2011 that limits the cumulative credit to $500 for all years after 2005.

Example: Daisy purchased a new home two years ago. In 2011, she installs energy-efficient windows at a cost of $4,000. She has never claimed the Non-Business Energy Property Credit on any prior return. She may claim the credit in 2011, up to $200 (the limit for windows). This reduces her tax dollar for dollar.

Residential Energy-Efficient Property Credit

This residential energy credit is also claimed on **Form 5695** (Part II of the form). *Unlike* the Non-Business Energy Property Credit, the Residential Energy Efficient Property Credit puts NO CAP on the amount of credit that can be claimed by the taxpayer (except in the case of fuel cell property). This is rare, because most credits have a pre-set limit. Congress designed this credit to spur investment in alternative energy equipment.

In 2011, this credit equals 30% of what a homeowner spends on qualifying property. Labor and installation costs are included when figuring this credit. This credit is only available for the following property:

- Solar electric property
- Solar water heating property costs
- Small wind energy property costs
- Geothermal heat pump property costs
- Fuel cells (principal residence only)

This credit is also different because it applies to items installed at a principal residence *or* a second home[61] (but does not apply to rental property). The residence must be in the United States. The maximum credit is 30% of qualifying costs.

The credit may be applied to labor costs, assembly and installation, and any wiring that is needed to install the energy-efficient item in the home. No credit is allowed for equipment that is used to heat swimming pools or hot tubs.

The taxpayer must reduce his basis in the property by the amount of the credit. This credit is not refundable, but unused amounts can be carried over to the following year.

The item installed must be new and not used. This credit is NOT limited by Alternative Minimum Tax (AMT). Unlike the Non-Business Energy Property Credit, unused credits may be carried over to future years.

Credit for Excess Social Security or Railroad Retirement Tax Withheld

This is a credit for workers who overpay their Social Security tax during the tax year. It usually happens when an employee is working two jobs and both employers withhold Social Security tax. If a taxpayer works for more than one employer during the year, each employer is required to withhold Social Security (or RRTA taxes). If the taxpayer's withholding for Social Security tax exceeds the annual maximum, he can request a refund of the excess amount.

During 2011, Social Security tax was 4.2% of the first $106,800 of an employee's taxable earnings. (In 2011, the withholding rate of 4.2% is lower than the 2010 rate of 6.2%.) Wages in excess of $106,800 are not subject to the Social Security tax. There is no limit on the Medicare portion of the FICA, so the combined Medicare tax for 2011 remains at 2.9% on all of an employee's earnings.

---

[61] The credit for fuel cells is only applicable to the taxpayer's primary residence.

Self-employed individuals are responsible for paying both the employee and the employer portions of the Social Security tax and the Medicare tax.

If only ONE employer withheld too much Social Security or RRTA tax, the taxpayer must ask the employer to correct the error. The taxpayer cannot claim the excess as a credit against his income tax.

A taxpayer claims this credit directly on **Form 1040** (line 69). This is a fully refundable credit.

Mortgage Interest Credit

(*Not frequently tested) Taxpayers who hold qualified Mortgage Credit Certificates under a qualified state or local government program may claim a non-refundable credit for mortgage interest paid. The credit is for homeowners who purchase low-income housing and was designed to help low-income individuals afford housing. This credit only applies to a main home. If the interest on the mortgage was paid to a related person (such as a personal loan from a family member), then the credit is not allowed.

The credit only applies to taxpayers who are issued a Mortgage Credit Certificate (MCC) by their local or state government. The MCC will show the rate the taxpayer must use to figure his credit. Taxpayers use **Form 8396**, *Mortgage Interest Credit*, to calculate the amount of the credit.

Other Credits

In this section, we will cover lesser-known credits. Most of these credits are limited to certain individuals, or are for certain types of asset purchases.

1. Health Coverage Tax Credit (refundable)
2. Foreign Tax Credit
3. Credit for Prior Year Alternative Minimum Tax (AMT)

Health Coverage Tax Credit

This credit was expanded for 2011, and it is refundable. The Health Coverage Tax Credit (HCTC) pays 72.5% of qualified health insurance premiums for eligible individuals and their families.[62] The HCTC was specifically established to help cover the cost of health insurance for workers whose pensions are trusteed by the Pension Benefit Guaranty Corporation (PBGC).

The HCTC is a federally funded program administered by the IRS that pays a portion of qualified health insurance premiums for eligible individuals and their family members. Only certain individuals qualify for this credit.

---

[62] Due to the *Trade Adjustment Assistance Extension Act of 2011*, the HCTC tax credit percentage increased from 65% to 72.5% *retroactively* to February 13, 2011. A taxpayer can claim 80% of payments for qualified health insurance premiums for January or February 2011 coverage and 72.5% of payments for March through December 2011 coverage.

In order to qualify for this credit, the taxpayer must be one of the following:
- Receiving Trade Adjustment Assistance (TAA) benefits
- Receiving pension payments from the PBGC and be 55 years old or older
- The spouse or dependent of someone who fell into one of the categories above at the time of Medicare enrollment, death, or divorce

There are a number of restrictions on this credit. Taxpayers who are already enrolled in Medicare do not qualify. Additionally, the following individuals do not qualify for the HCTC:
- Those who are not enrolled in a qualified health plan
- Those who do not pay more than 50% of their qualified health plan premium
- Incarcerated individuals
- A person who can be claimed as a dependent on another individual's federal tax return

An individual may receive the tax credit each month or at the end of the year for as long as he continues to meet eligibility requirements. Taxpayers can receive the HCTC in one of two ways:
- By registering for the monthly HCTC and receiving a reimbursement each month as health insurance premiums become due.
- By claiming the yearly HCTC as a credit on their federal tax return. The taxpayer will receive a tax credit as a refund or as a credit against taxes owed.

Since the HCTC is a refundable credit, it can create a refund even if the taxpayer has no tax liability for the year. Eligible taxpayers use IRS **Form 8885,** *Health Coverage Tax Credit,* to claim the yearly HCTC on their federal income tax returns.

Foreign Tax Credit

This credit applies to taxpayers who have paid foreign taxes to a foreign country on foreign-sourced income and are subject to U.S. tax on the same income. Many taxpayers have overseas investments or other foreign sources of income, and this credit is designed to prevent U.S. taxpayers from having to pay tax on their foreign-sourced income twice: once to the U.S. government and once to the government of the foreign country where the income was sourced.

U.S. citizens and resident aliens are eligible for the Foreign Tax Credit (FTC). Non-resident aliens are not eligible for the credit. Foreign tax paid is usually reported to the taxpayer by the financial institution on **Form 1099-INT** or **Form 1099-DIV**.

There are two ways to claim the Foreign Tax Credit. If the total foreign tax paid does not exceed $300 (or $600 for filing status MFJ), taxpayers may claim the credit directly on their **Form 1040.** In order to claim the Foreign Tax Credit on Form 1040, all the taxpayer's foreign source income must be "passive category income" (such as interest and dividends) and reported on a qualified payee statement.

A "qualified payee statement" includes **Form 1099-INT**, **Form 1099-DIV**, **Schedule K-1** (for **Forms 1041, 1065, 1065-B, 1120S**), or a similar substitute statement.[63]

If the tax paid exceeds $300 (or $600 for MFJ), then taxpayers must file **Form 1116,** *Foreign Tax Credit*, in order to claim the credit.

Four tests must be met to qualify for the credit:
1. The tax must be imposed on the taxpayer.
2. The taxpayer must have paid (or accrued) the tax.
3. The tax must be a legal and actual foreign tax liability.
4. The tax must be an income tax.

> **Example:** Arlene, who is single, owns a number of foreign stocks. In 2011, she received a 2011 **Form 1099-DIV** that shows $279 of foreign taxes paid. Arlene paid no other foreign taxes. She is eligible to claim the $279 Foreign Tax Credit on **Form 1040** and does not have to complete **Form 1116**.

> **Example:** Yusuf and Fatima are married and file jointly. Their **Form 1099-DIV** shows a foreign tax paid of $590. The couple is not required to complete **Form 1116,** because their foreign taxes are less than $600 (the limit for MFJ taxpayers).

> **Example:** Colette is a shareholder of a French corporation. She receives $300 in earnings from the corporation. The French government imposes a 10% tax ($30) on Colette's earnings. She must include the gross earnings ($300) in her income. The $30 of tax withheld is a qualified foreign tax for the purposes of the Foreign Tax Credit.

In most cases, it is to the taxpayer's advantage to take the Foreign Tax Credit. However, taxpayers have the option to itemize foreign taxes as "Other Taxes" on **Schedule A.** They may choose either the deduction OR the credit, whichever gives them the lowest tax, for all foreign taxes paid. Taxpayers cannot claim both the deduction and a tax credit on the same return. However, a taxpayer may alternate years, taking a credit in one year and a deduction in the next year.

The taxpayer may even change his credit to a deduction and vice versa by amending his tax return. The Foreign Tax Credit is non-refundable, so it can drop tax liability to zero, but not below that.

---

[63] This election is not available to estates or trusts.

> ***Note:** Do NOT confuse the Foreign Tax Credit and the Foreign Earned Income Exclusion! They are two different things. The Foreign Earned Income Exclusion allows a portion of the foreign earned income to be completely excluded from income, so it is not taxed. The Foreign Tax Credit, on the other hand, adds the taxpayer's foreign income to his taxable income and then *reduces* the U.S. tax by the credit amount. The Foreign Earned Income Exclusion only applies to income that is earned while a taxpayer is living and working overseas. The Foreign Tax Credit applies to any type of foreign earned income, including investments.

Non-Qualifying Expenses for the Foreign Tax Credit

The following expenses do not qualify for the Foreign Tax Credit:

- Any taxes that the taxpayer does not legally owe or that would be refunded by the foreign nation if the taxpayer filed a claim
- Any taxes on already-excluded income
- Taxes on foreign oil or gas extraction income
- Taxes from international boycott operations
- Taxes of U.S. persons controlling foreign corporations or partnerships
- Taxes imposed by sanctioned foreign countries or countries that are involved with international terrorism [64]
- Interest or penalties paid to a foreign country

The Foreign Tax Credit is a non-refundable credit, and the taxpayer is allowed a one-year carryback and a ten-year carry-forward of any unused credit.

Taxpayers may not claim the Foreign Tax Credit for taxes paid on any income that has already been excluded from income using the Foreign Earned Income Exclusion or the Foreign Housing Exclusion.

The Foreign Tax Credit is allowed in figuring the Alternative Minimum Tax.

Credit for Prior Year Alternative Minimum Tax (AMT)

The Alternative Minimum Tax, or AMT, is a separately figured tax that eliminates many deductions and credits, thus increasing tax liability. The AMT was originally adopted in order to prevent high income taxpayers from using elaborate deductions to reduce their income tax to zero. The AMT was designed to ensure that high income taxpayers pay at least a minimum amount of tax.

There is a special credit for prior-year minimum tax paid. This is because, with AMT, the taxpayer would be forced to pay taxes twice on the same items of income. A taxpayer can get a tax credit for Alternative Minimum Tax paid in a prior year. This credit is calculated on **Form 8801**, *Credit for Prior Year Minimum Tax*.

---

[64] The list of terrorist nations includes Cuba, the Sudan, and North Korea— if interested, you can see a full list of excluded nations in **Publication 514**, *Foreign Tax Credit for Individuals*.

Unit 11: Questions

1. All of these taxpayers contributed to their employers' 401(k) plan. Who qualifies for the Retirement Savings Credit based on their adjusted gross income?

A. Ed, who is Single and has an adjusted gross income of $35,200.
B. Sybil, who is Married Filing Jointly and has an adjusted gross income of $52,500.
C. Bert, who is Married Filing Separately and has an adjusted gross income of $30,600.
D. Carl, who is a Qualifying Widower and has a modified AGI of $29,000.

The answer is B. Sybil qualifies for the credit because her AGI is under $56,500, which is the threshold limit for Married Filing Jointly. Taxpayers who file as Single, Qualifying Widow, or Married Filing Separately (such as Ed, Carl, and Bert) cannot qualify if they have an AGI that exceeds the AGI limits. ###

2. Gail's earned income from wages is $7,000. She has interest income of $3,200. She is single and has a valid Social Security Number. She does not have any dependents. Which of the following is TRUE?

A. Gail qualifies to claim the Earned Income Tax Credit.
B. Gail does not qualify for the Earned Income Tax Credit.
C. Gail qualifies for the Earned Income Tax Credit and the Child Tax Credit.
D. None of the above.

The answer is B. Gail does not qualify for the EITC because her investment income exceeds $3,150 for 2011. ###

3. For the purposes of the EITC, which of the following types of income are considered to be "earned income"?
A. Alimony.
B. Household employee income reported on **Form W-2**.
C. Child support.
D. Interest and dividends.

The answer is B. Household employee income is considered earned income, because it is a type of wages. Alimony, child support, and interest and dividends are not considered earned income for the purpose of the EITC. ###

4. Orlando is a university senior who is studying to be an optometrist. Which of the following expenses is a qualifying expense for the American Opportunity Credit?

A. The rental of the vision equipment he will use in this program.
B. Student health fees.
C. Room and board.
D. A physical education course not related to his degree program.

The answer is A. Because Orlando's equipment rental fee must be paid to the university as a condition for enrollment, it is considered a qualified related expense. The other expenses do not qualify. Qualified tuition and related expenses do not include insurance or medical expenses (including insurance and student health fees), room and board, transportation or similar personal, living, or family expenses even if the fees must be paid to the institution as a condition of enrollment or attendance, or any course of instruction or other education involving sports, games, or hobbies, *unless* the course is part of the student's degree program. ###

5. Which of the following would be a qualifying child for the purposes of the Child Tax Credit?

A. An 18-year-old dependent who is a full-time student.
B. A six-year-old nephew who lived with the taxpayer for seven months.
C. A child actor who is 15 years old and provides over half of his own support.
D. A foster child who has lived with the taxpayer for four months.

The answer is B. A nephew that lived with the taxpayer for seven months may qualify. In order to qualify for the Child Tax Credit, the qualifying child must have lived with the taxpayer for more than six months and be under the age of 17. ###

6. Beatrice has three dependent children, ages 2, 12, and 18. All her children live with her. Assuming she meets the other criteria, what is the maximum Child Tax Credit she can claim on her 2011 tax return?

A. $0.
B. $1,000.
C. $2,000.
D. $3,000.

The answer is C. Beatrice can claim $2,000 as a maximum credit, or $1,000 for each qualifying child. For the purposes of this credit, she only has two qualifying children, because one of her dependents is already over 17 and therefore no longer eligible for the credit. ###

7. Scott is 43 and unmarried. Scott's half-brother, Taylor, turned 16 on December 30, 2011. Taylor lived with Scott all year, and he is a U.S. citizen. Scott claimed Taylor as a dependent on his return. Which of the following is true?

A. Taylor is a qualifying child for the Child Tax Credit.
B. Taylor is NOT a qualifying child for the Child Tax Credit.
C. Taylor is not a qualifying child for the Child Tax Credit because siblings do not qualify.
D. Taylor would only qualify for the Child Tax Credit if he is a full-time student.

The answer is A. Taylor is a qualifying child for the Child Tax Credit because he was under age 17 at the end of 2011. Siblings can be qualifying children for the purposes of this credit. ###

8. Lauren and Ralph divorced four years ago. They have one 12-year-old child, Amy, who lives with Lauren. All are U.S. citizens and have SSNs. Lauren and Ralph provide more than half of Amy's support. Lauren's AGI is $19,000, and Ralph's AGI is $39,000. The divorce decree does not state who can claim the child. Lauren signed **Form 8332** to give the dependency exemption to Ralph. Which of the following statements is TRUE?

A. Ralph can claim Amy as a dependent along with the tax benefits.
B. Ralph and Lauren need to choose who can claim Amy as a dependent and any other tax benefits.
C. Ralph can claim Amy as a dependent and the Child Tax Credit. Lauren can use Amy to file as Head of Household and claim the Earned Income Credit and the Child and Dependent Care Credit so long as she meets the requirements for those specific benefits.
D. Neither Ralph nor Lauren can claim Amy as a dependent or can claim any of the other benefits.

The answer is C. Since Lauren signed **Form 8332**, the dependency exemption, the Child Tax Credit is given to Ralph, the non-custodial parent. However, Lauren can still file as Head of Household and claim the Earned Income Credit, so long as she otherwise qualifies for them. ###

9. Clyde is single and his **Form 1099-DIV** shows a total of $423 of foreign tax paid. What is the easiest way for Clyde to deduct his foreign taxes paid?

A. By completing **Form 1116.**
B. By claiming the tax directly on his **Form 1040**.
C. Foreign taxes are not deductible.
D. By deducting the tax paid on **Schedule B**.

The answer is A. Clyde needs to complete **Form 1116** because his foreign taxes exceed $300. ###

10. Which of the following statements regarding the Foreign Tax Credit is correct?

A. The Foreign Tax Credit is a refundable credit.
B. The Foreign Tax Credit is available to U.S. citizens and non-resident aliens.
C. Taxpayers may choose to take a deduction for foreign taxes paid, rather than the Foreign Tax Credit.
D. Taxpayers can choose to claim both a deduction and a tax credit for foreign taxes paid, so long as the taxes were paid to different countries.

The answer is C. Taxpayers have the option to itemize foreign taxes on **Schedule A.** They may choose either the deduction OR the credit, whichever gives them the lowest tax, for all foreign taxes paid. Taxpayers cannot choose to claim both the deduction and a tax credit on the same return. ###

11. The Lifetime Learning Credit is different from the American Opportunity Credit. However, they do share some of the same requirements. Which of the following requirements is TRUE for BOTH education credits?

A. There is no limit to the number of years the credits can be claimed.
B. Expenses related to housing are allowed as qualified education expenses.
C. The credits are available for only the first two years of postsecondary education.
D. To be eligible for either of the education credits, taxpayers must use any filing status other than Married Filing Separately.

The answer is D. Taxpayers who use the filing status of Married Filing Separately are not eligible to claim either the American Opportunity or Lifetime Learning credits.###

12. Which form is used to claim education tax credits?
A. Form 8863.
B. Form 4136.
C. Form 8812.
D. Form 2441.

The answer is A. IRS **Form 8863** is used to claim education credits. The American Opportunity Credit and the Lifetime Learning Credit are both claimed on IRS **Form 8863.** ###

13. Which of the following items is NOT tax deductible as an education-related expense for the Lifetime Learning Credit?

A. Required books.
B. On-campus childcare in order to attend class.
C. Tuition.
D. Required fees.

The answer is B. Daycare is not a qualifying education expense. For purposes of the Lifetime Learning Credit, qualified education expenses are tuition and certain related expenses required for enrollment or attendance at an eligible educational institution. ###

14. Which of the following individuals is eligible for the American Opportunity Credit?

A. Betsy's son, Garrett, who is enrolled full-time as a postgraduate student pursuing a Master's degree in biology.
B. Lucy, who is taking a ceramics class at a community college.
C. Doug, who was convicted of a felony for distributing a controlled substance.
D. Beth, who is taking at least one-half of the normal full-time course load required for a computer science associate's degree program, attending classes the entire school year in 2011.

The answer is D. Beth is eligible for the American Opportunity Credit because she is taking at least one-half of the normal full-time workload for her course of study for at least one academic period beginning in 2011. Graduate courses do not qualify, and courses that do not lead to a degree, certificate (or other recognized credential) do not qualify for this educational credit. Persons with felony drug convictions cannot qualify for this credit. ###

15. In 2011, what is the maximum amount of the American Opportunity Credit?

A. $2,500 per tax return.
B. $2,500 per student.
C. $2,000 per tax return.
D. $1,000 per student.

The answer is B. In 2011 the maximum credit is $2,500 per student. The credit is per student per year, and the taxpayer's family may have more than one eligible student per tax return. ###

16. What is the maximum amount of the Lifetime Learning Credit in 2011?

A. $2,000 per student.
B. $2,500 per student.
C. $1,000 per student.
D. $2,000 per tax return.

The answer is D. The maximum credit is $2,000 per tax return. The credit is allowed for 20% of the first $10,000 of qualified tuition and fees paid during the year. The credit is per tax return, not per student, so only a maximum of $2,000 can be claimed each year, no matter how many qualifying students a taxpayer may have. ###

17. Samira and Rishi are married and file jointly. Their daughter, Amanda, was enrolled full-time in college for all of 2011. Samira and Rishi obtained a loan in 2011 and used the proceeds to pay for Amanda's tuition and related fees. They repaid the loan in 2012. Which year will they be entitled to claim an education credit?

A. They cannot claim an education credit.
B. 2010.
C. 2011.
D. 2012.

The answer is C. Samira and Rishi are eligible to claim an education credit for the year 2011. The credit should be calculated for the year in which the taxpayer paid the expenses, not the year in which the loan is repaid. ###

18. Edwin is a professional bookkeeper. He decides to take an accounting course at the local community college in order to improve his work-related skills. Edwin is not a degree candidate. Which educational credit does he qualify for?

A. The American Opportunity Credit.
B. The College Credit.
C. The Lifetime Learning Credit.
D. The Mortgage Interest Credit

The answer is C. Edwin qualifies for the Lifetime Learning Credit. He does not qualify for the American Opportunity Credit because he is not a degree candidate. The "College Credit" does not exist. The Mortgage Interest Credit is not an education credit. ###

19. In 2011, Tyrone paid $5,000 of his own funds to cover all of the cost of his college tuition. Tyrone also received a Pell grant for $3,000 and a student loan for $2,000, which he used for housing costs and books. For the purposes of figuring an education credit, what are Tyrone's total qualified tuition and related expenses?

A. $10,000.
B. $7,000.
C. $5,000.
D. $2,000.

The answer is D. The total qualified tuition payments are the net of the $5,000 tuition minus the grant of $3,000, which equals $2,000. The $3,000 Pell grant is tax-free, so it is not a qualified tuition and related expense and must be deducted from his overall qualifying costs.###

20. Based on the Child and Dependent Care Credit rules, which of the following individuals meets the eligibility test for a "qualifying person"?

A. Jeremy, 5, who is taken care of by his mother at home all day.
B. Destiny, 21, a full-time student supported by her parents.
C. Leroy, 80, who lives at home with his son, but is neither is disabled.
D. Leanne, 52, who is unable to care for herself and is married to Jake, an employed construction worker.

The answer is D. Leanne meets the qualifying person test because she is the spouse of someone who works, and she is unable to care for herself.###

21. Geraldine placed a $250 deposit with a preschool to reserve a place for her three-year-old child. Later, Geraldine changed jobs and was unable to send her child to that particular preschool. She forfeited the daycare deposit. She later found another preschool and had $4,000 in qualifying daycare costs. Which of the following is TRUE?

A. The forfeited deposit is NOT deductible.
B. The forfeited deposit is deductible.
C. The forfeited deposit is a deduction on Schedule A.
D. Geraldine may deduct the deposit because she took her child to another preschool.

The answer is A. The *forfeited* deposit is not for actual childcare and so is not a work-related expense. A forfeited deposit is not actually for the care of a qualifying person, so it cannot be deducted as a childcare expense and does not qualify for the Child and Dependent Care Credit. ###

22. Brett paid daycare for his five-year-old son so he could work. His childcare expenses were $3,000 in 2011. He also paid a deposit of $100 to the daycare and an enrollment fee of $35. Brett was reimbursed for $1,200 by his Flexible Spending Account at work. How much of the childcare expenses can he use to figure his Child and Dependent Care Credit?

A. $1,800.
B. $1,900.
C. $1,935.
D. $3,135.

The answer is C. Brett's childcare expenses are figured as follows: ($3,000 + $100 + $35) - $1,200 = $1,935. If a taxpayer has a reimbursement under a Flexible Spending Account, those amounts are pre-tax. The taxpayer cannot use reimbursed amounts to figure this credit. Fees and deposits paid to an agency or a daycare provider are qualifying expenses if the taxpayer must pay them in order to receive care. Only a *forfeited* deposit would be disallowed. ###

23. Nina pays for daycare for each of the following individuals so she can work. All of the following are qualifying individuals for the purposes of the Child and Dependent Care Credit, EXCEPT:

A. Nina's husband, who is totally disabled.
B. Nina's son, age 13, who is Nina's dependent.
C. Nina's nephew, age 12, who is also Nina's dependent.
D. Nina's niece, who is 35, lived with her all year, and is completely disabled.

The answer is B. Nina's son does not qualify, because he is over the age limit for the credit. To qualify for the Dependent Care Credit, the qualifying person must be UNDER the age of 13, OR completely disabled. ###

24. Which of the following is NOT a qualifying expense for the purposes of the Child and Dependent Care Credit?

A. $500 payment to a grandparent for childcare while the taxpayer is gainfully employed.
B. $300 payment to a daycare while looking for employment.
C. $500 childcare expense while the taxpayer obtains medical care.
D. $600 in daycare expense for a disabled spouse while the taxpayer works.

The answer is C. Childcare costs to obtain medical care are not a deductible expense. Deductible daycare costs must be work related and for a child under 13, a disabled dependent, or a disabled spouse of any age. Childcare so that the taxpayer can volunteer, obtain medical care, run errands, or do other personal business is not "qualifying childcare." ###

25. What is the maximum amount of the Adoption Tax Credit for 2011?

A. $11,150.
B. $12,150.
C. $13,170.
D. $13,360.

The answer is D. The maximum credit for 2011 is $13,360 *per child*. If a taxpayer adopts two children, he will be eligible for the full credit on each child. ###

26. Which of the following expenses is NOT a qualified adoption expense for the purposes of the Adoption Credit?

A. Court costs.
B. Re-adoption expenses to adopt a foreign child.
C. Attorney fees for a surrogate arrangement.
D. Travel expenses.

The answer is C. The cost of a surrogate is not a qualified adoption expense. Qualified adoption expenses are expenses directly related to the legal adoption of an eligible child. These expenses include adoption fees, court costs, attorney fees, travel expenses (including amounts spent for meals and lodging) while away from home, and re-adoption expenses to adopt a foreign child. ###

27. Which tax form is used to claim the Adoption Credit?

A. Form 8839.
B. Form 2815.
C. Schedule A.
D. Schedule C.

The answer is A. To take the Adoption Credit, a taxpayer must complete **Form 8839**, *Qualified Adoption Expenses*, and attach it to **Form 1040**. ###

28. In 2011, Dylan and Hannah adopt a special needs child who is completely disabled. Their adoption expenses are $7,000, and their travel expenses related to the adoption are $1,200. What is their maximum Adoption Credit in 2011?

A. $7,000.
B. $8,200.
C. $13,360.
D. None of the above.

The answer is C. Dylan and Hannah can take the full Adoption Credit because they adopted a special needs child. There is a special rule for taxpayers who adopt special needs children. The full amount of the Adoption Credit is still allowed, even if the taxpayer does not have qualified adoption expenses. ###

29. Austin is a U.S. citizen, and he is adopting a foreign child. His income in 2011 was $31,000. The adoption is almost final, and he has an ATIN for the child. The child lived with Austin all year. Which of the following is true?

A. Austin can claim the Earned Income Tax Credit because his child is a qualifying child.
B. Austin cannot claim the Earned Income Tax Credit in 2011.
C. Austin cannot claim the Earned Income Tax Credit in 2011, but Austin can elect to amend the tax return once a SSN is granted and the adoption is final.
D. The Earned Income Credit is not applicable to foreign-adopted children.

The answer is C. To claim the EITC, the taxpayer must have a valid SSN issued by the Social Security Administration. Any qualifying child listed on **Schedule EIC** also must have a valid SSN. An ATIN is not sufficient for the purposes of the EITC. However, the taxpayer can elect to amend the tax return once an SSN is granted and the adoption is final. ###

30. To qualify for the Earned Income Credit, which of the following is TRUE?

A. The taxpayer must have a dependent child.
B. The taxpayer must be a U.S. citizen or legal U.S. resident all year.
C. The taxpayer's filing status can be MFS if the taxpayer does not live with his or her spouse.
D. The taxpayer must have a valid SSN or ITIN.

The answer is B. The taxpayer must be a U.S. citizen or legal resident all year. Taxpayers do not need to have a dependent child in order to qualify for the Earned Income Credit; however, the EITC is greatly increased if the taxpayer has a qualifying child. Single taxpayers who are low-income may still qualify for the credit. A taxpayer cannot claim the EITC if his filing status is MFS. A taxpayer must have a valid SSN in order to qualify for the EITC. An ITIN is not sufficient. ###

31. For those claiming the Earned Income Credit in 2011, the taxpayer's interest or investment income must be _____ or less.

A. $2,950.
B. $3,100.
C. $3,150.
D. $4,000.

The answer is C. For the purpose of the EITC, interest or investment income must be $3,150 or less. For the EA exam, you must memorize this number—the amount of investment income that disqualifies a taxpayer from claiming the EITC has been tested on numerous prior exams. ###

32. Monty and Belinda are married and living together. Monty earned $12,000 and Belinda earned $9,000 in 2011. They have two minor children and have decided to file Married Filing Separately tax returns, each claiming one child as a dependent. Which statement is TRUE?

A. They can both qualify for the Earned Income Credit on their MFS tax returns.
B. Based on the information, they may qualify for the EITC on a joint tax return.
C. Monty can file "Single" and qualify for the EITC.
D. Belinda can file as "Head of Household" and claim the credit.

The answer is B. Since Monty and Belinda are married and live together, they can choose to file a joint return or each may choose to file separately. A taxpayer cannot qualify for the EITC on a MFS return, so Monty and Belinda must file jointly in order to claim the credit. ####

33. Which of the following filing conditions would NOT prevent an individual from qualifying for the Earned Income Credit for the year 2011?

A. MFS filing status.
B. A taxpayer with a qualifying child who is 23 and a full-time student.
C. Investment income of $3,300.
D. A taxpayer who is 68 years old without a qualifying child.

The answer is B. All the other choices are disqualifying for the purposes of the EITC. At the end of the tax year, the child must be under age 19, OR under age 24 AND a full-time student, OR any age and disabled. ###

33. On which tax form would a taxpayer claim the Credit for the Elderly or Disabled?

A. Schedule A.
B. Form 8063.
C. Schedule R.
D. Form 8812.

The answer is C. The Credit for the Elderly or Disabled must be claimed on Schedule R (Form 1040). The credit is not refundable. ###

34. The Residential Energy Efficient Property Credit is an enhanced energy credit for very specific energy systems or improvements. Which of the following items is NOT a qualifying item for the purposes of the credit?

A. Solar energy systems.
B. Fuel cells.
C. Small wind energy systems.
D. Asphalt roofs.

The answer is D. The Residential Energy Efficient Property Credit is a credit of 30% of the costs of solar energy systems, fuel cells, small wind energy systems, and geothermal heat pumps. There is no dollar limit on this credit. Asphalt roofs do not qualify for this credit, but they may qualify for the Non-Business Energy Property Credit, which is a different credit for energy-efficient items installed in a taxpayer's primary residence. ###

Unit 12: Basis of Property

> **More Reading:**
> Publication 551, *Basis of Assets*
> Publication 544, *Sales and Other Dispositions of Assets*

Understanding Basis

Almost everything a taxpayer owns and uses for personal purposes, pleasure, or investment is a capital asset. Examples include:

- A main home or vacation home
- Household furnishings
- Antiques
- A car or boat
- Stocks or bonds (except when held for sale by a professional securities dealer)
- Coin or stamp collections
- Gems and jewelry
- Gold, silver, coins, etc. (except when they are held for sale by a professional dealer)

The tax treatment of these assets varies based on whether the asset is personal-use, business property, or investment property.

When capital assets are sold, the difference between the asset's basis and the selling price is a **capital GAIN** or a **capital LOSS**.

In order to correctly calculate capital gains and losses, you must first understand the concept of "basis" and "adjusted basis." The basis of the asset is usually its cost.

"Cost basis" is the amount of money invested into a property for tax purposes. Usually this is the cost of the item when it is purchased. However, there are some instances where basis is different than the cost of the item. Basis is figured in another way when property is acquired by gift or inheritance. The cost basis of an asset can include:

- Sales taxes charged during the purchase
- Freight-in charges
- Installation and testing fees
- Delinquent real estate taxes that are paid by the buyer of a property
- Legal and accounting fees

All of these costs are added to an asset's basis. These costs are not deductible as an expense, whether or not the asset is business-use or personal-use.

> **Example:** Raoul purchases a new car for $15,000. The sales tax on the vehicle is $1,200. He also pays a delivery charge to have the car shipped from another dealership to his home. The freight charge is $210. Therefore, Raoul's basis in the vehicle is $16,410 ($15,000 + $1,200 + $210).

> **Example:** Hilda is a self-employed writer. She purchases a new scanner for her home office. The scanner costs $540. The sales tax on the scanner is $56. Therefore, Hilda's basis in the item is $596 ($540 + $56).

In order to correctly report a capital gain or loss, a taxpayer needs to identify:

- The asset's **basis** (or adjusted basis):
    - **Basis** is the original cost of the asset[65]
    - **Adjusted basis** includes original cost plus any increases or decreases to that cost (such as commissions, fees, depreciation, casualty losses, insurance reimbursements, etc.)
- The asset's **holding period**:
    - Short-term property is held one year or LESS
    - Long-term property is held MORE than one year (this is important because long-term capital gains are taxed at a lower rate than short-term capital gains)
- The proceeds from the sale

Basis of Real Property (Real Estate)

The basis of real estate usually includes a number of costs in addition to the purchase price. If a taxpayer purchases real property (a house, a tract of land, a building), certain fees and other expenses automatically become part of the cost basis. This also includes real estate taxes the seller owed at the time of the purchase, if the real estate taxes were paid by the buyer.

> **Example:** Lawrence purchases a home from Tara for $100,000. Tara lost her job and fell behind on her property tax payments. Lawrence agrees to pay the delinquent real estate taxes as a condition of the sale. The delinquent property tax at the time of purchase totaled $3,500. The IRS does not allow a taxpayer to deduct property taxes that are not his legal responsibility. Therefore, Lawrence must add the property tax to his basis. Lawrence's basis in the home is $103,500 ($100,000 + $3,500).

If a property is constructed rather than purchased, the basis of the property includes the expenses of construction. This includes the cost of the land, building permits, payments to contractors, lumber, and inspection fees. Demolition costs and other costs related to the preparation of land must be added to the basis of the land.

---

[65] Beginning in 2011, brokers must report cost basis on **Form 1099-B**.

> **Example:** Wanda purchases an empty lot to build her home. The lot costs $50,000. Wanda also pays $2,800 for the removal of tree stumps before construction can begin. There was also an existing concrete foundation on the lot that Wanda dislikes, and she has the foundation demolished and removed in order to build a new foundation that she prefers. The demolition costs are $6,700. All of these costs must be added to the basis of the land (NOT the basis of the building). Therefore, Wanda's basis in the land is $59,500 ($50,000 + $2,800 + $6,700).

Adding Settlement Costs to Basis

Generally, a taxpayer must include settlement costs for the purchase of property in his basis. The following fees are some of the closing costs that can be included in a property's basis:

- Abstract fees
- Charges for installing utilities
- Legal fees (including title search and preparation of the deed)
- Recording fees
- Surveys
- Transfer taxes
- Owner's title insurance

Also included in a property's basis are any amounts the seller legally owes that the buyer agrees to pay, such as back taxes or interest, recording or mortgage fees, charges for improvements or repairs, and sales commissions. A taxpayer cannot include fees incidental to getting a loan.

How to Figure Adjusted Basis

This section discusses how to figure adjusted basis in property. Before figuring gain or loss on a sale or exchange, a taxpayer must usually make adjustments to the basis of the property. The result is the adjusted basis. The most common concepts when discussing basis are:

- **Cost basis:** The basis of property a taxpayer buys is usually its actual cost.
- **Adjusted basis:** Sometimes, a taxpayer must make increases or decreases to the cost of the property. The result is the property's "adjusted basis."

> **Example:** Brian buys a house for $120,000. The following year, he paves the driveway, which costs him $6,000. Brian's *adjusted basis* in the home is now $126,000 ($120,000 original cost + $6,000 in improvements).

> **Example:** Whitney purchases a commercial washer for her pet grooming business. She does not plan to use the washer for anything other than her business. The washer costs $1,230. The sales tax on the washer is an additional $62. There are also freight and installation charges of $96. Finally, there is a manufacturer's rebate on the washer of $300. Whitney sends in the rebate slip along with a copy of the receipt and receives the rebate check two weeks later. Her basis in the washer is figured as follows:
>
> | | |
> |---|---|
> | Cost: | $1,230 |
> | Sales tax: | $62 |
> | Installation: | $96 |
> | Rebate: | ($300) |
> | **Basis:** | **$1,088** |
>
> In this case, the washer is a business asset, and therefore, a non-capital asset.

Basis "Other Than" Cost

There are times when a taxpayer cannot use *cost* as the basis for property. In these cases, the fair market value or the adjusted basis of the property can be used. Below are some examples of times when an asset's basis will be something other than cost.

Property Received in Exchange for Services

If a taxpayer receives property in payment for services, he must include the property's FMV in income, and this becomes the taxpayer's basis in the property. If two people agree on a cost beforehand, and it is deemed reasonable, the IRS will usually accept the agreed-upon cost as the asset's basis.

> **Example:** Cassidy is an Enrolled Agent who prepares tax returns for a long-time client named Katie. Katie then loses her job and cannot pay Cassidy's bill, which totals $450. Katie offers Cassidy an antique vase in lieu of paying her invoice. The fair market value of the vase is approximately $520. Cassidy agrees to accept the vase as full payment on Katie's delinquent invoice. Cassidy's basis in the vase is $450, the amount of the invoice that was agreed upon by both parties.

The basis of gifted property and inherited property is also calculated on the basis "other than cost." Inherited property and gift property are covered later.

Basis After Casualty and Theft Losses

If a taxpayer has a casualty loss, he must decrease the basis of the property by any insurance proceeds. A taxpayer may increase the basis in the property by the amount spent on repairs that restore the property to its pre-casualty condition.

> **Example:** Ira paid $5,000 for a car several years ago. It was damaged in a flood. He does not have flood insurance on the car. Ira spends $3,000 to repair the car. Therefore, his new basis in the car is $8,000 ($5,000 + $3,000).

Remember, after a casualty loss, insurance reimbursements DECREASE basis, while out-of-pocket repairs INCREASE basis.

Assumption of a Mortgage or Loan

If a taxpayer buys property and assumes an existing mortgage on it, the taxpayer's basis includes the amount paid for the property PLUS the amount owed on the mortgage. The basis also includes the settlement fees and closing costs paid for buying the property. Fees and costs for getting a loan on the property (points) are not included in a property's basis.

> **Example:** Sondra buys a building for $20,000 cash and assumes a mortgage of $80,000 on it. Therefore, her basis is $100,000.

Basis Adjustments after an Involuntary Conversion

An involuntary conversion occurs when a taxpayer *involuntarily* gives up, sells, or exchanges property. An involuntary conversion can happen after a disaster, such as a house fire, drought, or a flood. Involuntary conversions may also occur after casualties, thefts, or the condemnation of property. If a taxpayer receives replacement property as a result of an involuntary conversion, the basis of the replacement property is figured using the basis of the converted property. A taxpayer may also have to figure gain if the amount of the insurance reimbursement exceeds his basis of the asset.

> **Example:** Joy receives insurance money of $8,000 for her shed, which was destroyed by an earthquake. Joy's basis in the shed was $6,000. She uses $6,000 to purchase a new shed. Joy needs to recognize a $2,000 gain, since she realized a gain of $2,000 from the conversion ($8,000 - $6,000) and only used $6,000 of the $8,000 insurance proceeds to replace the shed.

Basis of Property Received as a Gift

The basis of property received as a gift is figured differently than property that is purchased. To figure basis in property received as a gift, the taxpayer must know the adjusted basis of the property just before it was gifted, its fair market value, and the amount of gift tax paid on it, if any. Gift taxes are always paid by the giver (donor), not the receiver (donee) of the gift.

Do NOT confuse this concept with the basis of "inherited property," which is property that is passed on to another person after the owner of the property has died. Inherited property will be covered later.

Generally, the basis of gifted property is the same in the hands of the donee as it was in the hands of the donor. This is called a "transferred basis." For example, if a taxpayer gives his son a car and the taxpayer's basis in the car is $2,000, the basis of the vehicle remains $2,000 for the son. However, some adjustments must be made in cases where the taxpayer pays gift tax, or other adjustments.

Example: Alicia's father gives her 50 shares of ABC stock. The fair market value of the stock is currently $1,000. Her father has an adjusted basis in the stock of $500. Alicia's basis in the stock, for purposes of determining gain on any future sale, is $500 (transferred basis).

Figuring Basis on a Gift: Examples

If the FMV of the gifted property is less than the donor's adjusted basis, the donee's basis for gain is the same as the donor's adjusted basis. If the donee reports a loss on the sale of gifted property, the basis is the lower of the donor's basis or the fair market value of the property on the date of the gift. The sale of gifted property can also result in no gain or loss. This happens when the sale is *greater* than the gift's FMV but *below* the donor's basis.

Example: Russell receives a gift of 500 shares of stock from his Uncle Hugh. Uncle Hugh's basis in the stock was $1,000 when he gave it to his nephew. However, the FMV of the stock at the time of the gift is only $900 because it had lost some value. Russell sells the stock two months later for $920. Russell does not have any gain or loss for tax purposes. This is because Russell's basis for figuring GAIN is $1,000. However, Russell's basis for figuring LOSS is $900 (the FMV at the time of the gift). This is an example of a sale of gifted property resulting in **no gain or loss.** This happens when the sale ($920) is above the gift's FMV ($900) but below the donor's basis ($1,000).

Example: Charlie's grandmother, Leslie, bought 20 shares of Ford stock many decades ago. Leslie gifts her grandson the stock when the current FMV is $7,500. Charlie's grandmother's basis in the stock is only $1,000. Therefore, Charlie's basis in the stock is the same as his grandmother's: $1,000. During the year, Charlie sells the stock for $7,500. He must report a taxable gain of $6,500. The answer is figured as follows: ($7,500 sale price - $1,000 basis = $6,500 capital gain).

Example: Benny's Aunt Roberta bought 100 shares of Business Corp. stock when it was at $92. Roberta's basis for the 100 shares is $9,200. Roberta then gives the stock to Benny when it is selling at $70 and has an FMV of $7,000. In this case, Benny has a "dual basis" in the stock. He has one basis for purposes of determining a gain, and a different basis for determining a loss. Here are three separate scenarios that help illustrate how the gain or loss would be calculated when Benny sells the gifted stock:

Scenario #1: If Benny sells the stock for MORE than his aunt's basis, he will use Roberta's basis to determine his amount of gain. For example, if he sells the stock for $11,000, he will report a gain of $1,800 ($11,000 - $9,200).

Scenario #2: If Benny sells the stock for LESS than the FMV of the stock at the time of the gift ($7,000 in the example), he must use that basis to determine the amount of his loss. For example, if the stock continues to decline and Benny eventually sells it for $4,500, he can report a loss of $2,500 ($7,000 - $4,500).

> **Scenario #3:** If Benny sells the stock for an amount BETWEEN the FMV and the donor's basis, there will be no recognized gain or loss. For example, if Benny sells the stock for $8,000, there will be no gain or loss on the transaction.

Basis of Inherited Property

When someone inherits an asset, he is impacted by "basis" when he eventually sells the property. Basis of an asset is generally its cost. However, in the case of inherited assets, very different rules apply.

As we mentioned before, the rules for determining basis of inherited property are different than the rules for gifted property. Inherited property is also called property "inherited from a decedent."

This means that the original owner has died, and the property has passed on to another individual. Gifted property, on the other hand, passes to another individual while the original owner is still alive.

Usually, heirs use a "stepped up" basis for inherited assets. It doesn't matter what the deceased person actually paid for the asset. The basis of inherited property is generally the FMV of the property **on the date of the decedent's death.** This means that when the property is sold, the gain will be calculated based on the change in value from the date of death. However, this can vary if the personal representative of the estate elects to use the "alternate valuation date" (covered later).

Cash or property inherited from a deceased taxpayer is not considered income to the recipient. A taxpayer does not have to report inherited property as income on his tax return. However, if the taxpayer later earns income from the property (such as interest, dividends, or capital gain from the sale of the property), those amounts must be reported.

> **Example:** In January 2011, Phil's mother dies, and he inherits 300 shares of IBM stock from her. The value of the inherited stock is not taxable to Phil. However, in December 2011, IBM issues a taxable stock dividend of $100. The dividend is payable to Phil. Although the transfer of the stock was not a taxable event, the dividend that Phil earned after the stock transfer is taxable as ordinary income.

"Stepping Up" Basis on Inherited Property

A taxpayer's basis in inherited property is generally the fair market value of the property on the date of the decedent's death. In most cases the "valuation date" for the estate is the date of death.

This typically results in a beneficial tax situation for anyone who inherits property from a deceased person. This is because the taxpayer who inherits the property generally gets an increased basis. Tax professionals call this a "stepped-up" basis. However, there are cases where this rule can work against taxpayers. Although most property such as stocks, collectibles, and bonds increase in value over time, there are also occasions where the value of the property drops. Although this is rare, this would create a "stepped-down" basis.

Example #1: Sasha's uncle bought 300 shares of Giant Corp stock many years ago for $500. Sasha inherited the Giant Corp stock when her uncle died. On the date of her uncle's death, the value of the stock was $9,000. Therefore, Sasha's basis in the stock is $9,000. She later sells the stock for $11,000. She has a capital gain of $2,000 ($11,000 - $9,000). This is the concept of a "stepped-up" basis.

Example #2: With the same facts as above, if Sasha were to sell the stock for $8,000, she would have a capital loss of $1,000.

Example #3: Sasha's aunt also bought 100 shares of Enron stock many years ago for $10,000. Sasha inherited the Enron stock when her aunt died. On the date of her aunt's death, the value of the Enron stock was $150. Therefore, Sasha's basis in the stock is $150. She later sells the stock for $150. She cannot report a loss on the stock. That is because the basis of the stock was "stepped-down" for tax purposes. No one will receive a tax deduction for the loss in value of the stock.

Exception for an Alternate Valuation Date

Usually, the basis of an estate is figured on the date of death. However, there is a special rule that allows the executor of the estate to elect a different valuation date. If the executor makes this election, the valuation date is six months *after* the date of death.

Usually the executor will make this election in order to reduce the amount of estate tax that must be paid. The "alternate valuation date" is an election made by the executor, and is not required. For estate tax purposes, in order to elect the alternative valuation date, the estate value and tax must be LESS than on the date of the taxpayer's death.

Choosing to take an alternate valuation date will also affect the basis of the property that is passed on to the beneficiaries of the estate.

If a federal estate tax return (**Form 706**) does not have to be filed for the deceased taxpayer, the basis in the beneficiary's inherited property is the FMV value at the date of death,[66] and the alternate valuation date does not apply.

Basis of Securities

A taxpayer's basis in securities (stocks or bonds) is usually the purchase price, plus any additional costs (for example, brokers' commissions). In order to compute

---

[66] Most taxpayers are not subject to the estate tax and are not required to file an estate tax return upon their death. A filing is required for estates with combined gross assets and prior taxable gifts exceeding $5 million for taxpayers dying in 2010 (or later). This means that if the taxpayer's estate is valued at less than $5 million, then an estate tax return is not required.

gain or loss on a sale, taxpayers must provide their basis in the sold property. The basis of stock is usually its cost, but basis can also include other fees.

When a taxpayer sells securities, the investment company will send **Form 1099-B,** *Proceeds from Broker and Barter Exchange Transactions,* showing the gross proceeds of the sale. **Form 1099-B** does not usually include how much taxpayers paid; they must keep track of this information themselves. If taxpayers cannot provide their basis, the IRS will deem it to be zero.

Many taxpayers own shares of stock they bought on different dates or for different prices. This means they own more than one block of stock. Each block may differ from the others in its holding period (long-term or short-term), its basis (amount paid for the stock), or both.

In directing a broker to sell stock, the taxpayer may specify which block, or part of a block, to sell; this is called **Specific Identification**. The "Specific Identification method" requires good recordkeeping; however, this method simplifies the determination of the holding period and the basis of the stock sold, giving the taxpayer better control and versatility in handling an investment.

If the taxpayer cannot identify the specific block at the time of sale, shares sold are treated as coming from the earliest block purchased; this method is called "First In, First Out" (FIFO).[67]

FIFO Example:

Tia bought 50 shares of stock of Coffee Corp. in 2005 for $10 a share. In 2006, Tia bought another 200 shares of Coffee Corp. for $11 a share. In 2008, she bought 100 shares for $9 a share. Finally, in 2011, she sells 130 shares. She cannot identify the exact shares she disposed of, so she must use the stock FIFO method to figure the basis of the shares that she sold. Tia figures her stock basis as follows:

Shares purchased

Year	# of Shares	Cost per share	Total cost
2005	50	$10	$500
2006	200	$11	$2,200
2008	100	$9	$900

The basis of the stock that Tia sold is figured as follows:

50 shares (50 × $10) balance of stock bought in 2005	$500
80 shares (80 × $11) stock bought in 2006	$880
Total basis of stock sold in 2011	$1,380

---

[67] Specific Identification and First In, First Out (FIFO) are also common inventory methods that are used by businesses. You will learn more about how these inventory methods are used by businesses in Part 2 of the EA exam course books.

> **Example:** Amber buys two blocks of 400 shares of stock (800 shares total), the first in May 2009 for $11,200 and the second in June 2010 for $11,600. In September 2011, she sells 400 shares for $11,500 without specifying which block of shares she is selling. Because Amber did not specify a block of shares at the time of sale, the sold shares are treated as coming from the earliest block purchased. Since the basis and holding period defaults to the original block of shares, Amber realizes a long-term gain of $300 ($11,500 - $11,200).

Adjusted Basis of Securities

An "adjustment to basis" is an increase or decrease in the original basis of an asset. It may include commissions or fees paid to the broker at the time of purchase or sale. Stock is usually bought and sold in various quantities. The taxpayer is required to keep track of the basis per share of all stock bought and sold.

Events that occur after the purchase of the stock can require adjustments (increases or decreases) to the "per share" basis of stock. The original basis per share can be changed by events such as stock dividends, stock splits, and Dividend Reinvestment Plan (DRIP) accounts.

- **Stock dividends** are additional shares that companies grant to their shareholders. These additional shares increase the taxpayer's ownership so the original basis is spread over more shares, which decreases the basis per share.
- **Stock splits** occur when a corporation distributes more stock to its existing stockholders as a way to bring down the market price of its stock. For example, in a "2-for-1" stock split, a corporation issues one share of stock for every share outstanding. This then decreases the basis per share by half. The original basis of $200 for 100 shares becomes $200 for 200 shares.

> **Example:** Pepper pays $1,050 for 100 shares of Jolly Ice Cream, Inc. stock (including the broker's commission of $50). Her basis in the 100 shares is $1,100 ($1,050 cost + $50 broker's commission). Therefore, the original cost basis *per share* is $11 ($1,100/100). Pepper receives 10 *additional* shares of stock as a non-taxable stock dividend. Her $1,100 basis must be spread over 110 shares (100 original shares plus the 10-share stock dividend). So, adding 10 shares means her basis per share decreases to $10 ($1,100/110).

Basis after a Stock Split (Stock Dividend)

The way to figure basis after a stock split or a stock dividend is to divide the taxpayer's adjusted basis of the old stock between the shares of the old stock and the new stock. Basically, this means that if the old stock was priced at $10 per share, after the split each share would be worth $5. This is because the corporation's assets did not increase, only the number of outstanding shares.

Stock acquired in a non-taxable stock dividend or stock split has the same holding period as the original stock. If the original stock has a long-term holding period, stock received in a non-taxable stock dividend also has a long-term holding period. For example, if the original stock has a holding period of three months, the new stock immediately has a three-month holding period

A stock dividend and a stock split are not taxable events. However, both of these types of distributions do affect the taxpayer's basis in his stock.

After a split, taxpayers need to recalculate their basis for the newly acquired shares. The new basis per share is the total cost of the shares divided by the new share count.

> **Example:** Sean bought 100 shares of Mini Corp. for $50 per share. Sean's cost basis is $50 x 100 shares or $5,000. In 2011, Mini Corp. issues a stock dividend. Sean receives 100 additional shares of stock. Therefore, his new basis in each individual stock is $25 = ($5,000 ÷ [100+100]).

In rare cases, a stock dividend may be taxable. A taxable stock dividend occurs most often when shareholders have the option to receive cash or other property *instead* of stock. The holding period for stock received as a *taxable* stock dividend begins on the date of distribution.

Restricted Stock

If stock is granted to a taxpayer but is subject to restrictions, then the taxpayer does not have to report any income until the stock is either granted or sold (when it is taxable depends on the circumstances).

Restricted stock is stock that has been granted to a taxpayer (usually an employee of a company) that is non-transferable and subject to certain conditions, such as termination of employment or failure to meet certain performance targets. Stock-based compensation generally consists of either the transferring of stock or the issuance of stock options to an employee (or independent contractor) as part of a compensation package. Stock is considered "transferred" only if the employee has the risks and benefits of an owner of the stock. (The employee must be a bona fide owner and shareholder of the stock.)

Generally, restricted stock is not eligible for capital gains treatment, and the entire amount of the vested stock must be reported as ordinary income in the year of vesting. The amount that must be reported as ordinary income is calculated by subtracting the exercise price of the stock from the fair market value of the stock on the date of vesting. The difference is then reported as ordinary income by the shareholder.

If the shareholder decides to hold the stock and sell at a later date, then the difference between the sale price and the fair market value on the date of vesting is then reported as a capital gain or loss.

> **Example:** Natasha is a sales executive working for Big Corp. As part of her compensation package, she receives a restricted stock grant of 2,000 shares. The restriction on the stock is lifted once she reaches certain sales targets. At the end of the year, Natasha reaches her sales goals, and the stock is vested. On her grant date, the stock for Big Corp is trading at $15 per share. Natasha decides to declare the stock at vesting, so she must report $30,000 (2,000 shares X $15 per share) as ordinary income.

Basis of Property Transferred From a Spouse (or Former Spouse)

The basis of property transferred by a spouse (or former spouse if the transfer is incident to divorce) is the same as the spouse's adjusted basis.[68] Generally, there is no gain or loss recognized on the transfer of property between spouses, or between former spouses if the transfer is because of divorce. This rule applies even if the transfer was in exchange for cash, the release of marital rights, the assumption of liabilities, or other considerations.

There are some exceptions to this rule. The basis of the property must be adjusted for any gain recognized by the transferor on property transferred in a trust. Special rules also apply if the taxpayer's spouse (or former spouse) is a non-resident alien.

If the property transferred is a series E, series EE, or series I United States savings bond, the transferor must include the interest accrued to the date of transfer. The basis in the bond immediately after the transfer is equal to the transferor's basis increased by the interest income includible in the transferor's income.

> **Example:** Before they divorced, Demi and Layton jointly owned a home that had a basis of $50,000 and a fair market value of $250,000. When they divorced last year, Demi transferred her entire interest in the home to Layton as part of their property settlement. Layton's basis in the interest received from Demi is her adjusted basis in the home. His total basis in the home is their joint adjusted basis ($50,000).

> **Example:** Margot and Thornton divorced in 2011. Thornton owns stocks with a fair market value of $350,000 and a basis of $200,000. Pursuant to the divorce decree, Thornton transfers all of the stocks to his former spouse. The stock transfer is treated as a non-taxable transfer; therefore, no gain or loss is recognized by either party. Margot's basis in the stock is $200,000.

---

[68] For more information on property transfers incident to divorce, see **Publication 504**, *Divorced or Separated Individuals*.

Basis of a Non-Business Bad Debt

There are two kinds of bad debts—business and non-business. If someone owes you money that you cannot collect, you have a bad debt. Some non-business bad debts are deductible, and others are not. Business bad debt arises in a trade or business (such as when a customer fails to pay his bill), and it is treated differently than non-business bad debt. Business bad debt is covered in Part 2 of the EA exam.

To deduct a bad debt, the taxpayer must have a basis in it—that is, the taxpayer must have already included the amount in income or must have already loaned out the cash. If a taxpayer loans money to someone in a true debtor-creditor relationship that is unrelated to a business, the loan is a non-business debt. The debt must be a valid and enforceable obligation.

Taxpayers must prove that they have taken reasonable steps to collect the debt and that the debt is worthless. A debt becomes worthless when it is certain that the debt will never be paid. It is not necessary to go to court if the taxpayer can show that a judgment from the court would be uncollectible. A partially worthless debt is not deductible.

The taxpayer may take a bad debt deduction only in the year the debt becomes worthless, but a taxpayer does not have to wait until the debt comes due, if there is proof that the debt is already worthless (for example, if the debtor dies or declares bankruptcy).

Example: In January 2011, Stephanie loans her friend Jed $14,000 to buy a car. Jed signs a note and promises to pay the entire debt back with interest on December 31, 2011. Jed has a bad car accident in June 2011 and cannot pay his debts so he files for bankruptcy. Stephanie does not have to wait until the debt comes due. The bankruptcy means the loan has become worthless, since there is no longer any chance the amount owed will be paid. Stephanie can take the deduction for non-business bad debt.

For a legitimate bad debt to be deductible, the intent of the loan must be genuine. The transaction must be a true loan and not a gift. If a taxpayer lends money to a relative or friend with the understanding that it will not be repaid, it is considered a gift and not a loan. There must be a true creditor-debtor relationship between the taxpayer and the person or organization that owes the money.

Loan Guarantees

A *loan guarantee* is not a true debtor-creditor relationship. If a taxpayer simply guarantees a debt (by co-signing on the loan) and the debt becomes worthless, the taxpayer cannot take a bad debt deduction. If the taxpayer makes a loan guarantee as "a favor" to friends and does not receive any consideration in return, the loan payments are considered a gift and are therefore not deductible as a bad debt. There must be a profit motive in order for the loan to qualify as a true debtor-creditor relationship.

> **Example:** Lucas and Jason are co-workers. Lucas, as a favor to Jason, co-signs on an auto loan at their local credit union. Jason does not pay the loan and declares bankruptcy. Lucas is forced to pay off the note in order to maintain his credit. However, since he did not enter into a formal guarantee agreement to protect an investment or to make a profit, Lucas cannot take a bad debt deduction.

When minor children borrow from their parents, there is no genuine debt. A bad debt cannot be deducted for such a loan.

A legitimate non-business bad debt is reported as a short-term capital loss on **Schedule D, Form 1040**. It is subject to the capital loss limit of $3,000 per year. This limit is $1,500 if a taxpayer is married filing a separate return.

Holding Period (Short-Term or Long-Term)

The "holding period" is a very important concept to understand for the EA exam. When a taxpayer disposes of investment property, he must determine his holding period in order to figure gain or loss. Holding periods vary based on whether the property is purchased, inherited, or acquired as a gift.

The holding period determines whether any capital gain or loss was a short-term or long-term capital gain or loss. This is very important, because long-term capital gains rates are given more beneficial tax treatment.

If a taxpayer holds investment property for MORE than one year, any capital gain or loss is *long-term* capital gain or loss. If a taxpayer holds property for one year or LESS, any capital gain or loss is *short-term* capital gain or loss.

> **Long-term = OVER one year**
> **Short-term = One year or LESS**

To determine how long a taxpayer has held an investment property, he should begin counting on the date *after* the day he acquires the property. The day the taxpayer disposes of the property is part of the holding period. This is very important—the EA exam will usually have a few questions relating to holding period.

> **Example:** Nicky bought 50 shares of stock on February 5, 2010 for $10,000. She sells all the shares on February 5, 2011 for $20,500. Nicky's holding period is NOT more than one year and she has a short-term capital gain of $10,500. The short-term gain is taxed at ordinary income rates. A long-term gain is taxed at preferential tax rates. If Nicky had waited one more day, she would have received long-term capital gain treatment on her gains, and it would have saved her on income taxes.

Do not confuse the "trade date" with the "settlement date," which is the date by which the stock must be delivered and payment must be made.

Example: Stuart bought 100 shares of Huge Corp. stock on October 1, 2010 for $1,200. To determine his holding period, Stuart must start counting his holding period on October 2, 2010 (the day *after* the purchase). He sells all the stock on October 2, 2011 for $2,850. Stuart's holding period has been over one year, and therefore, he will recognize a long-term capital gain of $1,650 ($2,850 - $1,200).

Stock acquired as a stock dividend (also called a stock split) has the same holding period as the original stock owned.

Example: On September 10, 2008, Jamal bought 500 shares of Big Widgets Corporation stock for $1,500, including his broker's commission. On June 6, 2011, Big Widgets distributes a 2% non-taxable stock dividend (10 additional shares). Three days later, Jamal sells all his Big Widgets stock for $2,030. Although Jamal owned the 10 shares he received as a non-taxable stock dividend for only three days, all the stock has a long-term holding period. Because he bought the stock for $1,500 and then sold it for $2,030 more than a year later, Jamal has a long-term capital gain of $530 on the sale of the 510 shares.

Holding Period for Gifted Property

The holding period for a gift is treated differently than the holding period for inherited and purchased property. If a taxpayer receives a gift of property, then the holding period includes the donor's holding period. This concept is also known as "tacking on" the holding period.

Example: Marion received an acre of land as a gift from her Aunt Helen. At the time of the gift, the land had an FMV of $23,000. Helen's adjusted basis in the land was $20,000. Helen held the property for six months. Marion holds the land for another seven months. Neither held the property for over a year. However, Marion may "tack on" her holding period to her aunt's holding period. Therefore, if Marion were to sell the property, she would have a long-term capital gain or loss, because jointly they held the property for thirteen months, which is over one year.

Special Rule: Holding Period of Inherited Property

If a taxpayer inherits property, the capital gain or loss on any later disposition of that property is ALWAYS treated as a long-term capital gain or loss. This is true regardless of how long the beneficiary actually held the property. The taxpayer is considered to have held the inherited property for more than one year even if he disposes of the property less than one year after the decedent's death.

Example: Warren inherits an acre of land from his father, Rudolph, who died on April 3, 2011. At the time of his father's death, the land had an FMV of $18,000. Rudolph's adjusted basis in the land was $5,000. After Warren received the property, he sold it two weeks later for $18,500. Warren gets a "stepped-up" basis in the property and may use the FMV at the time of his father's death ($18,000) as the basis in the land. Therefore, Warren has a $500 long-term capital gain ($18,500 - $18,000 = $500).

The holding period of the deceased person does not matter. Inherited property is ALWAYS considered long-term, regardless of how long the original owner held the property, or how long the person who inherited the property holds it.

Example: Joni purchases 100 shares of Successful Corp on January 10, 2011. Joni dies two weeks later. Her father, Ronald, is Joni's only beneficiary. Ronald inherits the stock, and it is transferred to him on September 30, 2011. Ronald sells the stock one week later. Even though no one actually held the stock for over a year, Ronald gets long-term capital gain treatment on the sale, because the stock was inherited property.

Unit 12: Questions

1. On February 11, 2011, Henry bought 1,000 shares of Greenbrae Corporation stock for $4 each, plus paid an additional $70 for his broker's commission. What is Henry's basis in the stock?

A. $1,000.
B. $4,000.
C. $4,070.
D. None of the above.

The answer is C. Henry's basis in the stock is $4,070 ([1,000 X $4] = $4,000 + $70). ###

2. Brigit purchased 1,000 shares of Free Drive, Inc. on January 3, 2011. The original basis in the 1,000 shares of stock she purchased was $5,100, including the commission. On August 14, 2011, she sold 500 shares for $3,300. What is the adjusted basis of the stock she SOLD?

A. $5,100.
B. $2,550.
C. $3,300.
D. $3,255.

The answer is B. Brigit's original basis in the total stock was $5,100, which is $5.10 per share, so her basis in the 500 shares she sold is 500 X $5.10, or $2,550. ###

3. Tariq bought two blocks of 400 shares of stock. He purchased the first block in April 2007 for $1,200 and the second block in March 2011 for $1,600. In June of 2011, he sold 400 shares for $1,500 without specifying which block of shares he was selling. Tariq's sold stock represents a _____.

A. Short-term loss of $100.
B. Short-term gain of $300.
C. Long-term loss of $100.
D. Long-term gain of $300.

The answer is D. The basis and holding period would automatically default to the original block of shares, so Tariq realized a long-term gain of $300. ###

4. Consuela bought 40 shares of Giant Corporation for a total purchase price $1,540. She also paid a $20 broker's commission on the purchase. What is her initial basis PER SHARE?

A. $39.
B. $38.50.
C. $1,560.
D. $77.

The answer is A. Consuela's initial basis for this stock is $1,560, or $39 per share ($1,560 ÷ 40 shares). Cost basis includes the amount paid for the stock and any commission paid on the purchase. ###

5. On March 10, 2009, Hans bought 500 shares of Manufacturing Company stock for $1,500, including his broker's commission. On June 6, 2011, Manufacturing Company distributed Hans a non-taxable stock dividend of 10 additional shares. Three days later, Hans sold all his stock for $2,030. What is the nature of his gain on all the shares sold?

A. Long-term capital gain of $530.
B. Long-term capital gain of $500, short-term gain of $30.
C. Short-term capital gain of $530.
D. None of the above.

The answer is A. Although Hans owned the 10 shares he received as a non-taxable stock dividend for only three days, all the stock has a long-term holding period. Because he bought the stock for $1,500 and then sold it for $2,030 more than a year later, Hans has a long-term capital gain of $530 on the sale of the 510 shares. ###

6. Deirdre bought 100 shares of stock of Around Pound Corporation in 2004 for $10 a share. In January 2005 Deirdre bought another 200 shares for $11 a share. In July 2005 she gave her son 50 shares. In December 2008 Deirdre bought 100 shares for $9 a share. In April 2011 she sold 130 shares. Deirdre cannot identify the shares she disposed of, so she must use the stock she acquired FIRST to figure the basis. The shares Deirdre gave her son had a basis of $500 (50 × $10). What is the basis of the 130 shares of stock Deirdre SOLD in 2011?

A. $880.
B. $1,380.
C. $1,300.
D. $1,000.

The answer is B. If a taxpayer buys and sells securities at various times in varying quantities and she cannot adequately identify the shares sold, the basis of the securities sold is the basis of the securities acquired first (FIFO). Deirdre figures the basis of the 130 shares of stock she sold as follows:

50 shares (50 × $10)
Balance of stock from 2004: $500
80 shares (80 × $11)
Stock bought in January 2005 $880
Total basis of stock sold $1,380
###

7. Julian owned one share of common stock that he bought for $45. The corporation distributed two new shares of common stock for each share held. Julian then had three shares of common stock. What is Julian's new basis for each share?

A. $5.
B. $45.
C. $15.
D. $135.

The answer is C. Julian's basis in each share is $15 ($45 ÷ 3). If a taxpayer receives a non-taxable stock dividend, divide the adjusted basis of the old stock by the number of shares of old and new stock. The result is the taxpayer's basis for each share of stock. ###

8. Claire owned two shares of common stock. She bought one for $30 in 2006 and the other for $45 in 2007. In 2011, the corporation distributed two new shares of common stock for each share held (a "2-for-1" stock split). Claire had six shares after the distribution. How is the basis allocated between these six shares?

A. All six shares now have a basis of $12.50.
B. Three shares have a basis of $10 each and three have a basis of $15 each.
C. The shares are valued at $45 each.
D. Some other amount.

The answer is B. The shares now are valued as follows: three with a basis of $10 each ($30 ÷ 3), and three with a basis of $15 each ($45 ÷ 3). If a taxpayer receives a non-taxable stock dividend, he must divide the adjusted basis of the old stock by the number of shares of old and new stock. The result is the taxpayer's basis for each share of stock. ###

9. On her one-year anniversary at her new job, Faith's employer gave her restricted stock with the condition that she would have to return it if she did not complete a full five years of service with her company. Her employer's basis in the stock was $16,000, and its fair market value is $30,000. How much should she include in her income for the current year, and what would be her basis in the stock?

A. Income of $16,000; basis of $30,000.
B. Income of $10,000; basis of $30,000.
C. Income of $30,000; basis of $16,000.
D. Faith would not report any income or have any basis in the stock until she has completed five years of service.

The answer is D. The stock is restricted, so Faith does not have constructive receipt of it. She should not report any income until she receives the stock without restrictions. Constructive receipt does not require physical possession of the item of income. However, there are substantial restrictions on the stock's disposition because Faith must complete another four years of service before she can sell or otherwise dispose of the stock. ###

10. Stephen purchases a truck for $15,000. He puts $5,000 down in cash and finances the remaining $10,000 with a five-year loan. He then pays taxes and delivery costs of $1,300. He also pays $250 to install a protective bedliner. What is Stephen's basis in the truck?

A. $6,550.
B. $10,000.
C. $16,550.
D. $16,300.

The answer is C. Stephen's basis in the truck is the cost of both acquiring the property and preparing the property for use. Therefore, his basis is figured as follows: ($15,000 + $1,300 + $250) = $16,550. Any funds that are borrowed to pay for an asset are also included in the basis. ###

11. Mackenzie purchases an empty lot for $50,000. She pays $15,000 in cash and finances the remaining $35,000 with a bank loan. The lot also has a $4,000 lien against it for unpaid property taxes, which she also agrees to pay. Which statement below is CORRECT?

A. Mackenzie's basis in the property is $50,000, and she may deduct the property taxes on her Schedule A as property taxes paid.
B. Mackenzie's basis in the property is $19,000.
C. Mackenzie's basis in the property is $54,000.
D. Mackenzie's basis in the property is $46,000.

The answer is C. Her basis is figured as follows: ($50,000 + $4,000 = $54,000). Mackenzie may not deduct the delinquent property taxes on her Schedule A. This is because any obligations of the seller that are assumed by the buyer increase the basis of the asset, and are not currently deductible. Since Mackenzie did not legally owe the property taxes but she still agreed to pay them, she must add the property tax to the basis of the property. ###

12. Marilyn won the lottery and then made personal loans to several friends. The loans were a true debtor-creditor relationship, but not business related. She could not collect on many of these loans. How does Marilyn report these transactions?

A. The losses from the uncollectible loans are not deductible, since they were personal loans.
B. The losses are deductible as non-business bad debt on **Schedule D.**
C. The losses are deductible as a business expense on **Schedule C.**
D. The losses are deductible on **Schedule A** as casualty losses.

The answer is B. A non-business bad debt is reported as a short-term capital loss on **Schedule D.** It is subject to the capital loss limit of $3,000 per year. ###

13. Conrad purchased Blue-Chip Corporation stock in 2008 and sold it in 2011. In 2011, he also traded in a copy machine that he had been using in his business since 2007 for a new model. On December 15, 2011, Conrad's mother gifted him 35 shares of Energy Corp. stock that she had held for five years. Conrad sold the gifted stock two weeks after he received it from his mother. What is the holding period for all these assets?

A. All short-term.
B. Blue-Chip stock and copy machine are long-term and Energy Corp. stock is short-term.
C. All the stocks are long-term; the copy machine is short-term.
D. All are long-term.

The answer is D. All the property is long-term property. If a taxpayer holds investment property for more than one year, any capital gain or loss is a long-term capital gain or loss. If a taxpayer holds a property for one year or less, any capital gain or loss is a short-term capital gain or loss. If a taxpayer receives a gift of property, then the holding period includes the donor's holding period. Since Conrad's mother had already held the stock for a few years, it would receive long-term treatment in Conrad's possession. ###

14. When trying to determine the holding period for investment property, which of the following is important?

A. The cost of the property.
B. In the case of gifted property, the amount of the gift.
C. The date of acquisition.
D. The amount realized in the transaction.

The answer is C. To determine the holding period, a taxpayer must begin counting on the day after the acquisition date. If a taxpayer's holding period is not more than one year, the taxpayer will have a short-term capital gain or loss. The amount realized in the transaction has no bearing on the holding period. ###

Unit 13: Capital Gains and Losses

> **More Reading:**
> Publication 550, *Investment Income and Expenses*
> Publication 544, *Sales and Other Dispositions of Assets*

The sale of property is an important concept for the EA exam. The sale of assets (whether they are securities, such as stocks, or personal property, such as a main home) will result in a capital gain or loss. Learning how to calculate capital gains and losses is essential to understanding how property transactions are taxed.

Losses from the sale of "personal-use" property, such as a main home or a car, are not deductible. However, losses from the sale of investment property (such as stocks or bonds) are deductible up to a certain limit.

Investment property is also a capital asset. Therefore, any gain or loss from its sale or trade is generally a capital gain or loss.

Stocks, stock rights (also called "stock options"), and bonds are also considered capital assets (except when held for sale by a bona-fide securities dealer). Property held for personal use only, rather than for investment, is a capital asset, and a taxpayer must report a gain from its sale as a capital gain. However, a taxpayer CANNOT deduct a loss from selling personal-use property. Examples include a personal-use car or a television set.

Example: Liam owns a used Toyota sedan. It is his personal-use vehicle. He purchased the car two years ago for $2,500. In 2011, he sells the car for $2,100. Liam cannot claim a loss from the sale of the car, since it is his personal-use vehicle.

Example: Mason sold his personal computer to his friend, Adam, for $750. Mason paid $5,000 for the computer five years ago. Mason used the computer to play games and to balance his checkbook. He did not use the computer for business. Mason cannot deduct a loss on the sale of his personal computer.

Capital gains and deductible capital losses are reported on **Form 1040, Schedule D**, *Capital Gains and Losses*. **Schedule D** is used most commonly to report gains and losses from stock sales, but it is also used to report other types of capital gains and losses, such as taxable gains from the sale of a primary residence.

Example: Priscilla collects antique coins as a hobby. She is not a professional dealer. Two years ago, Priscilla gets lucky and purchases an antique Roman coin for $50. In 2011, she is offered $1,000 for the coin, and she promptly sells it. Priscilla has a taxable capital gain and she must report it on her tax return.

*Note: New for 2011, the **Schedule D** has been revised, and a new form for reporting the sale of capital assets has been added. The new **Form 8949**, *Sales and Other Dispositions of Capital Assets*, is now required as part of the reporting process.

In 2011, **Schedule D** was revised to allow for entries from the new **Form 8949** and changes made to **Form 1099-B**.

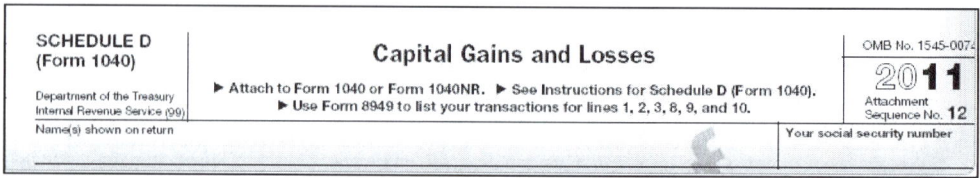

In previous years, capital gain transactions would only have been reported using IRS **Schedule D** (or **Schedule D-1**), but for tax year 2011 **Form 8949**, *Sales and Other Dispositions of Capital Assets* may also be required.[69]

Schedule D is still used to report gain or loss on the sale of investment property and other capital gain distributions, but additional detail on these transactions is first reported on **Form 8949**.

Form 8949 is used for the following transactions:
- Transactions reported on **Form 1099-B** (generally, these are sales of stocks, bonds, and other similar investments)
- Capital gains from an involuntary conversion of non-business assets (except in the case of casualty or theft)
- Non-business bad debts

Form 8949 requires the taxpayer to list the individual transactions by type, and then the totals are transferred to **Schedule D**.

---

[69] The **Schedule D** instructions also provide instructions for completing **Form 8949**.

> ### *Reporting Capital Gains and Losses: Summary*
> Short-term capital gains or losses (assets held for one year or less) are now reported on Part I of **Form 8949**.
>
> Long-term capital gains or losses (assets held for more than one year) are now reported on Part II of **Form 8949**.
>
> These amounts are then transferred to **Schedule D**.

Non-capital Assets

On the other hand, assets held for business-use or created by a taxpayer for the purpose of earning revenue (author's writings, copyrights, inventory, etc.) are considered *non-capital* assets. You may see references to non-capital assets on Part 1 or Part 2 of the EA exam.

Gains and losses from the sale of business property are reported on **Form 4797**, *Sales of Business Property*, and in the case of individual taxpayers the amounts flow through to **Form 1040, Schedule D**.[70]

> **Example:** Tony is a sole proprietor of a fitness club. He also owns stock in a few companies as an investment. In 2011, Tony sold used fitness equipment from his club in order to make room for new equipment. Since the fitness equipment was business property, the sale of these assets is reported on **Form 4797**, *Sales of Business Property*. Also during the year, Tony sold some Google stock at a substantial profit. He has a capital gain on the stock and must report the sale on **Schedule D**.

The following assets are non-capital assets:
- Inventory (or any property held for sale to customers)
- Depreciable property used in a business, even if it is fully depreciated
- Real property used in a trade or business (such as a commercial building or a residential rental)
- Self-produced copyrights, transcripts, manuscripts, drawings, photographs, or artistic compositions
- Accounts receivable or notes receivable acquired by a business
- Stocks and bonds held by professional securities dealers
- Business supplies
- Commodities and derivative financial instruments

---

[70] See **Publication 544**, *Sales and Other Dispositions of Assets*, for additional information on the sale of business property. Gains and sales of business property are covered more in Book 2.

> **Example:** Michael is a self-employed fisherman who reports his income and loss on **Schedule F**. In 2011, he sells some of his commercial fishing equipment, which was business-use only. The fishing equipment is a non-capital asset, and the sale must be reported on **Form 4797**, *Sales of Business Property*. Also during the year, Michael sells his vacation home and has a substantial loss on the sale. Unlike the fishing equipment, the vacation home is a capital asset, and since it is personal-use only, Michael cannot deduct the loss on the sale.

Capital Gains and Losses in General

Long-term capital gains are generally taxed at a lower rate than ordinary income. Short-term capital gains are taxed at the ordinary rate. This is why taxpayers prefer to have long-term capital gains, rather than short-term capital gains. The capital gains tax rate depends on the holding period, type of asset, and the taxpayer's ordinary income bracket.

If a taxpayer sells securities through a broker during the year, he should receive **Form 1099-B,** *Proceeds from Broker and Barter Exchange Transactions*, by January 31 following the end of the tax year.

Form 1099-S, *Proceeds From Real Estate Transactions*, usually reflects gross proceeds of real property transactions.

This statement shows the gross proceeds from the sale of securities. The IRS also receives a copy of **Form 1099-B** from the broker. If **Form 1099-B** does not include the basis, the taxpayer must provide this information. If the taxpayer cannot provide or calculate the basis of an asset, the IRS will deem the basis to be zero.

> **Example:** In 2011, Corbin sold stock. Corbin received **Form 1099-B** that shows a net sales price of $1,200 on the sale of 600 shares of Cuddly Inc. He bought the stock six years ago and sold it on September 25, 2011. His basis in Cuddly Inc., including commission, is $1,455. He has an overall loss on the stock, which he will report on **Schedule D**.

The sale and income (or loss) must be reported in the year the security is sold, regardless of when the taxpayer receives the proceeds from the stock sale.

The $3,000 Loss Limit and Loss Carryovers

Capital losses are always netted against capital gains. This follows the normal passive activity loss rules.[71] However, there is an exception for stock losses. *Up to $3,000* of excess capital losses is deductible against ordinary income in a tax year ($1,500 for married taxpayers filing separately). The allowable loss is referred to as the capital loss deduction limit. Unused losses are carried over to later years.

---

[71] Passive activity rules were covered earlier.

The carryover losses are combined with the gains and losses that actually occur in the next year. Short-term and long-term capital loss carryovers are reported on **Schedule D.**

The carryover retains its character as either long-term or short-term. A long-term capital loss carried over to the next tax year will reduce that year's long-term capital gains before it reduces that year's short-term capital gains.

> **Example:** Arthur purchased stock two years ago for $16,000. The stock declines in value and he finally sold the stock in 2011 for $12,000. Arthur has a $4,000 long-term capital loss. He also has $30,000 in wages in 2011. He may claim $3,000 of his long-term capital loss against his ordinary income, thereby lowering his gross income to $27,000 ($30,000 - $3,000). The remainder of the long-term capital loss must be carried forward to a future year ($1,000 carryover).

Unused losses may be carried over year after year until they are all deducted. There is no limit on how many times a capital loss can be carried over during the taxpayer's life.

Figuring Capital Gain or Loss

A taxpayer figures gain or loss on a sale or trade of stock or property by comparing the amount realized with the adjusted basis of the property.

- GAIN: If the taxpayer realizes more than the adjusted basis of the property, the difference is a gain.
- LOSS: If the taxpayer realizes less than the adjusted basis of the property, the difference is a loss.

> **Example:** Nadine purchased 50 shares of Big Auto stock five years ago for $5,000. Then, two years ago, she purchased 750 shares of Huge Utility stock for $8,200. In 2011, Nadine sold all her stock. Her Big Auto stock sold for $2,000, which means she had a loss. Her Huge Utility stock sold for $13,000, which means she had a gain. All of Nadine's gains and losses are long-term, because she held all her stock for over one year. Her long-term loss and long-term gain are "netted" against each other to figure her NET capital gain. Nadine's gains and losses are figured as follows:
>
> | Stock | Basis | Sale Price | Gain (or loss) |
> |---|---|---|---|
> | Big Auto | $5,000 | $2,000 | ($3,000) |
> | Huge Utility | $8,200 | $13,000 | $4,800 |
> | **Net Capital Gain** | | | **$1,800** |

A realized gain (or loss) is the amount realized that is above (or below, in the case of a loss) the adjusted basis of the property. This amount is not necessarily taxable. There are many instances where a taxpayer may have a realized gain that is not a taxable event. We will go over a number of these instances in this chapter.

A "recognized" gain or loss is the actual amount that must be included in income (or deducted from income) for tax purposes.

Worthless and Abandoned Securities

Starting in 2008, taxpayers could choose to "abandon" securities. Stocks, stock rights, and bonds (other than those held for sale by a securities dealer) that became worthless during the tax year are treated as though they were sold on the last day of the tax year. The taxpayer would report the loss as if he sold the shares for zero dollars on the last day of the taxable year.

Taxpayers report their losses from worthless securities on **Schedule D (Form 1040)**. This rule is helpful for a taxpayer who has a security that has declined in value so much that he wishes to take a loss on it rather than retain ownership.

Example: Reginald owned 500 shares of WorldCom stock. The company files for bankruptcy and the bankruptcy court extinguishes all rights of the former shareholders. Reginald learns of the bankruptcy court's decision in December 2011. Rather than wait for a formal notice from the court, Reginald chooses to abandon his WorldCom securities, knowing that his shares are worthless. He takes a capital loss on his 2011 tax return, reflecting the value of his worthless shares as "zero."

A taxpayer may "abandon" a security and treat it as worthless on his tax return. To abandon a worthless security, a taxpayer must permanently surrender all rights to the security and receive no consideration in exchange for it.

*Note: Worthless securities get special tax treatment. Unlike other losses, a taxpayer is allowed to amend a tax return up to **seven years** prior in order to claim a loss from worthless securities. This is more than double the usual three-year statute of limitations for amending returns.

Capital Gain Distributions and Mutual Funds

A mutual fund is a regulated investment company generally created by pooling funds of investors to allow them to take advantage of a diversity of investments and professional management. Mutual funds often sell profitable investments at certain times throughout the year. Owners of mutual funds may receive both **Form 1099-DIV** and **Form 1099-B**.

Form 1099-DIV reports capital gain distributions from the mutual fund. Profits of these sales are reported to the shareholders as capital gain distributions.

If taxpayers (shareholders) decide to sell any of their shares in the mutual fund itself, **Form 1099-B** will be issued. The taxable gain or loss from the sale or exchange of the taxpayer's shares in a mutual fund is reported on **Form 1040, Schedule D**.

What makes these types of distributions unusual, however, is that capital gain distributions are *always* taxed at long-term capital gains tax rates, *no matter how long* a taxpayer has personally owned shares in the mutual fund.

Capital gain distributions can be reported directly on **Form 1040** only if a taxpayer has no other capital gains to report. Otherwise, capital gain distributions must be reported on **Schedule D** along with a taxpayer's other gains and losses.

Qualified Small Business Stock (Section 1244)

There is a special type of stock called Section 1244 Small Business Stock (also called qualified small business stock[72] or QSBS). QSBS is stock in qualifying domestic corporations that is subject to special tax rules that are favorable to the shareholder. Congress has allowed for special treatment for this type of stock in order to spur investment in domestic corporations.

Losses on small business stock are considered ordinary losses (rather than capital losses) and any gain on a 1244 stock is a capital gain.

This means that the losses are not subject to the capital loss limit ($3,000 per year), but gains are still given favorable capital gains rates. The amount that can be deducted as an ordinary loss is $50,000 ($100,000 for joint filers). Ordinary losses are more favorable to the taxpayer because he can deduct this loss against his ordinary gross income.

Losses from the sale of qualifying small business stock are reported on **Form 4797**, *Sales of Business Property*.

In order to qualify, the shareholder must be an individual or partnership. Other entities do not qualify for this specialized treatment—that means that if a corporation buys small business stock, it does not get this type of special tax treatment.

Only the *original purchaser* of the stock can claim an ordinary loss. So, if this stock is inherited or gifted to another person, the special treatment for losses also does not apply.

*Special Rule: Excluded Gains on Small Business Stock

While losses on small business stock are given special treatment, gains on qualified small business stock are also given preferential treatment. This is intentional; in 2011, Congress extended a special exemption in order to stimulate investment in small U.S. corporations. It isn't often that Congress allows for complete exclusion of gain, but qualified small business stock is one of those instances.

The general rule is this:
- A taxpayer generally can exclude up to 50% of the gain from the sale or trade of qualified small business stock held for over five years.
- The exclusion can be up to 75% for stock acquired after February 17, 2009, and up to 100% for stock acquired after September 27, 2010. The stock

---

[72] A "qualified small business" is a domestic C Corporation, the gross assets of which do not exceed $50 million (without regard to liabilities).

must be held for over five years in order to qualify for this 100% exclusion of gain.

- The 100% exclusion for qualified small business stock was extended by Congress to include stock that was purchased after September 27, 2010 and before January 1, 2012 (if held more than five years). The new law eliminates the Alternative Minimum Tax preference for these sales.

So, for example, if a taxpayer purchased qualified small business stock on January 1, 2011, he would have to wait until January 2, 2016 to sell the stock in order to receive the 100% exclusion from gain (the stock must be held OVER five years in order to receive the 100% exclusion from gain).[73]

For its stock to qualify as "qualified small business stock," the corporation must be a small business corporation at the time the stock is issued. This means that the stock:

- Must be issued by a C Corporation with no more than $50 million of gross assets
- Must be held by a non-corporate taxpayer (usually an individual); and
- Must have been acquired by the taxpayer on original issuance. (If the stock is later gifted or inherited, the special treatment does not apply.)

Only stock in a domestic corporation qualifies for this special treatment. Corporate shareholders, estates, or trusts do not qualify for this special loss recognition treatment on the stock they own.

Gains from qualified small business stock are reported on **Schedule D (Form 1040).**

Wash Sales and Disallowed Losses

In general, a wash sale occurs when a taxpayer sells or otherwise disposes of stock or securities (including a contract or option to acquire or sell stock or securities) at a loss and, within 30 days before or after the sale or disposition, the taxpayer buys, acquires, or enters into a contract or option to acquire substantially identical stock or securities.

Example: Carlos sells 1,000 shares of Big Corp stock on December 4, 2010 and takes a loss of $3,200. Carlos has seller's remorse, and on January 1, 2011 he buys back 1,000 shares of Big Corp stock. Because of the IRS wash sale rules, all of the $3,200 loss is disallowed. He cannot take the loss until he finally sells those repurchased shares in some later year. He must add the disallowed loss to the basis of the newly-purchased shares, resulting in an increase to the basis.

---

[73] Under current law, the earliest tax year for which this 100% capital gain exclusion can be claimed is 2015.

A taxpayer cannot deduct losses from sales of securities in a wash sale. A "wash sale" is when a taxpayer sells securities and then turns around and:
- Buys identical securities,
- Acquires substantially identical securities in a taxable trade, or
- Acquires a contract or option to buy identical securities.

The wash sale rule time period actually lasts a total of 61 calendar days: the 30 days before the sale is made, the 30 days after the sale is made, and the day of the sale. To claim a loss as a deduction, the taxpayer needs to avoid purchasing the same stock (or similar security) during the wash sale period. For a sale on July 31, for example, the wash sale period includes all of July and August.

If a taxpayer's loss was disallowed because of the wash sale rules, he must add the disallowed loss to the basis of the new stock or securities. The result is an increase in the taxpayer's basis in the new stock or securities. This adjustment postpones the loss deduction until the disposition of the new stock or securities.[74]

For the purposes of the wash sale rules, securities of one corporation are not considered identical to securities of another corporation. This means that a person can sell shares in one corporation and then purchase shares in a different corporation, and this will not trigger a wash sale. In order for a wash sale to apply, the shares must be identical.

Similarly, "preferred" stock of a corporation is not considered identical to the common stock of the same corporation.

If the number of shares of identical securities a taxpayer buys within 30 days is either more or less than the number of shares sold, the taxpayer must determine the particular shares to which the wash sale rules apply.

A taxpayer does this by matching the shares bought with an equal number of the shares sold. A taxpayer must match the shares bought in the same order that he bought them, beginning with the first shares purchased.

Example: Chelsea bought 100 shares of Best Chocolate stock on September 24, 2010. On February 3, 2011, she sold those shares at a $1,000 loss. On February 10, 2011, Chelsea bought 100 shares of identical stock. Since she *repurchased* identical shares ten days after selling the stock, she cannot deduct her $1,000 loss. She must add the disallowed loss ($1,000) to the basis of the 100 shares she bought on February 10. This is a wash sale.

If a taxpayer sells stock and his or her spouse then repurchases identical stock within 30 days, the taxpayer has a wash sale. This is true even if the spouses file separate tax returns.

---

[74] Wash sale rules do not apply to trades of commodity futures contracts and foreign currencies.

Installment Sales

An installment sale is a sale of property where at least one payment is to be received after the tax year in which the sale occurs. If a taxpayer sells property and receives payments over a number of years, he is allowed to use the "installment method" in order to defer tax. Using the installment method means that the taxpayer would only report gains as each installment is received.

Each payment on an installment sale typically consists of the following three parts:

- Interest income
- Return of the basis in the property
- Gain on the sale

In each year the taxpayer receives a payment, he must include both interest income and gain on the sale. The taxpayer does not include in income the part that is the return of basis in the property.

This is the "installment method." If the taxpayer decides not to use the installment method, he must report ALL the gain in the year of the sale. Installment sale rules do not apply to property that is sold at a loss.

Installment sales are reported on **Form 6252**, *Installment Sale Income*, which is attached to **Form 1040**.

A taxpayer may also be required to complete **Schedule D** or **Form 4797**.

If the property sold is a capital asset, the taxpayer must include the capital gain on **Schedule D.** An example of a capital asset would be the sale of a vacation home.

If the property sold is business or rental property, the installment income is figured on **Form 6252** and then transferred to **Form 4797.** If the installment sale includes any income due to depreciation recapture, it is reported as ordinary income in the year of the sale.

> **Example:** Ernesto sells property in an installment sale at a contract price of $6,000. His gross profit is $1,500. The gross profit percentage on the sale is 25% ($1,500 ÷ $6,000). After subtracting interest, Ernesto reports 25% of each payment, including the down payment, as installment sale income. The remainder (balance) of each payment is the tax-free return of the property's basis.

> **Example:** In 2010, Chloe sold an empty lot with a basis of $40,000 for $100,000. Her gross profit was $60,000. In 2010, she received a $20,000 down payment and the buyer's note for $80,000. The note provides for four annual payments of $20,000 each, plus 8% interest, beginning in 2011. Therefore, Chloe's gross profit percentage is 60%. She must report a gain of $12,000 on each payment received.

The installment method cannot be used for publicly traded securities, such as stocks and bonds. This means that a taxpayer is forced to report gain on the sale of securities in the year of the sale, regardless of whether the proceeds are received until the following year.

Example: Dillon owns 500 shares of stock, which he sells at a gain on December 29, 2011. Dillon doesn't receive the proceeds until January 15, 2012. Dillon is required to report the capital gain on the sale of the stock on his 2011 tax return. He cannot delay reporting the gain, and the sale is not considered an installment sale.

The sale of inventory in the normal course of business is never considered an installment sale.

Installment sales are allowed to related parties. However, if a taxpayer sells property to a relative (a related party transaction, covered next) and the relative later sells or disposes of the property within two years of the original sale, the taxpayer will lose the benefit of installment reporting.

Example: Lou sells a plot of land to his daughter, Melanie. The sale price is $25,000, and Lou realizes a profit on the sale of $10,000. Melanie agrees to pay in five installments of $5,000. A year later, Melanie sells the property to another person. Lou must report the entire profit of $10,000 on the sale, even though he may not have received all the installment payments. The installment method is disallowed on this related party sale, because the property was disposed of before the two-year holding period.

There are exceptions to this rule. If the disposition is due to an involuntary conversion (such as a fire or other disaster), then the property will not be subject to the related party rule. Also, if the sale or exchange later occurs because of death, then the sale will not be subject to the related party transaction rule.

This rule does not apply to a second disposition, if the taxpayer can prove to the IRS's satisfaction that neither the first disposition to the related person nor the second disposition was primarily for the avoidance of tax.

Generally, an involuntary disposition will qualify under the "non-tax avoidance exception," such as when a creditor of the related person forecloses on the property or the related person declares bankruptcy.[75]

---

[75] Publication 537

Special Rules for No-Interest Loans on an Installment Loan

Interest earned on an installment agreement is called the "stated" interest. If interest is not charged or the interest rate is too low, there is a minimum amount of interest the seller is considered to have received. If the installment sale calls for payments in a later year and the sales contract provides for no interest, the taxpayer may have to figure unstated interest, even if it creates a loss on the sale. This "imputed" or "unstated" interest is taxable.

The rules regarding imputed interest were created in order to prevent a seller from increasing his sales price in order to offer a zero percent interest rate so that he might profit from a lower tax liability. The taxpayer must use the Applicable Federal Rate (AFR) to figure the unstated interest on the sale. The AFR must be applied to all loans of six or more months' duration.

The taxpayer then must report interest as ordinary income. Interest is generally not included in a down payment. However, the taxpayer may have to treat part of each later payment as interest, even if it is not called "interest" in the agreement with the buyer.

No gain or loss is recognized on the transfer of an installment obligation between a husband and wife if the transfer is incident to a divorce.

Dealer Sales are Not Installment Sales

Sales of property by a professional dealer who regularly sells the same type of personal property are NOT installment sales. This rule also applies to real property held for sale to customers in the ordinary course of a trade or business (inventory). The sale of inventory is never treated as an installment sale even if the seller receives payment after the year of sale.

However, the rule does not apply to an installment sale of property used for farming. (The taxation of farmers and other special rules that affect farming businesses are covered in Part 2 of the EA exam.)

Related Party Transactions and Capital Losses

Special rules apply to related-party transactions. These are business deals between two parties who are joined by a special relationship. If a taxpayer sells capital assets to a close family member or to a business entity that the taxpayer controls, he might not get all the benefits of the capital gains tax rates, and he may not be able to deduct his losses. The related party transactions were put into place to prevent related persons and entities from shuffling assets back and forth and taking improper losses.

"50% Control" Rule

If a taxpayer controls more than 50% of a corporation or partnership, then any property transactions between the taxpayer and the business would be subject to related party transaction rules.

In general, a loss on the sale of property between related parties is not deductible. When the property is later sold to an unrelated party, gain is recognized only to the extent it is more than the disallowed loss. If the property is later sold at a loss, the loss that was disallowed to the related party cannot be recognized. If a taxpayer sells or trades property at a loss (other than in the complete liquidation of a corporation), the loss is not deductible if the transaction is between the taxpayer and the following related parties:

- Members of immediate family, including a spouse, siblings or half-siblings, ancestors, or descendants (children, grandchildren, etc.). *Note: For the purpose of this rule, an uncle, nephew, stepchild, stepparent, or in-law is not considered a related party.
- A partnership or corporation that the taxpayer controls (a taxpayer "controls" an entity when he has over 50% ownership in it). This also includes partial ownership by other family members.
- A tax-exempt or charitable organization controlled by the taxpayer or a member of his family.
- Losses on sales between certain closely related trusts or business entities controlled by the same owners.

Example: Hillary buys stock from her brother, Leo, for $7,600. Leo's cost basis in the stock is $10,000. He cannot deduct the loss of $2,400 because of the related-party transaction rules. Later, Hillary sells the same stock on the open market for $10,500, realizing a gain of $2,900. Hillary's reportable gain is $500 (the $2,900 gain minus the $2,400 loss not allowed to her brother).

Example: Vicky purchases stock from her father for $8,600. Her father's basis in the stock is $11,000. Vicky later sells the stock on the open market for $6,900. Her recognized loss is $1,700 (her $8,600 basis minus $6,900). Vicky cannot deduct the loss that was disallowed to her father.

In the case of a related party transaction, if a taxpayer sells multiple pieces of property and some are at a gain while others are at a loss, the gains will generally be taxable while the losses cannot be used to offset the gains.

Summary: Capital Gains
Reporting a Capital Gain or Loss

Taxpayers must use **Form 8949** and **Schedule D** to report capital gains and losses on the sale of assets such as the sale of stock.

1. Almost everything a taxpayer owns and use for personal purposes, pleasure, or investment is a capital asset.

2. Taxpayers must report all capital gains, but not all capital losses are deductible. A taxpayer may only deduct capital losses on investment property, not on personal-use property.

3. The tax rates that apply to net capital gain are generally lower than the tax rates that apply to other income. For 2011, the maximum capital gains rate for most people is 15%. For lower-income individuals, the rate may be 0% on some or all of the net capital gain. Rates of 25% or 28% may apply to special types of net capital gain.

4. If capital losses exceed capital gains, a taxpayer may deduct the excess on his tax return to reduce other income, such as wages, up to an annual limit of $3,000 (1,500 if MFS).

Completion of **Form 8949** and **Schedule D** may require information from **Form 1099-B**, **Form 1099-S, Form 1099-DIV**, and information from taxpayer records. **Form 8949** is for reporting all capital gain and loss transactions. The subtotals from **Form 8949** are carried over to **Schedule D** where the gain or loss is calculated in aggregate.

Holding Period

- Short-term property is held one year or less.
- Long-term property is held more than one year.

Long-term capital gains are taxed at a lower rate than short-term gains, so it is always beneficial for a taxpayer to have a long-term holding period, rather than short-term.

Proceeds from a sale:

- **Form 1099-B** reflects gross or net proceeds for a stock or mutual fund.
- **Form 1099-S** usually reflects gross proceeds of real estate transactions. A taxpayer generally won't receive a 1099-S on the sale of a primary residence.

Stock Rules, Wash Sales, and Stock Splits

Stock acquired in a non-taxable stock dividend or stock split has the same holding period as the original stock owned.

If the original stock has a long-term holding period, stock received in a non-taxable stock dividend also has a long-term holding period. Similarly, if the original stock has a short-term holding period, the new stock also has a short-term holding period. A wash sale occurs when a taxpayer sells or otherwise disposes of stock or securities at a loss and within 30 days before or after the sale or disposition, the taxpayer buys identical stock or securities. Losses are disallowed on a wash sale.

Unit 13: Questions

1. Norma sells an empty lot with an adjusted basis of $20,000. Her buyer assumes an existing mortgage on the property of $15,000 and agrees to pay Norma $10,000, with a cash down payment of $2,000 and then $2,000 every year (plus 12% interest) in each of the next four years. The selling price is $25,000. What is Norma's gross profit and gross profit percentage on the installment sale?

A. The gross profit is $5,000, and the gross profit percentage is 50%.
B. The gross profit is $10,000, and the gross profit percentage is 100%.
C. The gross profit is $15,000, and the gross profit percentage is 20%.
D. The gross profit is $5,000, and the gross profit percentage is 100%.

The answer is A. Norma's gross profit is $5,000, and the gross profit percentage is 50%. Her selling price is $25,000 ($15,000 existing mortgage + $10,000 payment over four years). Therefore, Norma's gross profit is $5,000 ($25,000 − $20,000 installment sale basis). The contract price is $10,000 ($25,000 − $15,000 mortgage). Her gross profit percentage is 50% ($5,000 ÷ $10,000). Norma must report half of each $2,000 payment received as gain from the sale. She must also report all interest received as ordinary income. ###

2. What is the maximum number of years a taxpayer can carry over an unused capital loss?

A. One year.
B. Two years.
C. Five years.
D. As many times as required to receive the entire deduction.

The answer is D. Unused capital losses may be carried over year after year until they are all deducted. There is no limit on how many times a loss can be carried over during the taxpayer's life. ###

3. Five years ago, Marsha bought 100 shares of IBM stock. Her sale date was March 10, 2011. Marsha's original cost for the stock was $10,110, plus an additional $35 in broker's fees. When she sold the stock, she received gross proceeds of $8,859. What is the net gain or loss from this transaction?

A. $1,286 in long-term capital loss.
B. $1,286 in short-term capital loss.
C. $1,251 in long-term capital loss.
D. $1,251 in long-term capital gain.

The answer is A. The answer is figured as follows: The original basis is increased by the broker's commission. Therefore, Marsha's adjusted basis is $10,145 ($10,110 + $35). The gross proceeds from the sale is $8,859, which is subtracted from the basis, resulting in a long-term capital loss of $1,286 ($10,145 - $8,859).

4. Emeline purchased 200 shares of stock on January 2, 2011 for $1,000. She sold all the shares on December 31, 2011 for $2,500. On January 3, 2012, the stocks were delivered and payment was submitted to Emeline's account. How should this sale be reported?

A. $1,500 long-term gain on her 2011 return.
B. $1,500 short-term gain on her 2011 return.
C. $1,500 long-term gain on her 2012 return.
D. $1,500 short-term gain on her 2012 return.

The answer is B. The sale and income must be reported in the year the security is sold, regardless of when the proceeds were received. She held the shares for less than one year, so her gain is short-term. Therefore, Emeline has a short-term gain that must be reported on her 2011 tax return. ###

5. An individual taxpayer only has $500 in capital gain distributions from a mutual fund, and no other capital gains or losses to report. Which of the following satisfies the reporting requirements?

A. All capital gain distributions must be entered on Schedule C.
B. The amount may be entered on Form 1040.
C. All capital gain distributions must be entered on Schedule D.
D. If there are no other capital gains or losses, then capital gain distributions do not need to be reported.

The answer is B. Capital gain distributions from mutual funds can be reported directly on **Form 1040** if the taxpayer has no other capital gains to report. Otherwise, capital gain distributions are reported on **Schedule D** along with other gains and losses. ###

6. Ruben bought 100 shares of Excellent Corp. stock on October 1, 2010 when the share price was $26. He then sold them for $20 a share on October 1, 2011. How should this trade be reported, and what is the nature of Ruben's gain or loss?

A. Ruben has a short-term capital loss of $600.
B. Ruben has a long-term capital loss of $500.
C. This is a wash sale.
D. This is a short-term loss of $500.

The answer is A. Ruben has a short-term capital loss of $600 = (100 shares X $26) - (100 shares X $20). Ruben's holding period was not more than one year, which means that the loss must be treated as a short-term capital loss. To determine holding period, begin counting on the date *after* the date the taxpayer acquires the property. ###

7. Amit purchased 100 shares in Foresthill Mutual Fund in April 2011 for $750. He received a capital gain distribution of $120 in 2011. The $120 was reported to him on Form 1099-DIV. How should this be reported on his tax return?

A. Amit must reduce his stock's basis by $120.
B. Amit must report the $120 as interest income.
C. Amit must report the $120 as a long-term capital gain.
D. Amit must report the $120 as a short-term capital gain.

The answer is C. Mutual funds frequently distribute capital gains to shareholders. Capital gain distributions for mutual funds are always taxed at long-term capital gain tax rates, no matter how long a taxpayer has actually held the mutual fund shares. ###

8. Fred bought ten shares of Jixi Corporation stock on October 1, 2010. He sold them for a $7,000 loss on October 1, 2011. He has no other capital gains or losses. He also has $20,000 of wage income. How must Fred treat this transaction on his tax return?

A. Fred may deduct the $7,000 as a long-term capital loss on his 2011 return.
B. Fred may deduct the $7,000 as a short-term capital loss on his 2011 return.
C. Fred may deduct $3,000 as a short-term capital loss to offset his wage income on his 2011 return. The remaining amount ($4,000) must be carried over to future tax years.
D. Fred may not offset any of his wage income due to the passive activity rules. The entire loss must be carried over to future tax years.

The answer is C. Fred has a short-term loss because he did not hold the stock for over one year. He may deduct $3,000 of the loss in 2011, netting against his wage income. The remaining amount ($4,000) must be carried over to future tax years. The carryover retains its character as either long-term or short-term.###

9. What form is used to report an installment sale?

A. Form 6252.
B. Schedule C.
C. Schedule E.
D. Form 2848.

The answer is A. A taxpayer must use **Form 6252** to report installment sale income from casual sales of real or personal property during the tax year. ###

10. Dorian purchased 1,000 shares of Hometown Mutual Fund on February 15, 2008 for $15 per share. On January 31, 2011, he sold all his shares for $3.75 per share. He also earned $45,000 in wages in 2011. He has no other transactions during the year. How should this transaction be reported on his tax return?

A. Dorian has a short-term capital loss of $11,250. He will be allowed to offset $11,250 of his wage income with the capital loss.
B. Dorian cannot claim a capital loss because he has no passive income. He must carry over the entire loss to a future tax year and offset capital gains.
C. Dorian may take a $3,000 capital loss on his 2011 tax return and the remainder of the losses will carry forward to the following year.
D. Dorian may take a $5,000 capital loss on his 2011 tax return and the remainder of the losses will carry forward to the following year.

The answer is C. Dorian cannot deduct all his stock losses in the current year. Dorian may take a $3,000 capital loss on his 2011 tax return and the remainder of the losses will carry forward to following years. ###

11. Melissa purchased 1,000 shares of Devil Foods Company stock in 2009 at $10 per share. She sold 900 shares on January 15, 2011 at $9 per share, resulting in a $900 loss. Melissa's husband, Alex, purchased 900 shares on February 10, 2011. Alex and Melissa keep their finances separate and will file separately (MFS) in 2011. Which of the following is TRUE?

A. Melissa may deduct the $900 capital loss on her tax return.
B. Melissa has a wash sale and her loss is not deductible.
C. Alex may deduct the loss on his separate tax return.
D. None of the above.

The answer is B. The loss is disallowed. Melissa has a wash sale, because her spouse repurchased identical securities within 30 days. It doesn't matter if they file MFS. If a taxpayer sells stock and her spouse then repurchases identical stock within 30 days, the taxpayer has a wash sale. ###

12. Nikhil's adjusted basis in 500 shares of Wediku Corporation was $2,550. If Nikhil sold 500 shares for $3,300, then what is his reported sales price for the shares and the resulting gain or loss?

A. $3,300 sales price and $750 gain.
B. $3,300 sales price and $700 gain.
C. $3,255 sales price and $750 gain.
D. $2,550 sales price and $750 loss.

The answer is A. The sales price is $3,300, which is $750 more than the adjusted basis of the shares. ###

13. Kevin purchased 100 shares of Ford stock last year, for which he paid $1,200. He also paid his broker a $75 fee on the purchase of his stock. A few months later, Kevin sold the stock. His **Form 1099-B** shows $925 as the gross proceeds from the sale. What is the amount Kevin will report as his sales price?

A. $850.
B. $925.
C. $1,000.
D. $1,275.

The answer is B. The sales price of the stock always remains the same. The sales price (or gross proceeds) is never adjusted. The broker's commission is instead added to the stock's basis. ###

14. Kayla's cost basis for 600 shares of Fenway Corporation stock she purchased in December 2008 and then sold in September 2011 was $2,400. Kayla sold the 600 shares for $4,400 and paid a $100 broker's commission. Her broker reported the gross proceeds of $4,400 on **Form 1099-B.** What was the sales price for the shares and the amount and type of capital gain or loss?

A. $4,400 sales price and $2,000 short-term gain.
B. $4,400 sales price and $1,900 long-term gain.
C. $4,500 sales price and $2,100 short-term gain.
D. $4,500 sales price and $1,900 long-term gain.

The answer is B. The sales price was $4,400, which was $1,900 more than the adjusted basis of $2,500 ($2,400 cost + $100 commission) of the shares. ###

15. Colin purchases 100 shares of Entertainment Company stock for $1,000 on December 1, 2010. He sells these shares for $750 on December 22, 2010. Colin has seller's remorse, and on January 19, 2011 he repurchases 100 shares of Entertainment Company stock for $800. Which of the following statements is TRUE?

A. Colin may report his capital losses from the first sale of stock.
B. Colin has a reportable loss in 2010, and a taxable gain in 2011.
C. Colin may not deduct his stock losses and must add the disallowed loss to his basis.
D. Colin may report a $250 capital loss in 2011.

The answer is C. Because Colin bought substantially identical stock, he cannot deduct his loss of $250 on the sale. However, he may add the disallowed loss to the cost of the new stock to obtain his adjusted basis in the new stock. This is called the "wash sale rule." ###

16. If taxpayers cannot provide their basis in a property and the property is later sold, the IRS will deem the basis to be _____.

A. Zero.
B. Fair market value.
C. Actual cost.
D. Average cost.

The answer is A. In order to compute gain or loss on a sale, taxpayers must provide their basis in the sold property. The basis on property is usually its cost. If taxpayers cannot provide their basis in the property, the IRS will deem the basis to be zero. ###

17. Gerardo has 100 shares of Huge Corp stock, which he purchased five years ago for $1,500. In May 2011, Huge Corp issues a non-taxable stock dividend of 50 additional shares. Gerardo sells 60 shares on December 25, 2011. What is his adjusted basis in the 60 shares that he sold in December 2011?

A. $500.
B. $600.
C. $900.
D. $2,250.

The answer is B. Gerardo's basis in the original stock was $1,500 for 100 shares, so his original basis per share was $15 ($1,500/100). The addition of 50 shares means Gerardo's basis per share *decreased* to $10 per share ($1,500/150). Therefore, Gerardo's basis in the 60 shares he sold in December is $600 ($10 adjusted basis per share X 60). ###

18. Which form is used by financial institutions to report gross proceeds from the sale of securities to the taxpayer?

A. Form 1099-S.
B. Form 1099-B.
C. Schedule D.
D. Schedule C.

The answer is B. Brokers report information about the sale of stock shares and other securities on **Form 1099-B.** This form also includes sales price and basis information. ###

19. Which new form is required in order to report capital gain or loss from stock sales?

A. Form 1099-S.
B. Form 6252.
C. Form 8949.
D. None of the above.

The answer is C. All capital gains and losses are now detailed on **Form 8949**; none are reported directly on **Schedule D.** The subtotals from **Form 8949** are then carried over to **Schedule D**, where the aggregate gain or loss is calculated. ###

Unit 14: Non-Recognition Property Transactions

> **More Reading:**
> Publication 523, *Selling Your Home*
> Publication 544, *Sales and Other Dispositions of Assets*

This unit covers non-recognition property transactions. These are transactions where a taxpayer sells or exchanges property without any tax consequences. Some of these transactions are non-taxable, some are tax deferred, and some are considered non-taxable exchanges.

Taxpayers who sell property *usually* have a realized gain or loss on the sale. Taxpayers may also have a realized gain or loss when they trade property. Whether or not the taxpayer must pay tax on the gain or loss depends on the type of transaction.

There are many instances where taxpayers who have a gain on property are not required to recognize the income on their tax return. This chapter will review the most common non-taxable exchanges, which are called "non-recognition property transactions." The three most common transactions that result in "non-recognition" treatment are:

- Like-kind exchanges (Section 1031 exchange)
- Involuntary conversions (Section 1033 exchange)
- Sale of a primary residence (Section 121, excluded gain)

In some cases, these transactions are partially taxable.

Sale of Primary Residence (Section 121)

In many cases, a taxpayer may exclude the gain from the sale of a primary residence. The exclusion from gain is up to $250,000 from the sale of the home ($500,000 on a joint return in most cases). Generally, if the taxpayer can exclude all of the gain, it is not even necessary to report the sale. If all or part of the gain is taxable, then the sale must be reported on **Schedule D**.

A loss on the sale of a primary residence cannot be deducted.[76]

The Section 121 exclusion only applies to a "main home," and does not apply to rental properties or vacation homes. A taxpayer's "main home" is the residence where the taxpayer lives most of the time. It does not have to be a traditional house. The main home can be a:

- House
- Houseboat
- Mobile home
- Cooperative apartment
- Condominium

---

[76] Foreclosures and short sales are not covered in this section. For coverage of forgiven debt due to a foreclosure or short sale, see Unit 6.

In order to qualify as a "home," it must have sleeping, kitchen, and bathroom facilities. Vacation homes and second homes do not qualify for this special non-recognition treatment.

> **Example:** Wayne owns and lives in a house in the city. He also owns a beach house, which he uses only during the summer months. The house in the city is his main home; the beach house is not. Wayne sells the beach house and has $100,000 in gain. The gain cannot be excluded, because the beach house is not his primary residence.

Eligibility Requirements for the Section 121 Exclusion

To be eligible for the exclusion, taxpayers must:

- Have sold the home that has been their main home
- Meet the "ownership" and "use" tests
- Not have excluded gain in the two years prior to the current sale of their home

Taxpayers must report the portion of the gain that exceeds the allowable exclusion amount: $250,000 for individual taxpayers or $500,000 for Married Filing Jointly.

The Ownership Test and Use Test

To claim the exclusion on the gain from the sale of a home, a taxpayer must meet the *ownership test* and *use test*. This means that during the five-year period ending on the date of the sale, the taxpayer must have:

- Owned the home for at least two years (the ownership test), and
- Lived in the home as his main home for at least two years (the use test).

In order to qualify for the exclusion, the taxpayer must NOT have excluded gain on the sale of another home sold during the previous two years.

> **Example:** From the last six years, Lindsay has lived with her parents in the house her parents owned. On September 1, 2010, she bought the house from her parents. She continued to live there until December 14, 2011 when she sold it because she wanted a bigger house. Lindsay does not meet the requirements for exclusion. Although she lived in the property as her main home for more than two years, she did not own it for the required two years. Therefore, she does not meet BOTH the ownership and use tests.

There are special exceptions for Armed Forces, intelligence personnel, and Peace Corps volunteers in the application of the five-year period. We will cover these exceptions later in this unit.

The required two years of ownership and use do not have to be continuous. Taxpayers meet the tests if they can show that they owned and lived in the property as their main home for either 24 full months or 730 days (365 x 2) during the five-year period.

Example: In 2003, Rosie lived in a rented apartment. The apartment building was later changed to a condominium and she bought the condo on December 1, 2008. In 2009, Rosie became ill, and on April 14 of that year she moved into her daughter's home. On July 10, 2011, while still living in her daughter's home, Rosie sold her condominium. Rosie can exclude all the gain on the sale of her condominium because she met the ownership and use tests. Her five-year period is from July 11, 2006 to July 10, 2011 (the date she sold the condo). She owned her condo from December 1, 2008 to July 10, 2011 (over two years). She lived in the residence from July 11, 2006 (the beginning of the five-year period) to April 14, 2009 (over two years).

Ownership and use tests can be met during different two-year periods. However, a taxpayer must meet both tests during the five-year period ending on the date of the sale.

Example: Irene bought and moved into a house in July 2007. She lived there for 13 months and then moved in with her boyfriend and kept her house empty. They broke up in January 2010. She moved back into her own house in 2010 and lived there for 12 months until she sold it in July 2011. Irene meets the ownership and use tests because during the five-year period ending on the date of sale, she owned the house for four years and lived in the house for a total of 25 months.

Short, temporary absences, even if the property is rented during those absences, are still counted as periods of use. Short absences include vacations and trips. Longer breaks, such as a one-year sabbatical, do not.

Example: Katarina bought her home on February 1, 2008. Each year, she left her home for a four-month summer vacation. Katarina sold the house on March 1, 2011. She may exclude the gain (up to $250,000). The vacations are short temporary absences and are still counted toward her periods of use.

Married Homeowners

The ownership and use tests are applied somewhat differently to married homeowners. Married homeowners can exclude up to $500,000 if they meet all of the following conditions:

- They file a joint return.
- Either spouse meets the ownership test (only one is required to own the home).
- Both individuals must meet the use test.
- Neither individual must have excluded gain in the two years before the current sale of the home.

If either spouse does not satisfy all these requirements, the couple cannot claim the maximum $500,000 exclusion. The exclusion amount must be figured as if the couple were unmarried. In order to qualify for the full $500,000 exclusion, the couple must file a joint tax return.

Under the ownership test, each spouse is treated as owning the property during the period that either spouse actually owned it. However, BOTH spouses must meet the "use test."

> **Example:** Leigh sells her main home in June 2011, and she has $350,000 of gain. She marries Kelly in September 2011. Leigh meets the ownership and use tests, but Kelly does not. Leigh can exclude up to $250,000 of gain on her tax return for 2011, whether she files MFJ or MFS. The $500,000 exclusion for joint returns does not apply in this case because Kelly does not meet the use test.

> **Example:** Zaid owns a home that he has lived in continuously for eight years. In June 2008, he marries Annabel. She moves in with her husband and they both live in the house until December 1, 2011 when the house is sold. Zaid meets the ownership test and the use test. Annabel meets the use test, because only Zaid is listed as the owner of the property. On a jointly filed return, they may still claim the maximum $500,000 exclusion because they both meet the use test, and Zaid meets the ownership test.

In the case of an unmarried couple that lives and owns a home together, they would be able to take the $250,000 exclusion individually on their separate returns if they qualify for the use test and the ownership test. Sometimes this exclusion also applies to family members who own a home and live together.

> **Example:** Greta and Sydney are twin sisters. They are both widowed and decide to purchase a home and live together. If they were to later sell the home, then the ownership and use tests would apply to them as well. Each one would be able to claim an exclusion for their portion of the sale on their individual returns ($250,000 exclusion each).

Deceased Spouses and Home Sales

If a taxpayer's spouse dies, there are special rules. A taxpayer is considered to have owned and lived in a home during any period of time when the spouse owned and lived in it as a main home (this is provided that the taxpayer did not remarry before the date of sale). So, in effect, the holding period is "tacked on" for surviving spouses.

Beginning with home sales after 2007, a maximum exclusion ($500,000) by an unmarried surviving spouse is allowed if the surviving spouse sells the home within two years after the date of the spouse's death.

> **Example:** Alice has owned and lived in her home for the last seven years. She marries William in April 2011, and he moves into the home with her. Alice dies six months later, and William inherits the property. He does not remarry. William sells the home on December 1, 2011. Even though William did not own or live in the house for two years, he is considered to have satisfied the ownership and use tests because his period of ownership and use includes the period that Alice owned and used the property before her death. Furthermore, William may qualify to exclude up to $500,000 of the gain because of the special rule that applies to surviving spouses.

This exclusion also applies to a home that is transferred by a spouse if the transfer is part of a divorce. In the case of a divorce, the receiving spouse is considered to have owned the home during any period of time that the transferor owned it.

Five-Year Test Period Suspension for Military Personnel

Taxpayers can choose to have the five-year test period for ownership and use suspended during any period the homeowner (or either spouse if married) served on "qualified official extended duty" as a member of the armed services or Foreign Service of the United States, as an employee of the intelligence community, or as a member of the Peace Corps. This means that the taxpayer may be able to meet the two-year use test even if he and/or his spouse did not actually live in the home during the normal five-year period required of other taxpayers.

Taxpayers are considered on "qualified official extended duty" if they serve at a duty station at least 50 miles from their main home or live in government quarters under government order. Taxpayers are considered to be on extended duty when they are called to active duty for more than 90 days or an indefinite period.

> **Example**: Luis bought a home in 2001 and lived in it for two-and-a-half years. Beginning in 2005, he was on qualified official extended duty in the U.S. Army, and left the home vacant. He sold his home in 2011 and had a $12,000 gain. Luis would normally not meet the use test in the five-year period before the sale. However, Luis can disregard those six years, because of the special exclusion for military taxpayers.

This extension of time can also apply to taxpayers who have recently left the military.

Exception to the Use Test for the Disabled

There is an exception to the use test if, during the five-year period before the sale of the home, the taxpayer becomes physically or mentally unable to care for himself. The taxpayer must have owned and lived in the home for at least one year.

Under this exception, the taxpayer is still considered to have lived in the home during any time that he is forced to live in a medical facility (including a nursing home) because of medical reasons.

Qualifying for a Reduced Exclusion

Taxpayers who owned and used a home for less than two years (meaning they do not meet the ownership and use test) may be able to claim a "reduced exclusion" under certain conditions. These include selling the home due to a change in place of employment, health, or unforeseen circumstances.

Unforeseen Circumstances

If a taxpayer does not meet the ownership and use tests, he can still claim the exclusion for "unforeseen circumstances." The IRS allows for broad interpretation in qualifying for a reduced exclusion under this rule. The IRS will accept that a home sale has occurred primarily because of "unforeseen circumstances" if any of these events occur during the taxpayer's period of use and ownership of the residence:

- Death or divorce.
- Health reasons (for a spouse, child, or other related person, such as a father, sibling, etc. The related person does not have to be a dependent in order for the "special circumstances" to qualify for the exclusion.)
- Unemployment or a job change. (The "job related" exclusion qualifies if the new job is at least 50 miles farther than the old home was from the former place of employment. If there was no former place of employment, the distance between the new place of employment and the old home must be at least 50 miles.)
- Multiple births resulting from the same pregnancy.
- Damage to the residence resulting from a disaster, or an act of war or terrorism.
- Involuntary conversion of the property.

Any of these situations listed can involve the taxpayer, spouse, co-owner, or a member of the taxpayer's household to qualify. The regulations also give the IRS Commissioner the discretion to determine other circumstances as unforeseen. For example, the IRS Commissioner determined the September 11, 2001 terrorist attacks to be an "unforeseen circumstance."

This is called the "reduced exclusion," because the taxpayer must figure the amount of excluded gain based on the actual use of the home.

> **Example:** Justin purchased his new home in Florida in June 2010. Then he suddenly lost his job. He got a new job in North Carolina and sold his house in April 2011. Because the distance between Justin's new place of employment and the home he sold is at least 50 miles, the sale satisfies the conditions of the distance safe harbor. Justin's sale of his home is due to a change in place of employment, and he is entitled to claim a reduced exclusion of gain from the sale.

How to Figure the Reduced Exclusion

The "reduced exclusion" amount equals the full $250,000 or $500,000 (for married couples filing jointly) multiplied by a fraction. The numerator is the shorter of:

- The period of ownership that the taxpayer owned and used the home as a principal residence during the five-year period ending on the sale date, OR
- The period between the last sale for which the taxpayer claimed the exclusion and the sale date for the home currently being sold.

The denominator is two years (or the equivalent in months or days). Figure the amount of the reduced exclusion by determining the number of days the taxpayer actually owned and used the property, divided by either 730 days (two years) or 24 months (two years).

Example: Carrie purchases her home on January 1, 2011 for $350,000. Her mother is diagnosed with terminal cancer, and Carrie must move to care for her. Even though Carrie does not claim her mother as a dependent, the move still qualifies as an unforeseen circumstance. Carrie sells her home on May 1, 2011 for $430,000, realizing a gain of $80,000. She qualifies for the reduced maximum exclusion, and part of her gain is non-taxable. She owned and occupied the home for 121 days (January 1 to May 1). She may exclude $41,438 ($250,000 X [121 ÷ 730]). Therefore, Carrie's taxable gain is $38,562 ($80,000-$41,438). This amount would be a short-term capital gain since she owned the house for less than one year.

Example: Leah, a single taxpayer, lived in her principal residence for one full year (365 days) before selling it at a $400,000 gain in 2011. She qualifies for the reduced exclusion because she is pregnant with triplets (multiple births exclusion). Leah can exclude $125,000 of gain ($250,000 X [365 ÷ 730]).

Study Hint: The EA exam will always have a few questions regarding the sale of a primary residence. If you are asked to figure a reduced maximum exclusion, you will be given the number of days or months. You must then remember the formula.

Land Sale Only and Adjacent Lots

If a taxpayer sells the land on which his main home is located but not the house itself, he cannot exclude the gain. Similarly, the sale of a vacant plot of land with no house on it does not qualify for the Section 121 exclusion.

Example: Theresa purchases an empty lot in 2008 for $90,000, intending to build her dream home. The construction was delayed and her house was never completed. In December 2011, Theresa sells the land for $150,000. She owned the property for over a year, so she has $60,000 of long-term capital gain. None of the gain can be excluded from income, because there is no residence on the property.

However, if a taxpayer sells a vacant lot that is *adjacent to his main home*, he may be able to exclude the gain from the sale under certain circumstances. The home sale exclusion can include gain from the sale of vacant land that was used as part of the principal residence, if the land sale occurs within two years before or after the sale of the home.

The land must be adjacent to land containing the home, and all other requirements of Section 121 must be satisfied. The sale of the land and the sale of the home are treated as one sale for purposes of the exclusion.

Figuring the Gain or Loss on a Home Sale

Once a taxpayer is determined eligible for the exclusion, to figure the gain or loss on the sale of his home, you must know the following:

- Selling price
- Amount realized
- Basis
- Adjusted basis

Selling Price: The selling price is the total amount the taxpayer received for his main home. It includes money, all notes, mortgages, or other debts taken over by the buyer as part of the sale, and the fair market value of any other property or services that the seller received.[77] Real estate sales proceeds are reported on **Form 1099-S**, *Proceeds From Real Estate Transactions*. If a taxpayer does not receive a **Form 1099-S**, he must figure basis by using sale documents and other records.

Amount Realized: The amount realized is the selling price minus selling expenses. Selling expenses include commissions, advertising fees, legal fees, and loan charges paid by the seller, such as points.

Example: Eve is unmarried. She sells her home for $350,000 in 2011. She purchased the home twenty years ago for $50,000 and has lived in it continuously. She pays $4,000 in seller's fees to sell the home. Her amount realized in the sale is $341,000 ($350,000 - $4,000 = $346,000). Her basis is subtracted from her amount realized in order to figure her gain: ($346,000 - $50,000 basis) = $296,000. Eve's gain is $296,000, but she qualifies for a Section 121 exclusion, because she meets the ownership and use tests. Therefore, she may exclude up to $250,000 of her gain from tax. Her taxable gain is figured as follows: ($296,000 gain - $250,000 Section 121 exclusion) = $46,000 in long-term capital gain.

If the selling price or amount realized is $250,000 or less ($500,000 or less if filing jointly), there is no need to figure the realized gain, assuming the "ownership and use" tests are met.

Basis: The basis in a home is determined by how the taxpayer *obtained* the home. For example, if a taxpayer purchases a home, the basis is the cost of the home. If a taxpayer builds a home, then the basis is the building cost plus the cost of land. If a

---

[77] A loss on the sale of a personal residence is not deductible.

taxpayer receives a home through an inheritance or as a gift, the basis is either its FMV or the adjusted basis of the home.

If the taxpayer inherited the home, the basis is its FMV on the date of the decedent's death, or the later alternate valuation date chosen by the representative for the estate.

Adjusted Basis: The *adjusted basis* is the taxpayer's basis in the home increased or decreased by certain amounts. Increases include additions or improvements to the home. In order to be considered a basis *increase*, an addition or improvement must have a useful life of more than one year (example: putting on a new roof or an additional bedroom). Repairs that simply maintain a home in good condition are not considered "improvements" and should not be added to the basis of the property. Decreases to basis include deductible casualty losses, credits, and product rebates.

Formula for figuring adjusted basis:

Basis + Increases - Decreases = Adjusted Basis

Example: Immanuel purchased his home years ago for $125,000. In 2011, Immanuel added another bedroom to the property. The cost of the addition was $25,000. This *increased* the house's basis. Immanuel's adjusted basis is therefore $150,000.

If the *amount realized* is more than the adjusted basis of the property, the difference is a gain and the taxpayer may be able to exclude all or part of it. If the amount realized is less than the adjusted basis, the difference is a non-deductible loss.

Example: Pete sold his main home for $275,000. His selling expenses were $10,000. The amount realized on Pete's sale is $265,000 (selling price minus selling expenses). He purchased his home ten years ago for $180,000. Therefore, his gain on the sale of the house is $85,000 ($265,000 - $180,000). If Pete meets the ownership and use tests, then he can exclude all the gain from the sale of his home, and the sale does not have to be reported on his tax return.

Proceeds from the sale of a main home that meet the ownership and use tests must be reported *only* if the gain is greater than the taxpayer's allowed exclusion: only the excess gain must be reported. Gain from the sale of a home that is not the taxpayer's main home will generally have to be reported as income.

In both cases, the non-excludable gain is taxable gain and must be reported on **Schedule D**. If the home was used for business purposes or as rental property, the gain would be reported on **Form 4797**.

If the taxpayer owns a home for one year or less, the gain is reported as a short-term capital gain. If the taxpayer owns the home for more than one year, the gain is reported as a long-term capital gain.

> **Gain = Amount realized > Adjusted basis**
> **Loss = Amount realized < Adjusted basis**

If the amount realized is LESS than the adjusted basis, the difference is a loss. A loss on the sale of a primary residence cannot be deducted. A loss on the sale of business property can be deducted, but will be covered in Book 2 of the EA study guide.

The taxpayer cannot include the fees and costs for obtaining a mortgage in the home's basis. These fees are not deductible. They include any costs that the taxpayer would have had to pay even if he paid cash for the home rather than financing it. These fees include pest inspections, title fees, etc.

However, if a taxpayer pays "points," then the points can be deducted as mortgage interest on Schedule A. The IRS defines "points" as prepaid interest paid by a home buyer at closing in order to obtain a mortgage or to obtain a lower interest rate.

If the taxpayer took depreciation deductions because he used his home for business purposes or as a rental property, he cannot exclude the part of the gain equal to any depreciation allowed (or allowable) as a deduction. Section 121 applies only to the non-rental (or non-business) portion.

> **Example:** Erica owns a duplex. She lives in one side and rents out the other side. Both of the units are the same size. She purchased the duplex in 2004 for $200,000. In 2011, Erica sells the duplex for $340,000. She has a **total gain** of $140,000. Since only half of the duplex counts as her primary residence, she would have to split the gain based on the portion of the property that qualifies as her main home. Under Section 121, Erica may exclude one half of the gain ($70,000). The other half of the gain ($70,000) is long-term capital gain. The rental portion of the duplex is treated as a sale of rental property (business property). Erica also has the option to reinvest the proceeds of the sale of her rental property into a new property by executing a Section 1031 exchange (covered next).

Like-Kind Exchanges (Section 1031 exchange)

A like-kind exchange occurs when similar business property is exchanged. If a taxpayer trades business or investment property (such as a rental property) for similar property, he does not have to pay tax on the gain or deduct any loss until he disposes of the property he received. This is the concept of a Section 1031 exchange. To qualify for non-recognition treatment, the exchange must meet all of the following conditions:

- The property must be business or investment property. A personal residence does not qualify.
- The property must not be "held primarily for sale" (such as inventory).

- Securities such as stocks and bonds do not qualify for like-kind exchange treatment.
- Partnership interests do not qualify for like-kind exchange treatment.
- There must be an *actual exchange* of property (the exchange for CASH is treated as a sale, not an exchange).
- The property to be received must be identified in writing within 45 days after the date of transfer of the property given up.

The replacement property must be received by the earlier of:
- The 180th day after the date on which the original property was given up in the trade, or
- The due date, including extensions, for the tax return for the year in which the transfer of the property relinquished occurs.

The most common type of 1031 exchange is an exchange of real estate. Taxpayers must report a like-kind exchange to the IRS on **Form 8824**, *Like-Kind Exchanges*.

Rules Regarding Acceptable Like-Kind Exchanges

Some trades are not eligible for like-kind treatment. For an exchange to qualify as a Section 1031 exchange, the property must be "like-kind" property. For example, the trade of real estate for real estate or personal property for personal property is a trade of "like-kind property." Real properties (real estate) are generally acceptable as "like-kind," regardless of whether the properties are improved or unimproved. For instance, an exchange of a rental property for farmland would be an acceptable trade.

In order for the exchange to qualify as a Section 1031 exchange, the property must be the same "class" of property. For example, the trade of an apartment house for a store building or a panel truck for a pickup truck qualifies as a trade of "like" property. However, the exchange of a semi-truck for a plot of land would not qualify as a Section 1031 exchange, even if both properties were business properties.

Example: Casey exchanges a private jet with an adjusted basis of $400,000 for an office building valued at $375,000. This exchange does not qualify as a 1031 exchange. Private property (the jet) cannot be exchanged with real property (the building). Non-recognition treatment would be disallowed in this case.

The trade of a piece of factory machinery for a factory building is NOT a qualifying exchange. Also, any equipment or other business property used within the United States and property used outside the United States is not "like property."

However, exchanges of real property generally qualify for like-kind treatment, even if the property is dissimilar in actual use.

Example: Rebecca exchanges 100 acres of farmland for an apartment building in the city. This exchange does qualify for like-kind treatment.

The exception to this rule is for foreign property. Real estate located *inside* the United States and real estate located *outside* the United States is not "like property" and does not qualify for Section 1031 treatment.

A taxpayer cannot deduct a loss in a Section 1031 exchange transaction.

Unacceptable and Disallowed Trades

For the Enrolled Agent exam, you must know which types of trades are considered "unacceptable trades" by the IRS. Properties are "like-kind" if they are of the same nature or character, even if they differ in grade or quality.

Intangible assets, such as trademarks, may still qualify for like-kind exchange treatment. However, the following types of property will NOT qualify for Section 1031 treatment:

- Livestock of different sexes[78]
- Securities, bonds, stocks, or notes
- Currency exchanges
- The exchange of partnership interests

What is "Boot"?

Although the Internal Revenue Code itself does not use the term "boot," this term is frequently used in the tax field and in the IRS publications to describe property that is not "like-kind" property. The receipt of "boot" will cause a realized gain on an otherwise non-taxable exchange.

Usually this occurs when two people exchange property that is unequal in value. A typical transaction involves one party exchanging property with another party who exchanges property and some additional cash in order to make up the difference. The party that receives cash will have a partially taxable exchange.

The exchange is still valid, but the taxpayer who receives boot may have to recognize a taxable gain. Boot received can be offset by qualified costs paid during the transaction.

Example: Sloan wishes to exchange his rental property in a 1031 exchange. His relinquished rental property has an FMV of $60,000 and an adjusted basis of $30,000. Sloan's replacement property has an FMV of $50,000, and he also receives $10,000 in cash as part of the exchange. Sloan, therefore, has a realized gain of $30,000 on the actual exchange, but he is required to pay tax on only $10,000—the cash (boot) received in the exchange. The rest of his gain is deferred until he sells or disposes of the property at a later date.

If you receive boot in an exchange, its fair market value is recognized as taxable gain. However, this gain cannot exceed the amount of gain that would have been recognized if the property had been sold in a taxable transaction.

---

[78] The livestock exception has been tested on numerous prior exams.

Sometimes, boot is recognized when two people exchange property that is subject to a liability. Liabilities on property are "netted" against each other. The taxpayer is treated as having received "boot" only if he is relieved of a greater liability than the liability he assumes.

This is also called "debt reduction boot," and it occurs when a taxpayer's debt on the replacement property is less than the debt on the relinquished property. "Debt reduction boot" most often occurs when a taxpayer is "trading down" in an exchange (acquiring a cheaper or less valuable property).

Basis of Property Received in a Like-Kind Exchange

The basis of the property received is generally the adjusted basis of the property transferred.

Example: Adrian exchanges rental real estate (adjusted basis $50,000, FMV $80,000) for another rental property (FMV $80,000). No cash was exchanged in the transaction. Adrian's basis in the new property is the same as the basis of his old property ($50,000). Basis should be increased by any amount that was treated as a dividend, plus any gain recognized on the trade. Basis should be decreased by any cash received and the FMV of any other (additional) property received.

Example: Peyton bought a new diesel truck for use in her delivery business. She paid $43,000 cash, plus she traded in her old truck for $13,600. The old truck cost $50,000 two years ago. Peyton took depreciation deductions of $39,500 on the old vehicle. Even though she deducted depreciation of $39,500, the $3,100 gain on the exchange ($13,600 trade-in allowance minus her $10,500 adjusted basis) is not reported because the gain is postponed under the rules for like-kind exchanges.

The basis of any other or additional property received is its fair market value on the date of the trade. The taxpayer is taxed on any gain realized, but only up to the amount of the money and the fair market value of the "unlike" (or boot) non-qualified property received.

Example: Judy has a rental house with an adjusted basis of $70,000. In 2011, Judy trades the rental house for an empty lot with an FMV of $150,000. Judy's basis in the empty lot is $70,000, which is the adjusted basis from her previous property.

Property Plus Cash

If a taxpayer trades property and also pays money, the basis of the property received is the basis of the property given up, increased by any additional money paid.

Example: Jorge trades a plot of land (adjusted basis $30,000) for a different plot of land in another town (FMV $70,500). He also pays an additional $4,000 in cash. Jorge's basis in the NEW land is $34,000 (his $30,000 basis in the old land plus the $4,000 additional money he paid).

Section 1031 Exchanges Between Related Parties

Like-kind exchanges are allowed between related parties and family members. However, if *either* party disposes or sells the property within two years after the 1031 exchange, the exchange is usually disqualified; any gain or loss that was deferred in the original transaction must be recognized in the year the disposition occurs.

For the purposes of this rule, a "related person" includes close family members (spouses, siblings, parents, and children). There are some exceptions to this "two-year" rule:

- If one of the parties originally involved in the exchange dies, the two-year rule does not apply.
- If the property is subsequently converted in an involuntary exchange (such as a fire or a flood), the two-year rule does not apply.
- If the exchange is genuinely NOT for tax avoidance purposes, the subsequent disposition will generally be allowed.

Exchanges between related parties get close scrutiny by the Internal Revenue Service, because they are often used by taxpayers to evade taxes on gains.

Involuntary Conversions (Section 1033)

An involuntary conversion occurs when property is destroyed, stolen, condemned, or disposed of under the threat of condemnation. If a taxpayer's property is damaged or destroyed and the taxpayer receives an award, insurance money, or some other type of payment, then the taxpayer has an "involuntary conversion." Involuntary conversions are also called *involuntary exchanges*.

In order to qualify as an involuntary conversion, the property must be converted as a result of:

- Theft, destruction, or other disaster,
- Condemnation, or
- Threat of condemnation.

The destruction or condemnation must be beyond the taxpayer's control in order to qualify.

Gain or loss from an involuntary conversion of property is usually recognized for tax purposes unless the property is a main home. A taxpayer reports the gain or deducts the loss on his tax return in the year the gain or loss is realized. A taxpayer cannot deduct a loss from an involuntary conversion on personal-use property unless the loss resulted from a casualty or theft.

However, a taxpayer may be able to AVOID reporting a gain on an involuntary conversion. This type of conversion is called a "Section 1033" conversion.

He does not have to report the gain if he receives or invests in property that is similar to the converted property. The gain on the involuntary conversion is then deferred until a taxable sale or exchange occurs at a later date.

> **Example:** Denise owns a residential rental with an adjusted basis of $50,000. It is destroyed by a hurricane in 2011. Her property is insured, so the insurance company gives Denise a check for $100,000, which is the fair market value of the home. Denise buys a replacement rental property six months later for $100,000. Her "realized gain" on the involuntary conversion is $50,000 ($100,000 insurance settlement minus her $50,000 basis). However, Denise does not have to recognize any taxable gain because she reinvested all the insurance proceeds in another, similar property. This is an example of a "qualified" 1033 exchange.

If a taxable gain is realized from insurance proceeds or some other source, tax on the gain can be deferred by reinvesting the proceeds in property similar to the property that was subject to the involuntary conversion. The taxpayer generally has two years to make a reinvestment in similar property in order to postpone the recognition of the gain. Some property is allowed a longer replacement period.

The Replacement Period

The replacement period for an involuntary conversion generally ends two years after the end of the first tax year in which any part of the gain on the condemnation is realized.

> **Example:** Barney owns a dog grooming business. On September 1, 2011, a flood destroys a storage shed filled with his grooming supplies. Barney's insurance company reimburses him for the entire loss. Barney has until December 31, 2013 to replace the shed and supplies using the insurance proceeds he received. Barney is not required to report the insurance proceeds on his 2011 tax return. So long as Barney reinvests all the insurance proceeds in the replacement property, then he will not have any gain.

Real property that is held for investment or used in a trade or business is allowed a three-year replacement period. The replacement period is four years for livestock that is involuntarily converted because of weather-related conditions. If the property is subject to an involuntary conversion in a presidentially declared disaster area, then the replacement period can be up to five years.

Property Type	Replacement period
Most property except those noted below.	Two years
Real property that is held for investment or business use. This includes residential rentals, office buildings, etc.	Three years
Sale of livestock due to weather-related conditions.	Four years

If a taxpayer reinvests in replacement property similar to the converted property, the replacement property's basis is the same as the converted property's basis on the date of the conversion. The taxpayer will have a "carryover basis" in the new property.

Essentially, the taxpayer's basis in the new property will be its cost, reduced by any gain realized on the old property that was not recognized.

The basis may be *decreased* by the following:
- Any loss a taxpayer recognizes on the involuntary conversion
- Any money a taxpayer receives that he does not spend on similar property

The basis is *increased* by the following:
- Any gain a taxpayer recognizes on the involuntary conversion
- Any cost of acquiring the replacement property

Example: Paula paid $100,000 for a rental property five years ago. After factoring in her depreciation deductions, her adjusted basis in the property is $75,000 at the beginning of 2011. The property is insured for $300,000 and is destroyed by a flood in June 2011. On December 15, 2011, Paula receives a $300,000 payment from her insurance. She reinvests all the insurance proceeds, plus $5,000 more of her own savings, into a new rental apartment building. She qualifies to defer all of her gain. Her basis in the new rental property is $80,000 ($75,000 + $5,000 of her additional investment).

Example: Franco owns an apartment building in Florida with a basis of $150,000. The building was destroyed by a mudslide and Franco eventually receives an insurance settlement of $300,000. A year later, Franco decides to purchase another apartment building in Hawaii for $290,000. Franco's "realized gain" on the involuntary conversion is $150,000 ($300,000 - $150,000 basis). Franco must recognize $10,000 of gain, because he received an insurance payment of $300,000, but only spent $290,000 on the replacement property ($300,000 - $290,000). Franco must report $10,000 in capital gain and his basis in the new property will be $150,000, which is calculated as the cost of the new property in Hawaii minus the deferred gain ($290,000 - $140,000 = $150,000). If Franco had used all the insurance proceeds and invested it in the new property, he would not have to report any taxable gain.

Condemnations

A condemnation is a type of involuntary conversion. Condemnation is the process by which private property is seized from its original owner for public use, such as by a local government. The property may be taken by the government or by a private organization that has the legal power to seize it.

The owner generally receives a condemnation award (money or property) in exchange for the property that is taken. A condemnation is like a forced sale, the owner being the seller and the government being the buyer.

Example: The federal government is authorized to acquire land for public parks. The government tells Trevor that it is condemning his farmland in order to use it as a public park. Trevor goes to court to try to keep his property. The court decides in favor of the government, which takes Trevor's property and pays him $400,000 in exchange. Trevor's basis in the farmland was $80,000. He decides not to purchase replacement farmland. Therefore, he has a taxable event, and $320,000 would need to be recognized as income ($400,000 - $80,000 = $320,000). If Trevor were to purchase replacement property with the condemnation award, he would have a non-taxable Section 1033 exchange.

A condemnation award is the money that is paid for the condemned property. Amounts taken out of the award to pay debts on the property are considered paid to the taxpayer and are included in the amount of the award.

Example: The state condemned Gabriel's property in order to build a light rail system. The court award was set at $200,000. The state paid Gabriel only $148,000 because it paid $50,000 to his mortgage company and also $2,000 in accrued real estate taxes. Gabriel is considered to have received the entire $200,000 as a condemnation award.

Postponing Gain or Loss from an Involuntary Conversion

Gain or loss from an involuntary conversion is not recognized if the taxpayer receives similar property. The basis for the new property is the same as the basis for the converted property. The gain on the involuntary conversion is deferred indefinitely until a taxable sale or exchange occurs.

If a taxpayer has an involuntary conversion and then purchases replacement property, he can elect to postpone reporting gain on the conversion. The taxpayer can postpone reporting all the gain if the replacement property costs at least as much as the amount realized from the sale.

Example: Ayah is a self-employed tax preparer. She bought an office copier for $1,500 in 2008 and deducted $780 depreciation. In 2011, a small fire destroyed the machine and Ayah received $1,200 from her fire insurance, realizing a gain of $480 ($1,200 - $720 adjusted basis). She chose to postpone reporting the gain, but her replacement machinery cost only $1,000. The taxable gain under the rules for involuntary conversions is limited to the remaining $200 insurance payment. All the replacement property is depreciable business property, so the ordinary income that Ayah must recognize from the conversion on her tax return is only $200.

To qualify for non-recognition treatment, the *replacement property* must be obtained within a certain time period. The taxpayer has two years to roll over the condemnation or insurance proceeds from the involuntary conversion into a new investment. The replacement property must be "similar or related in service or use."

The replacement period is longer for business-use real property (real estate) and real property held for investment. In this case, the replacement period is three years. In both cases, the replacement property must be purchased before the end of the tax year in which the replacement deadline applies.

> **Example:** Joel owns a bar and pool hall. In 2011, the building is condemned by the city because of the discovery of asbestos in the building. Joel has until December 31, 2014 to replace the condemned pool hall with a similar building.

Condemnation of a Primary Residence

If a taxpayer has a gain because his main home is condemned, he can generally exclude the gain as if he had sold the home (the Section 121 exclusion). The taxpayer can exclude up to $250,000 of the gain (up to $500,000 if MFJ).

> **Example:** Lane and Candace are married and file jointly. They paid $100,000 for their home ten years ago. The house is insured for $700,000. Their home is destroyed by fire in 2011, so they receive an insurance payment of $700,000. They have a realized gain on the conversion of $600,000 ($700,000 - $100,000). But $500,000 of the gain would be excluded under Section 121 (the exclusion for the sale of primary residence), leaving $100,000 as taxable long-term capital gain. Lane and Candace can also choose to reinvest the insurance proceeds under the rules for involuntary conversions and defer all the gain.

Summary: Non-Recognition Property Transactions

Section 121: Sale of Primary Residence

To be eligible for the exclusion, taxpayers must meet the following conditions:
- The home they sold had to be their main home
- They meet the ownership and use tests
- They did not exclude gain in the two years before the current sale of the home

A main home is the place the taxpayer lived most of the time. The ownership and use tests require that, during the five-year period ending on the date of the sale, the taxpayers:
- Owned the home for at least two years (the ownership test), and
- Lived in the home as their main home for at least two years (the use test).

The required two years of ownership/use do not have to be continuous. The maximum that can be excluded is $250,000 or $500,000 for MFJ.

Section 1031 Exchange: Like-Kind Exchanges

Section 1031 only applies to business properties. Section 1031 does NOT apply to exchanges of inventory, stocks, bonds, notes, other securities or evidence of indebtedness, or partnership interests. Livestock of different sexes are not like-kind properties. Also, property used in the United States and property used outside the United States do NOT qualify as like-kind properties.

The property to be received must be identified within 45 days after the date of transfer of the property given up. The replacement property must be received by the earlier of:
- The 180th day after the date on which the original property was given up in the trade, or
- The due date, including extensions, for the tax return for the year in which the transfer of the property relinquished occurs.

The most common type of 1031 exchange is an exchange of real estate. Taxpayers must report a like-kind exchange to the IRS on **Form 8824,** *Like-Kind Exchanges.*

Section 1033: Involuntary Conversions

In order to qualify as an involuntary conversion, a property must be converted as a result of:
- Theft, destruction, or other natural disaster,
- Condemnation, or
- Threat of condemnation.

The gain on the involuntary conversion can be deferred if insurance or condemnation proceeds are reinvested. The taxpayer will have a "carryover basis" in the new property. Essentially, his basis in the new property will be its cost, reduced by any gain realized on the old property that was not recognized.

Unit 14: Questions

Sale of Primary Residence: Questions

1. Erik sold his home for $275,000. His selling expenses were $10,000. What is the amount realized on this sale?

A. $265,000.
B. $275,000.
C. $285,000.
D. Some other amount.

The answer is A. The amount realized on Erik's sale is $265,000 (selling price minus selling expenses). ###

2. Isaiah lived in and owned his home for fifteen months. In 2011, he decided to move in with his new girlfriend, so he sold his home for $285,000. His adjusted basis in the home is $160,000. What is the amount and nature of his taxable gain on the sale?

A. $0 (the gain is excluded under Section 121).
B. $160,000 short-term capital gain.
C. $125,000 long-term capital gain.
D. $125,000 short-term capital gain.

The answer is D. Since he does not meet the ownership or use tests, he cannot exclude any of his gain under Section 121. Therefore, the correct answer is $125,000, which is the result of subtracting the adjusted basis in the home from the amount realized ($285,000 - $160,000 = $125,000). Since he owned the property for less than a year, his gain is taxed as a short-term capital gain. ###

3. Uri bought his principal residence for $250,000 on May 3, 2010. He sold it on May 3, 2011 for $400,000 because he wanted to move to Hawaii. What is the amount and character of his gain?

A. Long-term ordinary gain of $650,000.
B. Long-term capital gain of $150,000.
C. Short-term ordinary gain of $250,000.
D. Short-term capital gain of $150,000.

The answer is D. Uri owned the home for one year or less, so the gain is reported as a short-term capital gain. He must start counting his holding period AFTER the date of purchase. ###

4. Lucille owns a home in the Vail ski area (the "ski home"). She stays at the ski home most weekends and spends the entire months of December, January, and February there. When she is not at the ski home, she lives in a four-room apartment that she rents in Denver. For over half the year, she lives in Denver. What is Lucille's primary residence for the purposes of the Section 121 exclusion?

A. Her ski home in Vail.
B. Her apartment in Denver.
C. She is considered a transient for tax purposes.
D. None of the above.

The answer is B. Lucille's main home is her rental apartment in Denver because she lives there most of the time. If she were to sell the ski home, she would not qualify for the Section 121 exclusion on the sale because it is a vacation home and not her primary residence. ###

5 Heather, a single woman, bought her first home in June 2001 for $350,000. She lived continuously in the house until she sold it in July 2011 for $620,000. Which of the following is TRUE?

A. Heather may exclude up to $250,000 in gain. The remaining amount must be reported and will be taxed as a long-term capital gain.
B. Heather may exclude all the gain. There is no amount that needs to be reported.
C. Heather may not exclude any of the gain.
D. Heather may exclude $250,000 in gain. The remaining amount must be reported as a short-term capital gain.

The answer is A. Heather is able to exclude the maximum amount of gain ($250,000) from the sale of her home. Her gain is $270,000 ($620,000 - $350,000). Her taxable gain is $20,000 ($270,000 gain - $250,000 exclusion). The $20,000 taxable gain must be reported as a long-term capital gain. ###

6. Mitchell purchased his primary residence for $350,000 on January 1, 2008. On January 3, 2011, he sells the home for $320,000, incurring a loss of $30,000. How is this transaction reported?

A. Mitchell has a short-term capital loss that can be reported on Schedule D.
B. Mitchell cannot deduct any loss from the sale of his home on his return.
C. Mitchell has a long-term capital loss that can be reported on Schedule D.
D. Mitchell has a deductible casualty loss.

The answer is B. If a taxpayer has a loss on the sale of a primary residence, he cannot deduct it on his return. Losses from the sale of a main home are never tax-deductible. ###

7. Which of the following would generally NOT be acceptable as "unforeseen circumstances" for a taxpayer to take a reduced exclusion on the sale of his primary residence?

A. The home is condemned by the city.
B. A divorce.
C. The birth of twin girls.
D. A move to a warmer climate for general health.

The answer is D. The move to a warmer climate would not qualify. All of the following events would be qualifying events in order to claim a reduced exclusion from a premature sale:
•A divorce or legal separation.
•A pregnancy resulting in multiple births.
•Serious health reasons. (The person who is sick does not need to be the taxpayer's dependent).
•The home is sold after being seized or condemned (such as by a government agency).
•The move is because of a new job or new employment.
If any of these exceptions apply, then the taxpayer may figure a reduced exclusion based on the number of days the taxpayer owned and lived in the residence. ###

8. Geoff sold his main home in 2011 at a $29,000 gain. He meets the ownership and use tests to exclude the gain from his income. However, he used one room of the home for business in 2008 and 2009. His records show he claimed $3,000 in depreciation for a home office. What is Geoff's taxable gain on the sale, if any?

A. $0.
B. $1,000.
C. $2,000.
D. $3,000.

The answer is D. Geoff can exclude $26,000 ($29,000 - $3,000) of his gain. He has a taxable gain of $3,000. He must report the gain from depreciation recapture. If a taxpayer took depreciation deductions because he used his home for business purposes or as a rental property, he cannot exclude the part of the gain equal to any depreciation allowed (or allowable) as a deduction. ###

9. Bob and Grace were married in January 2007. They purchased their first home in March 2007 for $150,000. In February 2011, Bob and Grace legally separated, and Grace was granted total ownership of the home by the divorce court as part of the divorce settlement. The divorce became final on June 2011, and the fair market value of the home at the time of the transfer was $370,000. Grace sells the house on December 23, 2011 for $480,000. What is Grace's taxable gain in the transaction?

A. $0.
B. $80,000.
C. $120,000.
D. $210,000.

The answer is B. Special rules apply to divorced taxpayers. Grace meets the ownership and use tests, and the basis in the property remains the same. Transfers related to a divorce are generally non-taxable, and the fair market value of the property at the time of the divorce has no bearing on the taxable outcome. The gain is figured as follows:

Original cost	$150,000
Sale price	$480,000
Total realized gain	$330,000
Sec. 121 exclusion	($250,000)
Taxable gain	$80,000

Since she owned the property for longer than one year, the taxable portion of Grace's gain would be reported as a long-term capital gain. ###

10. Alfred and Kaye are married and file jointly. They owned and used a home as their principal residence for 15 months. Alfred got a new job in another state and they sold their home in order to move for the new employment opportunity. What is the maximum amount that can be excluded from income under the rules regarding a "reduced exclusion"?

A. $22,727.
B. $250,000.
C. $312,500.
E. $500,000.

The answer is C. In this case, a reduced exclusion is available, even though the taxpayers did not live in the home for two full years. They qualify for a reduced exclusion because Alfred is moving for a change in employment. In this case, their "maximum reduced exclusion" is $312,500 [$500,000 x (15 months/24 months)]. The reduced exclusion applies when the premature sale is primarily due to a move for employment in a new location. ###

11. Shane and Phyllis move after living in their home for 292 days, because Phyllis became pregnant with triplets and they need a larger home. The gain on the sale of the home is $260,000. Since they have lived there for less than two years but meet one of the exceptions, what is the actual amount of their reduced exclusion? (Two years=730 days)

A. $60,000.
B. $200,000.
C. $260,000.
D. $500,000.

The answer is B. The couple has an exclusion of $200,000 (292/730 multiplied by the $500,000 exclusion available for married taxpayers). The remaining $60,000 would be considered taxable capital gain income and would be reported on Schedule D. This move qualifies for the "reduced exclusion," because multiple births from the same pregnancy are considered a "health related" move. ###

12. Regina bought a house for $189,000 in July 2007. She lived there continuously for 13 months and then moved in with her boyfriend. They later separated and Regina moved back into her own house in 2010 and lived there for 12 months until she sold it in July 2011 for $220,000. What is the amount and nature of her gain?

A. Regina has no taxable gain, because the sale qualifies for a Section 121 exclusion.
B. $31,000 long-term capital gain.
C. $31,000 short-term capital gain.
D. Some other amount.

The answer is A. This sale qualifies for Section 121 treatment. Regina meets the ownership and use tests because during the five-year period ending on the date of sale, she owned the house for four years and lived in it for a total of 25 months. The gain is not taxable and does not need to be reported. ###

Like-Kind Exchanges: Questions

13. How should taxpayers report Section 1031 exchanges to the IRS?

A. Form 8824.
B. Form 4787.
C. Schedule C.
D. Schedule D.

The answer is A. Taxpayers must report a like-kind exchange to the IRS on **Form 8824**, *Like-Kind Exchanges*. ###

14. Samson exchanged a rental building for another rental building. He had a basis of $16,000, plus he had made $10,000 in improvements prior to the exchange. He exchanged it for a building worth $36,000. Samson did not recognize any gain from the exchange on his individual tax return. What is Samson's basis in the new property?

A. $26,000.
B. $36,000.
C. $10,000.
D. $16,000.

The answer is A. Samson's basis in the new building is based on his basis in the old building, which was $16,000 + $10,000 additional improvements = $26,000 basis. ###

15. Which of the following transactions DO NOT qualify for a Section 1031 like-kind exchange?

A. An exchange of business city property and farm property.
B. An exchange of one trademark for another trademark.
C. An exchange of a business desk for a business printer.
D. An exchange of inventory for different inventory.

The answer is D. Inventory never qualifies for like-kind exchange treatment. The property must NOT be held "primarily for sale," such as merchandise, retail stock, or inventory. Generally, real property exchanges will qualify for like-kind treatment, even though the properties themselves might be dissimilar. ###

16. Allen is a flight instructor. He trades in a small plane (adjusted basis $300,000) for another, larger plane (FMV $750,000) and pays $60,000 in an additional down payment. He uses the plane 100% in his flight instruction business. What is his basis in the new plane?

A. $300,000.
B. $360,000.
C. $690,000.
D. $750,000.

The answer is B. Allen's basis is $360,000: the $300,000 basis of the old plane plus the $60,000 cash paid. The fair market value of the property has no bearing on Allen's basis in the new property. ###

17. Bailey exchanges his residential rental property (adjusted basis $50,000, FMV $80,000) for a different rental property (FMV $70,000). What is Bailey's basis in the NEW property?

A. $50,000.
B. $70,000.
C. $80,000.
D. $100,000.

The answer is A. His basis in the new property is the same as the basis of the old ($50,000). The basis of the property received is the same as the basis of the property given up. ###

18. Jacob exchanges a residential rental in Las Vegas with a basis of $100,000 for an investment property in Miami Beach valued at $220,000 plus $15,000 in cash. What is Jacob's taxable gain on the exchange, and what is the basis of the new property on Miami Beach?

A. Taxable gain:$15,000. Basis: $100,000.
B. Taxable gain:$0. Basis: $235,000.
C. Taxable gain:$15,000. Basis: $220,000.
D. Taxable gain:$15,000. Basis: $135,000.

The answer is A. Jacob's total realized gain on the exchange is $135,000 ([$220,000 + $15,000] - $100,000 basis in old property). Only the cash boot is taxable ($15,000). Jacob's basis in the new building will be $100,000 (the original basis in the land he gave up). ###

Involuntary Conversions: Questions

19. Katherine owns a yacht that she uses for personal use. Her purchase price was $150,000. The yacht is destroyed by a tsunami in 2011. Katherine collects $175,000 from her insurance company and promptly reinvests all the proceeds in a larger, new yacht, which costs her $201,000. What is her basis in the new yacht?

A. $175,000.
B. $176,000.
C. $201,000.
D. $226,000.

The answer is B. The answer is figured as follows: ($175,000 -$150,000) = $25,000: deferred gain; ($201,000-$25,000) = $176,000: new basis in the asset. Since Katherine purchased replacement property, the basis of the replacement property is the cost of the new yacht ($201,000) MINUS her deferred gain ($25,000). ###

19. A tornado destroyed Bryant's primary residence home on July 15, 2009. He wants to replace the home using a Section 1033 exchange for involuntary conversions. What is the latest year that Bryant can replace the property in order to defer any gain from the insurance reimbursement?

A. Bryant must make the election by December 31, 2011.
B. Bryant must make the election by July 15, 2012.
C. Bryant must make the election by July 15, 2011.
D. Bryant must make the election by December 31, 2012.

The answer is A. Bryant must acquire qualifying replacement property by December 31, 2011 (two years from the END of the gain year) in order for the involuntary conversion to be a qualified Section 1033 exchange. ###

21. Christian owns an office building with a $400,000 basis. The building was destroyed by a fire in 2011. Christian receives insurance money totaling $600,000. He purchases a new office building for $450,000 and then invests the rest of the insurance proceeds in stocks. Which of the following statements is true?

A. Christian has $200,000 in taxable gain he must recognize on his tax return.
B. Christian has $150,000 in taxable gain he must recognize on his tax return.
C. Christian does not have a taxable gain, because he reinvested all the proceeds in qualifying investment property.
D. Christian has $50,000 in taxable gain he must recognize on his tax return.

The answer is B. Christian's realized gain is $200,000 ($600,000 - $400,000) and his taxable gain is $150,000. He purchased another building for $450,000, so he may defer $50,000 of the gain under Section 1033 for involuntary conversions. The remainder of the gain, $150,000 ($600,000 - $450,000), must be recognized because he did not reinvest the remaining proceeds into "like-kind" property. If Christian had reinvested all the proceeds in the new building, then all of his gain would have been deferred, and he would not have to pay taxes on any of the amount. ###

Unit 15: The Estate Tax

> **More Reading:**
> Publication 559, *Survivors, Executors, and Administrators*
> Publication 950, *Introduction to Estate and Gift Taxes*

For Part 1 of the EA exam, you will be required to understand how estate and gift taxes affect individual taxpayers. For Part 2 of the exam, you will be tested on estates as well, because an estate is a type of entity.

Estates in General

For federal tax purposes, an estate is a separate legal entity that is created when a taxpayer dies. The person who inherits the property is not taxed on the transfer. Instead, the estate itself is responsible for paying any tax BEFORE the property is distributed to the heirs. The deceased taxpayer's property may consist of cash and securities, a primary residence, insurance, trusts, annuities, business interests, and other assets.

The estate tax is a tax on the transfers of property at death. It consists of an accounting of everything the taxpayer owned partially or outright at the date of death. When valuing an estate, the fair market value of the assets is used, not necessarily what taxpayer paid for them.

The Gross Estate

The total of all of these assets is called the "Gross Estate." The Gross Estate includes:

- The FMV of all property owned by the decedent at the time of death. This includes tangible and intangible property, such as copyrights.
- The full value of property held as joint tenants with the right of survivorship.
- The FMV of securities, even those that produce income that is exempt from tax, such as municipal bonds.
- Proceeds from life insurance.
- The value of any annuity or survivor benefits.
- The value of certain property that was transferred within three years before the decedent's death.

The Gross Estate does NOT include property owned solely by the decedent's spouse or other individuals. Lifetime gifts that are complete (no control over the gifts is retained) are not included in the Gross Estate.

Deductions from the Gross Estate

Once the Gross Estate has been calculated, certain deductions (and in special circumstances, reductions to value) are allowed in arriving at the "Taxable Estate." Deductions from the Gross Estate may include:

- Funeral expenses paid out of the estate.
- Administration expenses for the estate, including attorney's fees.
- Debts owed at the time of death.
- The marital deduction (generally, the value of the property that passes from the estate to a surviving spouse).
- The charitable deduction (generally, the value of the property that passes from the estate to a qualifying charity).
- The state death tax deduction (generally, any inheritance or estate taxes paid to any state).

*Note: Beginning in 2011, the Deceased Spousal Unused Exclusion (DSUE) amount may be added to the basic exclusion amount to determine the applicable exclusion amount. This is a new concept called "portability," which allows the surviving spouse's estate to use any portion of the exemption not used by the first spouse's estate. In the past, the estate and gift tax exemptions could not be passed to a spouse. The DSUE is an election, so it is only available if the election is made on the **Form 706** filed by the deceased spouse's estate.[79] The DSUE is not available to estates of those who died before 2011. The DSUE is only available for estate tax. It is not available for gift taxes.

Not Deductible from the Gross Estate

Certain items are not deductible from the Gross Estate. The payor's estate is not entitled to an income tax deduction for:

- Federal estate taxes paid.
- Alimony paid after the payor's death. (These payments would be treated as distributions to a beneficiary).

In addition, the marital deduction is limited if the surviving spouse is NOT a U.S. citizen. Property taxes are deductible only if they accrue under state law PRIOR to the decedent's death.

The Marital Deduction

There are special rules and exceptions for transfers between spouses, which are generally not subject to federal gift or estate tax. The marital deduction allows

---

[79] IRS Notice 2011-82, *Guidance on Electing Portability of Deceased Spousal Unused Exclusion Amount*.

spouses to transfer an unlimited amount of property to one another during their lifetimes or at death free of transfer taxes. The marital deduction is a deduction from the "Gross Estate" in order to arrive at the "Taxable Estate."

The unlimited marital deduction applies to both estate tax and gift tax. To receive an unlimited deduction, the spouse receiving the assets must be a U.S. citizen, a legal spouse, and have outright ownership of the assets. The unlimited marital deduction is not allowed if the transferee spouse is not a U.S. citizen (even if the spouse is a legal resident of the United States: a "green card holder"). If the receiving spouse is not a citizen, the marital deduction is limited to $136,000 in 2011.

Basis of Estate Property

Property that is jointly owned by a decedent and another person will be included in full in the decedent's Gross Estate unless the executor can show that the other person contributed to some of the purchase price. The surviving owner's new basis of property that was jointly owned must be calculated. To do so, the surviving owner's original basis in the property is added to the value of the part of the property included in the decedent's estate. Any deductions for depreciation allowed to the surviving owner on that property are subtracted from the sum.

If property is jointly held between husband and wife, there is only a "step-up" in basis of half the property's value. If the decedent holds property in a community property state, half of the value of the community property will be included in the Gross Estate of the decedent, but the entire value of the estate will receive a 100% "step-up" in basis.

Special Election for Decedent's Medical Expenses

Debts that were not paid before death are liabilities of the estate and are shown on the estate tax return (**Form 706**). However, if medical expenses for the decedent are paid out of the estate during the one-year period beginning with the day after death, the representative can elect to treat all or part of the expenses as paid by the decedent at the time they were incurred.

Estates and Credits

Estates are allowed some of the same tax credits that are allowed to individuals. The credits are generally allocated between the estate and the beneficiaries. However, estates are not allowed the Credit for the Elderly or the Disabled, the Child Tax Credit, or the Earned Income Credit.

Form 706: The Estate Tax Return

After the net amount of the estate is computed, the value of lifetime taxable gifts is added to this number and the estate tax is computed. The tax is then reduced by the available Unified Credit. A credit is an amount that reduces or eliminates tax. The "Unified Credit" applies to both the gift tax and the estate tax and it equals the tax on the applicable exclusion amount.

Any Unified Credit used against gift tax in one year reduces the amount of credit that can be used against gift or estate taxes in a later year. The "Unified Credit" on the basic exclusion amount for 2011 is $1,730,800 (exempting $5 million from tax).

Most relatively simple estates (such as estates comprised of cash, publicly-traded securities, and small amounts of other easily valued assets) do not have to file an estate tax return.

An estate tax return is filed using **Form 706**, *United States Estate (and Generation-Skipping Transfer) Tax Return.* The estate tax return is an extremely complex return, with more than 15 schedules.

The due date for **Form 706** is nine months after the decedent's date of death. The executor may request an additional six month extension of time to file by using **Form 4768**. However, the tax is still due by the due date and interest is accrued on any amounts still owed by the due date that are not paid at that time.

The estate tax rules that apply for the 2011 tax year are as follows:
- An estate will pay estate tax only if the taxable estate is valued at more than $5 million.[80]
- 2011 estates get a "stepped-up basis" in all inherited property.
- Portability applies to 2011 estates, which allows a surviving spouse to utilize any unused portion of the exemption amount.

In its current form, the estate tax only affects the wealthiest 2% of all Americans.

The assessment period for tax is three years after the due date for a timely filed estate tax return. The assessment period is four years for transfers from an estate.

The GST: Generation-Skipping Transfer Tax (Form 709)

Years ago, it was possible for grandparents to gift property or money directly to their grandchildren without any estate tax consequences. The GST tax put an end to that. Congress created the GST tax in order to make sure that no one could "skip out" on taxes by gifting money to their grandchildren or great-grandchildren.

The GST tax may apply to transfers occurring after the taxpayer's death, made to "skip persons." A "skip person" is a person who belongs to a generation that is two

---

[80] *The Tax Relief, Unemployment Insurance Reauthorization, and Job Creation Act of 2010* established a $5 million estate tax exemption and a 35% maximum federal estate tax rate. This rate is applicable from 2010 through the end of 2012.

or more generations *below* the generation of the donor. The most common scenario is when a taxpayer makes a bequest to a grandchild.

The GST tax is assessed when a property transfer is made, and the tax can be imposed before the death of the transferor (in the case of a gift) or after death (in the case of an inheritance).

The GST tax is imposed separately and IN ADDITION to the estate and gift tax. In 2011, the GST tax exemption is $5 million for individuals. The GST tax rate for 2011 and 2012 is a maximum of 35%.

Example: Patrick sets up a trust that names his adult daughter, Helene, as the sole beneficiary of the trust. In January 2011, Patrick dies, and the trust passes to Helene. However, later in the year, Helene also dies suddenly, and now the trust passes to her children (Patrick's grandchildren). Patrick's grandchildren are "skip-persons" for the purpose of the GST tax, and the trust fund monies may now be subject to the GST tax.

The GST tax is figured on the amount transferred to a skip person, after subtracting any GST exemption allocated at the maximum gift and estate tax rates. Each individual has a GST exemption equal to the basic exclusion amount, as indexed for inflation, for the year involved.

Any *direct* payments that are made toward tuition or medical expenses are exempt from gift tax or GST tax (we cover this exception in more detail in the next unit).

Example: Gordon wants to help support his grandchildren, but he wants to make sure that his gifts are not subject to gift tax, GST tax, or estate tax. So, in 2011, he offers to pay his grandchild's college tuition in full. Gordon writes a check directly to the college in the amount of $25,000. There is no tax consequence for this gift, and no reporting is required.

Requirements for the Executor of an Estate

After a person dies, an executor is usually chosen to manage the estate. The executor (or "personal representative") is generally required to settle the decedent's financial affairs.

A personal representative of an estate is the administrator in charge of the decedent's property. The personal representative is also responsible for filing the final income tax return and the estate tax return, if required.

The personal representative is responsible for determining the estate tax before the assets are distributed to any beneficiaries. The tax liability for an estate attaches to the assets of the estate itself, so if the assets are distributed to the beneficiaries before the taxes are paid, the beneficiaries may be held liable for the tax debt, up to the value of the assets distributed.

If there is no executor appointed to handle the estate, every person in actual or constructive possession of any property of the decedent is considered an executor and must file a return.

Either the personal representative or a paid preparer must sign the appropriate line of the return. Current IRS requirements require the executor of an estate to file the following tax returns:

- The final income tax return (**Form 1040**) for the decedent (for income received before death);
- Fiduciary income tax returns (**Form 1041**) for the estate during its administration; (if necessary) and
- Estate Tax Return (**Form 706**), if the fair market value of the assets of the estate exceeds $5 million.

Example: James was an unmarried wealthy landowner who died on April 20, 2011. His only daughter, Lily, was named as the executor of his estate. James earned wages in 2011 before his death. Therefore, a final tax return is required for tax year 2011. Lily asks her accountant to help prepare her father's final **Form 1040,** which will include all the money that James earned in 2011 while he was still alive. The accountant also helps Lily with the valuation of her father's estate. After adding up the fair market value of all her father's assets, they discover that James's Gross Estate is valued at $7 million. Therefore, an estate tax return (**Form 706**) is also required to be filed.

Income In Respect of a Decedent (IRD Income)

"Income in Respect of a Decedent" is any taxable income that was earned but *not received* by the decedent by the time of death. "IRD" is NOT taxed on the final return of the deceased taxpayer. IRD is reported on the tax return of the person (or entity) that receives the income. The beneficiary could be the estate, the surviving spouse, or some other beneficiary, such as a child.

Example: Carlos, the decedent, was owed $15,000 in wages upon his sudden death. The check for the wages wasn't remitted by his employer until three weeks later. Carlos's only beneficiary is his daughter, Rosalie. The wages are considered IRD, and Rosalie must recognize the same amount of income as Carlos would have recognized: in this case all $15,000 as ordinary income. Therefore, the $15,000 is IRD income.

Beneficiaries may take a deduction for estate tax paid on income earned before death but received AFTER the decedent's death. This deduction is taken by individuals as a miscellaneous itemized deduction on **Schedule A.** The IRD deduction is not subject to the 2% floor, as are most other miscellaneous itemized deductions.

IRD income retains the same tax nature after death as if the taxpayer were still alive. For example, if the income would have been short-term capital gain to the deceased, it's taxed the same way to the beneficiary. IRD can come from various sources, including:

- Unpaid salary, wages or bonuses,
- Distributions from traditional IRAs and employer-provided retirement plans,
- Deferred compensation benefits,
- Accrued but unpaid interest, dividends, and rent, and
- The accounts receivable of a sole proprietor.

There is no "step-up" in basis for IRD. If IRD is paid to the estate, it is reported on IRS **Form 1041**.

Example: Beverly died on April 30. Upon her death, she had accrued (but not yet received) $1,500 in interest on bonds and $2,000 in rental income. Beverly's beneficiary will include $3,500 in IRD in gross income when the interest and rent are received. The income retains its character as passive interest income and passive rental income.

Regardless of the decedent's accounting method, IRD is subject to income tax when the income is received by the beneficiary.

The Final Tax Return (Form 1040)

The unpleasant task of filing a deceased taxpayer's final return usually falls to the executor of the estate, but if no executor is named, a survivor must do it. This is usually a spouse or a family member. The return is filed on the same form that would have been used if the taxpayer were still alive, but "deceased" is written after the taxpayer's name. The filing deadline is April 15[81] of the year following the taxpayer's death, just like regular tax returns.

The personal representative must file the final individual income tax return of the decedent for the year of death and any returns not filed for preceding years. If an individual died after the close of the tax year but before the return for that year was filed, the return for the year just closed will not be the final return. The return for that year will be a regular return and the personal representative must file it.

Example: Stephanie dies suddenly on March 2, 2012. At the time of her death, she had not yet filed her 2011 tax return. She earned $51,000 in wages in 2011. She also earned $18,000 in wages between January 1, 2012 and her death. Therefore, Stephanie's 2011 and 2012 tax return must be filed by her executor. Her 2012 return would be her last individual tax return.

---

[81] In the 2011 tax year, the due date is April 17, 2012 instead of April 15, because April 15 is a Sunday and April 16 is the Emancipation Day holiday in the District of Columbia.

If a refund is due on the taxpayer's final return(s), the taxpayer's representative must also file a copy of **Form 1310,** *Statement of Person Claiming Refund Due a Deceased Taxpayer*. However, **Form 1310** is not required for a surviving spouse filing a joint return. On a decedent's final tax return, the rules for a personal exemption and deductions remain the same as for any taxpayer. The full personal exemption may be claimed on the final tax return, regardless of how long the taxpayer was alive during the year.

IRS Form 1041, U.S. Income Tax Return for Estates and Trusts

IRS **Form 1041** is used by a domestic decedent's estate, trust, or bankruptcy estate to report:

- The *current* income, deductions, gains, losses, etc. of an estate or trust[82];
- The income that is either accumulated or held for future distribution or distributed currently to the beneficiaries;
- Any income tax liability of the estate or trust; and
- Employment taxes on wages paid to household employees.

Form 1041 is often called a "fiduciary return."

It is also used to report the income that the deceased taxpayer had a right to receive but was unable to receive prior to his death (*frequently tested). Filing **Form 1041** is the responsibility of the decedent's executor, surviving spouse, or surviving heirs. **Form 1041** is also used to report the earnings on the decedent's property after death. For example, dividends or interest earned must be reported, even though a taxpayer may have died. Usually, investment property will continue to earn revenues even after a taxpayer has died, and those revenues must be reported. A Schedule K-1 is used to report any income that is distributed to a beneficiary. These schedules are filed with Form 1041, and a copy is also given to each beneficiary.

The due date for **Form 1041** is the fifteenth day of the fourth month following the end of the entity's tax year. An extension of six months can be filed.

The personal representative must file **Form 1041** for any domestic estate that has:

- Gross income for the tax year of $600 or more, or
- A beneficiary who is a non-resident alien (with any amount of income).

Summary: Estate Tax

The estate tax is a tax on the transfer of property after death. Estate tax returns are due nine months from the date of death, although the executor may request a six month extension of time to file.

The tax is still due on the due date. An estate tax return is filed on **Form 706,** *U.S. Estate Tax Return*.

---

[82] The taxation of trusts is covered in Book 2.

Unit 15: Questions

1. Which of the following is NOT "Income in Respect of a Decedent"?

A. Wages earned before death but still unpaid at the time of death.
B. Vacation time paid after death.
C. Taxable IRAs and retirement plans.
D. A royalty check that was received before death but not cashed.

The answer is D. Since the royalty check was received before the taxpayer died, it is not considered IRD income. Income in Respect of a Decedent is taxable income earned but not received by the decedent by the time of death. The fact that the royalty check was not cashed has no bearing on the nature of the income. ###

2. When is an estate tax return due?

A. Four months after the close of the taxable year.
B. Six months after the close of the calendar year.
C. Nine months after the date of death.
D. Twelve months after the date of death.

The answer is C. Estate tax returns are due nine months from the date of death, although the executor may request an extension of time to file. ###

3. Which form is used to report estate tax for the 2011 tax year?

A. Form 706.
B. Form 1040.
C. Form 1041.
D. Form 990.

The answer is A. An estate tax return is filed using **Form 706,** *United States Estate (and Generation-Skipping Transfer) Tax Return.*

4. Which of the following items is NOT an allowable deduction from the Gross Estate?

A. Debts owed at the time of death.
B. Medical expenses and taxes.
C. Funeral expenses.
D. Federal estate tax.

The answer is D. Federal estate tax is not deductible from the Gross Estate. All of the other items listed are allowable deductions from the Gross Estate. ###

5. Which form is used to report interest income that is distributed to a beneficiary?

A. Schedule K-1 (Form 1041).
B. Schedule B (Form 1041).
C. Form 1099-MISC.
D. Form 1099-INT.

The answer is A. A personal representative must file **Schedule K-1** to report income that is distributed to each beneficiary. These schedules are filed with **Form 1041**. ###

6. The executor of Ophelia's estate is her sister, Elise. Elise decides to make a distribution of 100% of the estate's assets before figuring and paying the estate's income tax liability. Which of the following is true?

A. The beneficiaries of the estate can be held liable for the payment of the liability, even if the liability exceeds the value of the estate assets.
B. No one can be held liable for the tax if the assets have been distributed.
C. The beneficiaries can be held liable for the tax debt, up to the value of the assets distributed.
D. None of the above.

The answer is C. The tax liability for an estate attaches to the assets of the estate itself, so if the assets are distributed to the beneficiaries before the taxes are paid, the beneficiaries can be held liable for the tax debt, up to the value of the assets distributed. ###

7. Delia's estate has funeral expenses for the cost of her burial. How should the executor deduct these costs?

A. Funeral expenses are an itemized deduction on Form 1040.
B. Funeral expenses are deducted on Form 1041.
C. Funeral expenses are deducted on Form 706.
D. Funeral expenses cannot be deducted as an expense.

The answer is C. No deduction for funeral expenses can be taken on **Form 1041** or **Form 1040**. Funeral expenses may only be claimed as an expense of the estate on **Form 706**. ###

8. Duncan died in 2011. Following his death, the executor of his estate paid the following bills. Which of these is NOT an allowable deduction in determining Duncan's taxable estate?

A. Administration expenses.
B. State inheritance taxes.
C. Charitable contributions.
D. Alimony paid after the payor's death.

The answer is D. Alimony paid after the payor's death is not deductible by the estate. Deductions from the gross estate are allowed for:
- Funeral expenses paid out of the estate
- Administration expenses for the estate, including attorney's fees
- Debts owed at the time of death
- The marital deduction
- The charitable deduction
- The state death tax deduction ###

Unit 16: The Gift Tax

> **More Reading:**
> Publication 950, *Introduction to Estate and Gift Taxes*

The gift tax is a type of excise tax imposed on the transfer of property by one individual to another. The tax applies whether the donor intends the transfer to be a gift or not. The donor is generally responsible for paying the gift tax.

In 2011, the estate tax and gift tax exemption amounts are unified. This means that there is a $5 million exemption applicable to gifts made in 2011. Since the estate tax and gift tax are unified in 2011, allocation of available gift tax exemption during one's lifetime will also reduce the estate tax exemption amount available upon death.

The maximum gift tax rate during 2011 is 35%. Gift tax is always imposed on the donor, not the receiver of the property. This means that the receiver of the gift does not pay the tax. The giver pays the tax (if any). However, under special arrangements the donee may *agree* to pay the tax instead.

Gift taxes are reported on **Form 709**, *United States Gift (and Generation-Skipping Transfer) Tax Return*. Although any gift could potentially be a "taxable gift," the following gifts are not taxable:

- Gifts that are not more than the annual exclusion. In 2011, the exclusion is $13,000 per person.
- Tuition or medical expenses paid for someone else, directly to the institution. These are called the educational and medical exclusions.
- Unlimited gifts to a spouse, so long as the spouse is a U.S. citizen.
- Gifts to a political organization for its use.
- Gifts to a qualifying charity.
- A parent's support for a minor child. This support is not considered a "gift" if it is required as part of a legal obligation, such as by a divorce decree.

These gifts are not subject to any annual limits.

Example: Alima gives her son, Dion, a gift of $13,000 in cash during the year. She also pays his college tuition, totaling $21,000. She writes the check directly to the college. Alima also pays for Dion's medical bills by issuing the check directly to his doctor's office. None of these gifts is taxable, and no gift tax return is required.

Example: Dave is single. In 2011, Dave gives his adult son, Noah, $15,000 to help start his first business. The money is not a loan, so Dave is required to file a gift tax return, since the amount exceeds the $13,000 annual exclusion amount.

Remember, "gifts" are made while the donor is still alive, while the estate tax applies after the taxpayer has died.

Form 709 is required for any of the following gifts:
- If the taxpayer gives more than $13,000 to one individual (except to a U. S. citizen spouse or charity)
- If the taxpayer "splits gifts" with a spouse
- If a taxpayer gives a future interest[83] to anyone other than a U.S. citizen spouse

If the taxpayer's spouse is not a U.S. citizen, a gift tax return is required in the following instances:
- Any gifts totaling more than $136,000 (limit in 2011)
- A future interest of any value

2011 Gift Exclusion Amounts
- The annual exclusion for gifts made to a donee during 2011 is $13,000.
- Unlimited gifts are allowed to a spouse so long as the spouse is a U.S. citizen.
- The maximum exclusion for gifts made to spouses who are not U.S. citizens has increased to $136,000 in 2011.
- The "lifetime exclusion" for 2011 is $5 million. This was increased by Congress for the 2011 and 2012 tax years.

The Marital Deduction

For U.S. estate and gift tax purposes, there are no tax consequences on gifts between spouses. The federal gift tax marital deduction is only available if the donee spouse (the person receiving the gift) is a U.S. citizen. If the spouse is not a U.S. citizen, the total lifetime gifts cannot exceed $136,000.

Gift Splitting

If a married couple makes a gift to another person, the gift can be considered as being one-half from one spouse and one-half from the other spouse. This is known as gift splitting.

In 2011, gift splitting allows married couples to give up to $26,000 to a person without making a taxable gift. Both spouses must consent to split the gift. Married couples who split gifts must file a gift tax return, even if one-half of the split gift is less than the annual exclusion.

Example: Harold and his wife, Margie, agree to split gifts of cash. Harold gives his nephew, Mark, $21,000, and Margie gives her niece, Nicole, $18,000. Although each gift is more than the annual exclusion ($13,000), by gift splitting they can make these gifts without making a taxable gift. In each case, because one-half of the split gift is not more than the annual exclusion, it is not a taxable gift. However, the couple must file a gift tax return. So even though each individual gift totals more than $13,000, they can do this and it's not taxable.

---

[83] A "future interest" is a gift that cannot be immediately used or possessed.

Example: Felicia gives her cousin, Jessie, $24,000 to purchase a new car. Felicia elects to split the gift with her husband, Rafael. One-half of the gift is deemed as coming from each spouse. Assuming they make no other gifts to Jessie during the year, the entire $24,000 gift is tax free. With the election, Rafael is treated as if he gave Jessie half the amount, or $12,000. Since they have decided to split the gift, they are required to file a gift tax return.

The Basis of Property Received as a Gift

For purposes of determining gain, a taxpayer generally takes a transferred basis when he receives property as a gift. This means that the taxpayer's basis in the property is the same as the donor's basis in the property. To figure the basis of property received as a gift, the taxpayer must know:

- The gift's adjusted basis (defined earlier) to the donor just before it was given to the taxpayer,
- The gift's FMV at the time it was given to the taxpayer, and
- Any gift tax paid on it.

Example: Darren's father gives him 20 shares of stock that are currently worth $900. Darren's father has an adjusted basis in the stock of $500. Darren's basis in the stock, for purposes of determining gain on any future sale of the stock, is $500. (This is the stock's "transferred basis.")

Generally, the "value" of the gift is its fair market value on the date of the gift. The value of the gift may be less than its fair market value to the extent that the donee gives the receiver something in return.

Example: Donald sells his son, Jared, a house for $10,000. At the time of the gift, the fair market value of the house is $90,000. Donald has made a gift to his son of $80,000 ($90,000 - $10,000 = $80,000).

Unit 16: Questions

1. In general, who is responsible for paying the gift tax?

A. The estate.
B. The donor.
C. The receiver of the gift.
D. The executor.

The answer is B. The donor is generally responsible for paying the gift tax. ###

2. Dustin pays $15,000 in college tuition for his nephew, Rich, directly to Rich's college. Which of the following statements is CORRECT?

A. The gift is taxable, and Dustin must report the gift tax on his individual tax return (Form 1040).
B. The gift is not taxable, but Dustin must file a gift tax return.
C. The gift is taxable, and Rich must file a gift tax return.
D. The gift is not taxable, and no gift tax return is required.

The answer is D. Because the payment qualifies for the educational exclusion, the gift is not taxable, and there is no reporting requirement. Tuition or medical expenses paid directly to a medical or educational institution for someone are not included in the calculation of taxable gifts. ###

3. In which case must a gift tax return be filed?

A. A couple filing jointly give a gift of $13,000.
B. A couple filing jointly give a gift of $15,000.
C. A single individual gives a gift of $4,000 to an unrelated person.
D. A wife gives a gift of $20,000 to her husband.

The answer is B. This is an example of "gift splitting." A married couple may split gifts, but they are required to file a gift tax return. Gifts to a spouse generally do not require a tax return. In 2011, gift splitting allows married couples to give up to $26,000 to a person without making a taxable gift ($13,000 from each spouse). ###

4. Shawn, a single taxpayer, has never been required to file a gift tax return. In 2011, Shawn gave the following gifts:

1. $18,000 in tuition paid directly to a state university for an unrelated person.
2. $13,500 paid to General Hospital for his brother's medical bills.
3. $50,000 in cash donations paid to his city homeless shelter, a 501(c)(3).
4. $15,000 as a political gift paid to the Republican Party (not a qualified charity).

Is Shawn required to file a gift tax return?

A. No.
B. Yes, because the donation to the political party is not an excludable gift.
C. Yes, because the total of the gifts exceeded $13,000 for the year.
D. Yes, because the political gift is a reportable transaction.

The answer is A. None of the gifts is taxable, and no reporting is required. Tuition or medical expenses paid for someone directly to an educational or medical institution are not counted as taxable gifts (the educational and medical exclusions). Gifts to a political organization for its own use are not reportable and not counted as part of the gift tax limit, even though the political organization is not a qualified charity. ###

5. In 2011, Jeffrey gives $25,000 to his girlfriend, Rachel. Which of the following statements is TRUE?

A. The first $13,000 of the gift is not subject to the gift tax, but the remainder is subject to gift tax, and Rachel is responsible for paying it.
B. Rachel is required to file a gift tax return and pay tax on the entire gift.
C. Jeffrey is required to file a gift tax return, Form 709.
D. Jeffrey may choose to report the gift tax on Form 1040, Schedule A.

The answer is C. Jeffrey is required to file a gift tax return. Gift tax is paid by the donor, not the recipient, of the gift. Jeffrey is responsible for filing the gift tax return. The first $13,000 of the gift is not subject to gift tax because of the annual exclusion. The remaining $12,000 is a taxable gift. ####

6. All of the following gifts are excluded from the determination of the gift tax EXCEPT:

A. A gift made to a political organization for its own use.
B. A cash gift given to a non-resident alien spouse of a U.S. Citizen.
C. A medical bill paid directly to a hospital on behalf of a relative.
D. A gift made to a qualifying charity.

The answer is B. Although a full marital deduction is allowed for a spouse who is a U.S. citizen, the marital deduction for a gift made to a non-citizen spouse is limited. ###

The Enrolled Agent Tax Consulting Practice Guide
Learn How to Develop, Market, and Operate a Profitable Tax and IRS Representation Practice

Available as a Kindle edition, paperback, and a Nook edition

About the Authors

Collette Szymborski is a Certified Public Accountant and the managing partner of Elk Grove CPA Accountancy Corporation. She specializes in the taxation of corporations, individuals, and exempt entities. Elk Grove CPA also does estate and elder care planning.

Richard Gramkow is an Enrolled Agent with over fifteen years of experience in various areas of taxation. He holds a Master's Degree in Taxation from Rutgers University and is currently a Tax Manager for a publicly held Fortune 500 company in the New York metropolitan area.

Christy Pinheiro is an Enrolled Agent, Accredited Business Accountant, and writer. Christy was an accountant for two private CPA firms and for the State of California before going into private practice. She is a member of the California Society of Enrolled Agents and National Association of Tax Professionals.

Made in the USA
San Bernardino, CA
23 November 2012